RUSSIA'S BITTER PATH
TO MODERNITY

RUSSIA'S BITTER PATH TO MODERNITY

A History of the Soviet and Post-Soviet Eras

Alexander Chubarov

Continuum
New York • London

2001

The Continuum International Publishing Group Inc
370 Lexington Avenue, New York, NY 10017

The Continuum International Publishing Group Ltd
The Tower Building, 11 York Road, London SE1 7NX

Printed in the United States of America

Library of Congress Cataloging-in-Publication Data

Chubarov, Alexander.
    Russia's bitter path to modernity : a history of the Soviet and post-
Soviet eras / Alexander Chubarov.
        p. cm.
    Continues: The fragile empire : a history of Imperial Russia.
    Includes bibliographical references and index.
    ISBN 0-8264-1350-1
    1. Soviet Union—History. 2. Russia (Federation)—History—1991–
I. Chubarov, Alexander. Fragile empire. II. Title.

DK266 .C474 2001
947.084—dc21

                                                    2001042321

For Marianna and Eugene,
the two best

Contents

Preface

This study seeks to provide a framework for the understanding of Russian history and politics over the past hundred years or so and finds it in the view of the Russian development as a fitful but ineluctable advance toward modern ideological, political, social, and economic patterns. Seen in this light, the socialist experiment, which began in 1917 and takes up, chronologically, just under nine-tenths of the period being examined, is interpreted as modernization in the broad sense of the word, including industrialization, urbanization, an educational (cultural) revolution, and the evolvement of a more "mature" or modern political culture and a secular mentality. The Soviet regime by its own policies had reared powerful forces of modernity that were destined to destroy it. The rapidly mounting complexity and diversification of all aspects of society created the ingredients of a systemic crisis that overwhelmed the Soviet leadership in the late 1980s.

The breakup of the Soviet Union was a political, social, and economic event comparable in scale to the 1917 revolution. Russia has emerged from the upheaval with tremendous geopolitical, economic, and demographic losses. In Russian history, reform periods have invariably been accompanied by immense suffering of the population and have always been protracted and painful. In this sense, the transitional era opened by Mikhail Gorbachev's *perestroika* (i.e., political and economic restructuring) and continued by Boris Yeltsin's liberal reforms conforms fully to the Russian tradition. Neither Gorbachev nor Yeltsin was able to achieve the goals he had set; the result of both reform efforts was a society in the state of an acute economic and political crisis.

Nevertheless, the era, opened by Gorbachev's *perestroika* and continued by Yeltsin's market reforms, has also brought about cardinal changes that Russia vitally needs in order to launch its remodernization. It has finished off the neo-Stalinist system of government, putting to rest the Communist Party's pretense to control the entire sociopolitical order. It has brought a substantial degree of democratization to society, including the legalization of public associations and political movements, ideological pluralism, the establishment of regular democratic elections, and the emergence of a multiparty system. It has disposed of the Soviet-type command economy, bringing in a vibrant private sector, the new business elites, and various other sections of the population, whose lives and well-being are now bound up with the continued marketization.

The analysis of these developments in the book is divided into an introduction, setting out the work's main argument, and three parts. Part One—"The Background"—gives overviews of the key aspects of Soviet ideology, society, and organization. Opening with a brief discussion of the legacy of imperial Russia, it then turns to its Communist successor, dealing with such themes as political culture, ideology, constitutional and political systems, nationalities, and economic setup. As implied in its name, the purpose of Part One is to provide a background and a structure for better understanding of the concrete historical periods of the Soviet and post-Soviet eras discussed in the subsequent two parts.

Part Two deals with the socialist experiment, that is, the attempt to build socialism and communism in Russia under the Soviet regime and the Communist rulers, and covers the period from the October Revolution of 1917 to the advent of Gorbachev in 1985. Each of the periods within this time frame—from Lenin to Stalin, to Khrushchev and Brezhnev—is analyzed in the complexity of its political, social, economic, and ideological aspects. Part Two concludes with an overview of the theoretical models and conceptual tools used by political scientists and historians to uncover the power mechanisms in the Soviet Union, including totalitarianism, pluralism, and corporatism. In particular, it looks at the rise of interest groups in the post-Stalin Soviet Union, accompanied by the growth of cultural and academic pluralism and the establishment of corporatist relations between the state and certain institutional economic interests. It offers a new interpretation of the outcomes of the significant postwar evolution of the relations between rising interests and the communist authorities.

Part Three covers the period 1985–2001, starting with Gorbachev's desperate and unsuccessful attempt to renovate the facade of the Communist system, through Russia's turbulent nineties under President Yeltsin, to the accession of Vladimir Putin and the impact the first year of his presidency had on the country. It analyzes key factors of the Soviet collapse, including the crisis of the command economy and the failures of *perestroika*'s economic strategies, the unforeseen results of Gorbachev's political reforms, and the rise of popular, nationalist, and proindependence movements in the constituent republics. It evaluates the course and results of the chaotic and muddled reforms under Yeltsin, including the Bolshevik-style attempt to destroy the Soviet economic system to its foundations in the hope that the phoenix of the market would rise from its ashes. Part Three concludes with a discussion of Putin's efforts to reinvigorate the Russian state, which has sustained a critical loss of authority during the Yeltsin era, and of whether this augurs well or not for the prospects of Russia's evolution toward a stable and developed democratic system and a more civilized form of capitalism.

Introduction

Russian history is commonly perceived, by Russians and foreigners alike, as something basically different from the norms and standards of the West. This popular view of Russia's "otherness" is epitomized in Winston Churchill's famous characterization of Russia as "a riddle wrapped in a mystery inside an enigma." Occasionally, misunderstanding of the Russian historical development generates suspicion and mistrust, leading to a tendency to see it as an aberration or regard certain periods of Russian history as blind alleys, that served only to lead the country to the periphery of world development.

One of the key factors contributing to the country's distinctiveness has been Russia's location in the center of the Eurasian landmass, straddling Europe and Asia. The dual nature of this Eurasian empire has given rise to unending efforts by the Russian political and cultural elites to define Russia's place in the surrounding world. What is the nature of Russia's mutual relations with the great civilizations of both the West and the East? What should be the orientation for Russia to follow in its political, socioeconomic, and cultural development? These questions have aroused public debates over the last two hundred years. They loomed particularly large at critical periods in the life of Russian society, when a radical transformation of social and political structures looked unavoidable and the country confronted the problem of choosing the path for its further development.

With Russian society torn by social and political divisions of the post-Communist transition, the traditional cultural schism has once again come to the fore. The invisible line divides Russians into those who lean toward Western values and way of life and think that Russia's troubles are caused by the insufficient emulation of these values and those who consciously or unconsciously oppose Western influences. One camp sees Western orientation as a single solution to Russian problems, whereas the other professes its belief in Russia's own distinct path of development.

Many of the roots of this disquiet and uncertainty about Russia's destiny and direction go back three hundred years to the reign of Peter the Great (1682–1725), whose image and example have been constantly invoked by Russian westernizing reformers over the recent decade.

Peter's transformation was launched in the period of early modern history, when the development of economic relations based on the market, new geographical discoveries, pioneering scientific inquiries, and the appearance of more efficient means of travel and communication were beginning to bind the world into a single civilization. The elements of this new civilization—countries and continents—now actively interacted with one another as parts of a system.

In this new epoch, a nation's economic or social backwardness and its inability to set up an effective system of government posed a real threat to the very sovereignty of the state. Increasingly, the government systems of more advanced countries provided models to be imitated and offered examples of desirable restructuring for their less developed neighbors. The attempt to "catch up" with more developed countries is usually described as modernization. Since early modern history, the advanced countries of Western Europe and of the West in general have been the models for modernization. For this reason, the "catching up" phase of development is also referred to as Europeanization or westernization. Peter's reform movement represents an important new departure in modern world history: it pioneered the process of modernization that was later to develop on a worldwide scale.

Since Peter's reign, competition with the West has become one of the key factors in Russian history. For the past three centuries, Russian history has been punctuated by reforms induced by the Russian government's efforts to catch up with and overtake its Western rivals. Peter's attempt to catch up with Russia's European neighbors would achieve full success later in the eighteenth century, during the reign of Catherine the Great (1762–96). By the end of the century, Russia was seen as one of the continent's three or four greatest military powers and was universally recognized abroad as being equal to Hapsburg Austria or Bourbon France. Napoleon's defeat by the forces of Alexander I (1801–1825) further increased the country's prestige, and in the first half of the nineteenth century Russia was generally perceived to be the continent's leading military power.

However, it was during that time—under the impact of the industrial revolution—that the factors that determined a country's power were undergoing fundamental change. Capitalism was transforming agrarian societies of the leading European states, revolutionizing their industrial bases, and increasing the size of urban populations. The persistence of traditional institutions—serfdom, in particular—now seemed to place Russia behind other countries of the continent. By the close of Nicholas I's reign (1825–55), the picture of a powerful Russia, dominating the international order, had disappeared. As Russia fell behind the rate of development of other nations, so its foreign policy became less successful, declining from the tremendous triumph over Napoleon to the disaster of the Crimean War (1853–56).

The Crimean War had demonstrated Russia's military and economic weaknesses to the Russian government in a shocking and humiliating fashion. Russia's ruling circles were compelled to accept the fact that in the second half of the nineteenth century it was no longer possible to retain serfdom and manage without a rationally organized legal system, local self-government, or modern army, and, at the same time, continue to aspire to the status of a leading European power. As a result, the government initiated the second great cycle of modernization, which lasted from the 1850s to the 1980s. This was Russia's attempt to remain a great power in the industrial era. The renewed process of catching up with the West, begun by the imperial regime and interrupted by the First World War and the revolution, was completed under the Communist government.

The revolution of 1917, starting with the collapse of tsarism in February and culminating in the Bolshevik takeover in October, was itself, to a large extent, engendered by the pressures of modernization. It engaged various sections of the population, including the bourgeoisie and the middle and working classes. Each group had its own political program. Some adhered to the collectivist principles of Russia's traditional society; others wished to emulate Western models of capitalism and democracy; still others advanced utopian Communist blueprints. Yet all felt the need to overcome the country's backwardness and catch up with the group of leading industrialized nations in various spheres, including technological progress, labor productivity, general literacy of the population, and the development of democratic institutions. Striving to accelerate Russia's development along the common vector of world civilization, Russia's progressives belonging to all classes understood that absolutism and the vestiges of feudalism were the main obstacles to the country's successful advance.

Under the circumstances, it was Vladimir Lenin and the Bolsheviks who had the upper hand. The new ruling elite pledged to build an entirely new type of government, the likes of which had never existed before. It claimed that for the first time in human history a government would serve the interests not of a privileged, exploiting minority, but of the overwhelming working-class majority of society. The deeply anti-capitalist Bolsheviks also set about the task of laying down the foundations of a socialist economy. To Lenin and his followers, this meant, first of all, the implementation of Marxist ideas about introducing a socialist mode of production based on public ownership and a planned economy.

Lenin realized that, in the economic sense, the new Soviet Russia was not ready for the introduction of socialism. But he was firmly convinced that Russia would not be left on its own and that its bold step toward socialism would be supported by the highly developed countries of Europe, which stood on the threshold of a world socialist revolution. This, however, did not happen, and the Bolshevik revolution remained isolated in a world dominated by "imperialist" powers. Soviet rulers became increasingly concerned that the country's economic weakness had serious implications for national security. In 1931 Joseph Stalin made this point quite clear: "We are fifty or a hundred years behind the advanced countries. We must make good this distance in ten years. Either we do it or we shall be crushed." Ten years later, Nazi Germany under Adolf Hitler invaded Soviet Russia determined to crush it; thanks to Stalin (despite his massive and unforgivable errors) and the heroism of the Soviet people, Hitler's plans were thwarted. Stalin's industrialization and the routing of Nazi Germany in 1945 marked the Soviet Union's achievement of great-power status in the industrial era.

Russia's postwar enhanced international standing rested firmly on the foundations of the economic, social, and cultural modernization laid down under Stalin. His rapid industrialization, in particular, had provided the Soviet Union with the industrial capacity and military might that enabled it to defeat Nazi Germany. Stalin's industrialization was totally "anti-Western" in its methods: it was not based on private enterprise, but was state-driven and ostensibly based on centralized directive planning. At the same time, there was much in it that drew upon Russia's traditional patterns. Ever since Peter the Great, the Russian government had played a key role in expanding the country's industrial capacity. The state in Russia had always directed the main forces of production and kept most important branches of industry under its control. It is highly significant that Russia's initial industrial boom in the 1890s, under the last two of the Romanov tsars, became possible mainly thanks to the government-sponsored railway construction program that created a big demand for metal, coal, and oil, leading to the rapid development of the metal and fuel industries.

Stalin's methods of financing industrial expansion also had parallels in the Russian past. Both under him and the last Romanov tsars it was the peasants who, of all the population groups, paid a particularly heavy price for the government's industrial policy. To finance economic modernization, the tsarist government relied on Russia's traditional fiscal structures, such as the village commune, which played a crucial role in the collection of government taxes. On top of the heavy fiscal burden of direct taxes, peasants also paid for the industrialization as consumers, through high tariffs on imported goods and rising indirect taxes on consumer goods. Similarly, under Stalin capital was forcibly squeezed out of the reluctant population, mainly the peasantry, through an arbitrary price system. But the most drastic solution of how to finance industrial expansion was found in creating on the basis of small and low-productive individual peasant farmsteads large-scale socialist collective farms. The collectivization of agriculture enabled the state to exercise direct administrative control over large collectivized farms, whose profits could be ploughed back into the construction of new industrial plants. The policy looked radical and unprecedented, yet it too, to some extent, drew upon the legacies of the past, including serfdom and the traditions of the village commune. The imposition of the collective-farm system was achieved partly due to state terror but also partly due to the vestiges of communal traditions and the egalitarian attitudes of peasants in the countryside.

It is obvious, then, that to understand the triumphs and failures of Russia's Soviet and post-Soviet development, it is essential to study them within Russia's own cultural and historical context. The true essence of the Soviet period of Russian history was modernization in the broad sense of the word, including industrialization, urbanization, and secularization of popular mentality.[1] The singularity of the Communist regime was that it pledged to carry out this vast transformation of society on the basis of Marxist ideology, that is, without private ownership that bred excessive exploitation of wage labor and other predatory capitalist practices. To a large extent, many of the Communist dogmas proved utopian and unrealistic, but it would be one-sided to reduce the process of Soviet modernization to a "revolution from above" imposed by a radical government on an unwilling population. The Bolshevik vision of socialism, including industrialization, urbanization, and cultural revolution, appealed to many sections of society as essential directions of the country's progress and evoked massive social support. It reflected aspirations of different social classes and groups and, in particular, the longing of the working classes for social justice. Many driven by enthusiasm were prepared to sweat at construction sites round the clock virtually for free. Young people, in particular, were deeply motivated by the idea that it was possible to build a better and fairer society relatively quickly, within their lifetime, by mounting a huge, exhausting effort and accepting hardships and self-sacrifice.

Under the banner of building socialism, the ruling Bolshevik Party
was transformed from the revolution's headquarters into a bureaucratic
machine, charged with mobilizing and channeling energies of society
into a massive modernization program. The role of the party-state structures as an instrument of building a modern society should also be
assessed not from the point of view of their compliance or noncompliance with standards of a "civilized" society of today, but in the context
of Russian civilization and on the basis of the understanding of the historical foundations of Russian statehood. For centuries, the class of "service nobility" constituted the spine of Russian statehood. In pre-Petrine
Russia, this ruling group was represented by the military landowning
class; in imperial Russia, by the state bureaucracy recruited from the
landowning nobility; and in Communist Russia, by the party-state elite,
known collectively as the *nomenklatura*.

The *nomenklatura* carried out its governing functions in ways and by
means, most of which had been foreshadowed by the actions of Russia's
administrative elites of the past. It used mobilization and centralization,
formulated public objectives, and fought for their implementation with
enthusiasm and self-sacrifice, by paternalism and repression, and
through coercion and terror. But its overarching goal was further
advance along the path of modernization. Naturally, as any other social
group, it also had its own "class" interests, but the best of its representatives were capable of articulating progressive aspirations of various
sections of Soviet society and of working staunchly for their realization.

There is little doubt that in many of its aspects Stalin's period
(1924–53) was brutal and harsh, but so was Russian society at large. The
Bolsheviks had inherited from the tsars an overwhelmingly peasant country, populated predominantly by a backward semifeudal mass—the "dark
people"—surviving into the dawning of the modern era. Moreover, as a
result of the harrowing experience of the First World War overlapping
with acute social conflicts of the 1917 revolution, then followed immediately by the brutal fratricidal civil war, the popular consciousness had
been badly upset. It combined, in a paradoxical way, the belief in a radiant Communist future with the blind conviction in effectiveness of violence as an instrument of modernizing society. The revolutionary
romanticism of the masses was blended with total disregard for human
life. The Bolshevik leaders themselves had not been raised in a test tube
but reflected all the flaws and imperfections of contemporary society.

It is against this background that certain negative phenomena, including high levels of state terror under Stalin, should be assessed: not to
condone such developments but to see them in their historical context.

Modernizations across the globe have given examples of great human achievement, elevating to the status of national heroes individuals as different as Henry Ford, Yuri Gagarin, and the founders of the Sony Corporation. But modernizations were also fraught with brutal and bloody conflicts, wars, colonial aggression, acute social antagonisms, and so on. Coercion and repression, jail and penal labor existed everywhere and are part of Western, Russian, and other nations' experience. The important thing in the study of history is to distinguish between those developments that were justified and necessary and those that do not easily lend themselves to interpretations on the basis of present-day wisdom and common sense.

The tremendous industrial growth achieved under Stalin's regime was the springboard for the expansion of Stalinism beyond the Soviet borders. After the Second World War, for the first time in history, Russia openly challenged the West's historical hegemony to furnish models of socioeconomic development for the rest of the world. The scale of Soviet achievement in the heavy industrial sector was particularly staggering. In a short period of time an industrial capacity was built characteristic of more economically advanced countries. In terms of its branch structure and technological sophistication, the Soviet economy now stood at a level comparable with the industrialized countries of the capitalist West. The USSR was now second only to the United States in its gross industrial output.

Western leaders were seriously concerned about the USSR's growing influence in the postwar world. The Soviet victory over a fascist capitalist state served to enhance the global appeal of Communist ideology. Following the postwar collapse of European overseas colonies, many of the newly independent countries in the third world adopted a socialist orientation. Soviet influence appeared to spread like a tidal wave across the entire globe: from Eastern Europe to China, from Vietnam to Cuba. Even within Western democracies themselves the popularity of Communist parties was far from negligible.

The extreme rivalry and distrust between the two antagonistic camps of states—one led by the USSR, the other by the United States—threatened repeatedly to engulf the world in a global conflagration. The world entered the era of the cold war that was to last for nearly a half century (1946–91). At its core was the intense military, economic, ideological, and political competition between the two socioeconomic models: the system of capitalism and the system of socialism.

By the 1970s the Soviet Union had achieved seemingly assured superpower status through military parity with the United States. Not since the days of Nicholas I had Russian power been rated so highly at home or abroad. Realities, however, were as deceptive in the Brezhnev era (1964–82) as they had been in the reign of Nicholas I. The factors of power in the world were changing quickly. In Nicholas's day, it had been the spread of the industrial revolution in Western Europe that had jeopardized Russia's status as a great power. Under Leonid Brezhnev, it was the revolution of the microchip and the computer.

In the postwar period, the leading industrialized countries of the West entered the era of scientific and technical revolution. This set the scene for rapid transition to a new, postindustrial stage of development. As the technological revolution advanced, it was becoming more and more obvious that certain inherent characteristics of the Soviet economic model stood in the way of technological progress. With the exception of the military-industrial complex, the latest scientific and technological achievements were slow to enter into production on a nationwide scale. Overcentralization, the absence of competition, and a lack of self-interest, motivation, and material incentives at all levels of the economy were the main impediments to technological progress. Moreover, Soviet planners needed to find ways of making the Soviet economic system more attentive to consumers. Endemic shortages of consumer goods, overcrowded housing conditions, primitive consumer services—all cried out for remedy. To continue to ignore consumers' needs was becoming more and more dangerous politically.

In the new conditions, the political and economic mechanisms created under Stalin began to reveal clearly their serious limitations. The habitual interference of party structures in matters of production became less and less effective; bureaucratic overcentralization could no longer cope with managing efficiently the increasingly sophisticated branch structure of the Soviet economy. When the Soviet economy showed the first symptoms of a slowdown, the system began to lose the very rationale it was based on. Economic growth, as the necessary condition for the creation of the material base of the future Communist society, was critical for justifying the system. As long as the economy delivered high growth rates, it commanded loyalty. But the declining economic performance began to corrode people's belief in the ability of the system to create the basis for a society of material plenty and therefore undermined the system's legitimacy.

All this put pressures on Nikita Khrushchev's and consecutive Soviet governments to shift away from the Stalinist economic model. After Stalin's death and until the USSR's collapse, the Soviet leadership for over thirty years was engaged in an almost continuous process of reforming the Stalinist system of socialist central planning. The objective of the reform programs of all Soviet leaders from Khrushchev (1953–64) to Mikhail Gorbachev (1985–91) was to make the economy more efficient and receptive to technological innovation and more responsive to consumer wants, while retaining its socialist character.

By the 1980s the Soviet Union had built a powerful economy of a distinctive type, second only to that of the United States. It was a world leader in many fields of science, including space exploration and civilian and military uses of nuclear power; it possessed an advanced educational establishment and a varied cultural scene; it evolved sophisticated industrial, social, and transportation infrastructures; and it had in place reasonably adequate housing and food supply systems. Contrary to the ideological claims that it developed in the direction of a socially homogeneous society, the social structure that emerged by the early 1980s was increasingly diverse and varied and was now dominated by distinctive groups of urban populations with their own interests, way of life, and mentality. Even more crucially, under the seemingly stagnating surface of an ostensibly "socialist" system, new trends and phenomena evolved, including an "administrative market" (bureaucratic accommodation of interests between economic departments and state planning agencies), a vast shadow economy, a certain diffusion of power, the emergence of privileged social groups, the rise of intellectual elites, an informal public opinion, cultural and intellectual pluralism, and ecological, nationalist, and dissident movements. All of these were impermissible from the point of view of the ossified ideology, but each reflected real modernizing trends affecting Soviet society.

By then it was clear that the Soviet Union had come to the point at which its legitimizing doctrines, institutions, and decision-making procedures were hopelessly outdated and no longer capable of meeting the growing demands and modern complexity of Soviet society. The bankruptcy of the neo-Stalinist system of government was obvious to any unprejudiced observer. The dominance of military leaders, central planners, and ideologists in determining priorities was called into question. The old Leninist ideology seemed no longer capable of incorporating the broad masses of the population into the Communist project. Thus, the Soviet regime by its own policies had nurtured powerful forces of modernity that in a matter of decades were destined to become the regime's own "gravediggers." It was exactly this rapidly mounting complexity and diversification of all aspects of society, including the economy, education, culture, communications, and interethnic and international relations, that created the ingredients of a systemic crisis that overwhelmed the Soviet leadership in the late 1980s.

Striking parallels exist between the collapse of the Soviet regime in 1991 and the downfall of tsarism in 1917. The peasant emancipation of 1861 under Alexander II inaugurated the era of the "great reforms" of a liberal nature that, instead of reinvigorating autocracy, sped it to its collapse. Because much of Russian life had been constructed around the institution of serfdom, its abolition inevitably necessitated liberalizing changes in areas including local government, the judicial system, and the military. The "great reform" laws of 1861–65 fundamentally altered the structure of the empire, launching Russia's transition from a semifeudal to something approaching a modern capitalist society.

In the final decade of the nineteenth century, the tsarist government sponsored a massive modernization program that boosted the development of capitalist relations across the empire and gave birth to modern classes of the bourgeoisie and the industrial proletariat. In the six decades between the peasant emancipation and the collapse of tsarism, the process of modernization of the country's social and economic structures brought about a more open, dynamic, and politically mature society. The First World War and revolution caught the tsarist empire in the middle of a process of transformation (industrial, agrarian, educational, and military), when most of the reforms were beginning to produce their first results. Yet the tsarist empire's political evolution could not keep pace with its rapid socioeconomic progress. The failure to adapt Russia's antiquated government structure to the fast-changing social, economic, and international conditions was among the principal reasons for the downfall of tsarism.

The Soviet regime picked up the torch of modernization and, in the late 1920s, launched its "socialist onslaught" that also lasted for six decades. Like the tsarist government before it, the Soviet Union collapsed not because its modernization efforts had taken it to the periphery of contemporary civilization or into a historical cul-de-sac. Both regimes crumbled under the burden of the contradictions that developed within an increasingly involved and complex modern society. In the Soviet society, great changes occurred in the two postwar generations, with the move to the cities and the rise of educational levels and standards of living. By the late 1980s, a new Russian urban culture had formed, founded on a large professional class, largely free of ideology and potentially supportive of liberal political values. In the economy, powerful interest groups had emerged that increasingly vied with the party bodies for control over policy in their area. In the republics and regions, local administrative and intellectual elites had substantially increased their political weight and cultural autonomy. The country was in need of Western-type democratic structures and new economic patterns that would be capable of channeling and accommodating the new interests and creating conditions for the forces of modernity to develop further.

However, despite some modifications to the Soviet political and economic systems following Stalin's departure and spanning the period of thirty years until the advent of Gorbachev, the fundamental nature of the regime remained practically unchanged. The party-state continued to claim a monopoly on power and strove to control the entire sociopolitical order. By the end of Gorbachev's *perestroika,* the regime's unreformability had become patently obvious. It proved incapable of providing leadership during the period of a radical transformation of the existing social relations, political structures, and ideological doctrines. The system of centralized planning proved inadequate for a modern economy. Mounting economic problems pushed the republics toward secession, bringing local elites and populations to the conviction that only by freeing themselves from the failed and seemingly unreformable system would they be able to find a way out of the Soviet impasse. As a result, in 1991 the Soviet authoritarian regime, like its autocratic predecessor in 1917, collapsed like a house of cards.

The breakup of the Soviet Union was a political, social, and economic event, whose dramatic repercussions were as great as those of the 1917 revolution. The scale of the upheaval was revealed in the depth of economic dislocation, explosions of interethnic violence escalating into local wars, pauperization of the mass of the population, the magnitude of human suffering, and other dramatic developments. Russia emerged from the upheaval with tremendous geopolitical, economic, and demographic losses: it still commanded the biggest territory—one-eighth of the world landmass—but had only half the population of the former USSR.

The adherents of the liberal school of westernizers hailed the collapse of the Soviet Union as an absolute triumph of their ideas and as the final proof that there were no alternatives to a pro-Western orientation. The new political forces that took control in Russia at the start of the 1990s under the presidency of Boris Yeltsin (1991–99) launched the reforms under the banner of the liberal westernizing ideology and pursued its precepts doggedly and uncritically. This blind faith that Western patterns could be introduced by the stroke of a pen and that they would resolve Russia's problems as if by magic was not based on any serious analysis of the actual economic, political, and sociocultural circumstances of the country. The "shock therapy" of the early 1990s was more like a surgical operation on Russia's distinctive economic and social organism: it inflicted great pain but gave little cure. It was a Bolshevik-style attempt to destroy an old economic system to its foundations in the hope that the phoenix of the market would rise from its ashes. This, however, did not happen. The results of the reform were mixed and provoked an anti-Western and nationalist backlash in many sections of the population.

Over centuries Russia has evolved as a Eurasian power with distinctive historical, economic, and political characteristics, and a way of life different from Western norms. Being open to influences from both the East and the West, Russia has always followed its own path. The attempt to create overnight a bourgeois society of a Western type and establish full-scale capitalist relations in a society, which for over seventy years had officially repudiated them, was an absurd idea that was doomed to fail. There is little doubt that the social and political system that will ultimately emerge from the post-Communist transition will be different from Western patterns. Russia needs to find its own model of development with Russian characteristics.

It follows from what has been said above that westernization, understood as a wholesale borrowing from or copying of the West's historical experience, cannot explain or define the deeper content and direction of Russia's modernization attempts. Russia's emulation of Western patterns, to a large extent, had a "technocratic" character and was mainly concerned with the acquisition of Western technical and organizational knowledge and the importation of modern technological expertise, including military know-how. Paradoxically, Russia was compelled to emulate Western advances in these and other areas to preserve its own sovereignty and independence and to continue to develop in its own way. Russia's bouts of westernization are usually catalyzed by security threats or direct military challenges coming from the West: the Northern War against Sweden in the reign of Peter the Great, the defeat in the Crimean War at the start of Alexander II's reign, and the intensification of military-industrial competition with the West in the final phase of the cold war are prime examples. Stalin's "socialist onslaught" itself was motivated by the need to prepare the country to hold its own against "capitalist encirclement" and involved massive imports of Western equipment and know-how to augment the country's industrial and military capabilities.

No doubt, global military and economic competition and technological change will continue to act powerfully on Russia. The country also can hardly escape the powerful pressure of such worldwide forces as globalization, privatization, and liberalization. Russia needs to emulate Western democratic procedures, such as free elections and multiparty parliamentarism, which are part and parcel of a modern state. Pluralist democracy is no longer seen as a mode of government suitable only for certain wealthy nations, but as one that brings universal benefits.

It is also clear, however, that the new Russia cannot turn its back on its Soviet experience. As the dust of the postwar ideological rivalry settles, it becomes clear that, far from being an aberrant phase, the Soviet period was an organic part of Russian history and was largely successful in turning Russia and most of the other Soviet republics (many of which have had no previous experience of independent statehood outside the Russian Empire) into modern states. The turbulent 1990s showed clearly that denigration of the Soviet achievement and uncritical copying of Western ways leads only to deindustrialization and demodernization and threatens to relegate the former superpower to the status of a raw materials supplier for Western multinationals.

At the start of the twenty-first century, Russia must find a synthesis of Western forms with Russian content that will take into account its national characteristics: a huge territory, a northern location, unreliable agricultural conditions, a peculiar economic structure, the traditionally significant regulatory role of the state, and the cultural, religious, and psychological makeup of its population. Russian political and intellectual elites must continue to engage in the "westernizers versus Slavophiles" debate about the correlation between national and "adopted" elements within Russian civilization to achieve a better mix of Western patterns with usable elements of the Russian past. Without all this, Russia will not be able to embark successfully on its remodernization to catch up with its Western competitors in the era of scientific and technical revolution and postmodern society.

Finally, Russia must capitalize on its indigenous experience of modernization and its tremendous achievements, both in the prerevolutionary era and under the Soviets, and not squander it in pursuit of the latest ideological fads. All the talk to the effect that Russia must decide which of its two "old regimes"—the tsarist or the Soviet—it wants to inherit is meaningless because it obscures the fundamental fact that both eras have been essential steps on Russia's path to modernity.

Part One

THE BACKGROUND

Chapter One

"Old Regime" Russia

Geopolitical Evolution of the Russian State

The Kievan Rus is believed to have been the first Russian state and the cradle of the three branches of the East Slavs: the Great Russians, the Ukrainians, and the White Russians (or Belorussians). The Kievan Rus emerged in the ninth century and, like most other barbarian kingdoms, rose to civilized status by adopting Christianity as its state religion in 988. In contrast to central and eastern Europe, however, Kiev's official religion was not the Christianity of the Latin world, but of the Greek world of Byzantium. The main reason for the adoption of the eastern form of Christianity, known also as Orthodox Christianity, was that the Kievan Rus maintained close cultural, economic, and political links with its powerful southern neighbor, the Byzantine Empire, with its center in Constantinople. One of the consequences of the conversion to Orthodox Christianity was the adoption of a written language from Bulgaria, based on Greek and Hebrew alphabets.

The Kievan Rus state expanded to a considerable size, but by the end of the twelfth century it had fragmented into smaller feudal principalities. In 1237 the Mongols, led by Batu, a grandson of the great Mongol leader Genghis Khan, were able to exploit this fragmentation, invaded the Russian lands, and established their lordship over them. This severed Russia's links with Western Europe and with the South. Only in 1480 were the Mongols finally expelled from Russia. Their legacy of 240 years was the introduction of a degree of barbarism into Russian life and a relative separation of Russia from the rest of Europe.

By the late fifteenth century, Moscow emerged as the capital of the fledgling centralizing state. It had successfully brought under its control formerly disunited Russian lands. By 1600 it had grown twelvefold to become the largest state in Europe.

By the middle of the seventeenth century, Russia acquired Siberia in the east, while in the southwest it reestablished its authority over the

Ukraine. In the eighteenth century Peter I and Catherine the Great annexed the present-day Baltic states and a substantial share of Poland, thus giving the Russian Empire its basic modern form. To assert the rising status of Russia among the European powers, Peter took the imperial title of old East Rome (Byzantium). In other words, he claimed for the Muscovite state the mantle of the successor to the Roman Empire. At Peter's command, Moscow had to yield its status of the capital city to the new imperial capital of St. Petersburg.

By 1800 Russia had conquered the Crimea, thus gaining access to the Black Sea. By the early nineteenth century, it had completed the incorporation of the whole of the Transcaucasian region. During the Napoleonic Wars, Finland and Bessarabia (a region in southeastern Europe) were seized. Russia annexed Vladivostok on the Pacific coast by 1860 and the Kazakh lands and central Asia by 1885.

By the second half of the nineteenth century, the Russian Empire's borders had assumed their settled contours. Russia had spread its authority over vast territories, stretching from the Danube's estuary in the west to the Pacific Ocean in the east, from the Eurasian tundra in the north to the borders of Turkey, Iran, Afghanistan, and China in the south. In its territory and population Russia was the biggest world power. Its population, according to the general census of 1897, was 128 million (178 million by 1914). In 1917 the Bolsheviks inherited from the tsars the world's largest landmass and one of the most populous countries.

EVOLUTION OF RUSSIAN STATEHOOD

9th–13th centuries	Kievan Rus
13th–15th centuries	Political fragmentation of the Russian lands
1240–1480	Mongol yoke
1462–1682	Muscovite state
1682–1917	Imperial Russia
1917–1991	Soviet Russia
1992–	Russian Federation

Paradoxes of Tsarist Russia

Tsarist Russia was an empire of great internal contradictions. It was a colossus, which had expanded over one-sixth of the earth's landmass, yet it was ever vulnerable to foreign invasion. It had one of the world's largest populations, yet the majority of its people lived in poverty and discontent. It commanded the world's richest natural resources, yet its productive forces were severely constricted by the remnants of feudalism. It strove to cement its multiethnic population by systematic Russification, but this only stimulated nationalist movements. It tried to portray its political system as a "people's autocracy" at a time when the regime was becoming increasingly detached from its people. The gigantic empire of the tsars became ever more fragile and vulnerable until it was shattered to pieces in the turmoil of war and revolution.[1]

The Beggarly Empire

In early Russia, the unification of the Russian principalities around Moscow proceeded mainly under the pressure of external political factors, such as the constant threat of military invasion. National security interests required from this poor, sparsely populated agrarian country the ability to mobilize all available resources at times of military emergency. The solution of how to maintain its military security was found in the creation of a special warrior class bound by the obligations of military service to the state. To provide them with an income and reward for their service, the state granted to members of the military class land and peasants to work it. A system thus took shape that featured a ruler with sweeping powers, a nobility based on service to the state, and a peasantry increasingly tied to land owned by the nobility.

Eventually, a considerable part of the Russian peasantry became bonded to their squires or the state. The Russian peasants were fully and completely enserfed by the articles of the new legal code of Tsar Alexis, father of Peter the Great, in 1649, the very year in which a "bourgeois" revolution occurred in England, bringing about the overthrow of the king. In the West, social progress was achieved mainly through the natural development of economic relations. By contrast, the Russian state drew its strength and vitality from the use of noneconomic methods. Force, coercion, and enserfment of the population became the chief means by which Russia developed its productive forces. The clearest illustration of this is Peter the Great's era. Under him, Russia built up its industry, expanded its military might, and established itself as one of the great powers of Europe. At the same time, Russia's peasants found themselves increasingly bound by the restrictions of serfdom. The population was treated by the despotic state merely as building material for the establishment of a grand empire.

The Russian peasants were given their personal freedom only in 1861 under the Tsar Liberator Alexander II. The peasant emancipation was a major turning point in Russian history, yet the government did all it could to compensate landowners for the loss of their servile labor and to make the peasantry shoulder this compensation. The emancipation conserved some of the elements and relations of the old serfdom system and hindered the development of the institution of small- and medium-scale private ownership, particularly the ownership of land.

In the early twentieth century, although capitalism was making rapid progress in Russia, the agrarian sector continued to dominate the national economy. About four-fifths of the population continued to live in rural communities. The overwhelming majority of the population (73.7 percent, according to the 1897 census) was illiterate. Socially segregated from the rest of society, the peasants, many of whom were born under serfdom, remained the "dark people"—a medieval element surviving into the modern era.

In towns, the continuing industrialization accelerated the growth of the class of urban wageworkers. Many of them were proletarians of the first generation, who had recently arrived from the countryside. The urban working class assumed an increasingly significant political role due to its high concentration in the two main nerve centers of the country, St. Petersburg and Moscow. At the beginning of the twentieth century, the Russian working class remained the most oppressed, impoverished, and discontented in Europe. Much of its dissatisfaction arose from Russia's lack of proper labor legislation, which would regulate relations between capitalists and workers. There was no legal provision for the operation of trade unions, for national insurance for illness and work-related accidents, or for a system of old-age pensions.

In Russia the divide between the working classes of peasantry and proletariat and the rest of the population was particularly deep, for here the remnants of feudal customs and practices were aggravated by the predatory methods of Russia's capitalism in the early stages of its development. The government's inability to regulate the relations between different social groups and to curb the excessive exploitation of wage labor heightened the rebellious mood of the people and forced them to adopt a more radical, revolutionary course of struggle for their legitimate demands.

In the early twentieth century, the unprecedented rise of popular discontent erupted into three revolutions in the space of twelve years from 1905 to 1917. Popular movements became breeding grounds for extreme, ultraradical elements. Russia's peasants and workers lent a ready ear to the radicals' call "Expropriate the expropriators!" and to the provocative Bolshevik battle cry "Loot the loot!" In February 1917 the protesting women in Petrograd bread queues ignited the social explosion that in a matter of days culminated in the inglorious collapse of the great empire of the tsars. Thus, to a great degree, the downfall of tsarism can be attributed to the government's failure to ensure basic rights and decent standards of living to the mass of its working population.

Polyethnic Monolith

Mounting ethnic tensions further compounded the social antagonisms that were tearing Russian society apart. Pre-Petrine Russia was a relatively homogeneous country in terms of its population (predominantly Slavic) and religion (Orthodox Christianity). Russia's continual territorial expansion, particularly starting from Peter the Great's reign onward, began to transform a Slavic state into a multiethnic empire. By the start of the twentieth century, the political map of the Russian Empire looked like a monolithic unitary state. Yet, in actual fact, it accommodated within its borders very different lands, from territories that were home to ancient civilizations to almost unpopulated areas to the east of the Ural Mountains. It had one of the most diverse and heterogeneous ethnic mixes in the world, with over a hundred peoples and dozens of distinct ethnic identities with distinctive ethnic, linguistic, religious, and cultural qualities. The peoples of Russia had very different pasts. Some used to have their own centuries-old statehood, others were at the stage of the disintegration of tribal society. They belonged to different races and linguistic families. They differed in national mentality and held different religions. Russia's Christians were Orthodox, Uniate, Catholic, and Protestant, not to mention numerous Christian sects. Significant sections of the empire's population adhered to Islam, Judaism, Buddhism, and other religions and creeds.

This multiethnic empire had evolved as a result of a contradictory process of state building that cannot be reduced to such simplified definitions as "voluntary reunification" and "forced annexation." Some peoples found themselves incorporated in the empire because of their geographical proximity, common economic interests, and long-standing cultural ties with Russia. To others, engaged in interethnic or religious conflicts with neighbors, Russia's protection offered a chance to survive. Still others had been incorporated as a result of conquest or collusion between Russia and the other great powers.

Russia's expansion, in particular, the incorporation of territories that lagged behind in socioeconomic development, was not always to Russia's advantage. Only by straining all its economic, demographic, and military resources could it sustain the status of a great power capable of playing an influential role in the international arena and controlling the numerous nationalities populating its huge territory. In a paradoxical way, the territorial expansion provided Russia with an impressive amount of men and materials to claim the status of a great power on the world stage. Yet the growth of the empire was achieved at a crippling social cost and caused mounting ethnic problems. In the final analysis, the territorial expansion was a factor that did more to constrain, rather than advance, the economic and sociopolitical development of Russia.

The great state, which accommodated the traditions and ways of life of so many different peoples, found it more and more difficult to cope with the pressures of ethnic assimilation and nationalism. With the collapse of the autocracy in February 1917, followed by the Bolshevik takeover in October, the seemingly monolithic structure of the Russian Empire rapidly unraveled. The national liberation movements on the fringes of the decomposing state spontaneously and instantly destroyed the tsarist colossus from within, splitting it into a multitude of large and small entities (the Russian Soviet Federated Socialist Republic, the Ukraine, Belorussia, Finland, the Baltic states, the newly created republics in Transcaucasia, the North Caucasus, the Volga region, Kazakhstan, and central Asia). Some lands, like Poland and Finland, gained full independence and became sovereign states. Most, however, succumbed to the recentralizing drive of the new Communist authorities in Moscow and were reincorporated into the Union of Soviet Socialist Republics. They escaped from the tight grip of Communist authoritarianism seven decades later, when in 1991 the tsarist empire's successor, the USSR itself, collapsed.

Unlimited Power Limited

Russian autocracy was a form of absolutist government that derived its sanctity from the concept of the traditional "God-given" power of the

Russian tsar and from the claim of the right of succession to the great empires of antiquity. An absolute monarch was the central element in the Russian political system. There were no recognized formal limits on his political authority and no rule of law to curb his arbitrary will. In Western Europe, even in the age of absolutism, monarchs had to reckon with the interests of powerful social groups such as the nobility and the bourgeoisie, and they often faced opposition in the form of a parliament, or municipal councils, or self-governing religious bodies. By contrast, the absolute rule of the Russian tsars met with no opposition from society. A state like the Russian autocracy completely dominates society and treats its subjects as its property. Although by the end of the nineteenth century parliamentary democracies and constitutional monarchies had been established throughout almost all of Europe, Russia, practically right to the very end of tsarism in 1917, remained firmly in the grip of autocracy.

Most of the tsars of the Romanov dynasty were personally well-educated and civilized men and women. Many of them came close to the realization of the need to transform Russia into a constitutional monarchy. Catherine the Great regarded highly Montesquieu's political ideas, including his concept of the separation of powers, and strove to transform Russia's tyrannical government into an enlightened one. Her grandson, Alexander I, entrusted his liberal-minded minister Michael Speransky to draw up plans of a complete overhaul of the Russian political system to allow for local self-government, civil rights for all sections of the population, and a national legislative assembly. His nephew, Alexander II, even seriously considered the introduction of a constitution, when his life was tragically cut short by a terrorist bomb. The great social upheaval of the revolution of 1905–7 finally compelled his grandson, Nicholas II, to institutionalize the principle of the separation of powers and to introduce basic civil freedoms. However, this change was too little and too irresolute to bring Russia's political system up to the standards of the European civilization of the twentieth century. Despite Catherine's "enlightened absolutism," Alexander I's liberal aspirations, the liberal reforms under Alexander II, and the constitutional experiment under Nicholas II, the basic, essential features of Russia's political system were still practically unchanged in the early twentieth century from what they had been in the seventeenth century.

Despite their worthy upbringing and European education, the Romanovs remained essentially a very Russian dynasty, whose mentality was deeply rooted in the conditions of life in Russia. Their ability to effect change was severely constricted by Russian realities, such as the special status of the nobility, the country's industrial backwardness, and the conservatism of many sections of the population. Russian absolutism has often been portrayed as the unchallenged authority of the supreme ruler. In actual fact, each of the Romanovs, despite the seemingly unlimited nature of his or her power, was not absolutely free to do what he or she liked and was often vulnerable and insecure both as a ruler and as a human being.[2] Few of the Romanovs lived to die peacefully. Some of them were murdered as a result of a coup d'état or an assassination (Peter III, Paul I, Alexander II); others were deposed and imprisoned and later killed, like Nicholas II. Still others passed away in rather mysterious circumstances (Peter I, Alexander I, Nicholas I).

Even more insecure and dependent on the fortunes and will of the ruler was the position of the tsars' ministers and favorites, such as Michael Speransky, Sergei Witte, and Peter Stolypin. These reform-minded officials usually had to elaborate their reform plans in the deep secrecy of government privy committees and were always in danger of incurring disfavor of their royal patron (Witte), or falling into disgrace and being sent into exile (Speransky) or assassinated (Stolypin).

In the end, the Russian Empire became neither a nation nor a bourgeois society. The incompetent and unpopular regime grew increasingly isolated, until it became completely detached from its people. The political bankruptcy of tsarism was starkly and disastrously revealed with the onset of the First World War. The war provided the last mighty push to bring the whole rotten structure tumbling down.

Leaps in Circles

Many contradictions of the modern age are due to the fact that peoples and countries had entered it at different levels of development. There was a "top league" of the industrialized nations of Europe and North America, which used their great industrial muscle to spread their political and economic domination over a considerable part of the globe. At the other end, there were colonial countries that extracted very few benefits from contact with Western civilization. There was also a third group of states, in Asia as well as in Europe, that had their own centuries-old history, yet had emerged as actors in the international scene relatively recently. Some countries of that group were semicolonies, others were themselves colonial empires, yet all of them had one thing in common: they were confronted with the historical challenge of closing the gap with the developed nations.

The countries in that middle group had fallen behind in rates of development for various reasons: Spain, because it had come to depend too much on the exploitation of its vast colonies in Latin America; Japan, due to its self-imposed isolation; Italy, because of political fragmentation; and so on.[3] But the main reason was that these states had been slow to modernize the traditional socioeconomic system inherited from the medieval era. They now faced the task of overcoming their backwardness by taking the path of capitalist modernization and following the lead of the advanced industrialized nations. Russia was one of these modernizing, developing states.

From the time of Peter the Great, Russia has made several modernization attempts at radical restructuring of all essential spheres of the country's life, from its economy to its political system. However, the problem with all of Russia's modernizing efforts was that reforms were launched too late, when the country was already in the grip of a social and political crisis and when the government was under intense direct pressure either from below, in the form of mass social discontent, or from an external threat or a military defeat. In such exceptional circumstances and under such great pressure the reforming government was compelled to act quickly and in great haste, often without enough time to think through its new policies and their consequences. As a result, none of the periodically undertaken reforms was carried out in a comprehensive and consistent manner. Each generation of reformers inherited unresolved problems from previous reform efforts and passed on its own unresolved problems to the next. As a result, every new generation of reformers had to deal with the backlog of accumulated past problems, as well as new ones. The inconclusive and contradictory nature of Russia's reform cycles may be described as "leaps in circles."

Such reformism induced by the pressure of circumstances resulted in ill-conceived policies that had not been properly prepared or explained clearly to the population. For example, the problem of setting up a representative assembly in Russia was first formulated in the blueprint of government reforms prepared by Speransky in the early nineteenth century, then shelved in secret government archives and forgotten. A hundred years later, on the eve of the revolution of 1905, the government still flatly rejected any proposals for the introduction of some form of parliamentary system in Russia. Then suddenly, just a few months later, the government was compelled to reexamine Speransky's plan, which had been gathering dust for nearly a century, and announce the convocation of a consultative state Duma. Some weeks later still, it was pushed into changing its mind again and promised a legislative state Duma. As a result, a representative parliamentary institution was introduced, as it were, overnight, and political parties were allowed to form in a country that had never had any parliamentary traditions or legal political parties before. It is hardly surprising that reform under duress failed to deliver a workable constitutional system. The inability of the authorities to implement vitally needed change at the right time opened the way for the advocates of revolution.

Chapter Two

Political Culture

The term *political culture* usually refers to certain values, perceptions of history, and fundamental political beliefs shared by a majority of the population. The question, which is often asked in connection with Russia's recent Communist experience, is, to what extent does Russian political culture hinder or help the transition to democracy? The seventy-four-year long Communist period itself carried on, in changed forms, Russia's prerevolutionary authoritarian tradition. How has the experience of centuries of authoritarian rule affected the Russian political culture?

At one extreme of responses to this question there is a view that treats Russian political culture as immature and unprepared for democracy. It argues that the historical experience has created a society in which ideas such as freedom, self-government, and rule of law are not ingrained in the collective consciousness. But there is also a positive view, which stresses the more recent experience of the Russian people and the impact of factors such as urbanization, rising educational levels, and opening up to the outside world. These are taken to have created a changed political culture and a people much more determined to stand up for democratic values. This has been further strengthened by the experiences of the period since the late 1980s, during which popular opinion and action changed an entire system.

Where does the truth lie? Is Russian political culture supportive of democratic values, or are the legacies of the autocratic experience likely to pervert the cause of democracy in Russia? To what extent does Russia's past weigh upon its present?

To begin with, it is useful to identify some of the most basic characteristics of the Russian traditional political culture, particularly those more enduring values that are not easily destroyed by revolutions and other major social and political upheavals. Many of them have to do with the traditional way of life of the people determined by the geographical, environmental, and climatic factors prevailing in the country. What were the important facts of life in Russia that shaped the mentality of Russians and affected their social and political behavior?

"Too Asiatic for the Europeans and Too European for the Asians"

Historians note a number of geopolitical characteristics peculiar to Russia that have been instrumental in shaping its historical development and the national mentality of its population. One feature of the country's geography, in particular, seems to have had a fundamental influence: Russia's location in the center of the Eurasian landmass. Russia's position between Europe and Asia has had a profound effect on the emergence of a distinctive civilization. It was Asiatic in the eyes of the Europeans and too European for the Asians. The Russian state found its fitting symbol in the double-headed eagle of Byzantium. One of its crowned heads is turned to the East and the other, to the West. It was adopted as the coat of arms of the Muscovite tsars, then of the Russian Empire, and now resurrected as a state symbol of post-Communist Russia. The double-headed eagle symbolizes the dual nature of a great state that extends for thousands of miles across two continents. This state accommodated the traditions and ways of life of its extraordinarily diverse mix of peoples with their distinct mentalities and political cultures that clashed and interacted within the confines of a great empire.

The dual nature of this Eurasian empire and its unique geopolitical location have given rise to unending efforts by the Russian political and cultural elites to define Russia's place in the surrounding world. What is the nature of Russia's mutual relations with the great civilizations of the West and the East? What should be the orientation for Russia to follow in its political, socioeconomic, and cultural development? These questions have aroused public debates over the last two hundred years. They loomed particularly large at critical periods in the life of Russian society, when a radical transformation of social and political structures looked unavoidable and the country confronted the problem of choosing the path for its further development.

One of the earliest and best known examples of such debates is the Slavophiles versus westernizers controversy of the 1840s. This great intellectual debate for the first time distilled two contrasting interpretations of Russia's past and future.

The Slavophiles, led by writers like Alexei Khomiakov (1804–60), Konstantin Aksakov (1817–60), and Ivan Kireevsky (1806–56), had been brought up in the traditions of European culture and did not question the many achievements of Western civilization. Nevertheless, they were unhappy with the westernizing orientation imparted to Russian culture since the time of Peter the Great because they saw it as damaging to the unity of the Russian nation. In the Slavophiles' view, Russia had for a long time been following a completely different path from that of Western Europe. European history was predicated on state despotism and the constant struggle between egoistic individuals and antagonistic social groups in the conditions of unfettered capitalism. By contrast, Russian society was founded on the collectivist principle of the commune united by common interests of its members. The next important element of Russian life was the Orthodox religion. Its precepts had strengthened even more the original ability of Russians to sacrifice their individual interests for the sake of a collectivist good and had taught them to help the weak and bear patiently the hardships of life. As for the state, it had traditionally looked after its people, defended the nation from aggressive neighbors, and maintained order and stability, but it had not interfered in the spiritual or communal life of the people. Slavophiles condemned the imported ideas and institutions as alien to the Russian people and called for the revival of Russia's old ways of social and state life.

The Slavophiles' opponents—the westernizers—were represented by two main strands: the liberals, such as Konstantin Kavelin (1818–85) and Boris Chicherin (1828–1904), and the radicals inclined to socialism, such as Alexander Herzen (1812–70) and Vissarion Belinsky (1811–48). What united this diverse group of thinkers was their rejection of the view that Russia was unique. They firmly believed that Russia advanced along the European path of development, which was the only possible way for a civilized country to go. Russia had taken this path later than most European countries—at the beginning of the eighteenth century—as a result of Peter the Great's reform efforts. Naturally, its level of development lagged behind that of the advanced countries of Western Europe. But Russia's progress in the "Western" direction would continue and would lead to the same changes as other European countries had already gone through. Both the liberal and the radical wings of westernizers were aware of the establishment in Western Europe of a new socioeconomic order and of its positive and negative effects. The difference in their attitude to the prospect of similar developments at home was that the liberals recognized that Russia lacked the conditions necessary for the establishment of capitalist patterns, and they called for the creation of such conditions. The radicals, by contrast, found the prospect of the importation to Russia of the European bourgeois system objectionable. In their view, Russia should not simply strive to catch up with the advanced countries of the West by borrowing uncritically their concepts and institutions, but should make a bold leap toward a totally new and in principle different system of life—socialism. Belinsky and Herzen saw the predominance of communal land tenure among the peasantry as a peculiarly Russian characteristic that made such a leap possible.

It is impossible to overestimate the impact of the westernizer–Slavophile controversy on the future intellectual and political history of Russia. Many of the later disputes and divisions between different factions, schools of thought, and political parties in Russia can be analyzed in terms of two camps. One camp saw Western orientation as a single solution to Russian problems, whereas the other professed its belief in Russia's distinct path of development.

In the final decade of the twentieth century, as the country entered a period of radical transformation of existing social relations, political structures, and ideological doctrines, the interest in the debate was rekindled with new intensity. The adherents of the liberal school of westernizers hailed the collapse of the Soviet Union as an absolute triumph of their ideas and as the final proof that there were no alternatives to the pro-Western orientation. The new political forces that took control in Russia in the early 1990s launched the reforms under the banner of the liberal westernizing ideology and pursued its precepts doggedly and uncritically. The results of the reforms have been mixed and have provoked an anti-Western and nationalist backlash in many sectors. The social and political divisions that tore Russian society in the 1990s have revealed the traditional cultural schism. The invisible line continues to divide Russian society into those who lean toward Western values and way of life and think that Russia's troubles are caused by the insufficient emulation of these values and those who consciously or unconsciously oppose Western influences. The debate about the correlation between national and "adopted" elements within Russian civilization is unlikely to subside in the foreseeable future.

Egalitarianism and Communalism

Egalitarianism and communalism are often cited as examples of archetypal characteristics of the Russian traditional political culture. They take their root in the communal foundations of village life in tsarist Russia. The collectivist ethos was itself conditioned by the influence of the ecological environment. Russia's harsh and inhospitable climate accounts for the fundamental difference in farming conditions between Russia and Western Europe. In central Russia the annual cycle of agricultural work was unusually short: just 125–130 working days from mid-April to mid-September. The soil was poor and required careful cultivation, for which there was not enough time. Time, weather, and primitive agricultural methods were the constraints that forced peasants to work day and night with little sleep or rest, using the labor of all available members of their families, including children, women, and the elderly. Even in the best of times the soil yielded a harvest that barely covered the basics. By contrast, farmers in Western Europe enjoyed the advantage of a much longer growing season. The winter break in farming in some countries of Western Europe was fairly short (December and January); consequently, the arable land could be cultivated more thoroughly.

Poor crop yields and the dependence of peasant labor on the weather conditioned the extraordinary tenacity of communal institutions in the Russian countryside. The peasant commune provided a collectivist safety net and a guarantee of survival for the mass of the rural population. Centuries-long experience of life and work in such adverse conditions had taught peasants to devise a whole set of measures to help those members of the community who were on the brink of ruin. Together, as a community, it was easier to find protection from natural calamities or to meet obligations imposed by the squire and the state. It was advantageous for the village to have common pasture and woodland, a common place for watering the cattle. The village community looked after orphans and childless old people. At regular intervals the land was redistributed among the peasant households in the village to ensure that each family had an amount of land commensurate with its size. Collective responsibility for periodic redistribution of land encouraged communal values and egalitarianism and reinforced conformity to group norms.

The measures of collectivist relief survived in the countryside into the early twentieth century. They outlived the tsarist regime that collapsed in 1917. Rural egalitarian traditions still existed in the 1920s and up to the start of Stalin's forced collectivization of agriculture at the end of that decade. The imposition of the collective- and state-farm system itself was achieved partly due to state terror but also partly due to the vestiges of communal traditions and egalitarian attitudes of peasants in the countryside.

Indeed, the type of socialism built in the Soviet Union had much in common with the primitive egalitarianism of Russian traditional rural communities. The Soviet system achieved equality in poverty by keeping living standards at a subsistence level for the majority of the populace. The Soviet system is sometimes referred to as "barracks-style socialism" to convey the idea of a regime that treats its subjects as conscripts, enforcing strict regimentation and the equality of servitude.

"Orthodoxy—Autocracy—Nationality"

The broad scope of state authority and the dominance of a state religion or ideology are often seen as key enduring aspects of traditional Russian political culture characteristic of both of the old regimes—the tsarist and the Soviet. The tsarist government regarded autocracy and Orthodoxy as the chief pillars that ensured political order and social stability in the empire. Its concern in protecting and maintaining these principles was seen in the great efforts it made to promulgate the official doctrine of "Orthodoxy—Autocracy—Nationality." The doctrine's first component proclaimed the essential role that the official Orthodox Church and its teachings occupied in Russian life. The second component proclaimed that Russia needed an absolute monarch as the central element in its political system (the word *autocracy* refers to a regime that concentrates power in the hands of an absolute ruler, or autocrat). The final component proclaimed the special character and value of the Russian people as an imperial nation unifying various ethnic groups of a gigantic empire.

Orthodoxy has left an indelible mark on Russian spiritual, cultural, and political traditions. Both Russia and the West represented predominantly Christian civilizations. However, Christianity reached them through different channels. Rome was the West's main mediator of Christianity, whereas in Russia's case it was the Byzantine Empire that acted as its Christian "godmother." Byzantium was the eastern part of the Roman Empire, and it saw itself as its heir after the collapse of the western part in 476. Catholicism (the western form of Christianity) reflected the peculiarities of Roman civilization, whereas Orthodoxy (the eastern form of Christianity) was imbued with the spirit of Greek civilization that dominated Byzantium at the time of the implantation of Christianity in Russia.

Central to Orthodox Christian beliefs was the concept of the joining together of the earthly and the heavenly order. The authority of the emperor was the power that linked these two worlds. When exercised properly, the emperor's power was capable of resolving all contradictions between the imperfect world of mortals and the ideal celestial order. It was able to bring this world into harmony with the next. For this reason, the authority of the "true" tsar was seen by the Orthodox religion as a guarantee of salvation after death.

In Western Europe, particularly after the sixteenth-century Reformation, the Christian religion motivated individuals to engage in some kind of profitable economic activity. Economic success strengthened the belief of the faithful that they were the "chosen" ones, destined for future individual salvation. Western Christianity roused Europeans to seek economic prosperity. It encouraged them to develop civil society as a means of protecting their business interests and civil rights. By contrast, in Russia the Orthodox religion promised its people not individual but collectivist salvation. The Russian people were prescribed by their religion to engage in a centuries-long quest for a "true" Christian tsar, to pin their hopes on his ability to resolve their grievances in this world and ensure their salvation in the next.

The gradual secularization of these beliefs crystallized into two divergent value systems. In the West, professional success became one of the chief criteria for the evaluation of a person's activity. In Russia, the idea of bringing closer the existing, imperfect world to the divine order resulted in the rise of a collectivist movement in search of a better future based on collectivist foundations. This luminous future was to be achieved not through individual enrichment but by strict adherence to the ideal of social justice. With the collapse of tsarism in 1917, the charismatic power of the Communist leader replaced the divine authority of the emperor as the force that showed the way to the radiant collectivist future.

The Orthodox Church by its precepts greatly enhanced the sanctity and legitimacy of the Russian autocracy. The tsar was not merely an absolute ruler but one whose authority was derived from God. There were no recognized formal limits on his political authority and no rule of law to curb his arbitrary will.

The state, like the Russian autocracy, which completely dominates society and treats its subjects as its property, is sometimes referred to as patrimonial.[1] It stifles the freedoms of private and public life and inhibits the emergence of organized associations and self-governing bodies that would represent the interests of different sections of society. In other words, it suppresses all those things that characterize modern forms of the political life of the state. Russia remained firmly in the grip of the autocracy practically right to the very end of tsarism in 1917, when it was supplanted by a Communist dictatorship.

Russian Contemporary Political Culture

The Soviet period in many aspects represented continuity with the pre-revolutionary period in that it was consistent with some key features of traditional Russian political culture—the autocracy, the supremacy of the state over society, the dominance of a state ideology, and an emphasis on egalitarianism and collectivism. However, in other aspects, the Soviet period represented a departure from elements of traditional Russian political culture. The peasant commune and other forms of traditional social life were destroyed by the Stalinist upheaval to be replaced by large state-run economic units such as collective and state farms. Atheism and Marxism were proclaimed the official doctrine, and attempts were made to turn Marxism into a sort of "secular" religion to replace Christianity and other religious creeds of the tsarist empire. The Orthodox Church itself was subject to severe restrictions during most of the Soviet period.

But the most significant shifts in Russian political culture of the Soviet period were connected with the transition from a predominantly rural, uneducated society to one that is overwhelmingly urban and literate. Prerevolutionary Russia was a land of peasants, with over 80 percent of its population living in rural communities. Today, the situation has been almost reversed: nearly three-quarters of the population of Russia is classified as urban. In the late 1920s and over the following six decades, the social and demographic changes connected with the processes of industrialization and urbanization transformed the passive neofeudal peasant society into an urban industrial society with a modern social structure and an increasingly articulate population. By the mid-1980s, a large urban middle class had developed, represented by a substantial professional, scientific-technical, and cultural intelligentsia with new cultural and material requirements.

The steadily rising educational levels of Soviet society were one of the consequences of Soviet urbanization. By the early 1980s, specialists with higher or secondary vocational education accounted for 40 percent of city dwellers. The rising educational levels brought about a cardinal change in the very notion of the intelligentsia. From a narrow intellectual elite it was transformed into a wide stratum of educated people incorporating diverse social categories and groups: engineers, administrators, academics, actors, teachers, and politicians.

In addition, the ever-growing pressures of the scientific and techno-logical competition with the West required the Soviet regime to accept a certain level of openness to outside influences. Scientific and cultural exchanges of people and ideas, though closely monitored, gradually broadened the channels through which the diverse influences of the out-side world filtered into the Soviet Union. In the 1970s and 1980s these external cultural influences assumed an ever greater importance in shap-ing Soviet political culture and public opinion.

The cumulative effect of urbanization, rising educational attainments, and the influence of global moral and technological trends was nothing short of a cultural revolution. Contrary to the Communist rulers' expec-tations, Soviet modernization did not result in strengthening the hold of socialist ideology in the popular consciousness. On the contrary, it led to the formation of a critically minded, alienated, and democratically ori-ented constituency for liberal reforms. The new "Soviet man" that the authorities sought to forge turned out to be an individualist and a prag-matist. His way of life, requirements, tastes, everyday behavior, and aes-thetic preferences more and more conformed to "Western" norms. The result of Soviet industrialization and urbanization was a population that was shedding fast its "communal" characteristics, transforming into a society of autonomous individuals. As socialist consciousness waned, alternative ideologies spread, and pro-Western, liberal democratic views gained growing popularity, particularly among the younger, urban, and educated sectors of the population.

When communism finally collapsed in Russia in 1991, many Russians were psychologically prepared to rethink their fundamental political val-ues. The Russian government itself embraced political and economic val-ues imported from the West. At the same time, the government and other political forces evoked images of the pre-Soviet period, evident in the naming of the parliament the Duma and the readoption of prerevolu-tionary names for many streets, squares, and cities. A crisis of Russian identity emerged both for elites and for average citizens. For the elderly in particular, the post-Communist changes appeared to mock the cher-ished egalitarian values of Soviet society. The generation of pensioners remains the main constituency of the neo-Communist parties, but it is gradually moving off the historical stage.

For millions of well-educated ex-Soviet citizens living in urban areas, the psychological transition has already been made. Thousands of entre-preneurs have taken advantage of the new laws allowing private enter-prise and have opened their own businesses. A new post-Soviet generation is rising to leading positions throughout the country. Many of its members, those in their early thirties today, have lived their entire professional lives in the world of Gorbachev's *perestroika* and the post-Soviet market economy. For this generation, the end of the Soviet era was the emancipation they had been waiting for.

Contemporary Russian political culture is a vibrant mixture of contradictory elements drawn from the prerevolutionary, Soviet, and post-Soviet periods, and enriched with global moral and intellectual influences. This is a culture in a state of flux: it combines a resurgence of Russian nationalism and Orthodox Christianity with survivals of the values of Soviet patriotism and collectivism and with high levels of support for principles associated with liberal democracy, including political and religious tolerance, political liberty, individual rights, rights of opposition and dissent, freedom of speech, and competitive elections.[2] It is a fluid culture, engaged in active processes of social modernization leading to a market economy, a law-governed state, and a civil society.

Chapter Three

Soviet Ideology

Main Tenets of Classical Marxism

In the Soviet Union, ideology was used to legitimate power. For this reason, political authority in the USSR was always closely linked to ideological doctrine. This doctrine was based on Marxism.

As a philosophical theory, Marxism represented a particular type of socialism. Its founders were two German philosophers, Karl Marx (1818–83) and his lifelong friend and collaborator Friedrich Engels (1820–95). In the course of several decades, starting in the turbulent 1840s, they had constructed a huge and comprehensive philosophical system. Their ideas were first presented in a systematic form in 1848 in the celebrated *Manifesto of the Communist Party*. They were then developed more thoroughly in the three volumes of Marx's *Capital*. The intellectual roots of Marxism included the eighteenth-century Enlightenment, classical economics, utopian socialism, and German idealistic philosophy—in other words, some of the main traditions of Western thought. Most importantly, Marx and Engels tried to find a rational formula that would sum up the evolution of humankind and indicate the course of its future development.

One of the key elements of their theory was the idea of the natural-historical character of social development. The essence of the theory was that society developed in accordance with its own intrinsic laws. The laws of social development were no less objective than the laws of nature. For this reason, each social formation appears only then and there, when and where appropriate conditions have matured for it. It subsequently gives way to a next formation when that new formation has been prepared by a different set of objective and subjective conditions. In this sense, Marx presented social development as a natural social-historical process. Similar to organic nature and living organisms, social systems are conceived, develop, and pass from one qualitative stage to the next in accordance with certain objective laws.

The second fundamental Marxist principle in the explanation of the historical process is materialism. Idealistic philosophical systems believe that consciousness determines existence. By contrast, materialism looks for objective foundations of consciousness itself. It finds them in the material life of people, in their concrete social conditions. Materialism led Marx to discover an economic base of society in the form of the mode of production. He argued that the mode of production of the material means of existence conditioned the whole process of social, political, and intellectual life. It was not consciousness that determines existence; on the contrary, social existence determines consciousness. The mode of production or relations of production of the same type generate similar sociopolitical structures and even ideological forms.

By using this approach, Marx singled out five socioeconomic formations: the primitive type of society, slavery, feudalism, capitalism, and communism. The capitalist stage and the capitalist mode of production and exchange were described and analyzed by him most exhaustively. Marx's main conclusion from his analysis of contemporary capitalism was that the bourgeoisie would be unable to control the rapid expansion of the productive forces unleashed by the capitalist mode of production. In addition, the bourgeoisie would completely antagonize the proletariat by driving it to utter destitution and poverty. On the basis of his analysis, Marx drew up the conclusion that capitalism was, inevitably, heading for self-destruction. He predicted that anticapitalist revolutions would occur in the most developed capitalist countries. The current phase of history would be terminated by a proletarian revolution. It would abolish the minority rule of the bourgeoisie and also do away with individual property as the economic foundation of its political power. Humankind would enter the era of communism with a workers' government running society in the interest of the majority of society.[1]

The spread of Marxist ideas in Europe coincided with the rising interest of the political and cultural elites in Russia in the issue of "Russia between Europe and Asia" and stimulated the ongoing discussion between westernizers and Slavophiles. Marx's theory seemed to fit neatly into the westernizers' ideological framework, particularly into more radical strands of "westernism." The Marxist teaching, as interpreted by its Russian followers, had certain appealing qualities. The doctrine seemed to explain clearly and logically the development of human society by the action of certain immutable laws. The knowledge of these laws allowed making "scientific" predictions of the direction, stages, and final goals of human progress. In other words, Marxism offered its followers a ready-made formula of social transformations suitable for any part of the world, including Russia.

The growing popularity of Marxism in Russia must be seen in the wider context of the modernizing processes that were beginning to affect the country at the end of the nineteenth century. The development of capitalism, the appearance of elements of civil society, and the government-sponsored industrialization of the 1890s seemed to indicate that Russia, after all, took the road followed by the leading group of industrialized nations. The western model of development appeared to display major advantages. It accelerated cultural, economic, and technological progress and led to the establishment of parliamentary systems and the expansion of democratic freedoms. All this gave credibility to the arguments of the Russian advocates of westernism.

As a result, Russian radicals began to see the process of westernization and Europeanization of Russia through the prism of Marxist theory. It should be noted that the conversion of Russian radicals to Marxism was, to a great extent, influenced by the successes of the Western European Social-Democratic movement. European social democracy in those days adhered to the theoretical tenets of Marxism. Russian radicals were convinced that the European Social-Democratic movement was an influential force contributing to democratization of Western European society. They saw positive signs of this democratization in the appearance of labor legislation and trade unions and the recognition of social and political rights of workers. These progressive developments represented real achievements in the struggle for social equality in the West, and they seemed proof enough for Russian intellectuals of the scientific correctness of Marxism.

Russian Social-Democrats, led by George Plekhanov (1856–1918) and Vladimir Lenin (1870–1924), believed that the introduction of capitalism in Russia would be made difficult by the vestiges of the feudal system. But the shining prospect of socialist society inflamed their imagination, and they were determined to attain it by means of a proletarian revolution that would sweep away both nascent capitalist patterns and feudal remnants. This deep conviction in the scientific correctness of Marxist predictions gave Lenin and his followers a sense of purpose that many other revolutionary or reform-minded groups lacked. In 1917 Lenin's Bolsheviks, who represented the radical wing of Russian Social-Democrats, took power in Russia. They hoped that by concentrating control over productive resources in their hands, they would be able to use their knowledge of the "objective laws" of human society to steer the country toward the "Communist" stage of development, when all property and power would be held in common and all people would be equal.

Marxism-Leninism

The collapse of the Communist experiment in the Soviet Union has seriously discredited the idea of socialism as an alternative to capitalism. Those who still cling to the socialist ideal as a model of social development try to dissociate Marx from Lenin, the founder of the Soviet state, insisting that the Bolshevik leader made a radical revision of classical Marxism and completely transformed it into a militant ideology of a totalitarian state. They find instances of complete reversals of Marx's conclusions, for example, in Lenin's assertion about Russia's readiness for a proletarian revolution. They say that Marx repeatedly emphasized that the new Communist society would be the result of a highly developed capitalism. In this regard, Russia was viewed by Marx as a very unlikely place in which to have a proletarian revolution, because the industrial revolution there had hardly started.

Many analysts, however, are convinced that Leninism rests firmly on the doctrinal foundations of classical Marxism. It is possible to list a range of Marxist principles by which Lenin was guided in his activities, first as the leader of the Russian proletarian revolution and later as the head of the victorious workers' government. These ideas formed part and parcel of Leninism and were thoroughly assimilated by it. They became the immutable dogmas that underpinned the construction of socialism in the former USSR. Only the most central of them will be summarized here:

- Humankind in its development passes through five formations, with communism being the highest and final of them.

- Humankind advances to communism, the essence of which will be "from each according to his abilities, to each according to his needs."

- Private ownership of the means of production is connected with exploitation; with the abolition of private property, exploitation will disappear.

- Class struggle is the essence of world development: "The history of all hitherto existing society is the history of class struggle" (Marx).

- Class struggle is waged by two main classes: the exploited working class and the exploiting class of the bourgeoisie.

- Due to its social position, the working class is naturally attracted to socialism.

- The state is an instrument created to protect the exploiters from the exploited.

- Democracy under capitalism is merely one of the forms of the exploiting bourgeois state.

- The road to socialism lies through a violent revolution, the aim of which is the destruction of the bourgeois state and private ownership and the creation of a workers' state—the state of the dictatorship of the proletariat.

- The state of the dictatorship of the proletariat is a necessary stage in the transition to a classless society, a society without the state.

- The essence of socialism and of the transition to communism is a gradual abolition of money-commodity relations (in other words, of the market).

- The essence of a socialist economy is a high degree of centralization and of planning in all aspects of the economy.

- The dictatorship of the proletariat is unthinkable without the Communist Party's dominant position within the state.

Marxist tenets with Lenin's amendments became gospel in the Soviet Union, and the ruling ideology was frequently referred to as "Marxism-Leninism." The Soviet model of socialism was not just the result of Soviet rulers' policies. It was a logical end product of the implementation of the principles elaborated by the founders of Marxism. Their ideas, such as a nonmarket economy, the dictatorship of one class, and the predominance of a single, Communist ideology, provided the cornerstones of the new social system. The practical implementation of these ideas in every country, which followed the Soviet model, led to the alienation of people from power, their estrangement from property, and the rise of an authoritarian state.

Marxism versus Human Nature

From 1917 on, Marxism-Leninism provided the foundations of Soviet ideology and organization until three-quarters of a century later, when the Soviet state faltered and suddenly crumbled to dust.

One of the main reasons why the Communist ideological foundations collapsed was that Marxism preached what even the early Christians did not believe was possible or practical. It advocated universal, forcible redistribution: paradise on earth was to be achieved by the abolition of property on which the capitalist mode of production was based. There is no doubt that Marx was largely right in identifying many ills of the capitalist society. But capitalism cannot be reduced to its evils. It makes and breaks people's destinies, plunging some to the very bottom of destitution and poverty while allowing others to develop their creative potential and enjoy life to the full. It has provided millions and millions with welfare and reasonable prosperity. On the whole, countries with developed capitalist patterns have been able to ensure living standards for the mass of the population unattainable under any other socioeconomic system that has ever existed. From the point of view of everyday human experience, this may be the most important and valuable advantage that distinguishes capitalism from all precapitalist socioeconomic systems.

In addition, capitalist patterns, however cruel some of them may seem, appear to be more in tune with basic human instincts and passions than the utopian egalitarian blueprints of the founders of Marxism. The Marxist picture of humankind's triumphant march upward through the five socioeconomic formations, from primitive society to communism, obscures the tremendous stability of some of the essential characteristics of human nature. In the course of biological evolution, even when humans ceased to exist as animals, when they acquired the ability to make tools and developed the power of abstract thinking, they still had preserved the sum total of their primordial instincts and inclinations. These instincts developed into human passions. They change little from century to century and even from millennium to millennium. An authoritative source provides a revealing catalog of some of the most enduring traits of human nature:

> Again Jesus called the crowd to him and said, "Listen to me, everyone, and understand this. Nothing outside a man can make him 'unclean' by going into him. Rather, it is what comes out of a man that makes him 'unclean.'
>
> "If anyone has ears to hear, let him hear."
>
> After he had left the crowd and entered the house, his disciples asked him about this parable. "Are you so dull?" he asked. "Don't you see that nothing that enters a man from outside can make him unclean? For it does not go into his heart but into his stomach, and then out of his body." . . .

He went on: "What comes out of a man is what makes him 'unclean.' For from within, out of men's hearts, come evil thoughts, sexual immorality, theft, murder, adultery, greed, malice, deceit, lewdness, envy, slander, arrogance and folly. All these evils come from inside and make the man 'unclean.'" (Mark 7:14–23)[2]

There is no reason to think that much has changed in human nature after two thousand years since these words were first spoken. The darker sides of human nature have not gone away. They remain part of people's everyday existence and continue to have a powerful influence on the course of human development.[3]

Marx and Engels, and their Russian followers after them, assumed that the abolition of private ownership and its replacement by public control would put an end to the influence of human instincts and passions on the economic and social life of society. People would somehow free themselves from the inborn characteristics of human behavior. The seventy-four-year-long Communist experiment demonstrated clearly the fallacy of this assumption. The "new" Communist man failed to shed human characteristics that have developed over thousands of years, including those associated with economic structures based on private ownership.

The underestimation of the importance of human instincts and passions by Marx and Engels in their vision of the Communist future is especially striking if we consider that both of them were experts in human history and were well aware of the place of human instincts and desires in it. Marx fully used his deep understanding of human nature in elaborating the political economy of capitalism. In particular, he singled out one powerful instinct as a driving force of capitalist accumulation: greed, the passion for accumulation, including the hoarding of gold. Indeed, greed, as an insatiable desire for wealth and gain, is one of the pillars on which his economic theory rests. In his *Capital*, Marx quotes Christopher Columbus to demonstrate how capitalist accumulation generates base passions and all-consuming desires and, at the same time, is driven by them:

With the possibility of keeping hold of the commodity as exchange-value, or exchange-value as a commodity, the lust for gold awakens. With the extension of commodity circulation, there is an increase in the power of money, that absolutely social form of wealth which is always ready to be used. "Gold is a wonderful thing! Its owner is master of all he desires. Gold can even enable souls to enter Paradise." (Columbus, in his letter from Jamaica, 1503)[4]

Marx also turns to the poetic genius of William Shakespeare to convey the power that money has over people and to demonstrate the extent to which it inflames passions and corrupts morals. He brings home the message with the help of a great passage from *Timon of Athens* (act 4, scene 3):

> Gold? yellow, glittering, precious gold? . . .
> Thus much of this, will make black, white; foul, fair,
> Wrong, right; base, noble; old, young; coward, valiant.
> . . . What this, you gods? Why, this
> Will lug your priests and servants from your sides,
> Pluck stout men's pillows from below their head;
> This yellow slave
> Will knit and break religions; bless the accursed;
> Make the hoar leprosy adored; place thieves,
> And give them title, knee and approbation,
> With senators on the bench; this is it,
> That makes the wappen'd widow wed again:
> . . . Come damned earth,
> Thou common whore of mankind.[5]

Marx sees capitalist accumulation as an "unceasing movement of profit-making" driven by the capitalist's "boundless drive for enrichment" and the "passionate chase after value."[6] Self-interest is not the preserve of the capitalist alone. The worker, too, is only human and not naturally imbued with altruism. Capitalism makes them both enter into certain relations with one another, in which each of them pursues his private interests. Marx makes a significant admission that something positive is achieved as a result of their self-centered interaction to benefit the whole of society:

> The only force bringing them [the capitalist and the worker] together, and putting them into relation with each other, is the self-ishness, the gain and the private interest of each. Each pays heed to himself only, and no one worries about the others. And precisely for that reason, either in accordance with the pre-established harmony of things, or under the auspices of an omniscient providence, they all work together to their mutual advantage, for the common weal, and in the common interest.[7]

There is hardly any point in arguing what came first: market or human passions. What is certain, however, is a definite correlation between the two. The very existence of the market and life in a compet-

The University of Te

Instructor:_____

Dept:_____

Course Title:

_____

e-mail address-----------------------------

F

O R D	CALL NO	AUTHOR

itive market environment, associated with profit hunting and rivalry, arouse many passions inside a human being. The market induces not just instincts directly connected with business activities. It also kindles feelings and desires normally associated with the spheres of leisure, entertainment, and sport. At the same time, the market moderates passions by giving vent to them.

The system, set up in Soviet Russia from the blueprints of Marx and his Russian followers, closed all the "pores" and "safety valves" that exist in a market economy. The imposition of strictly centralized planning and rigid regulation stifled personal initiative and entrepreneurial talent as the driving force of economic development. For decades, draconian restrictions and administrative constraints prevented those engaged in industry and agriculture from using their own creativeness and talent to achieve a desired level of prosperity. The Soviet economic model built up frustration and internal tensions and drove individuals to search for roundabout ways of fulfilling their potential. Individuals with entrepreneurial and mercantile habits of mind could apply their skills only in the illegal sector of the economy known as the "shadow economy" and risked being arrested and punished for their activities as common criminals. At the other extreme, social engineering of the Soviet type resulted in public apathy and indifference, breeding stagnation and the decay of the entire system.

Chapter Four

The Soviet Political System

Dictatorship of the Proletariat

Lenin's chief contribution to the Marxist canon was the development of Marx's concept of the dictatorship of the proletariat. In the writings of Marx and Engels the concept of the dictatorship of the proletariat was most clearly elaborated with regard to the experience of the Paris Commune of 1871. The founders of Marxism viewed it as the first proletarian revolution in human history because it brought to power a government of the working class, represented by the bloc of proletarian and petit bourgeois revolutionaries. This was government of a new type—the first example of a dictatorship of the proletariat in history. The main conclusion that the two founders of Marxism reached in their analysis of the lessons of the Paris Commune was that the chief reason for its downfall was an insufficient toughness on the part of the proletarian government. It was hesitant to suppress the counterrevolutionary forces, adopting the tactics of "passive defense."

Lenin attached great importance to the study of the lessons of the defeated Paris Commune and insisted on the form of an iron dictatorship that would be utterly ruthless and merciless toward the enemies of a workers' republic of the future. Lenin left no doubts about what he meant by dictatorship:

Dictatorship is rule based directly upon force and unrestricted by any laws.

The revolutionary dictatorship of the proletariat is rule won and maintained by the use of violence by the proletariat against the bourgeoisie, rule that is unrestricted by any laws.[1]

Lenin used the phrase "the dictatorship of the proletariat" to describe a government representing the majority of the population, but prepared to use force to control the minority that opposed it. According to him, immediately after the revolutionary overthrow of capitalism there would be an intermediate period on the road to socialism. During that transitional stage, the dictatorship of the proletariat would perform the function of suppression of the exploiting classes. It would include the destruction of the very foundations on which the activity of exploiters was based, such as private property, and even the physical annihilation of the exploiters themselves. But the new government would be more democratic than any that had existed previously, as it would represent for the first time in history the interests of most Russians, rather than those of a privileged minority.

In Lenin's view, the new proletarian government would need to build and maintain a coercive machinery of power and use it not just against its internal enemies, but also to repel "attempts on the part of the bourgeoisie of other countries to destroy the victorious proletarian socialist state." Only with the triumph of the proletarian-socialist revolution on a worldwide scale would class struggle finally be over, society become classless, and the coercive apparatus of the state no longer be needed. The state would die out (or, to use Friedrich Engels's famous phrase, simply "wither away"). The dictatorship of the proletariat would come to an end.

If the Paris Commune of 1871 was the first attempt in history to establish a dictatorship of the proletariat, then Russia in 1917 became the first country in the world where the dictatorship of the proletariat triumphed and consolidated under the determined leadership of Lenin and the Bolsheviks.

"All Power to the Soviets!"

In Russia the dictatorship of the proletariat took the form of a republic of soviets, and the tsarist empire was transformed into the Union of Soviet Socialist Republics (USSR), or Soviet Union for short.

The origins of soviets as proletarian governing bodies go back to the events of the revolution of 1905. During the general strike of that year, St. Petersburg workers set up the Soviet of Workers' Deputies to coordinate the strike action in the imperial capital. This quickly became the model of a new working-class organization that was reproduced across the empire. The Russian word soviet means advice or counsel, and was also applied to meetings, such as the peasant commune. Just as communes consisted of all heads of households in the village, so a soviet was elected from all workers in the town. In 1905 soviets were set up in towns and cities across the country. In some places they gained much wider powers than simple strike committees, spreading their control from working-class districts to entire towns and effectively acting as city councils or the local administration. The St. Petersburg soviet was by far the most important of them. It existed for about three months and was eventually suppressed by the tsarist government.

Twelve years later, following the collapse of tsarism in February 1917, soviets were resurrected. After the abdication of Nicholas II, two governments simultaneously had emerged contending for the right to provide political leadership: the official liberal provisional government and the unofficial government in the form of the Petrograd Soviet of Workers' and Soldiers' Deputies supported by the armed workers and soldiers of the capital. The provisional government had the support mostly of Russia's traditional elites, including the remnants of the tsarist bureaucracy and the high command in the army. The Petrograd soviet commanded the loyalty of urban workers and peasants, and spread its authority over other soviets that sprang up in the towns and villages and at the front.

Between February and October 1917 Lenin emphasized that the soviets were the "only possible form of revolutionary government." He vehemently castigated the idea of a parliamentary system and insisted that what Russia needed was "not a parliamentary republic—to return to a parliamentary republic from the Soviets of Workers' Deputies would be a retrograde step—but a republic of Soviets of Workers' and Peasants' Deputies throughout the country, from top to bottom."[2] Lenin understood that the Bolsheviks stood little chance of becoming a ruling party as a result of elections to a Western-style parliament. They had, however, a very good chance of coming to power by seizing control of the soviets. Lenin's strategy was vindicated in October, when the Bolshevik-led insurrection in Petrograd toppled the provisional government. By that time the Bolsheviks had already gained a majority in the soviets.

The Party of a New Type

From the start of his career as a professional revolutionary, Lenin believed that proletarian revolution was at hand and prepared for it carefully. He understood that in tsarism Russian Marxists had a formidable opponent, and for that reason he attached great importance to the preparation of organizational structures of a future Marxist party.

In 1902 Lenin produced *What Is to Be Done?* In this seminal work on the party's organization he laid down a detailed plan for the building of the party of the working class. Lenin severely criticized those within Russian social-democracy who argued that the party should concentrate the workers' attention on the economic struggle against capitalism. Lenin believed that this trend of "economism" within Marxism would encourage the workers to develop merely a "trade-union consciousness" and distract them from the vital political task of overthrowing tsarism.

In other words, Lenin believed that the workers, left to their own instincts, would choose reforms in wages and working conditions over political revolution. In his view, only a strong organization of revolutionaries could provide leadership to the spontaneous movement of the proletariat and transform its struggle into a genuine "class struggle." What the proletariat needed then was "a party of a new type." It would not simply drag at the tail of the labor movement, passively registering what the masses of the working class feel and think. On the contrary, the party would stand at the head of the movement, forming the "vanguard of the proletariat." It would be the party of a new type in the vital sense that it would not wait for the Russian proletariat to evolve into a fully fledged political class, but would assume an active and decisive role in shaping the working class itself and spearheading the proletarian revolution.

As far as the structure and composition of the party were concerned, Lenin insisted on a monolithic and militant underground organization of professional revolutionaries submitting to strict party discipline. It would operate as a revolutionary headquarters with a military-style commitment to subordination, unity, and secrecy. In short, the very organization of the party, centralized in the extreme, was a dictatorship on a small scale.

HISTORY OF THE PARTY'S NAME

1898–1917	Russian Social-Democratic Labor Party
1917–1918	Russian Social-Democratic Labor Party (Bolsheviks)
1918–1925	Russian Communist Party (Bolsheviks)
1925–1952	All-Union Communist Party (Bolsheviks)
1952–1991	Communist Party of the Soviet Union
1993–	Communist Party of the Russian Federation

Following the Bolshevik takeover, the Communist Party quickly ceased to be a political party in any conventional sense of the word because it no longer expressed the interests of any social group as such. The party evolved into an administrative, military, and industrial machine. It recruited its members from many social groups. Former workers, soldiers,

peasants, or officers, once they became Communists, were initiated into a
new social category in its own right. Their status in society, material position, access to privilege, and even food rations set them apart from the rest
of society. Party membership conferred on them the new identity of the
"vanguard of society." In effect, they were a new privileged elite.

The "Party-State"

The one-party dictatorship gradually forged a distinctive political system. In the pre-October period Lenin had repeatedly expressed his conviction in the ability of the masses to run the state directly through
soviets. This, in his opinion, would make redundant the civil service,
parliamentary institutions, the separation of legislative, executive, and
judicial powers, and many other structures of a democratic system of
government. In real life, however, the mass of the working population
was immediately restricted in its right to participate in democratic politics. Not just the "natural enemies" of the new regime—the bourgeoisie,
landowners, former tsarist civil servants, and the clergy—were denied
political rights. The Bolsheviks were suspicious of the overwhelming
majority of the country's population—the peasantry—and introduced
legal restrictions on their voting rights. From the start, the idea of "rule
by the people" through soviets was compromised, and the soviets themselves were gradually transformed into a decorative facade masking the
party's power monopoly. In real life, the notions "Soviet power" and
"Bolshevik power" converged.

Nevertheless, officially the power was divided between the soviets and
the Communist Party. The soviets were, ostensibly, the representative
organs of the popular masses, whereas the party "guided" the soviets. In
theory, the soviets embodied all state power in the Soviet Union. The
voters of every village, town, province, and republic elected representatives, called deputies, to the soviets to serve as representative bodies for
each territory. Deputies served on a part-time, voluntary basis and usually met two to four times a year, for a day or two at a time, to hear
reports and approve the proposed budget and plan. The large size of the
soviets and their infrequent sessions pointed to the ceremonious character of these bodies.

Voting for deputies to soviets was another indication of their ritual
and formal function. The "election" was uncontested, as generally only
one candidate ran for a given seat. All candidates were vetted and
approved by a party committee. The regime went to great lengths to

ensure that everyone cast a ballot with a single, preprinted name at a polling station. The massive turnout and near unanimous endorsement of the candidate were treated as signs of the unshakable unity of regime and people. For the authorities, such ceremonies were of great importance, serving to showcase the democratic character of the state, whereas for much of the population, voting in elections was regarded as part of the harmless pageantry of everyday life.

Once "elected," a soviet, in its turn, "elected" a set of executive officials to manage the government in its jurisdiction. In reality, the soviet simply ratified a choice that had been made by the Communist Party authorities. At lower levels of the soviet structures the executive arm of each soviet was called the executive committee. It consisted of a chairman, the deputy chairs, and the heads of government departments responsible for such areas as finance, transportation, social welfare, catering, and education. The executive officials were formally accountable to the soviets, but, in reality, they were answerable to two sets of superior authorities: higher level government executive officials and Communist Party officials.

Soviet Government

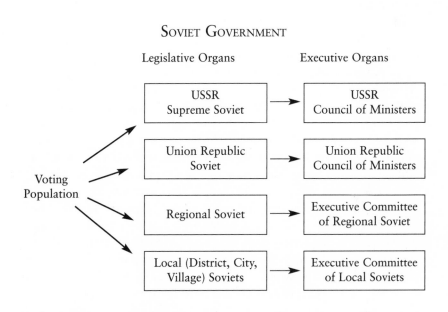

At the highest levels, such as the level of union republics' administration and the all-union central government, the model of soviet and
executive committee took on a more elaborate form. Instead of a
soviet, there was a Supreme Soviet; instead of an executive committee,
there was a Council of Ministers. The USSR Supreme Soviet had the
formal authority to enact laws, but its function was not in principle
different from the ceremonial character of lower-level soviets. The
Supreme Soviet met only twice a year, and then for a few days each
time, to hear official reports and rubber-stamp motions proposed by
the leadership. At the apex of the state executive was the USSR Council
of Ministers. Formally, it was equivalent to the cabinet of a parliamentary government in a Western democracy. In reality, all major
strategic decisions were taken by the Politburo of the Communist Party
of the Soviet Union (CPSU), in effect the cabinet, whereas the Council
of Ministers was, in effect, a committee of administrators entrusted
with carrying out the strategies of the Politburo and running the state
economy. A similar system was replicated in all constituent republics
of the Soviet Union.

The party's own structures paralleled that of the government and
were designed to supervise and direct it. Every territorial subdivision—
district, town, province, and so on—had a full-time party organization.
A CPSU committee of a city, for example, was comprised of functional
departments overseen by full-time senior party officials called secretaries. It was presided over by a first secretary. The first secretary of the
party organization worked closely with the chairman of the executive
committee of the city soviet. But the status of the party official was superior to that of the soviet official, and directives and guidance from the
party secretary were binding on the executive arm of the city soviet. At
each level of the territorial pyramid the pattern was repeated, with a full-
time Communist Party committee shadowing and supervising the governmental structure for the given territorial unit. Similar to each city,
each province or union republic had its own first secretary and party
organization. They ensured that government and social organizations
worked in unison following the leadership's overall policy directions.

At the top, ultimate power to decide policy rested in the CPSU
Politburo. The Politburo was a small committee made up of the country's most powerful leaders. It was presided over by the general secretary
of the CPSU. In effect, he was the real head of the country. The Politburo
also included the chairman of the Council of Ministers, senior secretaries
of the CPSU Central Committee, one or two of the first secretaries of the
Communist Party organizations in union republics, the minister of

STRUCTURE OF THE CPSU

```
┌─────────────────────────────────┐
│        General Secretary        │
└─────────────────────────────────┘

┌─────────────────────────────────┐
│            Politburo            │
└─────────────────────────────────┘

┌─────────────────────────────────┐
│   Secretariat and Departments   │
└─────────────────────────────────┘

┌─────────────────────────────────┐
│        Central Committee        │
└─────────────────────────────────┘

┌─────────────────────────────────┐
│    Republic Central Committee   │
└─────────────────────────────────┘

┌─────────────────────────────────┐
│    Regional Party Committee     │
└─────────────────────────────────┘

┌─────────────────────────────────┐
│      District or City Party     │
│            Committee            │
└─────────────────────────────────┘

┌─────────────────────────────────┐
│   Primary Party Organization    │
│          at Workplace           │
└─────────────────────────────────┘
```

defense, the chairman of the KGB (Committee of State Security, the Soviet political police and security agency), and the foreign minister.

The Politburo worked closely with the Secretariat of the Central Committee of the Communist Party. The Secretariat provided organizational support to the Politburo by helping to develop the agenda for its weekly meetings. Effectively, the Secretariat acted as the party's central headquarters. Its functional departments, presided over by secretaries, monitored the political and economic situation throughout the country and around the world, developing policy options for the

Politburo. In addition, the Secretariat managed the political careers of thousands of top political officials. It supervised the vast government bureaucracy, the army, the police, the law enforcement system, the KGB, and the governments of the republics and regions. Finally, it determined the ideological line that was to be echoed and reinforced throughout the country through the channels of party propaganda and the mass media.

The Politburo and the Secretariat issued their official decrees in the name of the CPSU Central Committee. The Central Committee was a larger body (it grew over the years from 25 members in 1921 to 307 in 1986) that included the most important and powerful figures in the country, such as regional party leaders and representatives of various economic and social interests. It was elected by the party congress, but this merely involved assenting to a list of candidates presented by the Politburo. Formally, the Central Committee was a party body, but it was the closest thing in the Soviet political system to a real parliament. It convened for its meetings (called plenums) only twice a year for a day or two and probably did not fulfill any important policy-making role. Yet it did serve to facilitate communication between the Politburo and the broader elite of the country.

Until the demise of the Soviet Union in 1991, the Communist Party had never been an ordinary social and political organization, or a political party in any conventional sense of the term. It was a mechanism to rule society and a key component of the Soviet political and economic system. At its peak, the Communist Party had around twenty million members, or around 9 percent of the adult population. But as a mass organization with a multimillion membership, the party did not elaborate national policy. This was the preserve of a narrow circle of top officials at the apex of the CPSU hierarchy and of the party's central apparatus that served it. Party structures at lower levels, rank-and-file Communists in particular, were accorded the role of mere executants of the will of the party's supreme leadership. The ordinary citizens, as well as the party rank and file, were effectively estranged from power, and potentially democratic institutions, such as the soviets, played the role of a smoke screen disguising an authoritarian regime.

The *Nomenklatura*

It is impossible to understand how the Communist Party maintained its grip on power without the mention of the role of the so-called *nomen-*

klatura principle. This denoted the party's monopoly on filling positions of power and authority in the party itself, in government, and in all organized areas of social life. All important posts in the country, from high state officialdom, army and police officers, to local and regional bosses and enterprise directors, were filled or "elected to" on the party's recommendation or approval. In this way, the Communist Party and ultimately its leader—the general secretary—managed to control the entire Soviet Union.

For this to be managed, the system of elite recruitment evolved in such a way that party bosses controlled the personnel policy at their corresponding levels. Bosses at various levels were responsible for a defined nomenclature of important jobs (hence the Russian word *nomenklatura*). High party officials controlled the higher reaches of the state, whereas regional and local party functionaries controlled appointments at their local or regional levels. The party itself was run on these principles—only trusted members were promoted to key full-time party posts by their superiors.

To occupy a *nomenklatura* position for the first time, a person had to have been approved by the appropriate party committee's personnel department. Once a person had succeeded in entering the ranks of the *nomenklatura*, however, he or she had a certain degree of job security and social status. *Nomenklatura* members tended to move up the career ladder to higher-level positions or, at worst, to other *nomenklatura* positions at the same level. Such people came to be regarded as members of a privileged social-political elite with access to power and material perquisites. In everyday language, they were collectively called the *nomenklatura* and thought of as a ruling class. They were, however, a ruling class with a difference, for they did not technically own productive resources but used their position of authority to grab the biggest share of social product.

The Communist Party's power monopoly and the *nomenklatura* principle with which it was enforced led gradually to the physical and intellectual degeneration of the leadership. Increasingly, people unsuitable for positions of responsibility controlled the levers of power. Bureaucratic blunders became an endemic disease of the system. This inherent flaw of the Soviet system has been described as "the law of a totalitarian pyramid." A leader selected his team on the principle "more stupid than I." As there was no regular mechanism for handing over power, the next leader could only be a person from his team. He, in turn, picked his inner circle in accordance with the same principle. As a result, the system aided the survival of the "unfittest," promoting to leadership positions individuals like Leonid Brezhnev (1906–82) and Konstantin Chernenko (1911–85) in the Soviet Union, or Erich Honecker (1912–94) and Nicolae Ceausescu (1918–89) in the Soviet bloc countries. A creeping degeneration and a lowering of the intellectual caliber of leaders affected not just politics but also the economy and culture: the regime promoted not the most talented people, but those who were prepared to work within its rigid administrative and ideological constraints.

SOVIET RULERS		
Figure	*Period in power*	*Reason for termination of office*
Vladimir Lenin	1917–24	Death
Joseph Stalin	1924–53	Death
Nikita Khrushchev	1953–64	Conspiracy
Leonid Brezhnev	1964–82	Death
Yuri Andropov	1982–84	Death
Konstantin Chernenko	1984–85	Death
Mikhail Gorbachev	1985–91	Revolution

The most serious flaw of the Communist regime was that it did not have a peaceful and regular system of the transfer of power from one leader to another. The struggle for power was particularly intense at the time of succession. Still, the enormous powers of the country's top leader—the general secretary of the CPSU—enabled him to stay in power as long as he could command the loyalty of the Politburo and the Secretariat. By appointing his supporters to leading party posts in the party leadership at the center and in the regions and by removing in time those who might oppose him, the general secretary could expect to stay in office until the end of his life. Most in fact did so. The result was a gradual aging of the entire ruling elite of the USSR.

Chapter Five

Soviet Nationalities

The "Red Federated Empire"

In Marxist teaching, "the nationalities question" played a subordinate role. Ethnic problems were considered to be a characteristic of the bourgeois capitalist world: as soon as capitalism gave way to socialism, all social roots of interethnic antagonisms would be eradicated and nations would come together in one supranational world community. In contrast to Marx, however, Lenin was aware of the revolutionary potential of the oppressed nationalities and was determined to use it. He referred to imperial Russia as "the prison of peoples" and incorporated the demand of the right of "national self-determination for all nations" into the first Bolshevik party program (1903).[1] Still, for Lenin and his followers, class struggle took priority, and they were firmly convinced that national problems would resolve themselves automatically in a socialist Russia. Somehow, at a stroke, the tsarist empire would be transformed into a proletarian internationalist state and skip the stage of the development of national states.

Following the October takeover, the Bolshevik government adopted the "Declaration of the Rights of the Peoples of Russia." The declaration facilitated the acceptance of Soviet power on the multiethnic fringes of the disintegrating empire by promising its peoples "equality and sovereignty" and reaffirming "the right to free self-determination, up to secession." Intoxicated with the idea of a world revolution and the "international solidarity of the proletariat," the Bolshevik leadership did not seriously expect the working masses of the ethnic periphery to claim self-determination. The declaration of the right to self-determination in theory and its denial in practice would determine the fundamental ambiguity of the Soviet regime's nationalities policy for many years to come.

The new constitutional structure, set up by the Bolsheviks, made important concessions to the principle of nationality. In 1918 the former imperial core territories were proclaimed a federation, called the Russian Socialist Federated Soviet Republic. A number of separate republics also sprang up on the imperial fringes that had fallen off from the Russian center during the revolutionary upheaval. They were tied to Russia by military treaties and economic agreements, but they remained for some time formally independent.

The Union of Soviet Socialist Republics was founded on 30 December 1922, five years after the October Revolution of 1917, on the ruins of the old empire but within much the same boundaries as imperial Russia. The formation of the USSR cannot be interpreted simply as a reunification of the peoples of the former empire forced on them from above by the Bolshevik leadership. The process of their reintegration into one state had deep historical, economic, political, and cultural causes and was supported from below, as well as directed from above. Moreover, the political regimes that had sprung up in the territories of tsarist Russia needed a union with the Russian heartlands to ensure their common survival in the face of a hostile international environment.

The breakup of the tsarist empire had led to the emergence of six socialist republics: Russia, Belorussia, Ukraine, Armenia, Azerbaijan, and Georgia. Formally these states were independent, but in reality they were parts of one country because they had joint command of the armed forces, a single currency, and joint people's commissariats (i.e., ministries) of transport, finance, labor, and foreign trade. Most importantly, they were subordinated to the central apparatus of the Russian Communist Party (Bolsheviks), which had always rejected the federal principle in its own structures. All that was needed was to formalize de jure the de facto unity of the soviet republics.

The task of working out proposals for a new constitutional structure was entrusted to Joseph Stalin, who at that time was the People's Commissar for Nationalities. Stalin proposed the incorporation of the Ukraine, Belorussia, Armenia, Georgia, and Azerbaijan as autonomies into Russia. Lenin disagreed with this plan of "autonomization," as he believed that to violate the proclaimed right of nations to self-determination would be a political mistake. It could spark serious conflicts, undermining the fledgling Soviet state. Lenin defended a different formula: "a voluntary union of equal independent republics."

Despite the difference of approach, however, both plans envisaged a centralized state with all the prerogatives of power concentrated in the hands of the central party bodies. To the Bolsheviks, whether they supported Lenin's or Stalin's viewpoint, and to the two leaders themselves, the class approach took priority over everything else. What really mattered was to find a solution to the nationalities issue that would help to advance the main strategic objective—the establishment of a socialist unitary state. Lenin's proposal was more in tune with the slogans of Communist propaganda and the goal of a world revolution. Lenin saw the Soviet Union as a bridgehead, from which the world revolution would begin to expand, incorporating ever-new national entities, into a "Socialist United States of the World." Lenin's plan emphasized the equality of the republics and opened the door to new countries to join the union. The invitation to other states to become members of the USSR was even incorporated in the first Soviet constitution, adopted in 1924. According to the constitution, the ultimate goal of setting up the Soviet Union was "uniting all the working people of all the countries" into one suprastate—a "World Socialist Soviet Republic."[2] Formally, the union was "open" both ways: republics were free to join, and they also had the right to secede. However, no legal mechanism was provided to enable the republics to exercise the right to leave.

The Central Committee approved Lenin's plan, and the administrative form of the Communist state took the shape of a federation, based on national ethnic groups. The ethnolinguistic principle of carving up administrative territories contradicted Russia's demographic realities: in many of its parts the ethnic mix of populations was too complex to allow a straightforward division of the territory into separate ethnolinguistic units. The task was particularly difficult in central Asia, where linguistic and ethnic diversity was especially profuse. Many ethnic communities found themselves arbitrarily divided between different republics, regions, or territories. For example, the autonomous territory of Nagorno-Karabakh was always largely populated by Armenians but was ceded to Azerbaijan by Stalin in 1921.

The federal structure incorporated several different levels of administrative units so as to take into account the size and level of development of the ethnic groups. At the top was the All-Union (federal) government of the USSR. Then followed governments of union republics. These included the major nationalities (called titular nationalities) that gave their republics their title. When the USSR was established in December 1922, it was comprised of four republics: the Russian Soviet Federated Socialist Republic, the Transcaucasian Soviet Federated Socialist Republic (comprising Armenia, Azerbaijan, and Georgia), and the Ukrainian and Belorussian Soviet Socialist Republics. Additional union republics were set up in subsequent years, bringing the total number to fifteen.

At the next level below the union republics, autonomous soviet socialist republics were set up to take account of ethnic groups located in a given republic and to give them a measure of political recognition and some elements of self-government. An autonomous republic was subordinate to its parent union republic. The overwhelming majority of autonomous republics—sixteen out of twenty—were located within Russia, two within Georgia, one within Azerbaijan, and one within Uzbekistan. The lower levels of this administrative structure incorporated eight autonomous provinces and ten autonomous districts, giving social identity to smaller ethnic groupings or national minorities within republics, such as Armenians in the Nagorno-Karabakh autonomous province within Azerbaijan.

UNION REPUBLICS OF THE USSR, 1990

Armenia	Lithuania
Azerbaijan	Moldavia
Belorussia	Russia
Estonia	Tajikistan
Georgia	Turkmenistan
Kazakhstan	Ukraine
Kirgiziya	Uzbekistan
Latvia	

AUTONOMOUS REPUBLICS OF THE USSR

(Within Russian SFSR)

Bashkiriya	Komi
Buryatiya	Mari
Checheno-Ingushetiya	Mordoviya
Chuvashiya	North Ossetiya
Dagestan	Tatarstan
Kabardino-Balkariya	Tuva
Kalmykiya	Udmurtiya
Karelia	Yakutiya

(Within Georgian SSR)

Abkhaziya	Adzhariya

(Within Azerbaijan SSR)
Nakhichevan

(Within Uzbek SSR)
Karakalpakiya

The state structure of the USSR was, on face value, a federation, and fifteen nominally sovereign republics were considered to be the constituent units of a federal union. The name of the nation—the Union of Soviet Socialist Republics—also implied the existence of a federal state. Most structures of power at the central level were replicated in the union republics: they had their own constitutions, national plan, and budget. However, there was one thing in the Soviet regime's setup that turned all the formal constitutional provisions of Soviet federalism into a moot issue. In the Soviet system, the party was the real source of all legislative policy and the controlling factor behind the formal governmental organs. But the centralized party hierarchy rejected the federal principle. The party organizations of the union republics were not national parties, but branches of the single unitary Communist Party of the Soviet Union. The party was the ultimate deciding factor on all matters of policy, and the central supreme party organs at the top in Moscow could always overrule or ignore any formal constitutional provisions.

The union authorities controlled major productive resources throughout the country, including land, natural resources, industry, and human capital, and made strategic decisions about economic development in the republics. The control of the money supply was also an exclusively central function. Apart from the party, other union-wide control structures such as the KGB, army, and economic bureaucracy penetrated into each republic and facilitated the center's supremacy. All this meant that, in reality, Soviet federalism was formal and ephemeral. The USSR was in fact a unitary state with a measure of administrative devolution. Genuine federalism was not viable in a state where the ruling party wielded absolute power.

Sorting out the "Nationalities Question"

In the 1920s the Bolshevik government's nationality policy was pragmatic and flexible enough to facilitate the integration of the non-Russian populations into the Soviet state. Unlike the late imperial period, when the tsarist regime discriminated against numerous non-Russian ethnic groups, the nationalities enjoyed formal political equality. This was seen as an important precondition for achieving equal socioeconomic and cultural standards across various peoples and helping less developed nationalities to overcome their backwardness. The Bolsheviks believed that this strategy would eradicate ethnic contradictions and settle the "nationalities question" for good.

In the localities the Soviet authorities pursued the policy of "indige-nization" (*korenizatsia*), designed to increase steadily the proportion of the representatives of the indigenous nationality in the local party and state administration (indigenization took the form of "Ukranianization" in the Ukraine, "Belorussianization" in Belorussia, and so on). In addi-tion, during the 1920s, the center actively co-opted representatives of non-Russian elites into central governing bodies. For example, a sub-stantial part of the new Soviet bureaucracy was recruited from mobile ethnic diasporas, such as the Jews. Alongside the Jews, the regime pro-moted Armenians and Georgians, many of whom had been active in the socialist movement and were well educated. As a result, Jews, Armenians, and Georgians featured prominently in top-level party and state bodies, as well as in the ranks of the new Soviet scientific and cul-tural intelligentsia, in the 1920s and 1930s.[3]

The early nationalities policy of the Bolshevik government displayed con-siderable tolerance of non-Russian languages and cultures and even system-atically encouraged the development of "minor" languages. New alphabets were invented for the first time for forty-eight ethnic groups, including the Turkmen, Chechen, and ethnic minorities of Siberia. Non-Russian lan-guages were increasingly used in lower-level administrative bodies, courts of law, and schools. The Communist authorities made great efforts to eradi-cate illiteracy by setting up schools, where students were taught in local lan-guages. Gradually, secondary and higher educational establishments were also set up with teaching in local languages. All this helped expand the ranks of non-Russian educated elites and led to a flowering of literature, the arts, and sciences in some of the republics and national autonomies.

There is no doubt that the Communist regime had very good reasons for pursuing liberal cultural policies. They served to ensure the stability of the multiethnic state by doing away with discrimination of non-Russians. They presented an attractive shop window to the rest of the world and, in particular, to Asian countries by demonstrating a fair treatment of the Muslim populations of central Asia. Finally, and most importantly, schooling and publishing in local languages facilitated the spread of the Communist gospel among non-Russians. Cultural workers of all nationalities were enjoined to produce works of literature and art that would be "nationalist in form and socialist in content."

The liberal language policies and the indigenization drive endured until the mid-1930s, helping to enlist the support of broad sections of non-Russian populations for the party and the Communist regime. More controversially, they accelerated the process of nation building among major nationalities and nudged some of the minor ones in the same direction. For example, the 1920s saw the consolidation of the Ukrainians as a nation: their language became entrenched in schools and local administration, and they evolved substantial Ukrainian-speaking educated elites, urban populations, and an industrial proletariat. The "indigenized" administrations tended toward greater independence from the center and craved greater national and cultural autonomy. They became breeding grounds for the spread of national communism in the republics as the desire to combine Communist ideas with national traditions. Contrary to the expectations of the Communist authorities, their policies did not do away with nationalism, but gave rise to nationalist ideologies and to gradual consolidation of nationalities into nations. It was clear that the evolving national elites would not remain content for long with formal equality and would sooner or later claim greater political rights to complement their cultural and language rights.

The onset of Stalin's revolution "from above" from the late 1920s onward signified a major turning point in the nationality policy from pragmatism and flexibility toward stringency and repression. In particular, Stalin's forced collectivization of agriculture in the early 1930s caused great upheaval and suffering both among Russian and non-Russian rural populations. The collectivization was probably the greatest disaster in Kazakh history and was accompanied by the enforcement of a settled way of life on the nomadic people and the destruction of traditional clan structures. The nomads resisted as much as they could by taking up arms, killing their cattle, or fleeing across the border into neighboring China. In the Ukraine, the administrative collectivization and the forcible requisitioning of crops in 1932–34 resulted in the famine that caused the deaths of several million people.

Stalin's radical policies were accompanied by purges among republican elites to curb any nationalist tendencies and "deviations." They soon escalated into an all-encompassing wave of terror that peaked in 1936–38. It dealt a crushing blow to the administrative elites in the republics. All members of the Ukrainian Politburo, for example, perished in the purge. The terror affected the elites of all nationalities, but its consequences in the union republics were particularly severe as it undermined many of the achievements of indigenization. Stalin's policies and the methods used to enforce them to a great extent put a chill on the process of nation building that had begun in the 1920s.

As a result of the Stalin revolution, many of the ideological imperatives of the Soviet nationality policy were transformed. In the 1920s the party leadership had sought to eradicate all vestiges of the imperial mentality of Russians, derided as "Great Russian chauvinism." Now the emphasis was reversed, and "local nationalism" was perceived a much bigger threat. The calls for international solidarity of proletarians were replaced by the new integrating ideology of Soviet patriotism and by the leader's cult. Both patriotism and the deification of the leader had, of course, deep roots in the prerevolutionary past. The officially sponsored patriotism had a certain base of support among the Russian population and, in particular, among the burgeoning numbers of Russian industrial workers and engineers. Many of them had come from rural communities and had achieved their new status and qualifications thanks to the policies of the Communist regime. As a result of industrialization and rising educational attainments, the new Russian nationalist movement began to take shape under the control of the central authorities. Consequently, Soviet patriotism had a distinctive Russian flavor.

The repressions against nationalities reached their peak in the mass deportations of entire peoples during the Second World War. When Soviet power was threatened by the Nazi invasion, Stalin accused the Crimean Tatars, the Volga Germans, and a number of Caucasian peoples of collaboration with the enemy, and deported nearly two million people in cattle trucks to eastern Kazakhstan, Siberia, and central Asia. About one-third of the deportees died en route or did not survive in the harsh conditions of the exile. The Molotov-Ribbentrop pact of 1939 and the Soviet victory in the Second World War allowed Stalin and his regime to complete the reintegration of the Russian lands lost at the time of the revolution and not only to take back the regions populated by East Slavs but also to reannex Estonia, Latvia, Lithuania, and Bessarabia. The "sovietization" of the reclaimed territories led to the deportation of tens of thousands to labor camps and exile.

After his death in 1953, the excesses of Stalin's treatment of nationalities did not reappear. At the same time, no conclusive and permanent break with Stalinist practices in this or any other sphere was made by his successors. Still, the post-Stalin leadership partially resuscitated some of the methods of the 1920s, including indigenization, greater reliance on non-Russian Communists in the union republics, and tolerance toward local languages and cultures. The concessions remained halfhearted, and the nationality policy oscillated between a more flexible, lenient tendency and repression.

On the whole, the union's various republics and national territories seemed to be obedient to Moscow in all essential matters. The level of visible conflict between national groups, or between nationalities and the center, was extremely low. The regime believed that it had been quite successful in molding "a new historic community of people—the Soviet nation." All citizens of the Soviet Union were members of a supranational Soviet people, subscribed to a unifying ideology (Marxism-Leninism), embraced a single political goal (communism), and communicated in a common language (Russian).

However, these hopes were never fulfilled. The relaxation of Communist controls after the death of Stalin and a limited decentralization that came with it rekindled the process of nation building stifled by Stalin's tyranny. The intelligentsia of various nation groups was growing more proactive, contributing to a revival of national languages, literatures, and self-awareness. The rising national elites were increasingly frustrated with restraints imposed by Moscow.

In the three decades following Stalin's death, non-Russians were able to use much better the opportunities implicit in the Soviet federal structures. From the 1960s they were fairly adequately represented in their republican leaderships and delegated their representatives to the center in Moscow. With time, members of the indigenous nationalities came to take certain rights for granted. These included the principles that the leader of the Communist Party organization in that republic was a member of the indigenous nationality, and that national cultural traditions were respected and developed as long as they did not directly clash with Soviet ideological doctrine. The steady rise in the population's educational levels over the decades of Soviet rule further contributed to the formation of a national intelligentsia and a national political elite in each republic. The growth of ethnic self-consciousness among various Soviet peoples fostered a tendency for the leaders and populations in the republics to think of the territory and institutions in their jurisdiction as "theirs." As a result, the national identity of the indigenous nationality became firmly bound with the territory that carried its name, even though some of the nationalities had had no tradition of independent statehood prior to the formation of the USSR.

The postwar period saw the rise of underground nationalist movements of varying intensity. The Crimean Tatars and the Germans voiced demands for the restoration of their territorial autonomies. Although their Volga autonomy was not reinstated, tens of thousands of ethnic Germans were able to emigrate to West Germany beginning in the 1970s. Similarly, the American patronage of the demands of the Soviet Jewry for the right of emigration helped to reach the level of over 200,000 Jewish emigrants leaving the Soviet Union by 1981.

However, the Crimean Tatars, German, and Jewish cases were special, as these were nation groups without territorial jurisdictions. In union republics nationalist activities of titular nationalities were usually limited to small circles of intellectuals. Opposition groups in Georgia, Armenia,

Major Nationalities of the Soviet Union, 1989[4]		
	In millions	*Percentage*
Entire population	285.7	100.00
Russians	145.2	50.80
Ukrainians	44.2	15.50
Uzbek	16.7	5.84
Belorussians	10.0	3.50
Kazakh	8.1	2.85
Azerbaijanis	6.8	2.37
Volga Tatars	6.6	2.30
Armenians	4.6	1.62
Tadjik	4.2	1.48
Georgians	4.0	1.39
Moldavians	3.5	1.22
Lithuanians	3.0	1.07
Turkmen	2.7	0.96
Kirgiz	2.5	0.89
Germans	2.0	0.71
Chuvash	1.8	0.64
Bashkirs	1.4	0.51
Jews	1.4	0.51
Latvians	1.4	0.51
Estonians	1.0	0.36
Chechens	0.9	0.33

Estonia, and Latvia focused primarily on language and cultural issues. Only Lithuania evolved a mass national movement in the 1960s and 1970s backed by the Catholic hierarchy. Some of the Lithuanian petitions to Soviet leaders contained over 100,000 signatures. Nationalism was also rife in West Ukraine, "reunited" with the rest of the republic during the Second World War. Many of its citizens sought to preserve and protect the Uniate Church banned by the Soviet authorities in 1946.

National aspirations of the Ukrainians were stamped out relentlessly for obvious reasons: the republic's demographic, economic, and geostrategic importance for the Communist empire was second only to Russia.

However, until the mid-1980s none of the national movements had sufficient strength to threaten the stability of the Soviet regime. To many observers, the CPSU's management of nationality relations looked successful enough to give credence to the Soviet leaders' claim that the "nationalities question" was close to being finally resolved. Few people could foresee that the Soviet federation was about to implode and the "nationalities question" would become utterly unmanageable. In practice, the assimilation of the various ethnic groups had not materialized in the way intended by Soviet leaders. As long as the central party-state authorities retained their coercive grip over society, it proved possible to prevent ethnic contradictions and tensions from getting out of hand. But once Gorbachev's liberalization began to undermine the power and authority of central institutions, the concealed ethnic divisions suddenly erupted to the surface.

Chapter Six

Serfdom—Capitalism—Socialism

Russia's Early Experience with Capitalism

Russia's prerevolutionary capitalist experience was brief and short-lived. In the thirteenth century the Mongol occupation cut Russia off from the West for over two hundred years and wrecked nascent roots of mercantile capitalism. Since the early fifteenth century Western Europe was developing a vigorous capitalism and strong bourgeoisie. By contrast, tsarist Russia lagged far behind with a bourgeoisie small and unimportant. Western notions of law, private property, and personal freedom were, to a large extent, unfamiliar to tsarist Russia. From the fifteenth to the seventeenth century the despotic tsars claimed absolute political power and were the chief owners of industry, mines, and the land. They held back the growth of capitalist tendencies by imposing royal monopolies on all lucrative enterprises.

Early industrialization from the seventeenth century on brought no introduction of capitalism. Russian "traditional" industrialization, as conducted under Peter the Great in the early eighteenth century, was alien to Western capitalist patterns. The state owned the means of production, appointed the management, set the price, and absorbed nearly all the output. The working force was not wage labor but the serfs tied in bondage to their factory. The state-licensed enterprises were assured of bonded labor and a market and had no incentive to rationalize production. In short, although a great surge took place in many branches of industry under Peter, his reforms did little to encourage private industrial capital.

At the beginning of the nineteenth century, while capitalism was only slowly beginning to affect Russia, it was revolutionizing Great Britain, Belgium, and France. It was transforming agrarian societies of the leading European states, rapidly expanding their industrial bases, and increasing urban populations. Yet the great industrial revolution spreading across the continent of Europe stopped short of the Russian borders. The government controlled the main forces of production, preventing the emergence of an urban bourgeoisie or commercial landed aristocracy. Private wealth was a function of government favor, when members of the nobility were rewarded with gifts of land and peasants by the government for their civil or military service. The gentry lived in the conviction that the government would provide them with an appointment and guarantee their livelihood. Few of them were familiar with or interested in commercial agriculture. At a time when the rest of Europe was undergoing rapid transformation under the influence of the developing capitalism, Russia lacked some of the basic institutional prerequisites for capitalism.

The Russian nobility was mostly impoverished, with a few very rich families. It lacked strong corporate spirit and could not prevent the government from implementing hostile policies like the 1861 emancipation of the serfs. The peasant emancipation accelerated the process of the economic decline of the nobility as it deprived them of the basic privilege of serf ownership and a guaranteed income gained through the exploitation of serf labor. Many nobles found it hard to adapt and to learn businesslike habits of mind. Some preferred to sell more of their land than to economize. By 1911 nobles owned only half of the land that was theirs in 1862.

The overwhelming majority of the Russian population were peasants. They were held in the condition of economic slavery by means of coercion, arbitrary punishment, and sheer brutality. There were two main groups of peasants—landlords' serfs and state peasants. The bigger group was landlords' serfs: they belonged to individual members of the nobility and lived on private estates. The remainder, state peasants, belonged to the government, but their existence was not far removed from the strict condition of serfdom. The serfs did not have legally recognized personal rights. They were a medieval and strongly anticapitalist element surviving into the modern era.

The peasant emancipation of 1861 gave Russian peasants their personal freedom. But the peasants were still kept socially segregated from the rest of the population: they were subject to corporal punishment, military conscription, payment of the poll tax, and certain other obligations from which other social classes were exempt. Most importantly, the land that they received at emancipation was granted not on an individual but on a collective basis—to the village commune. The commune had extensive powers over its members: taxes were communally collected and paid; the land was periodically redivided among the members in the commune; no peasant was free to leave the commune without the permission of the village elders. In other words, although the peasants had been freed from their bondage to the serf owners, they remained in bondage to the commune.

The retention of the commune was arguably the chief stumbling block that hindered the modernization of the agrarian sector and prevented capitalist development in rural areas. The practice of periodical equalization of landholdings between peasant households made it difficult for successful peasants to accumulate land and become small entrepreneurial farmers. The agrarian sector of the Russian economy more or less stagnated for the next forty years following the emancipation.

Tsarist Industrialization

Despite the inconclusive character of the emancipation legislation, it did lead to irreversible changes in all spheres of Russian life. It accelerated the process of the cleavage of the peasantry: more enterprising peasants increased their wealth and left the patriarchal commune, while others grew destitute and turned into dispossessed proletarians. As a result, mines and factories in rapidly developing industrial regions gained a steady flow of cheap wage labor. The natural economy was disintegrating. As a result, the Russian internal market's capacity increased, providing a powerful boost to the growth of industrial production. By the early 1880s the industrial revolution in Russia had finally arrived. Alongside the older, traditional branches of industry, new ones were created: coal mining, oil extracting, and machine building; the country was covered by a network of railways. The new social classes of bourgeoisie and industrial proletariat were rapidly developing. All strata of society were experiencing change.

In the final decade of the nineteenth century Russia's industrialization experienced remarkable acceleration under the guidance of Sergei Witte (1849–1915). He was an economic planner and manager of the type common in the governments of Western Europe and the United States, but rare in the high officialdom of imperial Russia. His background was unusual for a tsarist minister, because he was not a noble but had made his career in business and railway administration. Witte became the minister of finance under Alexander III and continued in that post under Nicholas II until 1903.

In 1897 he established a gold standard in Russia, thus fixing the value of the ruble against other currencies and against gold. This measure did much to add stability and prestige to Russian economic development and to attract foreign capital. Witte put into effect a massive state-sponsored program of railway building, including the construction of the Trans-Siberian Railway. The rapid growth of railways depended on government orders for iron, coal, locomotives, and equipment. All this boosted the development of Russian heavy industry and engineering. In the final decade of the nineteenth century the Russian government's strategy of economic development yielded spectacular rates of industrial growth: about 8 percent a year.

The state in Russia had always kept most important branches of industry under its control, and it continued to exercise control in the new conditions. In the early twentieth century special bodies were set up that reflected the close relationship between the government and leading capitalists, such as the Shipbuilding Council and the Congress of Transport Affairs. These organizations were comprised of industrialists and government officials. They oversaw the allocation of government orders, gave subsidies and tax benefits, and so on. For these reasons, the emerging Russian bourgeoisie had an ambivalent attitude toward the autocratic-bureaucratic regime. On the one hand, as its wealth increased, it began to crave political power and found itself in opposition to the autocracy. On the other hand, the continual financial support from the ruling bureaucracy and the dependence on government orders and other benefits made the bourgeoisie's opposition fairly weak and inconsistent. Because of its political servility, the bourgeoisie commanded little respect in Russian society.

The continuing industrialization accelerated the growth of the class of urban wageworkers. So novel was the class of factory workers to Russia that there was no legal provision to define its place in Russia's social structure: in their passports the workers were referred to by the traditional labels as peasants or town dwellers. At the beginning of the twentieth century the Russian working class represented an excellent example of a destitute and exploited labor force, characteristic of the early stages of capitalist development described so powerfully by Marx in *Capital*. Workers' wages were a quarter to a third of those in Western Europe; the proportion of well-paid workers was very small. The majority of Russian workers worked and lived in squalid conditions; hours of work were long, accident rates were high, and discipline was harsh. Not surprisingly, the Russian workers began to organize to better their lot. This restricted even further the bourgeoisie's freedom of maneuver and made it even more predisposed to political compromise. It saw the autocracy as less of a threat to itself than the revolutionary-minded working class.

Despite Russia's impressive economic growth, its per capita industrial production and per capita national income were still far behind the leading group of industrialized nations. Huge newly built modern industrial plants coexisted with thousands of small archaic mills. The agrarian sector remained dominant, and capitalist relations in agriculture developed at a slower pace due to the numerous vestiges of the old serfdom system. In 1913 only 18 percent of the population lived in towns, and industry still produced only 20 percent of national income.[1] Russia was still a mainly agricultural, underdeveloped country.

Ultimately, it was the social and economic backwardness of the countryside that was to have the most fatal consequences. The pace of the development of capitalist relations in agriculture lagged far behind the rapid growth of industrial production. After 1907, the Stolypin plan authorized the destruction of the commune. The tsarist prime minister's intention was to create a new class of independent, economically viable proprietors in the countryside attached to the principle of private property. This step, desirable as it was, was far too little and too late. The reform added new problems to the old by helping to stratify the peasant masses and creating hostility between different groups of peasants.

The government's inability to regulate the relations between different social groups and to curb the excessive exploitation of wage labor forced the working masses to adopt a radical, revolutionary course of struggle for their legitimate demands. Russia's peasants and workers lent a ready ear to the Bolshevik call "Expropriate the expropriators!" As for the middle class, it was too small to serve as a counterweight to radical, extremist slogans. The social explosion of February 1917 culminated in the inglorious collapse of the tsarist government and the end to the three-century-old rule of the Romanovs.

The Command Economy

In a few months' time control of the country passed into the hands of the deeply anticapitalist Bolsheviks. They immediately set about the task of laying down the foundations of a socialist economy. To Lenin and his followers this meant, first of all, the implementation of Marxist ideas of abolishing private ownership of the means of production and "socializing" private property. As a result, a socialist mode of production would be set up based on public ownership and a planned economy. Money-commodity relations would be replaced by the administrative distribution of commodities from a single center. The "socialization" of the means of production would be achieved through the "expropriation of the expropriators."

The Bolsheviks took these ideas from the founder of Marxism. The phrase "expropriation of the expropriators" itself belongs to Marx and provides an effective finale to the first volume of his *Capital*:

> The monopoly of capital becomes a fetter upon the mode of production which has flourished alongside and under it. The centralisation of the means of production and the socialization of labor reach a point at which they become incompatible with their capitalist integument. This integument is burst asunder. The knell of capitalist private property sounds. The expropriators are expropriated.[2]

This passage can be regarded as the final conclusion of Marx's entire theory. There is little doubt that these words fired the imagination of Lenin and his followers. The new rulers of Russia faced a huge task of transforming the relations of ownership and of organizing and managing production in a new way. They were determined to overhaul the country's life along socialist lines as quickly as possible and to institute a centrally planned economy. They wanted the state to control all economic activity: to define priorities, allocate resources, and determine prices and wages. In other words, from the beginning, the Soviet economy was conceived as a "command economy," that is, one based on instructions issued from above and not on the law of supply and demand.

The Bolsheviks' uncompromising and ruthless treatment of all opposition to their policies, such as the drive to "expropriate the expropriators," had made a civil war in Russia almost inevitable. In the civil war of 1918–20 the regime routed the remaining merchants and capitalists. Only during the New Economic Policy (NEP) retreat (1921–28) was some capitalism allowed, with private retail trade and a land-owning peasantry selling grain on an open market. But the NEP was a brief interlude, during which the state still regulated the economy and ran large-scale industry. In the early 1930s the Soviet authorities liquidated the capitalists as a class, drove peasants forcibly onto large state and collective farms, eliminated rural *kulak*s (well-to-do peasants), and nationalized over 97 percent of all the means of production. By the late 1930s, in its essentials, the Soviet economy already operated on the same principles on which it would function until the collapse of the USSR in 1991. These included

- virtually complete state ownership of the means of production

- severe curtailment of money-commodity relations (but not their total eradication envisaged in the Communist doctrine: money retained its use as a measure of exchange, financial accounting, and remuneration of labor)

78 *The Background*

- distortion of the law of value (prices were determined not on the basis of the market supply and demand but by bureaucrats at their office desks)

- extremely rigid centralization of economic planning and management with minimal economic decision-making powers left for republics and regions

- administrative distribution of resources and commodities

The enforced elimination of "commodity relations," that is, of a market economy, was unthinkable without the setting up of a hierarchical and bureaucratic system of centralized planning. This is because, if a market does not coordinate the millions of decisions taken by thousands of managers, the only alternative is an elaborate and complex command-bureaucratic structure. At the center of the planning system was the top economic planning agency of the Soviet state, the Gosplan (the State Planning Committee). It was charged with drawing up a blueprint for national economic activity, usually for a five-year period. The blueprint was driven by the major objectives set by the political leadership for the development of various branches of the national economy, such as electrification targets, agricultural goals, transportation networks, and the like. The five-year plan translated these broad objectives into industry-specific requirements (outputs of generators for electric stations, tractors and fertilizers for the countryside, steel rails and locomotives for railways). These general targets were then transmitted down to ministries charged with the management of the industries in question.

This mechanism displayed certain strengths at periods when the political objectives of the regime called for a kind of crash breakthrough in some branches of the national economy or when the country faced the emergency of war. The Soviet economy achieved remarkably rapid progress in its industrialization drive before the Second World War. It enabled the USSR to win the economic contest during the war with Nazi Germany by outperforming it in the production of military hardware. It was successful enough in repairing the devastation that followed the war. In the postwar period, in areas of intense rivalry with the West, such as nuclear power and space exploration, the planning system was able to concentrate skills and resources regardless of cost. This enabled the Soviet Union to match or better similar undertakings in the West.

The important point to make here is that the economic system created by the Communist regime could hardly function without a high degree of authoritarianism in the political sphere. Political despotism and economic overcentralization developed side by side, naturally complementing and mutually reinforcing each other. The regime's total political control allowed it to dispose freely of the country's entire demographic and material resources. In turn, the consolidation of the centralized system of state planning and management greatly strengthened the powers of the state and entrenched authoritarianism in politics. In short, political and economic power became closely intertwined in the Soviet system.

Of all the different reasons that brought about the collapse of the USSR, the economic factor was probably most decisive. In the 1980s the economic system that had enabled the Bolsheviks to transform the predominantly agrarian Russian Empire into a great industrial power and then to turn it into one of the world's two nuclear superpowers seemed to have lost all its vitality and was rapidly going into decline. In the case of the Soviet Union, the failure of the command-bureaucratic model of socialism was especially embarrassing, as the country possessed all human and natural resources necessary for building a highly developed economy.

A number of characteristics of the Soviet economy help explain the causes of its decay and ultimate collapse. First, the monopoly of state ownership of the means of production stifled innovation and competition. Enterprise managers were under intense pressure from central planners and local party bosses to fulfill their plan targets, and they habitually tried to cut corners by reducing quality. The incentives faced by heads of enterprises tended to militate against improvement, entrepreneurship, and innovation. The result was technological stagnation: the system had no incentives to upgrade continually the technological base of production and to raise labor productivity.

Second, the management monopoly of the party-state bureaucracy bred recklessness, irresponsibility, and arbitrariness in economic policy making. The prime examples are the administrative collectivization of the late 1920s, the superindustrialization of the 1930s, and the complete liquidation of peasants' small private land allotments in the 1950s. Paradoxically, the Soviet system of centralized planning did not have any built-in mechanisms to prevent arbitrariness and unpredictability in economic decision making. No amount of the most careful planning could override authoritarianism and willfulness as the cornerstones of the command-bureaucratic system.

Third, the eradication of market mechanisms and of private ownership deprived the economy of vital driving forces such as self-interest. Lack of personal motivation and material incentives affected all structural levels of the economy. In a Soviet-type economy, the worker is provided with no stimulus to work better and to increase labor productivity. As a result, state coercion and similar pressures of noneconomic character become the main driving forces of the economy.

Fourth, the Soviet economy was extravagantly wasteful and "uneconomical." The system favored extensive growth, that is, growth by increasing inputs of labor, raw materials, factories, and investment capital. In the 1930s and 1940s the Soviet Union had a large pool of unemployed workers, seemingly infinite supplies of oil, coal, and other raw materials, ample land for cultivation, and capital squeezed from the rural sector through collectivization. But in the postwar decades the USSR no longer enjoyed surplus labor, land, or capital resources waiting to be exploited. New gains in production had to be achieved through intensive growth—that is, through more efficient use of existing resources—by increases in labor productivity, automation, mechanization, and the application of new technologies. All of the reforms introduced by successive postwar leaderships—from Khrushchev to Gorbachev—attempted to shift away from the Stalinist model of extensive growth, but all produced little or no effect.

Fifth, the system of centralized planning seriously failed Soviet consumers. Endemic deficits of consumer goods, chronic food shortages, overcrowded housing conditions, and primitive consumer services became the hallmarks of a Soviet-type economy. All attempts by Soviet leaders to find ways of making the system more responsive to consumer wants proved futile. In contrast to the capitalist economy, with its periodic crises of overproduction, the command-bureaucratic economy could never overcome the underproduction and constant deficit of consumer goods despite all the promises and exhortations of Soviet leaders.

Finally, the Soviet system was severely handicapped as a result of its tendency toward self-isolation. No modern national economy can develop successfully without many ties to the economies of other countries, and without participating in the global economic division of labor. The Soviet system was isolated not only as a result of ideologically motivated political decisions of its Communist leadership but also on account of its technological backwardness and inability to compete with the more advanced economies.

Part Two

THE SOCIALIST EXPERIMENT

Chapter Seven

The Beginnings of the Socialist Transformation

Consolidating One-Party Dictatorship

Within a short period of time, from October 1917 to February 1918, the Bolsheviks consolidated their control over the greater part of the territory of the former Russian Empire. One of the chief reasons for this, to use Lenin's phrase, "triumphal march of the Soviet power" across the country, was, undoubtedly, the mass support of the first Soviet decrees. Their general democratic character met centuries-old expectations of the majority of the Russian population. In the conditions of an economic dislocation and unpopular war a radical program of rapid and sweeping reforms appealed to many social groups. The Decree on Land sanctioned the transfer of the gentry's land to the peasants, ensuring the loyalty of rural communities. The Decree on Peace gave hope of a speedy end to the war with Germany to the demoralized and exhausted army. The "Declaration of the Rights of the Peoples of Russia" promised equality, sovereignty, and the right to free self-determination to all nationality groups and facilitated the acceptance of Soviet power on the multiethnic fringes of the empire.

The political system that the Bolsheviks were forging in the months following the October takeover was distinctly different from the original idealistic blueprints of a "proletarian dictatorship." Before taking control of Russia, Lenin had spoken of doing away with the punitive machinery of state and replacing it by "direct arming of all the people." The population would be armed to defend the country from any external threat, while the resistance of the former propertied classes inside would be overcome with the help of the organs of popular democracy, such as soviets and people's militia.

However, the brutal logic of holding on to power compelled the Bolsheviks to establish their own secret police, the All-Russian

Extraordinary Commission for the Struggle against Counterrevolution, Sabotage, and Speculation (better known by its Russian acronym Cheka). Set up in December 1917 under the leadership of Felix Dzerzhinsky, Cheka was granted wide powers from arrest and investigation to passing and executing sentences. Its arsenal of repressive measures also included property confiscation, withdrawal of food coupons, blacklisting individuals as "enemies of the people," and expelling people from the country into external exile. Cheka evolved into a formidable instrument of the "proletarian dictatorship," suppressing resistance not only of the Bolsheviks' natural enemies, such as the propertied classes, but also of their former allies, including moderate socialists and anarchists.

Moreover, the new regime soon realized that it would not survive without a modern army to defend the new state. In January 1918 the Bolshevik government announced the formation of the Workers and Peasants' Red Army to be recruited on a voluntary basis. In a short period of time a network of military commissariats was set up in localities, and, by May 1918, the Red Army was expanded into a formidable 300,000 strong military force.

Lenin's concept of the dictatorship of the proletariat left no place for other political parties in the new state system. It accorded the Russian Communist Party of Bolsheviks (as it became officially called in March 1918) the role of the core of the proletarian dictatorship. The party directed activities of all governmental and nongovernmental organizations. It tolerated other socialist groupings only if they recognized the legitimacy of Soviet power and the supremacy of the Bolsheviks as the ruling party. In practice, this led inevitably to the emergence and rapid consolidation of a one-party system.

Civil War and War Communism: 1918–20

The Bolsheviks' uncompromising and ruthless treatment of every shade of opposition to their policies had made a civil war in Russia almost inevitable. The slide toward the war was precipitated by radical steps taken by the Communist authorities, including the dishonorable Brest-Litovsk treaty with Germany (March 1918) that hurt the patriotic feelings of many Russians.

In the economic sphere the Bolsheviks' initial experiments had involved the setting up of "workers' control" at private companies. Guided by the Bolshevik slogan "Factories to the Workers!" the workers proceeded to seize factories, mines, and other enterprises and to administer them through spontaneously elected factory committees. The problem, however, was that the revolutionary zeal of the workers could not substitute for the expert knowledge of the former managers and engineers. Not unnaturally, many company owners and industrialists were categorically against workers' control. To break the owners' resistance, the Bolsheviks launched a "Red Guard attack on capital" (October 1917–spring 1918). The strategy was designed to impose a comprehensive state control over the national economy by speeding up nationalization in industry and introducing the monopoly of foreign trade. As a result, the banks, railways, foreign trade, mercantile fleet, and all large enterprises in all branches of industry—coal, metal, oil, chemicals, machine building, textiles, sugar, and so on—were nationalized. In December 1917 a Supreme Council of Economy was set up with the responsibility to run the newly nationalized state sector. Conceived as the "chief headquarters of socialist industry," it marked the beginnings of an administrative system that would develop into a bureaucratic leviathan controlling all aspects of the Soviet economy.

In the countryside the Bolshevik Land Decree abolished the private ownership of land. Millions of peasants received free of charge over 450 million acres of land that had previously belonged to the gentry, bourgeoisie, monasteries, and the crown. Although it met the centuries-long expectations of the peasantry, the decree aggravated social tensions in the village, leading to conflicts between well-to-do peasants and their poorer brethren. As each group of peasants sought to divide the land to its own advantage, the Soviet government took the side of poor peasants. In June 1918 it issued a decree providing for the creation of Committees of the Poor Peasants. The committees distributed confiscated land, collected food surpluses from richer peasants (*kulak*s), and recruited for the Red Army. They played a significant role in helping to consolidate Soviet power in the countryside and acted, to use Stalin's phrase, as "strongholds of the dictatorship of the proletariat in the villages."[1]

The Bolshevik support of poor peasants alienated the wealthy *kulak*s, the main producers of marketable grain. In order to collect the grain for the cities and the army, the Bolsheviks had to resort to repression against them. In May 1918, the Bolshevik government declared a "food dictatorship." Special food detachments of armed workers and soldiers were dispatched to the countryside to confiscate grain surpluses from well-to-do peasants. The *kulak*s' economic position was severely undermined, but so too was agricultural production as a whole. The Bolshevik policies aroused the deep hostility of grain producers.

Thus, various sectors of the Russian population were increasingly compelled to take to arms to defend themselves against the strong-armed tactics of the new Communist dictatorship. As for the Bolsheviks, they did not see a civil war as anything out of the ordinary. The Communist leaders considered the armed confrontation of antagonistic political and social forces as a justifiable and legitimate form of "class struggle." Millions of armed, embittered, and illiterate workers and peasants turned a ready ear to revolutionary agitators, who stirred up class hatred and incited mobs of boorish soldiers and sailors to senseless acts of violence. From mid-1918 on the fighting escalated into an all-out war waged by diverse armed units: from regular armies to numerous guerrilla detachments and bandit gangs. Some thought of themselves as "Reds" (the traditional color of Communist revolutionaries), or pro-Bolshevik; others joined the "White" (the traditional color of the conservative supporters of the old order) movement that united diverse anti-Bolshevik forces from monarchists to socialists. Others still, including many members of moderate socialist parties, found themselves vacillating between the Bolshevik commissars and the White generals. Finally, there were disparate peasant detachments operating in different parts of the country that switched sides between the Reds and the Whites or even fought against both of them. The civil war dragged on for nearly three years until the end of 1920, imposing even greater hardships on the Russian people than those of the world war.

Ultimately, the loyalties of the peasantry that formed the bulk of the population proved decisive for the outcome of the civil war. To the majority of peasants, the agrarian policies of the White governments were unacceptable, because they wanted to reintroduce the old property rights of the landed gentry on the territories under their control. The peasantry had to choose between two evils: the grain appropriation and the ban on free trade, imposed by the Bolsheviks, or the restoration of the gentry's property rights. The Bolsheviks seemed to many to be the lesser of two evils. The peasants were convinced that the land that was given to them as the result of the revolution would remain theirs in case of a Bolshevik victory, whereas the Whites' victory would almost certainly mean the repossession of the land by former owners. The peasantry's pro-Bolshevik leanings enabled the Communist authorities to boost the strength of the Red Army to five million men toward the end of the war. The maximal strength of the White armies during the civil war did not exceed 800,000 men.

Apart from winning the support of the majority of the population, the Communist victory in the civil war also depended on the new regime's ability to keep the economy going when some of the vital food- and fuel-producing territories were temporarily outside its control and when tsarist Russia's former Western allies, intervening on the side of the anti-Bolshevik forces, sought to enforce an economic blockade of Soviet Russia. In this situation, the Bolshevik government adopted emergency economic measures, which became known collectively as war communism.

War communism pursued two principal objectives: first, to prevent total collapse of the economy and, second, to mobilize all available resources for the struggle against the domestic and foreign enemies of the new regime. War communism involved the nationalization of the country's entire industrial resources. In addition to large-scale industry nationalized in the course of the "Red Guard attack on capital" in the first six months following the October Revolution, the Soviet government put under its control all small and middle-size companies. In the countryside, a state monopoly of the grain trade was introduced, which prohibited the private sale of grain. A surplus-appropriation system was enforced. This meant that all food surpluses in the hands of the peasants were to be recorded and bought by the state at fixed prices. This helped to accumulate a store of grain for the provisioning of the army and the workers. Finally, a universal labor conscription was imposed on all classes of the population.

The prohibition of free trade had placed the burden of rationing food to the urban population and supplying the peasants with industrial goods on government agencies. Goods and foodstuffs were distributed centrally, usually without payment in exchange for coupons; the railways were obligated to transport goods free of charge; and essential communal services in the cities and medical care were also free. In theory, this system made money unnecessary. During war communism, the Bolsheviks toyed with the idea of abolishing money altogether, but all their experiments in this direction merely contributed to the chaos and rampant inflation that made the ruble practically worthless.

The majority of the population was unwilling to submit to the discipline of the state-run, moneyless economy, and many could survive the hardships of that period only by disobeying the strictures imposed on them by the Bolshevik regime. Those who stayed in hunger-stricken cities managed to survive thanks, to a great extent, to the activities of the so-called sack pushers (*meshochniki*), that is, people bringing sacks with food for sale or personal consumption. The authorities tried to curb the burgeoning black market by posting armed detachments at city gates to catch "sack pushers" and confiscate "surplus" foodstuff. Despite all the attempts to eradicate the black market and its inflated prices, about half of all food supplies in the cities were delivered by the "sack pushing" profiteers who, effectively, saved the urban areas from total extinction.

War communism was introduced as a temporary measure, which was necessitated by the exceptionally difficult conditions of national defense. It helped the Bolsheviks to prevail over the anti-Bolshevik movement. However, many of the party leaders soon began to see war communism as a necessary stage in the rapid transformation from capitalist to Communist patterns. The attraction of war communism to many Communists was that its economic policies were implicit in the doctrine of revolutionary Marxism. They rested on the same fundamental principle that, as the Bolsheviks believed, was to be the cornerstone of the socialist mode of production: a market economy, in which production was carried out by independent, autonomous producers for exchange on the open market, was to be replaced by a centrally planned, state-controlled economy. War communism seemed to have already made big strides toward achieving that objective: private ownership was virtually abolished, production and distribution were put under full control of the state, and the market and even money seemed almost redundant. To many Communists, it looked as if the first and most essential steps on the road to communism had been taken. Even as the civil war came to an end, they no longer considered the policies of war communism as temporary measures to survive and win the war, but began to see them as an important breakthrough in the direction of a genuinely nonmarket socialist economy.

The problem was that this was not the view of war communism shared by the Russian population. Angered by the continued confiscations of their crops, the peasants responded with armed antigovernment rebellions in different parts of the country. From peasants the discontent spread to the armed forces. In March 1921 in Kronstadt, the biggest naval base of the Baltic fleet situated on an island in the Gulf of Finland some twenty miles off Petrograd, 16,000 sailors and soldiers rose in an open armed revolt against the Communists. They demanded free elections to the soviets, freedom for all socialist parties, and broad freedom for the peasantry to farm and to dispose of the results of their labor as they chose. The insurgents were brutally crushed by troops loyal to Bolshevik authorities. Yet the population's widespread resistance to the government's plans to institute centralized planning compelled the Bolsheviks to reverse war communism.

New Economic Policy: 1921–28

At the Tenth Congress in March 1921 Lenin formulated the two principal lessons of Kronstadt. The first concerned the need to make concessions to the rural population: "Only an accommodation with the peasantry can save the socialist revolution in Russia." The second lesson emphasized the need to step up the struggle against any vestiges of ideological opposition, including moderate socialists, anarchists, and others, and ensure that the opposition was effectively prevented from agitating among the masses. The adoption of Lenin's strategy by the congress ushered in a period of several years (1921–28) of relatively peaceful development, known as the New Economic Policy (NEP).

During this period the government sought to conduct its domestic policy along two not easily compatible directions. On the one hand, the economic policy was revised and the economy was freed from the total state regulation of war communism. On the other hand, no liberalization was permitted in the political sphere: all attempts to democratize society were relentlessly stamped out. The discrepancy between economic liberalization and political dictatorship constituted the main contradiction inherent in the NEP.

The NEP brought with it a major reversal of the original tenets of Bolshevism, including the utopian idea of doing away with money. The government was compelled to reverse to a market economy, or money economy, and to the economic patterns that were acceptable and familiar to the masses. In 1925 the old, worthless ruble was withdrawn and exchanged for a new ruble, based partially on gold. The growth of a money economy increased the demand for credit. From 1922 on, a network of state banks for financing commercial and industrial enterprises was set up.

In the countryside, the food appropriation detachments were disbanded, and the surplus-appropriation system was replaced by a tax in kind. The introduction of a tax in kind meant that the peasants were now free to sell surplus produce on the market. The reestablishment of freedom of trade resulted in a rapid revival of small traders and of thousands of marketplaces and traditional fairs. The middlemen, who under war communism had a precarious existence as "speculators" and "profiteers" or "enemies of the people," could now openly apply their entrepreneurial skills.

The new economic system affected property relations both in agriculture and in industry. If the peasants were to produce more food, they had to be granted a measure of security in the form of reasonably long land tenure. This was done by a series of concessions to the peasants embodied in the Land Code of 1922. Although the principle of land nationalization was reaffirmed, peasants were declared long-term tenants. Leasing of the land was allowed; later, even the hiring of additional labor (previously condemned as an evil capitalistic practice) was permitted under certain conditions. These measures led to the rapid increase in the food supply that permitted the abolition of food rationing.

Soon the liberalization of agriculture began to have beneficial effects on industry. To induce peasants to sell their surpluses to the cities, industries had to have something to offer in return. Development of consumer industry, commercial enterprises, and service shops was soon tolerated and even encouraged. Licenses were granted for private enterprise; many small industrial enterprises, previously nationalized, were now returned to their previous owners or leased on certain strictly defined conditions to private entrepreneurs, who became known as Nepmen. As a result, the industries rapidly revived.

On the whole, the NEP remained a mixed economy of a dual market-administrative character. Although the money-commodity relations were allowed to revive, the so-called commanding heights—political power, the financial system, large-scale industry, transport, and foreign trade— remained in the hands of the Soviet state. The ultimate goal of creating a nonmarket socialist economy was not abandoned. The NEP envisaged a relatively long-term coexistence of socialist patterns alongside nonsocialist ones (i.e., capitalist and peasant economies), with the gradual displacement of nonsocialist structures from the national economy.

The NEP had many achievements to its credit. To begin with, it was successful in bringing the economy back to its prewar condition. By 1923–24 the hyperinflation of the civil war had been reigned in and financial stability restored. By 1926–27 the prewar levels of agricultural and industrial production had been achieved. The revival of market relations in the countryside allowed the peasant economy to grow, making the twenty-five million peasant households the main beneficiaries of the NEP. The peasantry gained three things: security of land tenure, freedom from requisitioning, and a free hand in selling agricultural surpluses. By making these concessions, Lenin admitted that the Soviet regime could ill afford to disregard the interests of some 80 percent of the population. But the Communists' retreat also gave them a much-needed six-year breathing spell after which they would resume their onslaught on the countryside.

The truth is that the NEP's reliance on market and money-commodity relations was alien to the interests of the new bureaucratic Communist hierarchy. The NEP system encouraged the growth of the class of small and medium-size entrepreneurs, including shopkeepers, owners of service shops, cafes, and restaurants. Communists were to coexist competitively with these small capitalist Nepmen, learn from them how to be efficient and productive, and eventually demonstrate the superiority of the socialist system. In everyday practice, however, the capitalists proved their superior efficiency and flexibility. The state-controlled industries, by contrast, were lagging behind both in volume of production and in quality. The fact that the private initiative represented by the Nepmen was doing better than the nationalized sector was unendurable in the long run, because it disproved the doctrines on which the Bolsheviks based their claim to power. It was obvious that either the market-based forces of the NEP would corrode the Soviet system or the system would have to destroy them in order to survive.

The Communist administrators' disapproval of the NEP was shared by broad sections of the impoverished urban and rural masses. As a result of hardships and privation imposed by war, famine, and economic adversity, their numbers had swelled considerably. The idea of a centrally administered economy that envisaged a primitive egalitarian distribution of wealth appealed to these population groups. Socialism to them meant nothing more than total equality at a subsistence level, whereas economic relations that promoted talented and enterprising people were frowned upon. These population groups eagerly supported the negative view of the NEP, articulated by some of the Communist leaders. They saw the return to capitalist patterns as a retreat from their vision of socialism.

The main reason for the vulnerability of the NEP was that it was based on an unstable balance of two sectors, private and public. It represented a shaky compromise between communism and capitalism, between collectivism and individualism. The expansion of private initiative and market relations was unacceptable to the Communist authorities as it meant the curtailment of state control over the economy. By the late 1920s the NEP supporters within the Soviet leadership were politically isolated and the NEP itself curtailed. The economic methods of running the economy were supplanted by the total domination of administrative, coercive, and extraordinary measures. The vestiges of the NEP were completely eradicated by the early 1930s, and by the mid-1930s it was completely displaced by a strictly hierarchical command-bureaucratic system.

Chapter Eight

"Great Leap" to Socialism

The Rise of Stalin

Iosif (Joseph) Vissarionovich Dzhugashvili (Stalin) (1879–1953) was of a solely proletarian origin: his father was a poor cobbler in a provincial Georgian town in the Caucasus and his mother, a former serf. Before he became a Marxist revolutionary and a Bolshevik party functionary, he had studied for five years at an Orthodox seminary. In 1914 he took the pseudonym of Stalin, "man of steel."

Stalin had risen in the party to the position of one of its recognized leaders thanks, in large measure, to Lenin's support. Lenin personally endorsed or suggested each step of Stalin's accumulation of power both before and after the revolution of 1917.[1] Stalin seemed to Lenin to encapsulate all the qualities of a professional revolutionary. He was a good organizer and was well trained in conspiratorial technique. After the revolution, Stalin was made Commissar for Nationalities, and in 1919, Commissar for the Workers' and Peasant Inspection, a body that was supposed to ensure public accountability by closely scrutinizing all activities of departments of government. He was, simultaneously, a member of the Communist Party's Central Committee and of its policy-making Politburo.

While Lenin was alive, the Bolshevik regime was characterized by oligarchic rule within the framework of a ruling party. The Communist Party did monopolize power and suppress its rivals, including other socialist parties, but within the party, with Lenin at its head, there was open controversy, debate, and compromise. The main levers of power were in the hands of the so-called Bolshevik old guard: approximately 10,000 party members who had joined the party before the October Revolution. The "Bolshevik guard" included many professional revolutionaries with considerable political experience. Sometimes they proposed different solutions to arising problems, which often led to the creation of factions within the party. The inner party contradictions of conflicting policies and personal ambitions were reconciled thanks to the integrating role of the top oligarch, Lenin. As a leader with great personal authority, Lenin had his way on many policy issues. However, on some questions he suffered defeat and saw himself obliged to accept the views of the majority. In a word, early Bolshevism contained an element of pluralism and was more an oligarchy than a personal dictatorship.

Originally, all major issues were discussed and resolved by the party's Central Committee. As long as the Central Committee membership was only ten or twenty persons, this practice was realistic. But as party membership grew, the Central Committee expanded and was no longer able to function as before. Consequently, the Politburo and the Orgburo (Organization Bureau) were created to guide the party during the intervals between Central Committee plenums. Gradually, these organs assumed absolute power while the power of the larger body—the Central Committee—diminished.

The Politburo and Orgburo formed the inner core of the party leadership alongside one more important body—the Secretariat of the Central Committee. Initially, it had a subordinate role of providing organizational and technical support for the work of the Central Committee. The activities of the Secretariat were directed by a number of party officials known as secretaries, while its head was referred to as first secretary. In March 1922 Stalin was proposed for a job in the Secretariat.

By that time Stalin had attained important standing in the leadership and enjoyed a reputation as one of the party's preeminent organizers. To reflect Stalin's stature, the post of the head of the Central Committee was renamed general secretary instead of first secretary. In his new post Stalin was able to exert greater influence on the agenda of the Politburo meetings and the wording of its resolutions, because their drafts were prepared inside the Secretariat. In addition, he was able to control the recruitment of the ruling elite, overseeing the placement and promotion of all responsible party officials.

In the struggle for power that ensued after Lenin's death in January 1924, Stalin showed what it meant to rule over the apparatus. His position in the Secretariat allowed him to expand his base of support in localities and at the center by ousting his opponents and filling all more or less important posts with his own appointees. Stalin selected people who were personally loyal and obedient to him. At the same time, they tended to be leaders inclined to tough administrative methods. Most of them had joined the party during the civil war and had received their primary political schooling in the conditions of war communism.

The new breed of Communists rejected the more liberal principles of the NEP, condemning them as deviations from a "true revolutionary path" to socialism. They wanted to build the new society quickly, relying on administrative pressure, military-style organization, and directives from above. These were the methods that had stood them in good stead in the postrevolutionary period of war communism and the civil war. What they lacked in education and culture was compensated by "revolutionary impatience": the desire to achieve the cherished goal of socialism at one stroke, in one great leap, skipping intermediate stages. Their optimism was sustained by the belief in their class superiority, conferred on them by Marxism.

The interests of the rising new party-state bureaucracy came into conflict with those of the old political elite—the Bolshevik old guard. As a result, a power struggle ensued within the ruling Bolshevik oligarchy. Stalin's elevation was due to his ability to promote the new ruling elite and express its interests. By relying on his cadres, he sought by every available means to undermine the authority of the more important of the Bolshevik leaders, who could be real or potential rivals in the struggle for power. He skillfully manipulated the party debate on the theory and practice of socialist construction, branding the views of his opponents as anti-Leninist. This allowed him to revile and demote all outstanding party intellectuals, including Lev Trotsky (1879–1940), Grigory Zinoviev (1883–1936), Lev Kamenev (1883–1936), and Nicholas Bukharin (1888–1938). By the end of the 1920s, they would be removed from positions of power and their supporters purged from the party and state bodies and replaced wholesale by Stalin's followers.

Stalinism is usually associated with the period of Soviet history that began in the early 1930s and led to the "great terror" in the second half of that decade. However, in many essentials Stalinism had been in evidence as early as 1926–27. Already at that time Stalin's personal qualities and his unscrupulous politicking in the bid for absolute power had led to the emergence of a new kind of authoritarianism based on the characteristics of the evolving Soviet political system. The new regime claimed to be the dictatorship of the proletariat but was in effect a dictatorship of the party that was quickly transformed into a dictatorship of its central apparatus. In the late 1920s and early 1930s Stalin put the party and government apparatus under his undivided control and established a personal dictatorship.

The Industrialization Debate: 1925–28

By the mid-1920s, thanks to the economic liberalism of the NEP, the country had, to a great extent, recovered after the dislocation of the First World War and the civil war. But this economic recovery meant merely the attainment of the prewar levels of economic development of tsarist Russia. Even in 1913 Russia had not been an economically advanced or developed country. A decade later its economic backwardness was even more acute. In essence, the country appeared even more agrarian than before.

Bolshevik leaders saw the rapid acceleration of economic development as a vital means of overcoming the backwardness inherited from tsarist Russia and creating the material base of a socialist society. The task of accelerating the country's economic development was felt particularly urgently, because the "proletarian dictatorship" ruled in an overwhelmingly agrarian country. In addition, the Bolsheviks were concerned that the country's economic weakness had serious implications for national security. The Bolshevik revolution remained isolated in a world dominated by "imperialist" powers. The breaking off of diplomatic relations by Britain in 1927 was just one example of the hostility of most Western powers to the Bolshevik regime. The same year saw the worsening of Russia's diplomatic relations with Poland, China, and other countries.

In the period 1925–28 two rival factions emerged within the party leadership that clashed over the issue of industrialization. There was the right wing, led by Bukharin, and the left wing, led by Trotsky, with Stalin playing one faction off against the other for his own political gain. In other words, the industrialization debate was also closely connected with the struggle for power and, first and foremost, with Stalin's all-consuming ambition to consolidate his position as leader of the party by any means and to rule as a dictator. However, it would be incomplete to reduce the industrialization debate in the Bolshevik leadership to the personal struggle for leadership. The political struggle at the top was affected by a combination of various circumstances arising from the domestic situation and international pressures and also by the predominant attitudes of various sectors of the population, from the lower classes to the ruling echelons.

Both factions within the party were committed to industrialization, but both disagreed on the methods, rates, and means of financing industrial development. Put briefly, the main distinction was that the Right advocated a more evolutionary and cautious development, whereas the Left insisted on a more rapid and ambitious investment program in heavy industry. Bukharin, as the main spokesman of the Right, counseled the continuation of the two parallel sectors: the state sector holding the "commanding heights" of the economy, and the private one represented by small-scale industry, handicraft, and individual peasant farming. Bukharin believed that the continuation of the more peasant-friendly policies would help to strengthen the worker-peasant alliance and would make Soviet power more stable by making it acceptable to the bulk of the population—the peasant masses. In short, his stand envisaged a more balanced development of the industrial and agrarian sectors and implied an almost indefinite continuation of a mixed economy, which was the essence of the NEP.

This economic program was branded as a *"kulak* deviation" by the propaganda of the Left. According to Trotsky and his adherents, all of this meant the appeasement of the petit bourgeois forces represented by the mass of the peasantry. Bukharin's program meant the strengthening of the capitalist elements and would lead to the restoration of capitalism. The Left was against making any concessions to the peasants and insisted upon speedy industrialization by increasing the tax burden on the peasantry and channeling the bulk of resources into state-owned industries.

Stalin used the controversy between the Left and the Right to his personal advantage. He swung easily from one political flank to the other and back again when this promised gains in the power game. In 1925–26 he had posed as an enthusiastic supporter of the NEP and an ally of Bukharin in order to undermine his previous political allies Zinoviev and Kamenev. In 1928–29 he went all the way to the extreme Left, this time to defeat the Right and Bukharin. Stalin realized that the adoption of radical economic policies designed to curtail the NEP would almost inevitably turn Bukharin and his supporters into oppositionists. By defeating Bukharin's group in 1929, he achieved absolute personal power.

More importantly, Stalin's strategy appealed to the predominant attitudes in the party as a whole. Most Communists lacked the education to appreciate the finer theoretical differences that split the political leadership. With the civil war experience behind them, they were better equipped to deal with economic problems by coercive and administrative measures, rather than learn the intricacies of market mechanisms. Many Communists favored accelerated rates of industrialization and a radical overhaul of the economy. They accepted Stalin's argument that Soviet Russia could not afford spreading industrialization over a period of several decades, as was implied in the program advocated by Bukharin.

There is no doubt that the implementation of Bukharin's alternative based on the rejection of the idea of forced and rapid expansion of heavy industry would have postponed the USSR's rise to the position of one of the world's most powerful industrial nations for an indefinite period of time. Stalin's rapid industrialization provided the Soviet Union with the industrial capacity and military might that enabled it to defeat Nazi Germany in the Second World War. From that point of view, of the two alternative models of industrialization, Stalin's approach appears to be more historically justified. However, Stalin's triumph also meant the entrenchment of a regime of personal dictatorship associated with high Stalinism. It dealt a shattering blow to the freedom of discussion within the party and resulted in the abandonment of the NEP and the reanimation of the practices of war communism.

Collectivization of Agriculture

The adoption of Stalin's model of industrialization, with its emphasis on the rapid expansion of heavy industry, very quickly sharpened the contradictions inherent in the NEP Russia. The transition to rapid industrialization beginning in 1927 was accompanied by massive ruble emission to finance capital investments in large-scale industry. As a result, the Soviet currency depreciated and lost convertibility. At the same time, prices of consumer goods went up, fueling shortages. Almost immediately the government was confronted with difficulties in grain procurements. The problem was that the peasants were losing incentives to sell their grain on the market or to the state, because money could not buy them necessary consumer goods and because the state procurement prices were set too low.

In 1927–28, as the cities and the army faced the threat of hunger, the authorities had to reintroduce food rationing. To resolve the food crisis, the government revived the experience of the war communism years, resorting again to the coercive methods of grain appropriation. Grain procurement detachments were once again sent to the countryside to confiscate agricultural produce by force and repression. The countryside responded with the killings of party activists, sporadic revolts, and uprisings, but the grain was collected. In 1929 the crisis situation recurred, as the unwilling peasantry had reduced areas under tillage.

The failure of state grain procurements not only posed a threat to social stability in the cities by creating food shortages but also undermined the government's grandiose plans of rapid industrialization. To implement its industrial projects, the Soviet Union relied on regular purchases of machines and equipment from abroad. This required additional financial resources that were to be gained by exporting raw materials and agricultural produce. Grain was the country's chief export commodity. Without sufficient stocks of grain to export, the government would have to either scale down significantly its ambitious industrialization rates or resort to extraordinary measures to squeeze grain out of unwilling peasants. The Communists increasingly perceived the peasantry as an obstacle to their plans of rapid socialist transformation.

Stalin's policy of forced collectivization of the countryside, launched at the end of 1929, was designed to overcome this obstacle by destroying the private sector in agriculture and putting the countryside under his unrestrained control. His collectivization of agriculture sought to achieve two interconnected objectives: one was political and the other, socioeconomic. Politically, collectivization was to solve once and for all the vexing problem of the persistence of "capitalist elements" in the village embodied in small individual farming. It allowed the regime to "liquidate the *kulak* as a class," that is, to eradicate those groups of the village population that were capable of challenging the regime and putting up resistance to its policies. The second, socioeconomic, reason was to create on the basis of small and low-productive individual peasant farmsteads large-scale socialist collective farms. It would be much easier to exercise direct administrative control over large collectivized farms than over some twenty-five million individual farmsteads. The new state-controlled agricultural units would be unaffected by the vagaries of market forces and would generate profits that could be ploughed back into the development of heavy industry.

SOCIAL STRATIFICATION OF THE PEASANTRY, 1927[2]		
Social categories	*Million people*	*Percent*
All peasants	108.0	100.0
Poor peasants	21.1	19.5
Middle peasants	81.0	75.0
Prosperous peasants (*kulaks*)	5.9	5.5

In less than two years, starting in November 1929, the regime used the army and the police to remove from villages by force all groups of the peasant population capable of resisting collectivization. The "dekulakization," as it was known, was ostensibly directed against the *kulaks* and successful middle peasants, who were usually the more hard-working and industrious of villagers. In real life, the line between different groups of peasants was not always clear-cut, and many middle and even poor peasants fell victim to arbitrary dekulakization.[3] The property of the *kulaks*, including their houses, was confiscated, while they them-selves were arrested and transported with their families under duress into remote and inhospitable regions of the north and Siberia. Historians estimate that 1.1 million peasant households were liquidated in this manner, with over a third of that number of dekulakized families force-fully resettled.[4]

The peasants rebelled, killed Communists and collective farm bosses, slaughtered cattle, burned down collective-farm property, or fled to the cities. However, as all political opposition had been routed, intimidated, or demoralized, there were no forces capable of transforming these spontaneous eruptions of popular discontent into an organized revolt and providing it with leadership. Millions of peasants showed their pas-sive resistance by fleeing to towns: in 1931 alone over four million people voted with their feet against collectivization. The rest of the peas-ants were induced by force or cajolement to join collective farms, where they had to work for a pittance. On the whole, the tragic saga of collec-tivization was over by the mid-1930s. By the end of 1939 collective and state farms had integrated 93 percent of all peasant households.[5]

The consequences of the destruction of the old economic structure in the countryside were severe. The productive forces of agriculture were undermined for many years to come: in 1929–32 the total number of cattle and horses fell by one-third and of sheep and pigs, more than twofold. The collectivization resulted in mass famine, caused not so much by a poor harvest as by the government's drive to appropriate all grain output of collective farms, including seed stocks, to feed the cities and sell for export. Starving peasants were reduced to pilfering grain from collective-farm fields and granaries. To combat this, a law was enacted in 1932 that imposed harsh penalties for stealing collective-farm property. Any theft, however small—be it merely a handful of seeds—was punished by a prison sentence of ten years minimum or a death sen-tence. Tens of thousands of people fell victim to this draconian law.

The human costs of the collectivization were catastrophic: the Ukraine, Kazakhstan, North Caucasus, the Volga regions and the South Urals region—in other words, some of the key grain-producing areas—were consumed by a devastating famine. The tragedy of the situation was that the authorities refused to acknowledge officially the existence of the famine. Troops were sent in to cordon off the affected areas to prevent the famished peasants from escaping to the cities, because their begging and appearance would immediately dispel the official tales about the happy life in collectivized villages. As a result, millions were condemned to starvation: three to four million people died of hunger in 1932–33.

However, to the Communists the end justified the means, as they celebrated a big victory on the road to socialism. Despite the fact that the peasant population fell by a third and grain output was down by 10 percent, the state procurement of grain in 1934 was double the level of 1928.[6] The agrarian sector was now transformed into an integral arm of the command-bureaucratic economy.

Stalin's extraordinary agricultural policies had momentous effects for the country's subsequent development and sounded the death knell for the old peasant Russia. The collectivization drove millions of peasants out of the countryside to the cities and construction sites, providing inexhaustible cheap labor to accomplish the great industrial leap. Until the end of his days Stalin prided himself on the achievements of his collectivization, referring to it as the "Second Revolution" after the October Revolution. The Soviet leadership saw its agricultural policy as subordinate to the needs of the industrial restructuring of the country. The collectivization enabled it to supply the expanding industries with raw materials, feed the factory workers, accumulate financial resources by exporting grain, and maintain a constant flow of surplus rural population to man new construction sites and industrial units.

The state could now dictate its mandatory procurement plans for agricultural produce and industrial crops that were increased from year to year. These compulsory deliveries were burdensome for the peasants, as the state procurement prices were set many times lower than the market value. On the positive side, the collective farms benefited from industrialization by receiving more machinery to substitute for the workstock lost during the collectivization. As the output of tractors, combine harvesters, trucks, and other machinery picked up, it became possible to set up so-called machine-tractor stations that specialized in providing mechanized services to collective farms.

In the long run the triumph of Soviet power in the countryside turned out to be a Pyrrhic victory. Despite Stalin's "socialist transformation of agriculture," no genuine modernization of the agrarian sector took place during the 1930s. Despite decades of "building socialism," the country that had been one of the world's main grain producers and exporters before the revolution was unable to produce enough grain for domestic consumption and was obliged to begin to import grain beginning in 1963. The chronic backwardness of the agrarian sector and its inability to meet growing consumer demands fueled discontent in Soviet society.

Chapter Nine

Stalinism

Industrialization

Industrialization is part and parcel of a modernization process in any country. However, in Soviet Russia the launching of "socialist industrialization" was highly politicized: it was presented by official propaganda as an essential and indispensable step in building the material foundations of socialism. The next important distinction was that Stalin's industrialization was not based on private enterprise, but was totally state-driven and was ostensibly based on centralized directive planning. Finally, the doctrine of "socialist industrialization" put great emphasis on a massive expansion of heavy industry, particularly the means of production, as a necessary first step on the way to the technological restructuring of the entire economy. Only after a massive surge in heavy industrial capacity had been achieved would it be possible to embark on a more balanced economic strategy, including the development of consumer-oriented light industry. As a result of a whole number of factors, the Soviet industrialization would be confined, for the most part, to the one-sided priority development of heavy industry.

Another peculiarity of Stalin's industrialization was that the country's international isolation meant that the USSR could not rely on foreign credits and external assistance to finance its ambitious industrial expansion. The financial resources for the construction of new industrial plants had to be found within the country and were to come from a number of domestic sources. First, the revenues from light industry and, in particular, from agriculture were to be used to finance the expansion of the industrial branches of the economy. Second, hard currency earnings from the state monopoly on foreign trade, including the export of grain, timber, gold, furs, and other goods, were to be used to buy state-of-the-art equipment for the newly constructed industrial enterprises. Third, the surviving Nepmen were to be subjected to heavy taxes. The crippling taxation of private enterprise together with the mounting administrative pressure would stifle private initiative in both industry and commerce by 1933.

Additional savings were to be gained by reducing the output of consumer goods and by restricting food consumption of both the urban and rural populations. This was to be achieved by raising retail prices, using goods rationing, and similar measures. Capital was forcibly squeezed out of the reluctant population, mainly the peasantry, through an arbitrary price system. By the exercise of ruthless dictatorial power, Stalin succeeded in diverting a huge percentage of the national income to industrial investment and defense purposes. As a result, living standards of blue- and white-collar workers plummeted two- or threefold. Consumer goods production all but ceased, and every available resource was pressed into the program of rapid industrial expansion in capital-intensive heavy industry, such as steel, coal, and machinery.

Ultimately, the most crucial resource of Stalin's industrialization was the abundance and inexhaustibility of cheap labor. It was provided by millions of trained workers, by millions of peasants driven to towns by the collectivization, by millions of labor camp inmates, and by 1.5 million of the former unemployed (unemployment disappeared in 1930).[1] Many were driven by enthusiasm, prepared to sweat at construction sites around the clock virtually for free. Young people, in particular, were deeply motivated by the idea that it was possible to build a better and fairer society relatively quickly, within their lifetime, by mounting a huge exhausting effort and accepting hardships and self-sacrifice.

This was Soviet Russia's period of great austerity, as reflected in a number of popular stories characteristic of the popular mood that people usually whispered in secret:

> An Englishman, a Frenchman, and a Russian were arguing about the nationality of Adam and Eve.
>
> "They must have been English," declares the Englishman. "Only a gentleman would share his last apple with a woman."
>
> "They were undoubtedly French," says the Frenchman. "Who else could seduce a woman so easily?"
>
> "I think they were Russian," says the Russian. "After all, who else could walk around stark naked, feed on one apple between the two of them, and think they were in paradise?"

Five-Year Plans

Stalin's industrialization was planned as a series of five-year programs for industrial expansion. A five-year plan became the "law" of the life of Soviet society. The transition to centralized directive planning led to the revival of certain characteristics of the war communism era. It entailed the elevation of the role of the Gosplan—the state planning authority—that had been in existence since the early 1920s. Gosplan was directly subordinated to the government and charged with drawing up the five-year plans in accordance with the leadership's political objectives. The plans set targets of output and production to be reached ranging across the whole of Soviet industry. The First Five-Year Plan covered the period from October 1928 to December 1932. It was launched with great fanfare in an atmosphere of officially sponsored optimism. The first apparent successes pushed the leaders to adopt the slogan "The five-year plan in four years!" But soon numerous difficulties began to crop up. The industrialization was embarked upon too hastily, with insufficient resources and with a limited pool of skilled labor. It was severely handicapped by the country's general backwardness in technological and economic terms and in social and cultural development. Moreover, overcentralized planning did not always work in practice. Untrained workers often could not operate the complicated, largely imported machinery, which was frequently put in unsuitable locations.

At the end of 1932, it was officially announced that the overall objectives of the First Five-Year Plan had been achieved ahead of time. Even now, after seven decades, it is difficult to judge to what extent the triumphant declaration corresponded to reality. The newspapers were allowed to report only "outstanding achievements" of the USSR's advance toward socialism. Local state agencies were prohibited from publishing any economic data apart from the official figures issued by the Gosplan. According to these, the output of machinery and electric equipment expanded by 157 percent over the 1929 level. Whatever the veracity of the Soviet statistics, in the industrial field the overall achievements of the plan were impressive. Two new important industrial centers were established, one in the Urals (Magnitogorsk) and the other in southern Siberia (Kuznetsk). Entirely new branches of industry were developed, such as aviation, plastics, and synthetic rubber. The plan constituted an important milestone in the process of the socioeconomic transformation of Russia.

The Second Five-Year Plan—from January 1933 to December 1937—also gave priority to heavy industry. One of the weaknesses revealed during the First Five-Year Plan was that of the Soviet infrastructure, especially roads, railways, and canals. Consequently, the second plan also provided for reconstruction and double tracking of the principal lines, starting with the Trans-Siberian Railway. The widening of old canals and the construction of new ones (like the Moscow-Volga canal) was another vital task assigned to the new plan. By 1933 the altered international position of the USSR resulting from Hitler's seizure of power was reflected in a rapid expansion of armament production. The armed forces were gradually reshaped into an increasingly professional, modern fighting machine, comparable to those of other great powers. Between 1933 and 1936, the size of the Red Army tripled, from 562,000 to 1.5 million, exceeding the size of the imperial army in 1913.

As with the First Five-Year Plan, the second was also officially declared completed nine months ahead of time, in 1937. Again, however, not all of its goals were achieved. Among the items that surpassed their estimated targets were steel and the automotive industry, created practically from scratch. Tanks and armored cars were given priority over civilian vehicles. The most striking failure was consumer goods production.

The first two five-year plans increased the industrial capacity of the USSR dramatically in all major fields—steel, coal, and electric power— and created new manufacturing sectors indispensable to any great power—automobiles, aviation, chemicals, and plastics. Consequently, the first two five-year plans laid the foundation of the industrial might of the Soviet Union, especially in the military field.

Industrial expansion and often forcible relocation involved a massive shift of sometimes unwilling citizens, mostly from the countryside to the cities. Between 1926 and 1939 the overall percentage of urban dwellers nearly doubled, from 18 to 33 percent.[2] During the first two five-year plans nearly twelve million people moved from the countryside to the cities. History had rarely seen migrations on such a scale. Most of the migrants left the countryside during the First Five-Year Plan as a result of the collectivization and the policy of "liquidation of the *kulak* as a class." The dramatic increase in the number of city dwellers represented in itself a major aspect of the Stalin revolution, leading to rapid urbanization of Soviet society.

On the whole, the government's modernization effort, despite its Russian peculiarities, reflected some of the more general global trends of the twentieth century and evoked cooperation of different sectors of the population. Thousands participated in the "great construction project of socialism" with a will to self-sacrifice, accepting hardship with a real sense of comradeship. Many were inspired by the Bolshevik vision of socialism and gave it their full support. The wave of labor enthusiasm was reinforced by carefully stage-managed propaganda campaigns leading to the appearance of "socialist emulation" as a form of competition for greater labor productivity among workers. The Stakhanovite movement, named for the record-breaking coal miner Aleksei Stakhanov, is perhaps the best-known example of the shock-worker competition of that period.

In a speech made in 1946 Stalin explained the causes of the Soviet victory in the Second World War by the rapid economic progress achieved in an incredibly short period of time during the prewar decade. He claimed that by the start of the war Soviet Russia had been transformed from an agrarian country into an industrial one, ready for the defense against the Nazis. The comparison of economic indicators of tsarist Russia in 1913 with those of the Soviet Union in 1940 brought him to the following conclusion:

> Such an unprecedented growth of production cannot be regarded as a simple and ordinary development of a country from backwardness to progress. It was a leap, with the help of which our Motherland had been transformed from a backward country into an advanced one, from an agrarian country into an industrial one. [3]

This historical transformation, according to Stalin, had been accomplished in an incredibly short period of time. It had required about 13 years starting from 1928.

Stalin claimed that industrialization and collectivization were the twin cardinal policies of the Communist Party that made this feat possible. The scale of achievement in the heavy industrial sector was particularly staggering. From 1928 to 1941, 9,000 large-scale industrial plants were built, or 600 to 700 each year.[4] In a short period of time an industrial capacity was built characteristic of the more economically advanced countries. In terms of its branch structure and technological sophistication the Soviet economy now stood at a level comparable with the industrialized countries of the capitalist West. The industrialization enabled the Soviet Union to mass-produce aircraft, trucks, cars, tractors, combine harvesters, synthetic rubber, and different types of equipment designed primarily for the expansion of heavy industry and military might. In the years of the "great leap" industrial production grew at an average annual rate of 10 to 16 percent, displaying the remarkable dynamism and seemingly boundless potential of the new economic system. By 1937 the USSR was second only to the United States in its gross industrial output (in 1913, fifth place).

Characteristics of Stalinism

In December 1936 a new Soviet constitution was adopted, hailed by official propaganda as a "constitution of the victorious Socialism." The
period of transition from capitalist to socialist patterns was now
declared over. The "socialist offensive" had resulted in the creation of a
socialist society and the completion of the first phase of communism,
socialism. The constitution formalized the new ownership relations and
the rights and obligations of Soviet citizens. It referred to soviets of people's deputies as the political foundation of the USSR, while public ownership of productive resources was proclaimed to be its economic base.
It guaranteed the rights to work, rest, education, and many others. In its
content, the constitution appeared to be an epitome of democracy. The
electoral system to soviets of all levels was also changed: suffrage
became universal, equal, and direct with secret ballot; and no categories
of the population, except the mentally ill and convicted, could now be
excluded from voting.

In reality, however, the pseudo-democratic facade of "victorious
socialism" masked a system in which the state exercised unlimited control, from politics to the economy. The economic basis of this system
was proclaimed to be socialist on the claim that it was based on "public
ownership." In fact, the term *public ownership* masked the monopoly of
state ownership, with the state acting as the supreme manager of nationalized productive resources. The state exercised control not just over the
means of production but also over the very physical and spiritual existence of the individual. Stalin's officials dominated the lives of ordinary
citizens not only through terror but also because the state they represented became virtually the sole employer.

By the second half of the 1930s the Soviet economy had taken on a
significant labor-camp flavor. Forced labor acquired massive propor-
tions, turning into a major factor of economic development. It was organized in the networks of reformatory camps and settlements run by the
Chief Directorate of Reformatory Camps, better known by its Russian
acronym, GULAG. The camps were set in remote and inhospitable areas
of the arid steppe and above the Arctic Circle and provided cheap labor
to develop new territories and natural resources in extreme climatic conditions. The convicts dug canals, laid rail track, built factories, mined
gold, and felled timber. They produced nearly half of all Soviet gold, at
least a third of platinum and timber, and contributed to one-fifth of
major construction projects. Entire new towns were conjured up out of
the ground by forced labor.

From the late 1920s on, Stalin actively encouraged and drummed up adulation of himself by official propaganda. Slavish admiration of the leader was obviously seen by him as an important prerequisite for establishing a direct personal dictatorship. It served to justify Stalin's absolute prerogatives by extolling his allegedly exceptional, outstanding, and even superhuman qualities as leader. The officially sponsored idolatry was inflated to ridiculous extremes that defied all common sense. An extract taken from a speech of one of the deputies to the Congress of Soviets in 1935 conveys the extent of the deification of the tyrant, for whom no vulgar glorification of his person could be too extravagant:

> Thank you, Stalin. Thank you because I am joyful. Thank you because I am well. . . .
>
> Thy name is engraven on every factory, every machine, every place on earth, and in the hearts of all men. . . .
>
> Every time I have found myself in his presence I have been subjugated by his strength, his charm, his grandeur. . . .
>
> I write books. I am an author. All thanks to thee, O great educator, Stalin. I love a young woman with a renewed love and shall perpetuate myself in my children—all thanks to thee, great educator, Stalin. I shall be eternally happy and joyous, all thanks to thee, great educator, Stalin. Everything belongs to thee, chief of our great country. And when the woman I love presents me with a child, the first word it shall utter will be: Stalin.[5]

The immoderate fanning of the leader's cult went hand in hand with massive ideological indoctrination of the populace. The regime sought to turn Marxism into a new socialist religion to serve as an emotional and intellectual substitute of Orthodox Christianity. The Orthodox Church itself was under constant attacks from the officially enforced state atheism, and its role considerably declined. Stalin himself posed as "high priest" of the new atheist church. He shaped Marxism-Leninism into a rigidly dogmatic and authoritarian ideology, designed to regulate all aspects of social life and to serve and justify his policies. His brand of Marxism was characterized by sketchiness and oversimplification, calculated to appeal to the broad masses of the working people. His earlier theological background as a seminarist may account for his ability to find a popular form to express ideas. Catchy and aphoristic slogans, clear and unambiguous ideological definitions, and a knack to present arguments in the form of clear-cut points were hallmarks of his public speeches and written articles. In 1938 Stalin's *Short Course of the History of the Communist Party* was published, giving the masses the "authorized" encyclopedia and gospel of the socialist religion.[6] Its author himself was now almost a living god and an object of ritual worship.

Base adulation of the leader and enforced ideological conformity were inseparable from the atmosphere of fear and intimidation fanned deliberately beginning in 1928. In March 1928, fifty-five engineers and administrators of the town of Shakhty in the coal-mining region of Donbass were arrested on charges of sabotage, allegedly sponsored from abroad. They were accused of trying to disrupt the operation of the coal industry and cause workers' unrest. At the public show trial that followed many of the defendants were made to confess their alleged crimes. Eleven death sentences were served, five of which were carried out. The rest of the alleged saboteurs received long prison sentences. The Shakhty affair set a precedent and a pattern for future demonstrative denunciations and show trials.

It has now been established beyond doubt that the whole affair was fabricated by Stalin's secret police. Most probably, Stalin used it to infuse the political life with elements of social confrontation to drum up support for his radical economic measures. The trial enabled him to discredit Bukharin's plan of class cooperation and counter it with the diametrically opposite idea of the intensification of class struggle. Stalin claimed that resistance of the enemies of the Soviet power would only intensify with the country's advance toward socialism. The population should be constantly vigilant against concealed wreckers and saboteurs, whose activities were allegedly directed by the capitalist West. From 1928 on official propaganda spared no efforts in driving home the perverted logic of the "intensification of class struggle": as socialism is getting stronger, its enemies do not wish to surrender. Instead, they strive to unite and put up growing resistance; they are like mortally wounded animals, which are especially dangerous. But equally dangerous are all those who do not appreciate the new policies or dread them; all those who lack faith and spread panic should be dealt a shattering blow, regardless of the posts they occupy.

Stalin's ominous theory prepared the population psychologically for the moment when he would point his accusing finger at leaders who strayed from "the party line" and thereby obstructed the nation's progress toward the shining goal of socialism. It enabled the regime to maintain constant ideological tension in society. The tiniest shades of dissidence, diverging views, and independent opinions were relentlessly smashed. From 1928 until the end of Stalin's period in power, stage-managed witch-hunts and show trials against alleged "enemies of the people," fabricated jointly by the secret police (known by the Russian acronyms OGPU and, from 1934, NKVD) and judicial bodies, practically never ceased. These horrendous activities were designed to maintain the "enemy image," which lay at the heart of the system of ideological terror and intimidation used to enforce complete ideological conformity of Soviet society.

In addition, from the mid-1930s on, the allegations of conspiracy and wrecking were increasingly used by the regime to explain the difficulties that accompanied the implementation of the industrialization plans. Although the targets of the Second Five-Year Plan were more realistic than the initial reckless onslaught of the first plan, chronic problems of delays and bottlenecks persisted. Soviet leadership interpreted them as resistance to "the party line" designed to derail industrialization, and it threatened administrators in the localities with reprisals. Not unnaturally, local bosses did their best to unmask as many "saboteurs" and "enemies of the people" as they could, scapegoating thousands of innocent people for the failures of the system of centralized planning and for their own mismanagement.

In 1937–38 terror reached a pathological level, extending to all social classes, and various professional and ethnic groups. This peak of mass repression is associated with the name of Nikolai Yezhov, head of the NKVD (People's Commissar for the Interior) at the time. Later Stalin would scapegoat Yezhov, blaming him for the "excesses" of the campaign of the "exposure of the enemies of the people" and branding his methods as "Yezhovshchina." In reality, Yezhov acted merely as a zealous executor of the directives issued by Stalin and his inner circle. In 1937 over 900,000 people were arrested and in 1938, more than 600,000. The overwhelming majority of them—almost 90 percent— were political prisoners arrested on charges of counterrevolutionary activity. Almost 700,000 death sentences for "counterrevolutionary crimes" were served during those two tragic years.[7]

It is highly significant that the surge of mass terror in the form of "Yezhovshchina" coincided with the triumphal official statements to the effect that the country had entered full-blown socialism. The blatant discrepancies between the official promises and the realities of life in "victorious socialism" caused mounting frustration and disaffection. In these conditions, the regime sought to shift the blame for persistent difficulties at work and at home on the machinations of "enemies of the people": administrators and specialists who had allegedly betrayed the cause of socialism. In this sense, "Yezhovshchina" had an antibureaucratic and populist aspect and served to vent the pent-up frustration of the credulous masses.

Stalinism, with "Yezhovshchina" as one of its hallmarks, also had deep roots in postrevolutionary Soviet history. Many of the important ingredients of the Stalinist system are detectable in the early Bolshevik regime as it evolved under Lenin, including the Communist Party's power monopoly, the destruction of all political opposition, the elevation of terror into an instrument of state, ideological indoctrination, and growing ideological dogmatism and intolerance. Stalin transformed these seeds into his own brand of extreme authoritarianism based on the party's central role in the political system and the state monopoly over productive property. He established an ideological dictatorship, propped by mass terror, the leader's cult, and the invoking of the enemy image. In doing all this, he amplified the authoritarian features of Leninism by taking them to an extreme.

Chapter Ten

From World War to Cold War

The Soviet-German Nonaggression Pact

The Second World War began on 1 September 1939, when Nazi Germany invaded Poland, and ended six years later, on 2 September 1945, with the unconditional surrender of Germany's ally, Japan. The surrender ceremony took place on board the USS *Missouri* in Tokyo Bay and was attended by delegations of the victorious Allied powers, including the United States, Britain, the Soviet Union, France, China, Australia, Canada, the Netherlands, and New Zealand.

The Soviet Union was engaged in the Second World War from its outbreak. In September 1939 the Red Army entered Poland; from 30 November 1939 to 12 March 1940 Soviet troops waged war against Finland; and on 22 June 1941 the USSR itself became a victim of aggression by Germany. From the moment of the German invasion and up to the final victory over Germany in May 1945, the Soviet people fought their Great Patriotic War for liberation from the German occupation. By courageously defending their country, they made a decisive contribution toward the final defeat of Germany. In May 1945 their four-year struggle was crowned by the seizure of Berlin. Three months later, implementing the agreements with its war allies, the Soviet armed forces contributed to the routing of Japan.

With the end of the war, Soviet official propaganda did everything to amplify the heroic liberation struggle of the Soviet people following the German invasion on 22 June 1941 and to efface the uncomfortable fact that the day of the German attack had been preceded by nearly two years of "friendly relations" between Communist Russia and Nazi Germany. Their cooperation had been officially established by a nonaggression pact, signed by Joachim von Ribbentrop, the German foreign minister, and Vyacheslav Molotov, the People's Commissar for Foreign Affairs, on 23 August 1939 in Moscow. The news of the Molotov-Ribbentrop Pact, as it became known, came as a great surprise to the Soviet public accustomed to the antifascist rhetoric of the Soviet media. It also caused grave concern in the West, for only a few weeks earlier, in the summer of 1939, Soviet-British-French talks had been held in Moscow intended to work out an international security agreement that would restrain Germany's aggressive aspirations. The talks ended on 2 August 1939 with a draft agreement on mutual assistance by the three powers. The Soviet nonaggression pact with Germany followed three weeks later and clearly signaled a major change in Soviet foreign policy.

One of the main reasons for this sudden reorientation toward Germany was the deteriorating situation close to the Soviet borders. On 22 March 1939 Germany had occupied the Lithuanian port of Klaipeda, forcing Lithuania to conclude a humiliating treaty. A large-scale German invasion in the Baltic area seemed to be in the offing. Moreover, the governments of the three Baltic states of Lithuania, Latvia, and Estonia took an openly anti-Soviet stand; and two of them—Latvia and Estonia— signed friendly nonaggression treaties with Germany. The Soviet leadership had grounds to fear that Germany was preparing to launch an attack on the USSR from the territories of the three Baltic states and Poland. The security situation at Soviet borders was jeopardized further because of the escalating military tension in the Far East, where the Red Army was involved in large-scale military operations against Japan in the summer months of 1938 and 1939.

Under these circumstances, Stalin and Molotov made the decision to terminate the talks with Britain and France and to conclude a nonaggression treaty with Germany. The main advantage of the pact seemed to Stalin to be that it gave the USSR a much-needed strategic respite to augment its military-economic capabilities. Moreover, it kept the Soviet Union out of the fray that was about to engulf "imperialist" capitalist nations. Moscow would be able to watch from the sidelines how its class antagonists fought with one another until they bled themselves white. In the meantime, the USSR would pursue some of its own imperial ambitions by expanding its borders farther west in accordance with the treaty's secret protocol. In addition, Moscow hoped to use Germany's influence over its Japanese ally to put pressure on Tokyo to restrain its aggressive anti-Soviet intentions in the Far East. Hitler's own objectives in securing the treaty with the Soviet Union were also strictly pragmatic. He wanted to neutralize the USSR as a possible adversary for a period of about two years. This would give Germany enough time to achieve its military-strategic objectives in western and central Europe.

Stalin's intelligence agents had informed him of Hitler's secret designs, including the plan to invade the Soviet Union in a few years time. Yet this did not deter the Soviet dictator from making a deal with Hitler. Several days after the pact had been signed, it was ratified by a rubber-stamp vote of the USSR's Supreme Soviet. The deputies approved the treaty without even knowing that the pact had an additional secret protocol that defined the spheres of interests of the Soviet Union and Germany in eastern and southeastern Europe. The protocol envisaged that in the event of a German-Polish armed conflict the German troops would occupy western and central Poland, while the remaining part of eastern Poland, together with Finland, Estonia, Latvia, and Bessarabia, would fall into the Soviet sphere of influence.

On the day after the ratification of the treaty by the USSR's Supreme Soviet, Germany, without declaration of war, invaded Poland. The Soviet government bided its time for two weeks and on 17 September sent its troops across the Polish border under the credible pretext of coming to the rescue of the East Slavs—Ukrainians and White Russians—living in eastern Poland and now threatened by the German occupation. Poland was swiftly routed under the blows from west and east, and Molotov and Ribbentrop endorsed the results of its partition in the new Soviet-German treaty on "friendship and borders" signed on 28 September. The secret addenda to the new treaty further clarified the victors' spheres of influence. The Soviet sphere was augmented by the inclusion of Lithuania in addition to the territories specified in the secret protocol of 23 August.

Following the signing of the German-Soviet nonaggression pact, the antifascist agitation in the Soviet media was toned down, as the two countries were now engaged in large-scale economic cooperation that constituted an important part of the "friendly relations." In the two years following the conclusion of the treaty and up to the day of Germany's sneak attack on the USSR, the German economic and military machine benefited substantially from trade with its future victim. Germany received about 2.2 million tons of grain, 1 million tons of oil, 0.1 million tons of cotton, 80 million cubic meters of timber, and other strategic commodities.[1] On the very night that German troops were completing their final preparations for the surprise attack on the Soviet Union, ships and trains carrying grain, oil, and other commodities were in transit from the USSR to Germany.

Stalin's government equally sought to exploit the provisions of the Soviet-German treaties to its advantage. The Soviet troops entered Estonia, Latvia, Lithuania, and Bessarabia. These territories used to be part of tsarist Russia but broke away following the 1917 revolution. Now they were speedily sovietized and reincorporated into the USSR as union republics. In addition, the USSR unleashed a war against Finland, which also had been designated part of its "sphere of influence." The Soviet propaganda strove to present the aggression against Finland as the liberation of the Finnish working classes from the yoke of landowners and capitalists. So convinced were Stalin and his generals in the swift victory over the Finns that the Russian troops were sent to Finland unprepared for a long military campaign. Dressed in light summer uniforms and suffering from severe frostbite, the Red Army soldiers soon found themselves embroiled in a long-drawn-out "Winter War."

Despite the overwhelming advantage over the Finns in men and equipment, the Red Army failed to score an early and impressive victory and was bogged down in a lengthy conflict. During the 105 days of the war, it lost nearly 290,000 men, including 74,000 dead.[2] This was the cost the Soviet Union paid to persuade Finland to give up a number of small territories along the Soviet-Finnish border. The staunch resistance of the Finns helped Finland to avoid sovietization enforced in the other Baltic states. The relations between the Soviet Union and Finland were irreparably damaged: following the German attack on Russia in June 1941, Finland took Germany's side in the war.

In contrast to the Red Army's uninspiring performance in the Finnish campaign, the German army scored one lightning victory after another in the initial stages of the war. It subjugated Poland in thirty-six days, defeated the combined British and French troops in May 1940 in just twenty-six days, and conquered Greece and Yugoslavia in eighteen days. The tactical ineptitude of the Soviet high command and the heavy casualties sustained by the Red Army in the war against Finland raised serious doubts about its combat readiness. It is highly probable that its poor showing in Finland may have influenced Hitler's decision to invade the USSR and strengthened his confidence in a swift conquest. He now considered seriously the possibility of routing Russia ahead of Germany's decisive attack on Britain. On Hitler's orders German generals drew up the plan for a blitzkrieg—a lightning strike—against the USSR. The conquest of the Soviet Union would spell the end of the Communist state and constitute an important step toward the attainment by Germany of global supremacy. The Nazis' objectives in the east also envisaged that the mass of Slavic, Jewish, and other nationalities that populated the Soviet Union would be enslaved or physically exterminated as an "inferior race."

The Great Patriotic War: 1941–45

The initial phase of the Russian campaign, following Germany's massive surprise attack on 22 June 1941, was extremely successful for the aggressor and catastrophic for the Soviets. The size of the invading army had no precedent in history: over 5.3 million men, over 4,000 tanks, 4,500 aircraft, and over 47,000 pieces of ordnance, attacking along an 1,800-mile-long front.[3] In the first five months of the invasion German armored units drove deep into Soviet territory, advancing to some 750 miles at some points past the Russian front. They reached the outskirts of Moscow, captured most of the Ukraine and the Crimean Peninsula in the south, and encircled Leningrad in the north, imposing a blockade on Russia's second largest city. The Red Army suffered losses unparalleled in military history: by 1 December 1941 it had lost 7 million (dead, missing, or taken prisoner), about 22,000 tanks, and nearly 25,000 military aircraft.[4] In practice, nothing remained of the Red Army units formed prior to the German invasion.

The catastrophic defeats and losses of the initial stage of the war were clearly the result of the fundamental miscalculation of the Stalinist leadership that had chosen to ally the Soviet Union with the Nazi regime. The collusion with Hitler had deprived Russia of the critical buffer of Poland, allowing Germany to amass troops along the Soviet border and launch the surprise attack. In addition, the Soviet troops, deployed in the recently annexed eastern provinces of Poland, did not have enough time to set up powerful defensive positions. Stalin had received numerous warnings from his intelligence agents and Western governments about the imminent surprise attack, but he chose to discount them. He may have believed that countermeasures by the Soviet Union could only provoke the Germans. He also may have dismissed the warnings as attempts to poison his relations with Germany. Had he heeded those signals, he could have saved much of his troops by ordering them to prepare for action. In any event, the Germans achieved a complete tactical surprise, while the Soviets' forward deployments exposed them to the full force of the Blitzkrieg.

The humiliating defeats were a tragic consequence of the political system, in which the supreme leader with absolute authority completely dominated strategic decision making. Stalin's own dictatorial disposition and the inclination to use terror to suppress dissenting opinions discouraged his administration from contradicting his own analysis of the situation. Moreover, the years of Stalin's overinflated cult had created a psychological environment, when even top political and military figures were too awed to contradict him or believed unquestioningly in his infallibility.

Stalin's reputation as a military leader is a hotly contested issue. He appointed himself the People's Commissar for Defense in July 1941 and the commander in chief of the Soviet armed forces in August. As commander in chief, Stalin presided over the Supreme Command headquarters charged with the overall supervision, planning, and coordination of all military operations. Stalin possessed certain qualities, including a sharp memory, the ability to get to the root of the matter, and tremendous willpower, that distinguish military leaders. However, he lacked formal military education and military experience. Too often Stalin relied on the crude tactics of throwing masses of soldiers into frontal attacks that resulted in the prodigal waste of manpower.

Many commentators blame Stalin for the incompetent meddling in military decision making during the first year of the war and for the exorbitant cost that the Red Army paid for their commander in chief's "crash course" in military science. Despite the success in repelling the Nazis from Moscow in December 1941, the series of defeats continued into the first half of 1942. Germans took some of the vital agricultural areas and came close to seizing Stalingrad (now Volgograd) on the Volga and occupying North Caucasus. The situation at the front began to improve for the Soviets only from around August 1942. Significantly, this turnaround coincided with the establishment of the post of deputy to commander in chief and the appointment of Army General Georgy Zhukov to it. From that time on, Stalin increasingly relied on his deputy's superior military knowledge and expertise in planning military operations.

In addition to his supreme military authority, Stalin continued to wield absolute political power, which he had concentrated in his hands during the 1930s. With the start of the hostilities, he set up and chaired the State Defense Committee as the top executive body in charge of the overall supervision of the national war effort. Alongside Stalin, it included a score of prominent Politburo members, such as Vyacheslav Molotov, Lavrenty Beria, Kliment Voroshilov, and Georgy Malenkov. In the autumn of 1941 it authorized the setting up of a network of city defense committees in cities along the front line, charged with organizing defense. They were headed by first secretaries of district or city party committees and were comprised of four to five officials each. City defense committees played a vital part in mobilizing for the building of defense fortifications, overseeing the formation of volunteer units, and organizing military production at local enterprises.

Having overcome the initial shock of the surprise attack, the Soviet administrative machine was soon able to orchestrate an unprecedented economic effort that defeated Germany and its satellites in armaments production. The achievement was especially remarkable in view of the fact that in 1941–42 the USSR lost to the enemy over half its industrial capacity and countless skilled workers. To appreciate the Soviet spectacular economic effort in the war, it is important to note that the task was not simply of switching over from civilian to military production but also of moving massive productive resources to the safety of the country's eastern regions. The Soviet leadership had never planned for a war that would be waged in Russia's industrialized heartlands, with the Soviet rear turned into a battlefield. To salvage its key productive resources from the rapidly advancing enemy in 1941, the Soviet leadership organized mass evacuation and redeployment of its industry to the Urals and the Asian hinterland. It was an exceptional relocation of human and material resources over a distance of from one thousand to two thousand miles, involving millions of workers and over 2,500 enterprises.[5]

As a result, Soviet armaments production boomed and had even surpassed its prewar level by 1944. In the course of the war the Soviet Union produced submachine guns 4.7 times more than the enemy, artillery 1.5 times more, tanks 2.2 times more, and military aircraft 1.1 times more.[6] The Soviet Union mass-produced armaments of equal or better quality than those of the enemy, including the famous T-34 tanks and the awesome Katyusha barrage rockets.

There is still no conclusive answer to the question of the extent to which Stalin's brutal industrial revolution of the 1930s, with all the enormous sacrifices it entailed, had created the foundations for the victories of 1941–45. What is clear, however, is that in the extreme conditions of war the overcentralized command economy displayed formidable mobilizing capabilities, overturning the calculations of German strategists at attaining a speedy conquest of Russia.

The greatest credit for repelling the aggressor goes to the Soviet people. In the first week of the war, 5.3 million men joined the Red Army. In total, 31 million officers and soldiers were enlisted during the four years of the hostilities.[7] Millions of Soviet citizens applied to join the Red Army as volunteers or served in the people's volunteer corps, providing an important reserve for the regular army. The volunteers fought courageously side by side with the regular troops in defending major cities including Kiev, Leningrad, Odessa, Moscow, Sebastopol, and Kursk.

The official propaganda sought to bolster the morale and fighting

spirit of the population and the army by extolling Stalin's great states-
manship and military genius. People were brainwashed into believing in
Stalin's infallibility, but they also drew moral strength from their trust in
the leader. As the war went on and the strategic advantage began to tip
to the Red Army's favor, the Soviet authorities inflated Stalin's godlike
image even more. The unfortunate defeats of 1941–42 were glossed
over, the triumphal victories of 1943–45 were attributed to the party and
the personal leadership of the supreme commander in chief, Stalin. His
name was made synonymous with the sacred word *rodina* (motherland):
the soldiers went into battle with the cry "For Motherland, for Stalin!"
modeled on the old Russian battle cry "For Orthodoxy, for the Tsar, for
Fatherland!"

Stalin himself sought to strengthen popular morale by appealing to
the patriotic and historical traditions of the imperial nation of Russians.
The emphasis on the nationalist side of the war played down the
Communist ideology. The reintroduction of military uniforms and
insignia modeled on those of the prerevolutionary imperial army served
to amplify nationalist and patriotic attitudes. Tsarist history and the rit-
uals of the Eastern Orthodox Church were invoked in efforts to raise
patriotic sentiments to the highest possible pitch. The theme of Russian
patriotism and national pride was adumbrated in works of Soviet writers, journalists, and filmmakers throughout the war.

The common tragedy united the whole nation in a fight for its very
survival. But the rise of patriotism did not signify abandonment by the
Soviet regime of its customary repressive practices. On the contrary, the
punitive apparatus shored up national unity by its own methods, suppressing all symptoms of dissidence, lack of faith, or questioning of the
leadership's actions. The GULAG network continued to function: labor
camps and prisons provided recruits for the Red Army and were, in turn,
replenished by those, returning from the German captivity (the regime
declared surrender to the enemy tantamount to treason), or those who
had stayed behind in the occupied territories (they were automatically
suspect of collaboration with the enemy), or those arrested for "anti-
Soviet attitudes and gossip" at the front and in the rear.

Entire nationality groups were singled out for punishment for alleged
collaboration with the enemy, including the Crimean Tatars, the Volga
Germans, and a number of Caucasian peoples, such as the Ingushetians,
Ossetians, and Chechens. They were evicted from their home territories
by the interior ministry troops and resettled in the central Asian regions,
Kazakhstan, and Siberia. These repressive operations, which victimized
nearly two million people, required a massive number of railway car-

riages and trucks, so badly needed to move supplies to the front. Many of the deportees perished en route to their destinations or did not survive the harsh conditions of the exile. Despite the efforts by Stalin's successors—from Khrushchev to Gorbachev—to right the wrongs inflicted on these nationality groups, the consequences of the wartime repressions would continue to have negative effect on interethnic relations within Russia even to the present day.

Turning the Tide

The German surprise attack on Russia reversed overnight the direction of Soviet foreign policy. The recent "friend" was now a deadly enemy, while its enemies became the Soviet Union's allies in the common struggle. Many in the West equally sympathized with the newly emerged force of resistance to the Nazi scourge. On the day of the undeclared assault by Hitler on the Soviet Union, political and public leaders in many countries voiced their support of the USSR. British Prime Minister Winston Churchill pledged his country's firm backing of the Russian war effort. President Franklin D. Roosevelt of the United States said that the American government was prepared to provide necessary assistance. The Soviet pact with Hitler and the manifest blemishes of Stalin's regime were quickly forgotten, replaced by the growing admiration for Soviet military achievements.

Obviously, the war did not resolve the contradictions that existed between the USSR and its capitalist allies, such as Britain and the United States. But for the moment all differences receded in the face of the fascist threat. Motivated by the common resolve to attain the full and unconditional defeat of Nazi Germany, the "big three" Allied powers set about creating and consolidating the antifascist coalition of states. One of the first steps was the Anglo-Soviet agreement of 12 July 1941, pledging the two countries to assist one another and to abstain from making any separate peace with Germany. The creation of the wartime coalition of the "big three" was finalized by the agreement on an Anglo-Soviet alliance of 26 May 1942 and the similar Soviet-American agreement of 11 June 1942. More generally, the Allies included all twenty-six signatories to the Declaration of the United Nations of 1 January 1942 (the number of signers would grow as the war went on).

The USSR played a key role in the antifascist coalition as the country which withstood the most powerful onslaught of the German military machine and made a decisive contribution toward victory over Nazism.

The turning point of the Great Patriotic War and of the Second World War in general was the Battle of Stalingrad (summer 1942–2 February 1943), waged deep in the Russian heartland. The suburbs of Stalingrad marked the farthest extent of the German advance into the Soviet Union. As a major industrial center, the city was an important prize in itself. In addition, German control of Stalingrad would have severed Soviet transport links with southern Russia via the Volga River, thus facilitating the conquest of the oil-rich Caucasus. It also would have opened the way to the enemy's advance to the east of the Volga toward the chief munitions-producing region of the Urals.

The 200-day-long Battle of Stalingrad involved over two million men on both sides at some of its stages and was waged over a territory of 40,000 square miles.[8] By September 1942 the Germans had reached the city's center, where they encountered stiff resistance from the Red Army. In the constant street fighting the Soviet soldiers defended each street and house and, although driven almost to the Volga, prevented the Germans from crossing the river. On 19 November 1942 the Red Army launched a counterattack in the form of pincer movements north and south of the city, and by the twenty-third they had encircled a substantial part of the enemy troops, including the Sixth Army under Field Marshal Friedrich Paulus. The surrounded troops finally surrendered on 2 February 1943, when Paulus and the last of his remaining 91,000 troops turned themselves over to the Soviets. In the course of the Battle of Stalingrad the Wehrmacht lost a staggering 1.5 million men.[9] The total Axis losses (Germans, Romanians, Italians, and Hungarians) at Stalingrad amounted to over one-fourth of all its troops in the Soviet-German theater of war.

The Stalingrad disaster put an end to Germany's offensive role in the Soviet Union. German forces at the Russian Front lost momentum, while the Red Army began to push the Germans back from the western portions of the Soviet Union. In the winter of 1942–43 the Soviets pushed the Germans more than 400 miles to the west, liberating millions of Soviet citizens and reclaiming the territories rich in coal, oil, and grain. From then on, the Red Army's offensive drive would remain unstoppable until the end of the war. Many major battles still lay ahead, but the war's outcome was no longer in doubt.

The Battle of Stalingrad proved a decisive victory that turned the tide of war and changed the global military and political balance in favor of the Allies. It was appraised as the greatest battle of the Second World War by the whole world and inspired the rise of resistance movements in the countries of Europe and Asia under Axis occupation.

In the summer of 1943, despite the Stalingrad debacle, the Nazi leadership still had under its control almost the whole of Western Europe, most of the Ukraine, the whole of Belorussia, the Baltic region, and some of the Russian western regions. In this situation Hitler, still hoping to revive Germany's military fortunes, took the decision to mount a major assault on the Soviet salient around the city of Kursk in western Russia. The salient was a bulge in the Soviet lines that stretched 150 miles from north to south and protruded 100 miles westward into the German lines. The German high command planned a surprise attack on the salient from both north and south, hoping to surround and destroy the Soviet forces within the bulge.

The Germans had amassed over 900,000 men for the Battle of Kursk (5 July–23 August 1943). However, the chief role in the assault was accorded to the panzer (tank) divisions: armed with 2,700 tanks and mobile assault guns, they were to break through the Soviet defense lines and make deep incursions into the Soviet rear. But the Soviet military command had surmised the German plan beforehand and had withdrawn their main forces from the vulnerable positions within the salient. The German assault started on 5 July but was soon slowed to a halt by deep antitank defenses and minefields, which the Soviets had prepared in anticipation of the attack. At the height of the battle on 12 July the Red Army began to counterattack, having built up by then a marked predominance of both troops and tanks. The Soviets soon developed a broad offensive that recovered the nearby city of Orel on 5 August and that of Kharkov (now Kharkiv, Ukraine) on 23 August. The battle entered military annals as the biggest tank battle in history, involving some 6,000 tanks: 3,306 Soviet tanks against 2,700 German tanks.[10]

The Battle of Kursk marked the decisive end of the German offensive capability on the Russian Front and cleared the way for the great Soviet offensives of 1944–45. The Kursk victory put the strategic initiative firmly in the hands of the Red Army. Following only six months after the Stalingrad triumph, it demonstrated to the whole world that the defeat of Nazi Germany was now just a matter of time. To compensate the heavy losses suffered under Kursk, the German command was obliged to relocate ever more fresh divisions to the Russian Front. For instance, it felt compelled to transfer to Russia many of its panzer divisions stationed in Italy, replacing them with the heavily depleted infantry units routed by the Soviets. All this created favorable conditions for the USSR's Western Allies, which were able to invade southern Italy and launch the British-American advance into Italy's central regions. The Kursk victory, the landing of British and U.S. troops in Italy, and the expulsion of the Italian and German armies from North Africa were all potent signs of the radical turn in the war.

On the Eastern Front, the major Soviet offensive of December 1943–April 1944 routed the German armies in western Ukraine and allowed the Red Army to reach the Soviet western border. The Red Army then pursued the enemy by advancing into Romania at the end of March 1944 and Poland at the end of July of that year. Military operations were now increasingly planned in coordination with the Western Allies. Following the opening of the second front in France, the cooperation between the Allies entered its most fruitful stage. By 6 June 1944—the day of the Western Allies' landing in Normandy—about two-thirds of the more combat-worthy Wehrmacht divisions were striving in vain to defend against the Red Army offensive in eastern Europe. In the autumn of 1944 the German troops were expelled almost entirely from the Soviet territory, and the Red Army advanced into Bulgaria, Yugoslavia, Czechoslovakia, Hungary, and Norway.

In the winter of 1944–45 the war against Germany and its allies in Europe entered its final phase. Squeezed between the two fronts, Germany had to counter the concerted assaults of the Allies. By mid-April 1945 the Soviet troops had pushed the Germans out of Poland, Hungary, and the eastern parts of Czechoslovakia and Austria, and occupied the eastern one-third of Germany. The last-ditch Battle of Berlin, despite the fierce resistance of the million-strong German forces, failed to repel the Soviet onslaught. At the climax of the German collapse, with Berlin encircled by Soviet troops, Hitler committed suicide on 30 April; two days later, the Berlin garrison capitulated. On 8 May the surrender of all German forces was signed.

Stalinism versus Fascism

For decades the Soviet authorities prohibited delving into the real cost of the Soviet victory or scrutinizing the causes of the military defeats at the start of the war. Soviet losses were deliberately played down in official statistics. Only with the advent of greater openness under Gorbachev did the true extent of the tragic mistakes of the Soviet leadership and of the human toll exacted for the victory become known.

The USSR bore the brunt of the war against Nazi Germany. From June 1941 to May 1945, the Soviet-German front was the main line of battle. In battles with the Red Army the Wehrmacht lost over 73 percent of its manpower, 75 percent of its tanks and artillery, and over 75 percent of its aircraft. The human cost of the Soviet victory was immense. The country lost one-seventh of its prewar population, which declined from 197 million in June 1941 to only 171 million at the end of 1945. Its total human losses are estimated at 26 to 27 million people. This number includes 8 to 9 million soldiers, who were killed in action or died of wounds or disease. The rest were civilian deaths caused by illness, malnourishment, and ill treatment in occupied territory, in captivity in German-occupied Europe, and in the harsh conditions of the Soviet rear. In just one episode of the war—the 900-day-long siege of Leningrad—800,000 civilians died of undernourishment and bombardments. The Soviet human toll was a demographic catastrophe that exceeded by far German losses (13–14 million) or those of its Western Allies, Britain (370,000) and the United States (300,000).[11]

The direct material damage wrought by war amounted to one-third of the country's entire national wealth. Over 1,700 cities and towns and over 70,000 villages were completely or partially destroyed, leaving 25 million people without homes. Many major cities, such as Stalingrad, Sebastopol, Novorossijsk, Voronezh, Novgorod, Pskov, and Smolensk, lay in ruins, with many completely razed to the ground. The Soviet industry lost 32,000 large- and medium-scale enterprises, while agriculture sustained immense losses in livestock slaughtered or requisitioned for the needs of the occupying armies.[12]

The war had an ambivalent effect on Stalin's regime. The initial disastrous defeats had nearly pushed Stalin's personal dictatorship to the brink of collapse. His despotism and unaccountability were clearly the main reasons for the tragic miscalculations at the start of the war. However, the turnaround in the USSR's military fortunes and the subsequent glorious victory allowed the regime to obscure the negative sides of the absolutist rule. The great military victory was used to consecrate command-administrative methods, mask the deficiencies of the Soviet socioeconomic system, and drum up the "great historic advantages" of the Stalinist model of socialism.

To this day, Stalin's ultimate triumph in the war with Hitler is used by some as grounds for exonerating Stalinist practices. A typical pro-Stalin argument asserts that, for all his sins and crimes, Stalin presided over Russian victory in the Second World War. But this claim is easily refuted. If Stalin had been rational, all those millions who were made to starve in the great famine of 1932–33 or liquidated as a result of Stalin's ideological intolerance would have been available to Russia as able-bodied men and women to put their shoulders to the wheels of agricultural and industrial production and carry rifles in the war. The purges of the 1930s crippled the Red Army and were largely responsible for its great reverse in the war with Finland and then in the first phase of the Soviet-German war. In a sense, the Soviet people won the war despite Stalin and his policies rather than thanks to him.

Moreover, Stalin and Bolshevism may be charged with indirectly assisting the rise of fascism. The Bolshevik leaders had always regarded the October Revolution as the dawn of a world socialist revolution. Despite what Lenin, Trotsky, or Stalin said about the "right of nations to self-determination," their actual policies were aimed at bringing near "world revolution." Having resurrected the Russian empire under a new name, they sought to spread the socialist gospel with the help of the international organization of Communists, known as the Communist International, or Comintern. From the time of its creation in 1919 until its inglorious dissolution in 1943, the Comintern was dominated by the Russian Communist Party and was seen by the Bolsheviks as "world revolution's headquarters."

The Bolshevik dominance over the Comintern may have had dire consequences for the world Communist movement and even for the world at large. At its Sixth Congress in 1928 Stalin enforced a critical switch in the Comintern's policy. By that time, the economies of the advanced capitalist nations had become embroiled in a deep crisis. It looked as if capitalism was in its death throes. The Soviet media was full of reports about the crisis of overproduction in the West, which was accompanied by hunger, poverty, unemployment, and the deliberate destruction of unsold commodities. Only socialism seemed to be capable of putting an end to the capitalist predicament. The rise of fascism in Germany seemed also to confirm that periods of economic instability contributed to increased aggressiveness of "imperialist" capitalist nations. The Soviet leaders interpreted the mounting economic and political problems in the West as a significant symptom of the approaching war and revolution.

It was against this background of escalating political and economic problems in the West that Stalin directed foreign Communists' energies not so much at combating fascism as at isolating Social-Democratic movements in their countries. Social-Democrats were now declared enemies along with fascists. They were denounced as "social-fascists" and "social-traitors," as they advocated gradual reforms, which only delayed the outbreak of revolution. On Moscow's instructions the Comintern forbade German Communists to enter blocs with German Social-Democrats. The Comintern's proscription for Communists to form political alliances with Social-Democrats undermined the unity of working-class movements and facilitated the rise of fascist and military dictatorships in a number of European countries. All this has led some analysts to the conclusion that Stalin's political intrigues in the world Communist movement helped indirectly Hitler's ascendancy.[13] A united front of German Communists and Social-Democrats might have blocked his rise to power.

By attacking the USSR, Hitler sought to realize his bloody racial fantasies and aspirations of enforcing the German Reich's domination over the entire world. By defeating Hitler, Stalin, on the other hand, hoped to achieve world revolution that would transform the world or its substantial part into the Kremlin's empire. There is even a fully argued theory that Stalin intended to use Hitler as an "icebreaker" of the world Communist revolution.[14] According to this hypothesis, Hitler, by subjugating the nations of Europe and destroying their military capabilities, was unwittingly doing groundwork for the Soviet dictator. Stalin was biding his time, waiting for Nazi Germany to overstretch itself in its global conquests. As soon as the Nazis had exhausted themselves in battles in Europe and elsewhere, the Red Army would be ready to launch a preventive war against Germany. The liberation of German-occupied countries by the Soviets would trigger Communist takeovers across Europe. According to this theory, Stalin's plan was foiled only because Hitler had surmised Stalin's intentions and preempted him by launching his own attack.

There has yet been no conclusive evidence either to prove or refute the theory about Stalin's plan of a preventive war against Hitler. But even if there was no such plan, it is clear that Stalin's vision of the world's future was dictatorial and inhuman. Bolshevism and Stalinism played a vital and positive historical role by routing fascism in alliance with the Western democracies. In its turn, fascism may have impeded the expansion of Communism into the global arena and prevented world revolution. Communism outlived fascism, but only by a few decades: by the late 1980s communism itself had collapsed.

The Onset of the Cold War

The "Grand Alliance" (to use Winston Churchill's phrase) forged by the USSR, the United States, and Britain in the extreme conditions of war, was critical in upholding freedom and sovereignty of its member states and of many other nations all over the world. Germany, Japan, and their allies suffered a total defeat, and the territories they had occupied were liberated. The struggle against fascism brought together world leaders of seemingly incompatible political and cultural backgrounds. They were compelled to overlook their differences to protect human and democratic interests of their populations against the racist aspirations of fascism.

The titanic struggle against Nazism obscured the contradictions between Western democracies and Stalinist Russia. Western leaders forgot about their prewar declarations that it was impossible to enter into agreements with the repressive Soviet regime. The American and British media were now full of articles and radio broadcasts brimming with goodwill toward the Russian ally and admiring the courage and skills of the Red Army. The prewar portrayal of Joseph Stalin as a cruel dictator now gave place to sugary references to "Uncle Joe." In its turn, Soviet propaganda refrained from invoking its prewar denunciations of "bourgeois" democracy. In the war's final phases hundreds of thousands of Soviet officers and soldiers, liberating European states, gained firsthand experience of the capitalist West, while their Western counterparts got to know real Soviet people and discarded some of the prewar stereotypes about the Soviets.

However, deep political antagonisms, which had colored the relations of the Soviet Union and Western democracies in the 1920s and 1930s, did not go away entirely but were only subdued. The inherent hostility was generated by irreconcilable ideological differences and clashing national interests. With victory in sight, these differences quickly resurfaced. Having routed their common enemy, the victorious powers lost the unity of purpose that had held together their wartime alliance.

Ironically, it was the conclusion of a series of agreements between the Allies in the final phases of the war that led to the reappearance of these centrifugal tendencies. The Yalta accords of the "big three" (February 1945) and subsequent agreements defined, in a veiled form, the postwar spheres of influence. Presented ostensibly as the foundation of a postwar peaceful settlement, they, in actual fact, sowed the seeds of future rivalry at the global and regional levels between Russia and its Western allies, and first of all, the United States.

The Yalta agreements endorsed a new balance of power that had formed toward the end of the war. As a result, the Soviet Union and the United States had developed powerful military and economic capabilities, which both were now tempted to use to attain their global political objectives. The United States had the necessary economic power augmented by its nuclear might. In its turn, the Soviet Union sought to exploit its impressive military presence in eastern and southeastern Europe and eastern Germany, as well as southeast Asia. In a way, the Yalta agreements had laid the foundations of the future bipolar world.

It was clear that each of the two sides would seek not just to maintain its presence in its corresponding sphere of interest, but also to expand it. Diametrical ideological differences and imperial cravings of the two aspiring superpowers made confrontation between them almost inevitable.

The uneasy wartime alliance between the United States and Britain on the one hand and the Soviet Union on the other began to unravel soon after the surrender of Nazi Germany. Western leaders were seriously concerned about the USSR's growing influence in the postwar world. The Soviet victory over a fascist capitalist state served to enhance the international appeal of the Communist ideology. The Americans and the British feared the Soviet domination of eastern Europe and the threat of Soviet-influenced Communist parties coming to power in the democracies of Western Europe. Less than a year after their grand common victory, the Allied powers found themselves on the opposite sides of an "iron curtain," to use the famous phrase coined by the former British prime minister Winston Churchill in his speech made in Fulton, Missouri, in March 1946:

> A shadow has fallen upon the scenes so lately lighted by the Allied victory. . . . I have a strong admiration and regard for the valiant Russian people and for my wartime comrade, Marshal Stalin. . . . It is my duty, however, . . . to place before you certain facts about the present position in Europe.
>
> From Stettin in the Baltic to Trieste in the Adriatic, an iron curtain has descended across the Continent. Behind that line lie all the capitals of the ancient states of Central and Eastern Europe . . . subject in one form or another . . . to a very high . . . measure of control from Moscow. . . . [T]his is certainly not the liberated Europe we fought to build up.[15]

The Soviets were determined to maintain control of eastern Europe to safeguard against any possible renewed threat from Germany, and also for the ideological reasons of spreading communism worldwide. By 1948 local Communists, directly or indirectly supported by Soviet bayonets, took power in East Germany, Poland, Czechoslovakia, Hungary, Romania, Bulgaria, Yugoslavia, and Albania.

Soviet expansion into eastern Europe led to counteractions by the Western powers designed to curb any further enlargement of the Soviet sphere of influence and the spread of the Communist ideology. These included the Truman Doctrine of containment of Soviet expansion proclaimed in March 1947 by U.S. President Harry S. Truman and the offer in June of that year by U.S. Secretary of State George Marshall of a recovery program to Europe. Containment of communism was enforced by setting up a network of U.S. military bases close to the USSR's borders in Greece and Turkey and by support of anti-Soviet elements in the Soviet bloc countries. The Americans also sought to establish a military-political alliance of Western nations under their leadership. This was successfully achieved in 1949 with the setting up of the North Atlantic Treaty Organization (NATO) as a unified military command to resist the Soviet presence in Europe. The political and military integration of the West was facilitated by the massive economic assistance provided to Western Europe under the Marshall Plan. It helped to integrate those countries' economies with the United States' economy, thus bringing Western Europe under American influence.

Moscow interpreted the American strategy of containment as part of a master plan to encircle and subjugate the Soviet Union and responded by measures designed to consolidate the alliance of the socialist bloc countries. In 1949 it set up the Council for Mutual Economic Assistance (Comecon), charged with coordinating economic assistance to Communist regimes. In 1955 several Comecon countries established a military-political alliance—the Warsaw Pact—to counterbalance NATO. However, the USSR did not possess economic muscle to enable it to compete on equal terms with its powerful trans-Atlantic antagonist. The world war had opposite effects on the economies of the two countries: the Soviet economy was exhausted, whereas the American economy was revitalized. Despite its relative economic weakness in comparison to the United States, the USSR scored some success in projecting its global influence through its support of foreign Communist parties, including those in Western countries. Moscow also backed national-liberation movements in the third world, where the collapse of European overseas colonies often led to the emergence of countries of "socialist orientation." Finally, Moscow did not refrain from using armed force to suppress antisocialist risings in some of the Soviet bloc countries.

The intense rivalry and mistrust between the two camps led by the USSR and the United States threatened repeatedly to engulf the world in a new global conflagration. The world entered the era of the cold war that was to last for nearly half a century (1946–91). At its core was the intense military, economic, ideological, and political competition between the two antagonistic camps: the system of capitalism and the system of socialism. Several previously united nations were split as a result of this overwhelming rivalry. Thus, Germany was divided into two states following the establishment of the Federal Republic of Germany

(West Germany) in 1948 and the German Democratic Republic (East Germany) in 1949. Divided nations would become a tragic symbol of the world torn between the two hostile camps for several decades, affecting the peoples of Germany, Korea, Vietnam, and several others.

Finally, there were serious internal considerations that compelled Stalin to put a chill on Soviet relations with the West. The regime had grounds to fear that the wartime contacts with the Allies had encouraged the spread of pro-Western attitudes in various sections of Soviet society. The positive perceptions of the West put into question the integrity of Soviet propaganda that had always condemned capitalism and strove to instill animosity toward Western political and cultural institutions and way of life. As the country began rebuilding its war-ravaged economy, the regime proceeded to tighten its ideological screws. The wartime patriotic rhetoric was again infused with themes of "class struggle." A massive ideological campaign was launched to combat apolitical "cosmopolitism" and reprehensible "cringing to the West." It was directed against all those who hoped for some liberalization of the country's internal life, as well as for improved relations with the West. Thus, the growth of repression inside the country was intrinsically connected with the onset of the cold war and the mounting confrontation with the West.

Chapter Eleven

Khrushchev and De-Stalinization

Stalin's Legacy

In the postwar period the capitalist world confronted the Soviet system with a powerful economic challenge. In the late 1940s and early 1950s, the leading industrialized countries of the West entered the era of a scientific and technological revolution. This opened a period of rapid transition to a new, postindustrial, stage of development. As the technological revolution advanced, it was becoming more and more obvious that the inherent characteristics of the Soviet economic model stood in the way of technological progress. With the only exception of the military-industrial complex, the latest scientific and technological achievements were slow to enter into production on a nationwide scale. Overcentralization, the absence of competition, and a lack of self-interest, motivation, and material incentives at all structural levels of the economy were the main impediments to technological progress.

During the war, overcentralization and planning, as the chief underlying principles of the Soviet economic system, had been developed to the utmost. In the extreme conditions of war they stood the Soviet Union in good stead, allowing to redeploy the country's industrial capacity to the safety of the eastern regions and to concentrate all available economic resources for the attainment of victory. But the retaining of that system after the war was hardly justified economically. Nevertheless, the Soviet government continued to pump huge resources into the military-industrial complex and the development of new types of weapons. In 1949 the USSR successfully tested the atomic bomb, and in 1953 it overtook the United States in the development of nuclear weapons by being the first to test the hydrogen bomb. In the early 1950s direct military expenditures accounted for 25 percent of the Soviet budget. Heavy industry was the next priority, second only to the defense sector, with machine-building, metallurgy, and energy generation allocated the biggest share of state investment.

As a result of the regime's obsession with continued expansion of the USSR's military and heavy industrial capabilities, Soviet agriculture, the light and food industries, and the services sector were severely underfunded. Particularly desperate was the plight of the peasants. Agricultural production had been seriously undercut by the war and the severe drought of 1946. The wages the peasants received in collective farms were a pittance. The villagers survived mainly thanks to the minute patches of land that had been left to them by the state for their individual use as household plots. These privately owned allotments were a concession that Stalin had been obliged to make to the collectivized peasants in the 1930s in the face of violent and widespread resistance to collectivization. During the war, when the state's grip on agriculture had somewhat relaxed, the peasants had been able to chip off strips of the collectivized field to augment their private plots. In 1946–47 this creeping privatization was uncovered, and the strips were reconfiscated. Yet the miniature individual plots, amounting to some 3 percent of all cultivated land, remained the key element of the subsistence economy in the village and also supplied agricultural produce to peasant markets in the cities. Peasants' household plots were also used to support privately owned livestock. Overall, they produced nearly half of all Soviet meat, milk, and green vegetables. By contrast, the work on collective and state farms was, by and large, performed carelessly and inefficiently. By the early 1950s state-controlled agricultural production had managed to reach its prewar level only to enter a period of drawn-out stagnation.

The West's technological advances had important implications for domestic life in the industrialized capitalist nations. They led to improvements in living standards, the growth of the middle classes, and greater social stability. In addition to economic and social benefits, Western populations enjoyed broad democratic rights and freedoms. By contrast, the Stalinist system was not geared to meet the needs of ordinary citizens. The people, the consumers, came last on the regime's priority list. Endemic shortages of consumer goods, overcrowded housing conditions, primitive consumer service—all these cried out for remedy.

From 1945 to 1953 the people's natural desire for improvement in living conditions and the authorities' inability to meet these expectations stoked domestic tensions. The Soviet people, who had sacrificed everything for the sake of victory, felt they deserved better. To continue to ignore consumers' needs was becoming more and more dangerous politically. Unable to follow the West's lead in creating a more democratic and consumer-oriented society, the Soviet leaders chose to seal the

USSR off from the West's "temptations" by an almost impenetrable "iron curtain."

In the immediate postwar years the internal pressures for change were also generated by new perceptions of themselves and of the wider world that many Soviets had acquired during the war. Ten million Soviet citizens had taken part in the Red Army's victorious liberation campaign in Europe, and over five million had been repatriated from German captivity. In other words, over fifteen million people had come face to face with "the capitalist realities" to discover a significant gap in the living standards between their country and the more industrialized capitalist nations. The experience was often a cultural shock compelling many to reconsider Soviet propagandist stereotypes.

More importantly, the historic victory reawakened patriotism and self-pride in millions of people. Public atmosphere was charged with great expectations and a desire for change. In villages, rumors spread of the impending dissolution of collective farms and of greater economic freedom. In towns, the intelligentsia hoped for democratization of the political regime. In the recently sovietized territories, including the Baltic republics and the western reaches of the Ukraine and Belorussia, Soviet punitive bodies confronted pockets of open armed resistance, mopping up guerrilla detachments of die-hard nationalists determined not to submit to Soviet rule.

Stalin's leadership responded to the new public attitudes with a combination of concessions and repression. On the one hand, it strove to create a semblance of some democratization: soviets at all levels resumed their regular work, and congresses of public, cultural, and professional organizations were reconvened after periods of prolonged inactivity. In 1948 the First Congress of Composers was held; in 1949 the Congress of Trade Unions was convened after an interval of seventeen years and the Congress of the Young Communist League for the first time in thirteen years. Positive developments took place in education, science, and culture. New universities and research centers were set up, and academies of science were founded in Kazakhstan, Latvia, and Estonia. In 1952 compulsory education was extended to seven years for all Soviet children, and a network of evening schools was set up for young people in jobs. Soviet television began its regular broadcasts.

In 1952 the Nineteenth Party Congress made the decision to rename the All-Union Communist Party of the Bolsheviks as the Communist Party of the Soviet Union (CPSU). This was a symbolic gesture that consigned to history the words *Bolshevik* and *Bolshevik Party*, associated in the popular consciousness with the years of Stalinist repression. The purge of political vocabulary also involved the terms *people's commissar* and *people's commissariat*, replaced by the more conventional *minister* and *ministry*.

However, the state-sponsored democratization was only skin-deep. Intimidation and repression remained the regime's main instruments of ruling society. In the late 1940s a new purge was under way disguised as the campaign against "cosmopolitism" and "cringing to the West." It was used to fan anti-Western attitudes and anti-Semitism, mirroring, to some extent, the anti-Communist hysteria that gripped the United States at about the same time. Stalin's equivalent of a "witch-hunt," however, had a far more ambitious aim of reimposing comprehensive ideological and political control over society. It was an attempt to resuscitate the "enemy image," which had faded somewhat during the war, and to provide ideological justification for a new spiral of terror. Until Stalin's death in 1953, state repression remained at an intolerable level, extending to various social, professional, and ethnic groups, including the party leadership itself, the intellectual community, and the Jews.

The "Secret" Speech

The domestic pressures, stoked in the period 1945–53, rose to the surface soon after Stalin's death. The dictator's departure compelled the Soviet leadership to weigh arguments in favor of some liberalization. Certain steps in that direction were taken in 1953–56, but the more public examination of Stalin's legacy would begin only in 1956, after Nikita Khrushchev (1894–1971) emerged as the country's undisputed leader and Stalin's successor.

Khrushchev had made his career under Stalin as a party secretary and one of his most devoted lieutenants, utterly dazed by the charismatic leader. After Stalin's death he rose to become the Soviet leader who sponsored substantial liberalization of Soviet society, put an end to mass terror, and attempted to discredit his former idol. Khrushchev's elevation was in large measure due to chance. Stalin himself had involuntarily facilitated the rise to power of his future denunciator, by promoting Khrushchev from one rung of the career ladder to the next. Ironically, the overly suspicious dictator had failed to discern in his protégé the political tendency that he had so ruthlessly crushed during his own rise to absolute power. It had been associated with leaders such as Bukharin and others who had favored continuation of the NEP and democratization, and strongly objected to the use of coercive methods in running the economy. Despite brutal repressions, that moderate political trend and its representatives had never been completely eradicated. In this sense, the rise of Khrushchev was not accidental, but represented a revival and a vindication of an alternative to Stalin's tyranny.

Of all Soviet leaders, Nikita Khrushchev had perhaps the most colorful personality. Lacking formal education, he was able to achieve a meteoric career rise from a village shepherd to the leader of a world superpower. Like thousands of other young Russian peasants he had left the countryside hoping to find a better life in the city. In tsarist Russia on the eve of the revolution, workers in the first generation, coming from a peasant background, were the fastest growing sector of the working class. Many of them enthusiastically accepted the Bolsheviks' simple black-and-white vision of society. Based on class hatred, it divided the world into "us," the workers, and "them," the bourgeoisie and landowners. By taking power from the exploiters and crushing their resistance, the workers would somehow manage to build a shining paradise on earth.

Having embraced this rigid class struggle approach in the period of his revolutionary youth, Khrushchev would never be able to discard it. The world to him remained divided by the barricades, with capitalists to one side and Communists to the other. The struggle between the socialist and capitalist camps was uncompromising and ineluctable, waged on the principle "either we bury them, or they bury us."

Khrushchev began his rise to the pinnacle of the party hierarchy as an enthusiastic young Communist in the 1920s, then as head of the Moscow party organization in the 1930s and leader of the Ukrainian party organization in the 1940s. For over two decades he had been one of Stalin's closest associates, and he had been in Stalin's inner circle from 1949. Placed at the head of the party after Stalin's death, Khrushchev immediately engaged in a fierce power struggle to defeat the conspiracy of Lavrenty Beria, who had been preparing to seize power in 1953. After Stalin died, Beria held in his hands the whole centralized machinery of repressions, including the Ministry of State Security and the Ministry of the Interior. Khrushchev, however, moved first and arrested Beria by enlisting the support of the leadership of the army, including Marshal Zhukov. Following Beria's imprisonment, all establishments of state security in the union republics and in the provinces were reorganized. Several months later, the Committee of State Security, better known by its Russian abbreviation of KGB, came into existence. The reorganization ensured that the secret police was now completely subordinate to the party leadership. As for Beria, he was tried and executed on standard Stalinist charges of espionage and state treason.

The fundamental problem, which confronted the Soviet leadership after Stalin's death, was what was to be done about the atrocities committed under his leadership. How much could be revealed without undermining the stability of the state and without running the risk of an outburst of mass anger against the system, which had permitted the crimes? The additional uncomfortable problem was that all the current leaders were deeply implicated in the repressive policies conducted under Stalin; therefore, any criticism of Stalinism would immediately subject them to considerable political risks.

All these worrying considerations made the Soviet leadership pause, until finally Khrushchev mustered the courage to address this problem at the Twentieth Party Congress held in February 1956. On the final day of its work Khrushchev unexpectedly announced a fresh closed session, at which he delivered a four-hour-long speech about Stalin's crimes toward the party and the whole nation.[1] The speech about the iniquities committed during the period of the "cult of personality" shocked and startled the delegates. Thanks to this unannounced speech, the Twentieth Congress entered history as the congress that gave a start to the process of de-Stalinization.

The reasons for Khrushchev's decision to come forward with the posthumous denunciation of Stalin were complex and contradictory. On the one hand, this was a considered political move, allowing him to claim the mantle of a bold and determined reformer and to undermine the position of his potential rivals in the leadership, such as the Stalinist hard-liners Molotov and Malenkov. Moreover, it projected the image of Khrushchev as a daring and enthusiastic reformer to the Communist delegations from all over the world attending the congress, and thus helped assert the Soviet leadership's supreme authority in the world Communist movement. It is also possible that Khrushchev was responding to the attitudes from within the Communist Party, including the desire of its leaders to protect themselves from any repetitions of Stalin's atrocities. There was also much in Khrushchev's determined move that was emotional and impulsive. It had much to do with the personal qualities of Khrushchev: his humanity, honesty, and compassion, which had not been totally obliterated in his character by his earlier involvement in the atrocities of Stalin's period.

Khrushchev conceived the speech as a broad attack on the personality and some of the policies of Stalin. Briefly, its main points were the following. He accused Stalin of having violated the Leninist principle of collective leadership. Moreover, Stalin had developed the cult of personality, accompanied by "loathsome adulation." Stalin had falsified the party's history by claiming that he had been Lenin's main collaborator. Khrushchev's chief indictment was that Stalin had "victimized" innocent people in his attack on the party that started in the mid-1930s. Khrushchev devoted a large part of the speech to the rehabilitation of prominent party and military figures. He denounced the continuation of the purges after the war and the preparations for a new purge in 1953. More importantly, Khrushchev condemned the ideological justification of the purges: the Stalinist principle "that the closer we are to socialism, the more enemies we will have." He argued that to apply this principle was absurd, especially after 1934, when "the exploiting classes were generally liquidated, when the Soviet social structure had radically changed. . . when the ideological opponents of the party were long since defeated politically."[2]

To damage Stalin's stature even more, Khrushchev attempted to tarnish his reputation as a war leader. He accused him of the misconduct of the war against Nazi Germany and, in particular, of the fatal misreading on the eve of the war of Hitler's intentions to launch a surprise attack. Khrushchev also condemned the wholesale deportation toward the end of the war of peoples who had been under German occupation and who were accused of collaboration. According to Khrushchev: "The Ukrainians avoided meeting this fate only because there were too many of them and there was no place to which to deport them."[3]

The chief limitation of the speech was that Khrushchev restricted himself to describing the Stalinist atrocities and failed to analyze the political system that had made them possible. The indictment is restricted to the years after 1934, leaving out forced collectivization and industrialization. In other words, Stalin's twin cardinal policies and the way in which they were conducted were accepted as necessary and justified. Khrushchev was careful to dissociate the party from Stalin, presenting it as a victim rather than an accomplice in his crimes. The party was the source of all that was positive under Stalin, whereas all that was negative was the fault of the dictator. Khrushchev said little about the sufferings of the peasantry during the collectivization and the repression against ordinary citizens. Even prominent party and government figures were rehabilitated selectively. The main contenders for power following Lenin's death, such as Trotsky and Bukharin, who had lost to Stalin, were mentioned only to be condemned. The victory of Stalin in the power struggle and the reckless policies that had helped him achieve it were therefore accepted. In other words, the party line pursued under his leadership was accepted as basically sound, but the way he abused his power was condemned.

The main weakness of the speech was that it failed to provide any theoretical or historical explanation for the emergence of the Stalin phenomenon. The cult of personality and the repressions connected with it were blamed on the bad temper of the leader and not on the nature of the Communist system. The speech did not give any consistent analysis of the legal, political, ideological, or institutional foundations of Stalinism. On the contrary, its moral censure of Stalin effectively exonerated the party and the system as victims of the tyrant's paranoiac will. Stalin's style of leadership was forcefully distinguished from that of Lenin and was condemned as a distortion of the true Leninist principles.

Khrushchev's partial exposure of Stalin left many areas in the dark. If the party had been innocent of the reckless policies and purges under Stalin, why had it not resisted them? Why had the Communists allowed such things to happen? One apocryphal story provides an explanation. Khrushchev was addressing a meeting and speaking of Stalin's crimes. A member of the audience shouted: "And what were you doing?" Khrushchev snapped back: "Who said that?" Silence. "Well," he replied, "that is what I was doing too, keeping silent."

Khrushchev's criticism of Stalinism could not be consistent for many reasons. First, he himself was a product of the Stalinist system and had made his career in it. Second, he himself had been implicated in Stalin's crimes: as first secretary of the Moscow Party Committee and then of the Central Committee of the Ukrainian Communist Party he had been in charge of the purges in Moscow and the Ukraine. However determined he might have been to cleanse the tarnished image of socialism, he remained part of the system that he tried to reform from within. Under the circumstances, Khrushchev's partial denunciation of Stalinism was an act of courage and a major personal victory. All people, closely connected with the many acts of violence and repression committed by Stalin, were still strongly entrenched in the supreme party leadership, including Stalin's henchmen such as Molotov and Lazar Kaganovich.

Although it was never actually published in the Soviet Union until the relaxation of censorship controls under Gorbachev, the speech could not, of course, be kept secret. Moreover, following the Twentieth Congress, local party committees were instructed to read it at the meetings of Communists, and its content soon became known to the majority of the adult population of the Soviet Union. The weightiest consequences of the Twentieth Congress for the country's internal life were the return of millions of ex-prisoners and the posthumous rehabilitation of many millions more. By 1959 the number of persons confined to camps, colonies, and special settlements fell to just under one million from over 5.2 million just before Stalin's death in 1953.[4]

Khrushchev's revelations exposed him to great personal risks. The hard-liners in the party leadership, such as Malenkov, Molotov, Voroshilov, and Kaganovich, who were closely tied to the Stalinist system, directed the efforts of party conservatives to overthrow Khrushchev. In June 1957 they formed a majority in the Politburo (called the Presidium during Khrushchev's period in office) of the party's Central Committee and demanded his resignation. Khrushchev fought back by demanding that the party's Central Committee settle the issue. His survival now depended on the regional party leaders who were heavily represented in this larger body. With their support he was able to defeat his opponents, condemn them as an "antiparty group," oust them from their positions in Moscow, and demote them to minor managerial posts far away from the capital. The fact that they were allowed to survive was highly significant in itself, indicating that Khrushchev wished to avoid a return to Stalinist terror.

"Khrushchevism"

In the years immediately following the Twentieth Party Congress, Khrushchev's power and prestige were at their peak. His policies, like the project to develop vast virgin lands in Kazakhstan, were popular and seemingly successful. In October 1957 the launch of the Soviet space satellite *Sputnik* inaugurated the exploration of outer space. In 1961 it was followed by the first manned space flight of the cosmonaut Yuri Gagarin. As a result, the Soviet Union established itself as a world leader in science and technology.

These indisputable achievements were admired all over the world and served to heighten further Khrushchev's personal prestige. They also seemed to have reinforced Khrushchev's Marxist-Leninist fundamentalist beliefs. Khrushchev was the last Soviet leader who was a product of the revolutionary epoch and retained some of its epic fervor. He never was a profound ideologist or a deep theoretician, and his faith in communism was perhaps naive and simplistic. His idea of communism was akin to the traditional peasant dream of having enough to live in comfort. For the first time since the NEP of the 1920s, he pursued policies designed to appeal to Soviet consumers. The rapid construction of prefabricated buildings, for example, enabled millions of Soviet families to move from hostels and communal flats into tiny but separate apartments.

Khrushchev's vision of a workers' state was reflected in the adoption of a new party program in 1961. It summed up the party's achievements and outlined highly ambitious plans for the future. They envisaged that the Soviet Union would catch up and overtake the United States economically by 1970, and within twenty years (by 1980) the USSR would become a Communist society:

> In the current decade (1961–1970) the Soviet Union, in creating the material and technical basis of communism, will surpass the strongest and richest capitalist country, the USA, in production per head of population; the people's standards of living and their cultural and technical standards will improve substantially; everyone will live in easy circumstances; all collective- and state farms will become highly productive and profitable enterprises; the demand of Soviet people for well-appointed housing will, in the main, be satisfied; hard physical work will disappear; the USSR will have the shortest working day.
>
> The material and technical basis of communism will be built up by the end of the second decade (1971–1980), ensuring an abundance of material and cultural values for the whole population; Soviet society will come close to a stage where it can introduce the principle of distribution according to needs, and there will be a gradual transition to one form of ownership—public ownership. Thus, a Communist society will in the main be built in the USSR.[5]

The new party program committed Soviet leadership to the promise that the next generation of Soviet people would live under communism. Khrushchev thus opened himself to bitter criticism as the economic problems in the final years of his period in power made clear that these utopian goals could not be achieved. His revolutionary ardor encountered growing skepticism and derision, reflected in many popular jokes:

> President John Kennedy comes to God and says: "Tell me, God, how many years before my people will be happy?" "Fifty years," replies God. Kennedy weeps and leaves. Charles de Gaulle comes to God and says: "Tell me, God, how many years before my people will be happy?" "A hundred years," replies God. De Gaulle weeps and leaves. Khrushchev comes to God and says: "Tell me, God, how many years before my people will be happy?" God weeps and leaves.[6]

From the late 1950s onward, Khrushchev suffered a series of obvious and embarrassing failures at home and abroad. At home, the economy failed to reach the goals he had set, notably for food production. His dramatic declarations that the Soviet Union would soon surpass the United States in production of milk and meat were never realized. His earlier successes in ploughing up the virgin lands turned out to be of little value over the long run. The newly opened lands suffered soil erosion and could not be farmed regularly. The clearest sign of agricultural crisis came in 1963, when, following a poor harvest, the Soviet government was compelled to buy huge quantities of grain from foreign countries, including the United States.

Khrushchev's relations with the party and government bureaucracies also came under increasing strain. Khrushchev's populism and egalitarianism were not readily appreciated by many of his colleagues who had grown accustomed to privilege and had a vested interest in maintaining their position and authority. He deeply offended party functionaries by requiring that personnel in important party committees be rotated regularly. He also called for dividing the party into two structures: one would direct agriculture, the other, industry. He contemplated equally radical plans for restructuring the government. His reckless reorganizations encountered increasing opposition, as they threatened the privileges and stability of the ruling *nomeklatura*.

Within the larger Communist world Khrushchev's attempts to build "socialism with a human face" were not universally appreciated. The Chinese leader Mao Zedong, in particular, openly disapproved of his attacks on Stalin and increasingly challenged the Soviet leadership of the world Communist movement. In Europe the "iron curtain" was breached in Berlin, with thousands of East German refugees fleeing to the western part of the city. The massive drain on skilled labor that was created by this exodus was crippling East Germany's economy. The crisis came to a head in 1961, when the East German authorities, on Khrushchev's instructions, erected a monumental wall to separate the city's eastern part from West Berlin. The wall was a poor advertisement for communism, but it helped to avert the economic collapse of East Germany.

In relations with the capitalist West Krushchev's policy of "peaceful coexistence" had failed to prevent diplomatic conflicts and military standoffs. The most serious clash between the world's two superpowers came in 1962 over tiny Cuba. The Cuban leader, Fidel Castro, who came to power in 1959, openly proclaimed his ties to Marxism and Leninism. To protect his new ally and to assert the Soviet military presence at the United States' doorstep, Khrushchev placed in Cuba offensive missiles capable of launching nuclear weapons. President John

Kennedy's administration responded by establishing a naval blockade of the island. A full-scale American invasion of Cuba seemed to be in the offing. In the face of American demands, Khrushchev reversed his plans and removed the missiles. In return, the American government promised not to invade Cuba. Khrushchev would never admit his failure in the Cuban crisis, but this apparent debacle undercut his prestige among the topmost leaders of the party.

Khrushchev's mistakes at home and abroad made his rivals (including his protégé Leonid Brezhnev) determined to act. In October 1964 the party-state *nomenklatura* rebelled against the troublesome leader. Practically the whole of the Politburo of the Central Committee conspired against him. Confronted by the hostile majority, Khrushchev was forced to resign. He was permitted to remain in Moscow, where he lived as a private citizen until his death in 1971.

Khrushchev committed many mistakes and misjudgments during his period in power. His competence as the leader of a world superpower was often in question. His political style was dubbed by his opponents "voluntarism," that is, policy making in a willful, foolish, and erratic manner. Khrushchev was notorious for advocating harebrained schemes and chasing impractical ideas, such as his insistence on massive expansion of the sown areas of maize, including territories beyond the Arctic Circle. (A popular joke commented on this obsession of his thus: "We shouldn't let Khrushchev go to the moon—he would plant maize there.")

Other hallmarks of political "Khrushchevism" were populism and overoptimistic, utopian objectives. His optimism stemmed from his Leninist fundamentalism and the belief that socialism, when cleansed of Stalinist distortions, would be able to prove its historic superiority over capitalism. However, Khrushchev's denunciation of Stalin and his quest for "socialism with a human face" failed to create conditions for genuine democracy in the party and the country. Khrushchev's reforms were, in the main, limited to the adjusting of the system established by his predecessor. The basic structures and the apparatus forged by Stalin continued to rule, and no institutional or political barriers were erected against a revival of Stalinism. The CPSU remained the dominant political institution, and the curbs on the KGB and the de-Stalinization process itself proved to some extent reversible.

All his limitations notwithstanding, Khrushchev's main historic merit consists of the fact that he was able to muster courage to mount the platform of the Twentieth Congress and reveal the crimes of the Stalinist regime against its own people. The speech dealt a crushing blow to

Stalinism but could not defeat it entirely. In changed forms it survived for a long time and even tried to raise its head under Brezhnev's creeping re-Stalinization. But the ferment engendered by Khrushchev's speech would continue. It ensured that there would be no return to high Stalinism as an extreme form of authoritarianism, based on tyrannical power, a leader's cult, and mass repressions. The conservative leaders who replaced Khrushchev were unable to reanimate that extreme type of tyranny.

Khrushchev would be remembered for his more consumerist approach and for the guarantees of basic freedoms he granted to Soviet citizens. The peasants' bondage to the collective farms was relaxed, and they were given freedom of movement within the country. The educated elites were allowed, on certain strictly defined conditions, to make contacts with foreign colleagues and even occasionally travel abroad. Finally, Khrushchev, despite all his blunders in the international arena, made a decisive contribution to the establishment of peaceful coexistence between the Soviet Union and the United States, and between East and West in general. These achievements endured under his successors.

Finally, the fact that the first secretary could become a private citizen so peacefully was in itself a remarkable achievement of Khrushchev's de-Stalinization. His nonviolent retirement was another sign that the system had moved away from the murderous brutality of Stalin's days, when the only way out from the top was to prison or before the firing squad. It demonstrated that Khrushchev had managed to introduce some elements of legality into the Soviet political system.

Chapter Twelve

Brezhnev's "Mature Socialism"

Advent of Brezhnev

It is unlikely that Leonid Brezhnev (1906–82) was the mastermind behind the conspiracy that saw Khrushchev peacefully voted out of office. As an extremely cautious politician, Brezhnev was hardly suitable for the part of a coup ringleader. However, his position in the supreme leadership, including his membership in the Politburo, required his active involvement for the plot to be successful. Significantly, following Khrushchev's removal from his post, Brezhnev repaid generously his backers with promotions, honorary titles, and other rewards.

Brezhnev's accession marked the beginning of a new stage in Soviet history. The top echelons of the state and party hierarchy were now fully dominated by a new generation of Soviet leaders. Their political careers were launched during Stalin's violent cadres revolution of the late 1930s, when they were promoted to replace Communists, who perished in the bloody purges of 1937–38. Their older colleagues had been different: imbued with revolutionary ardor, they had thought of themselves as a cohort of staunch party warriors leading the masses to a radiant future. By contrast, the new generation of leaders, represented by Brezhnev, were brought up, trained, and promoted entirely within the Stalinist system. Most of them were pragmatic and mediocre functionaries, a product of a long-term personnel selection carried out by the dictator. They were not inclined to take risks or follow through on big objectives, but excelled in bureaucratic intrigues and politicking. Their intellectual and psychological makeup explains, to a large degree, the indeterminate, half-and-half nature of the policies of the post-Khrushchev leadership.

Brezhnev seemed to be the embodiment of the typical characteristics of this new generation of Soviet administrators. He personified an average first secretary of the regional level and lacked many qualities necessary to be a national leader. No doubt, he was good at "apparatus politics" and bureaucratic intrigues, but this was hardly enough to compensate for his lack of education and strategic foresight. He enjoyed little respect among the Soviet people, who remembered the thrill with which Brezhnev used to pin medals on Khrushchev's chest. He was seen as an ungrateful man, who turned against the very person who had promoted him to the top. The best that could be said about Brezhnev was that, at least, he was not a malicious or cruel person.

In his private life Brezhnev enjoyed a good meal, was a keen huntsman, and relished a fast ride in a car. He introduced the habit for leaders to race through the streets of Moscow at the speed of 90 miles an hour. However, as a politician, Brezhnev did not like sharp turns and preferred to apply brakes rather than accelerate too briskly. He came to power without a political program or an action plan of his own. Instead, he strove to project the image of a sober and levelheaded leader, who never took important decisions without consulting his Politburo colleagues. In practice, this approach spawned an unwieldy bureaucracy that stifled innovation and initiative and accumulated unresolved problems. Brezhnev's basic strategy was to muddle through by balancing in the political middle and by rejecting both de-Stalinization and a full-scale return to Stalinism.

Brezhnev became general secretary because he suited almost everyone in the top leadership. His co-conspirators in the plot to oust Khrushchev regarded him as a temporary figure and would have never thought that he would be able to stay in power for as long as eighteen years. Brezhnev, however, was shrewd enough to know how to play the power game at the top political level. To understand how he was able to consolidate power, it is important to bear in mind that the CPSU had always contained within itself not one, but two parties. There was the outer party, which at that time had more than twelve million rank-and-file members; and there was the inner core comprised of several hundred thousand professional functionaries. The outer party of rank-and-file Communists had practically no say in deciding party policies and therefore the country's destiny. Real power was concentrated in the inner party or the *apparat* structures.

The inner party consisted of a legion of party secretaries—from the district, through regional and union republics' levels. Brezhnev began each working day by spending two hours on the phone ringing first party secretaries in the regions and the republics and cultivating good relations with them. More importantly, Brezhnev skillfully built up his base of support within the party's central apparatus, especially in its supreme body, the Politburo, where he was able to consolidate and enhance his authority. Brezhnev took considerable care to expand his influence by promoting his old cronies to the top party and state circles. Individuals whom he knew from the period of his work as party secretary in Moldavia and the Ukraine were persistently promoted to the top. Many of them were of very modest intellectual and cultural endowments, but had an overdeveloped taste for perks and privileges. Even a quick look at Brezhnev's inner circle is enough to see that it was comprised of self-centered politicians with a narrow provincial outlook, who were poorly equipped to run the country when the need for change was more and more obvious.

Roots of Stagnation

First of all, there was an urgent need to reexamine yet again the direction of Soviet economic development. In the 1960s the Soviet economy continued to follow the trajectory imparted to it by Stalin's forced industrialization launched in the 1920s. Its main objectives remained largely the same as they had been under Stalin: expanding the country's industrial and military capacity and restructuring the entire economy on the basis of machine production. In this sense, the industrialization process during the Soviet period was not confined to the initial five-year plans, but lasted for almost five decades. In effect, the economic development under Khrushchev and Brezhnev represented the deepening of industrialization and the attempt to spread it to all branches of the economy.

The Soviet Union continued to industrialize at a time when the industrialized capitalist countries were entering a postindustrial stage, reaping the benefits of the technological revolution. While advanced Western countries began utilizing new and intensive technological methods, the Soviet economy continued to develop in the extensive way, by putting ever more human and natural resources into production. This resulted in a labor deficit and even led to the growing demand for unskilled manual labor. In a country that had pioneered space flight and was a world leader in some spheres of science and technology, manual workers accounted for 40 percent of the entire labor force in industry, 60 percent in construction, and about 70 percent in agriculture.[1] Even in more mechanized branches of industry serious problems developed, caused by poor management and the low discipline and motivation of workers. The time-honored practice of wage leveling at the expense of more enterprising and better qualified workers and engineers led to the virtual disappearance of people with top skills and qualifications. The attempts to replace material incentives with "socialist emulation" failed to stimulate production. Apathy and indifference to matters of production were widespread among all groups of the working population.

In addition, bureaucratic overcentralization could no longer cope with managing efficiently the increasingly sophisticated branch structure of the Soviet economy. From 1965 to 1985 the number of ministries and economic departments with all-union competence increased 5.5 times, reaching a total of 160. The economic ministries became true citadels of Soviet bureaucracy, running branches of the economy under their command as absolute monopolies. They not only controlled from the single center all productive resources but also directly administered all companies and enterprises belonging to their branch across the entire country. Their enormous economic power allowed them to exert pressure on party and state structures at all levels and to lobby their departmental interests.

However, members of the party-state-managerial *nomenklatura* did not have any strictly economic interests of their own, as they were not private owners of productive assets. Their real interest was in maintaining at any cost their privileged position in society because it allowed them to grab the biggest share of the national product. The chief criteria of personnel selection within the *nomenklatura* were not competence or professionalism, but obedience and personal loyalty to leaders at the higher level. Administrators and managers were not elected or even rotated, but were appointed through the *nomenklatura* networks of patronage and nepotism. The ruling elite was increasingly transformed into a privileged caste and an antielite, whose members stood above the law and the rest of society.

Some analysts explain the prolonged nature of stagnation under Brezhnev with the help of the concept of "social contract."[2] This is interpreted as a tacit bargain or a set of unspoken mutual expectations that began to arise in the relations between the regime and society. The state committed itself to providing job security, social benefits, and relative income equality in exchange for quiescence and compliance from society. This strategy on the part of the political elite was matched by a complementary response in mass behavior, resulting in the emergence of a relatively stable conglomerate of diverse social forces that provided the social base of stagnation. It consisted of inefficient government and economic elites, semieducated white-collar workers, unskilled blue-collar workers, and, finally, collectivized peasants deprived of incentives to improve agricultural productivity. The forces of stagnation cared little about scientific and technological progress or intensification of production. They were content with the status quo and did not desire any far-reaching structural reforms in the economy and politics.

The Soviet Decline

By the early 1980s the country's economy had entered the stage of terminal decline. Its predicament contrasted sharply with the new phase of the technological revolution, which was unfolding in the industrialized countries of the West. New scientific achievements led to the establishment of microelectronics and biotechnology as the main directions of the technological revolution. The Soviet Union had achieved military parity with the most powerful industrial nation of the modern world, but its stagnating economy made maintaining this military equilibrium more and more strenuous. The cost of the arms race aggravated technological backwardness in most other branches of production. Consumer industries and agriculture were neglected. The population's living standards froze.

The deteriorating economic situation went hand in hand with an intellectual and physical decline of the Soviet leader and the ruling clique. Having suffered a stroke, Brezhnev was hardly fit to continue in his role of the national leader. His slow, unsure movements and indistinct speech at televised public meetings and official receptions betrayed his deteriorating physical condition. Yet the ruling party hierarchy continued to prop up the invalid leader at the top of the party-state pyramid. Throughout his almost two-decade-long period in power, the Politburo membership stayed practically unchanged. In the 1970s the average age of Politburo members reached 70 years old. Brezhnev's entourage became too infirm to endure even twenty-minute Politburo meetings. But the old men in the Kremlin continued to cling to power with all the strength left in them, blocking the way to the top to younger and more educated rivals.

The ruling circle grew increasingly aware of the looming crisis, but its self-centered interests prevailed over the strategic interests of the country. Some sporadic and timid attempts at reform were still periodically launched, but all this had little or no effect. It became common practice to juggle figures and to massage statistics to simulate nonexistent success. Such "creative accounting" was not regarded as something reprehensible. Systematic falsification of economic data and bogus, fraudulent statistics in economic plans, reports, and accounts became widespread. Deceit and whitewash at all levels were now the chief mode of the functioning of the administrative apparatus. The low living standards for millions of people, the absence of any incentives to raise labor efficiency, and a sharp increase in the alcohol consumption level were all signs of decay and disaffection within Soviet society. The country came face to face with a crisis of the entire socioeconomic system that the ruling elite refused to acknowledge or see. Moreover, the authorities sought to divert public attention from real problems by massive propaganda of militarism and by pushing the country into reckless military adventures, such as the war in Afghanistan.

In this parlous state the Soviet Union entered the 1980s and the time to meet the party's "solemn promise" made in 1961 that in 1980 the Soviet people would live under communism. Obviously, the promise was not and could not be kept. Soviet ideologists had to use all their ingenuity to explain away the embarrassment, and they came up with the neat idea of "developed" or "mature" socialism. This was presented as an indefinitely long stage of historical development. The implication was that the promised land of communism was no longer at hand and that generations of Soviet people should now be prepared to stick with "developed" socialism for as long as it takes to reach communism. As party documents unconvincingly explained:

> The extensive experience of socialist and communist construction in the USSR incontrovertibly demonstrates that our advance to communism is being accomplished through the stage of a developed socialist society. This is a necessary, natural, and historically long period of the formation of the communist system. This conclusion was drawn and elaborated by the Party in recent years and, unquestionably, it should be duly recorded in the Party Program.

The state's propaganda system tried hard to persuade the Soviet people of the correctness of party doctrine, but its attempts were now increasingly met with cynicism and derision. In the conditions of mounting deficit, which affected practically the entire consumer goods and services sectors, and which was further aggravated by the abnormal distribution system, skewed in favor of the privileged *nomenklatura,* many Soviet citizens began to question the proposition that the Soviet system did indeed offer an alternative model of economic development and social justice to that of capitalism. Soviet leaders became unable to persuade the population that the bright future of communism would ever arrive. A popular joke of the time posed a question: "What sort of a job should you take, so as never to be unemployed?" The answer was characteristic of the disdain in which people now held party promises: "Climb up the Kremlin wall and watch for the approach of communism."[3]

The party's demand for full loyalty to its doctrines prohibited any alternative ideas from being aired in public life and stifled serious discussion of trends and processes affecting society. Any attempts at a critical analysis of negative phenomena and social contradictions, even made by individuals loyal to the regime, were stamped out as provocative insinuations, hostile to the socialist system. Such critics were branded "anti-Soviet dissidents" who dared to deny the "historical advantages of socialism." The entire philosophy of stagnation was based on turning one's back on real problems, ignoring the realities, which cried out for radical changes in the economy and in foreign and domestic policies. All those who dared to say the unpalatable truth had to be muffled or silenced. The essence of the Brezhnev regime's twilight years has been well captured in the following Russian joke:

> Stalin, Khrushchev and Brezhnev are traveling in a train. The train breaks down. "Fix it!" orders Stalin. They repair it, but still the train does not move. "Shoot everyone!" orders Stalin. They shoot everyone but still the train doesn't budge. Stalin dies. "Rehabilitate everyone!" orders Khrushchev. They are rehabilitated, but still the train won't go. Khrushchev is removed. "Close the curtains," orders Brezhnev, "and pretend we're moving."

The regime's obsession with maintaining stability even at the cost of stagnation appeared to Soviet progressives to stand for extreme conservatism. Yet Russia's subsequent turbulent periods of reform and revolution, starting with Mikhail Gorbachev's *perestroika* and continuing with Boris Yeltsin's controversial market reforms of the 1990s, have made many reconsider their views of Brezhnev's period in power. In the 1990s, in particular, when Russian society struggled to preserve the remnants of stability in the economy and politics, many began to look back to Brezhnev's days with nostalgia, realizing that stability in life had its own definite value and that, at times, "stagnation" was more desirable than reforms and changes.[4] Some even claim that Brezhnev's era was the pinnacle of Russia's achievement, when the country enjoyed the elevated international status of one of the world's two superpowers.

There is no doubt that Brezhnev's era was the high point of state socialism in Russia. Soviet socialism had accomplished a great feat by bringing into being a modern society that in its occupational composition and educational level was comparable to the industrialized countries of the West. However, in the late 1970s and early 1980s, the Soviet social structure, characteristic of a postindustrial society, came into conflict with the conservative instincts of the Soviet system. Dogmatic and inflexible, state socialism sought to perpetuate outmoded socioproductive relations and economic patterns, inherited from Stalin's era and geared to the technological level of the 1920s and 1930s. Its conservatism was no longer compatible with the aspirations of an increasingly urbanized and better-educated population, which was tired of sweating for the abstract and ever-receding prospect of communism and wanted to be treated as consumers rather than "builders of communism."

In the first half of the 1980s Soviet politics revealed an astonishing paradox: the frail and ailing supreme leader seemed to be the key to ensuring the stability and strength of the system. A brutal and tyrannical leader like Stalin was no longer required to maintain the regime. The "cult of personality" gave place to a "cult without personality" and a nominal leader, who ensured bureaucratic consensus by showing due respect for the rights and privileges of the party elite. The advent of the more activist and strong-minded leader Yuri Andropov (1914–84), who succeeded Brezhnev in 1982, sent shock waves through the system, threatening to undermine its conservative foundations. However, his tenure was too short to effect any lasting change: in February 1984 Andropov himself died. His brief era at the top of the Soviet system led to an even shorter interlude under Konstantin Chernenko (1911–85). His accession was hailed by extreme conservatives in the Soviet leadership as a return to the cherished certainties of the Brezhnev era. Indeed, Chernenko seemed to fit perfectly the system in the final phase of decay: senile and physically frail, he did little more than stand as a figurehead for a year. In March 1985 he died.

By then it was clear that the Soviet Union had come to the point when reform could no longer be postponed. Its legitimizing doctrines, institutions, and decision-making procedures were hopelessly outdated. The bankruptcy of the neo-Stalinist system of government was obvious to any unprejudiced observer. The dominance of the military leaders, central planners, and ideologists in determining priorities was called into question. The institutions and groups affiliated with traditional policies were damaged by the policy failures of the strategies they advocated (for instance, mistakes of the military in relation to the policy toward Afghanistan). Finally, the old Leninist ideology seemed no longer capable of incorporating the broad masses of the population into the Communist project.

Chapter Thirteen

Cracks in the Soviet Monolith

Models of Soviet /Russian Power

The term *totalitarianism* is widely used to describe the system created by Stalin. Under him, the Soviet Union was run by means of a personal dictatorship backed by mass terror and other blatantly oppressive means. Some analysts believe that the term can equally be applied to the post-Stalin period and that the crude totalitarianism of Stalin only foreshadowed the more subtle totalitarianism practiced under Brezhnev. They say that the post-Stalin USSR remained a monolith run by a narrow group of top party officials headed by the supreme party leader.

In their definition of totalitarianism the American political analysts Carl Friedrich and Zbigniew Brzezinski identified six key elements of a totalitarian system: (1) an official ideology intended to achieve a "perfect final stage of mankind"; (2) a single mass party, closely interwoven with the state bureaucracy and typically led by one man; (3) the party's control over the military; (4) the party's monopoly of the means of effective communication; (5) state terror enforced by a ubiquitous secret police; and (6) central direction and control of the entire economy.[1] Although some supporters of the "totalitarian" approach later recognized the existence of group interests in the postwar Soviet Union, they insisted that group activity did not play any significant political role in the pre-Gorbachev times. They claimed that group interests stood practically no chance of reaching an "organized" stage and having any effect on the distribution of power in the Soviet political system. Almost throughout its history the Soviet Union remained a totalitarian state, in which the party-state leadership exercised unlimited control over society and did not tolerate autonomous political activity. The adherents of this school for a long time simply ignored the problem of interest groups as irrelevant to the study of the Soviet political system.

From the late 1960s, however, some commentators began to question the applicability of this concept to Brezhnev's USSR. They pointed to new developments in Soviet politics, which signaled a departure from the "classical" totalitarian model, including the end to mass terror, the replacement of one-man rule by the emphasis on "collectivist" leadership, and a certain liberalization of the regime. But the chief argument on which their critique of the totalitarian concept was based concerned the qualitatively new level of interest groups' activity in the post-Stalin era. The rise of interest groups in Soviet society allowed this school of analysts to speak of a special type of "Soviet pluralism." One of the founders of the "pluralist model" of Soviet politics, the Canadian-American scholar Gordon Skilling, maintained, in particular, that Communist politics was based on an interplay of interests.[2]

The American analyst Jerry Hough further developed the pluralist group approach in relation to the Soviet system. He believed that Brzezinski's claim that the Soviet political system was unique and had nothing in common with Western political systems was too sweeping and not suitable to describe the post-Stalin stage of Soviet development. Hough described the political process in the USSR as "bureaucratic conflict" that involved specific interest groups, such as ministries and economic departments in charge of the more important branches of the economy, the military-industrial complex, the Central Committee departments, which often defended the interests of economic sectors under their tutelage, and the regional party-state elites. As for Western-style autonomous interest groups, such as trade unions and other public organizations, they either did not exist or had a negligible influence on Soviet politics.[3]

In Hough's model the top party-state leadership played the part of "final arbiter," reconciling these bureaucratic interests rather than imposing dictatorially its will on the lower power structures and society. Describing his model as "institutional pluralism," Hough claimed that it restricted the power of the general secretary and the Politburo, forcing them to follow the advice of specific bureaucratic groups and mediating conflicts between them.[4] In practice, the elaboration of policies was often delegated to interested bureaucracies. In other words, the principles of policy formulation and decision making in the Soviet Union were not that different from pluralist politics in Western countries. The main distinction was in the type of interest groups: in the West they were mostly voluntary public associations, whereas in the USSR they were represented by institutional structures formed within the system.

In the late 1970s and early 1980s the debate on the nature of the

Soviet political system between the supporters of the totalitarian and pluralist schools was reinvigorated by the appearance of a new, "corporatist" approach. Most fully the views of the corporatist strand of Soviet studies were presented in the works of Valerie Bunce and John Echols.[5] Like pluralists, the corporatists recognized the existence of organized interests in the USSR and a certain adjustment of the post-Stalin regime. However, they disagreed strongly with the pluralist interpretation of the role of these interests and the nature of the changes. In particular, they objected to the central proposition of the pluralist model that downgraded the role of the top party-state leadership to that of a passive broker mediating institutional interests. The corporatists argued that this view ignored the fundamental differences between the role of the government in pluralist democracies of the West and in Brezhnev's USSR.

The supporters of the corporatist theory insisted that the Soviet authorities retained their immense prerogatives and were actively involved in the decision-making process. Soviet interest groups were not autonomous and independent, but instead were organic parts of the system and bound to follow the "rules of the game." In other words, their functioning was based on the corporatist, rather than the pluralist, model. In corporatist politics the more important interest groups are incorporated into the policy process by the state and its leaders. State corporatism allows the organization and articulation of interests, particularly those connected with heavy industry and the military, but only under the tight control of the state.

It is clear now that the Soviet reality was too complex, multifaceted, and contradictory to allow its essence to be captured in a single word, be it *totalitarianism, pluralism,* or *corporatism.* However, by focusing on particular aspects of the regime, the adherents of each of the three schools of thought contributed to a better understanding of the power mechanisms in the Soviet Union. In particular, the emphasis by the pluralist and corporatist schools on the study of interest groups helped to gain important insights into their structure and political role in the pre-Gorbachev period and laid the foundation for subsequent research into the growth of pluralism under Gorbachev and the evolution of organized interests in post-Soviet Russia.

One of the most important contributions of the group approach to the understanding of Communist systems was the discovery of institutional interest groups and the analysis of their unique role in Communist political systems. In the more liberal atmosphere of Gorbachev's *perestroika,* when the rigid ideological constraints were relaxed, Soviet analysts were able to draw upon some of the findings and approaches of their Western colleagues and to contribute to the ongoing debate. The issue of interest groups, in particular, attracted the attention of some market-oriented Soviet economists. In 1986 the economists V. Naishul and V. Konstantinov advanced their own theory of Soviet directive planning. In their view, the formulation of state plans relied on a bureaucratic accommodation of interests between economic departments and also between them and the state planning agencies. This coordination evolved in the direction of the growing autonomy of departmental interests.[6] Naishul later developed his ideas with the help of such concepts as "accommodation economy" and "administrative market" that challenged the widespread perception of the postwar Soviet order as a command-administrative system.

In the 1990s Russian analysts were able to uncover more detailed information about Soviet organized interests and investigate the extent of their influence. In particular, they were able to clarify the list of the more influential "complexes" of ministries and departments, lobbying in the common cause and thus constituting an interest group. These included the military-industrial complex, comprised of nine military-industrial ministries; the construction industry complex, comprised of seven all-union ministries; the mining and metallurgical complex, represented by two ministries and several economic departments; the fuel and energy complex, comprised of four all-union ministries; the chemical industry complex, with three all-union ministries; the agro-industrial complex, with four all-union ministries and one department; the machine-building industry complex; and the transport and communications group. The remaining ministries and economic departments in charge of the production of consumer goods, pharmaceuticals, and other light industries did not have any significant weight in bureaucratic wrangling for investment and resources.[7]

The Rise of Cultural and Academic Pluralism

Alongside institutional interest groups, whose growing influence was "softening" and "thawing" the Soviet monolith, other groups began to appear that were less formalized and yet increasingly assertive, voicing concern over various aspects of Soviet development. The appearance of these informal groups of writers, journalists, scientists, and other intellectuals became possible when the quarter-of-a-century-long "deep freeze" of Stalinist tyranny was replaced by the more liberal cultural and ideological atmosphere of the Khrushchev period. The direction and essence of changes that would rock the Soviet Union in the final phase of its history under Gorbachev were, to a significant extent, prepared by the ideas and activities of these groups. From the mid-1950s this relative liberalization affected literature and cinematography, painting and music, and natural and applied social sciences. All this served to transform the monotonous cultural landscape of the Stalin era, leading to the development of cultural and academic pluralism.

In particular, the autonomous activity of writers and journalists led to the appearance of a number of groupings of the literati usually clustered around major literary magazines, such as *Novyi Mir, Nash sovremennik, Oktiabr', Yunost'*, and *Molodaia gvardia*. Artists, filmmakers, composers, and actors also had their own informal groupings. Despite being poorly structured, these diverse interests and their representatives articulated independent opinions and beliefs and sought to express them in their artistic explorations. All this enabled Soviet art and culture of the 1970s to develop into a rich and varied scene.

The Soviet authorities, no doubt, were aware of the dangers of cultural autonomy for the purity of the obligatory "party spirit" that had to permeate works of Soviet artists and writers, yet they refrained from rooting out resolutely all shoots of cultural pluralism. Partly, this was because they hoped that the growing cultural diversity might help diffuse tensions in society by channeling the emotional and social energies of the better-educated and socially active citizens into creative search and cultural activities. Partly, it was an attempt to compensate for the growing disenchantment of the intelligentsia with Communist ideals and to fill in the spiritual void that was opening up in an increasingly demoralized society.

New trends connected with the rise of informal interest groups began to affect also the applied social sciences and, to some extent, the study of philosophy. Some of the more substantial adjustments of Soviet political, social, and economic thought during Brezhnev's times occurred, in particular, in the fields related to the study of international relations and world economy. During the 1960s, when the CPSU had to engage in a fierce ideological dispute with the Chinese Communist Party, or in the 1970s, when Brezhnev sought to normalize relations and ease tensions with the West through the policy known as détente, the Soviet leadership felt a growing need for specialist information and expert advice to help elaborate its policies in the international arena. As a result, foreign policy–oriented research institutes and regional and area studies think tanks within the USSR Academy of Sciences, such as the Institute of World Economy and International Relations (better known by its Russian abbreviation IMEMO), the USA and Canada Institute, and the Asia and Africa Institute, were allowed to engage in relatively unfettered research and were soon transformed into "oases of creative thought" (to use the phrase coined by Georgy Arbatov, the former director of the USA and Canada Institute).

Scholars from the academic think tanks were often required to do policy-relevant work for state and party agencies, such as the Ministry of Foreign Affairs, the KGB, and the Central Committee. This ranged from a short briefing paper to a detailed forecast of possible developments in a specific country, region, or area of international relations to drafting official party documents and writing speeches for Soviet leaders. Such cooperation of the party-state leadership with specialists flourished under Brezhnev. As coordinating procedures were steadily refined, a division of labor between the party-government apparatus and the think tanks evolved. The party set the parameters of intellectual discourse by promulgating certain ideological axioms; the scholars could debate with relative freedom their specialist issues as long as they kept within those general parameters.

Foreign affairs specialists exploited the sanctioned leeway to describe the outside world in new ways, foreshadowing some of the ideas that would later inform Gorbachev's "new thinking." Readers of Soviet specialized journals were presented with a more rational picture of the West, no longer automatically militaristic and predatory. Scholars conducted debates on a number of important international relations issues, including the third world problems, regional conflicts, global issues, and arms control. The concepts of globalization and interdependence, which would become key themes of Gorbachev's policies, were also popular with Soviet foreign policy experts and some economists, who argued that international cooperation was essential if humankind was to survive.[8]

It is important to emphasize that the research specialization of the academic think tanks and the expert advice they provided to the leadership did not turn them into genuine pressure groups. Even when they were headed by progressively minded directors, such as Anushavan Arzumanian (directed IMEMO in the late 1950s and the first half of the 1960s), Georgy Arbatov (longtime director of the USA and Canada Institute from 1967 to 1995), and Evgeny Primakov (in the 1970s and 1980s directed first the Institute of Oriental Studies and then IMEMO), the research institutes' influence on the party-state leadership was limited and depended on the experts' ability to persuade political leaders, by the strength of their arguments, to take their recommendations seriously.[9] Often their advice simply could not reach the intended addressee.

In the closing years of Brezhnev's occupancy written recommendations were prevented from being forwarded directly to the supreme party-government officials. Instead, all mail had to be sent to the General Department of the Central Committee to be sifted through by nameless functionaries. As a result, experts' proposals often ended up in a waste bin, or were occasionally forwarded to the Central Committee departments, and only rarely reached the desks of the top leaders.

All these difficulties notwithstanding, the expansion of a scholarly community strongly oriented toward policy questions prepared the necessary groundwork for significant changes in foreign and domestic policy decision making introduced in the late 1980s. A pool of human resources was created that could be used in posts more directly involved in policy making. Economists especially were sometimes drawn into the Ministry of Foreign Affairs; politically oriented scholars were more often recruited for work in the Central Committee apparatus, especially in the groups of consultants of the Central Committee, working full-time on long-range questions.

Until the advent of Gorbachev, however, the movement of scholars into posts in policy-making bodies was not large. The party continued to guard jealously its power monopoly and treated with suspicion the activities of the elite groups, which could undermine its self-assigned leading role in society. Despite some leeway they enjoyed, Soviet experts remained relatively unimportant as a political force. The official world continued to manipulate traditional doctrinal stereotypes of class struggle, cold war, and xenophobia. Decision-making practices favored established institutions like the military. Obsessive security-mindedness and compartmentalization of debate restricted the flow of information and discussion.

Although the impact on Soviet politics of the new "revisionist" thinking, generated by the academic community, is not always easy to quantify, in certain other areas of Soviet public life under Brezhnev the involvement of experts and scientists produced certain tangible achievements. Scholars were at the forefront of the Soviet ecological movement that began to develop in the 1960s. Specialists from different fields—soil science, law, biology, ethnography, economics, and so on—drew public attention to a variety of ecological problems and campaigned against mindless grandiose projects, initiated by empire-building central ministries regardless of the effects their schemes might have on the environment. Experts were first to raise the issue of the massive soil erosion caused by the sowing of vast areas of western Siberia—the so-called virgin lands. Scientists were involved actively in the environmental battle against the construction of cellulose factories on Lake Baikal that would have damaged the purity of the world's largest reservoir of fresh water. They fought successfully over the proposed diversion of Russia's northern rivers to provide irrigation for the cotton-growing areas of central Asia, warning that it would lead to incalculable economic and social side effects.

Thanks to the efforts of scientists, these and other environmental issues began to be aired in the Soviet press and found reflection in documentary and feature films, as well as in works of Soviet writers such as Valentin Rasputin and Vasily Belov. The environmental campaigns of the 1970s and 1980s did much to raise public awareness and reawaken public opinion. The ecological issues became the battleground where for the first time public interests openly stood up to narrow ministerial interests and, as in the case of Lake Baikal and the proposed river diversion, actually prevailed. With the onset of Gorbachev's *glasnost,* ecological issues became the crucial starting point for the criticism of defects of the Soviet system, especially following the 1986 explosion at the Chernobyl nuclear power station.

The work and activities of Soviet writers, artists, filmmakers, scientists, academics, and other intellectuals had prepared the soil for the rebirth of civil society in the late 1980s and its emancipation from tight party-state control. In the conditions of Brezhnev's Soviet Union these small circles of like-minded intellectuals were not yet pressure groups in the full sense. Their intellectual explorations and aesthetic search were conducted within the permissible leeway, prescribed explicitly or implicitly by the authorities. Attempts to go beyond the allowed limits of creative or academic freedom by such groups and their individual members were not tolerated: such "trespassers" were branded "dissidents" and subjected to repression.

Even the privileged "oases of free thought" that flourished in the academic think tanks remained insecure. In the early 1980s conservative elements in the Soviet leadership attacked the USA and Canada Institute, the reform-minded economists from the Novosibirsk branch of the USSR Academy of Sciences, and the Economic-Mathematical Institute in Moscow. A crackdown at IMEMO was also planned, following the arrest by the KGB of two members of its staff accused of distributing leaflets that criticized the official interpretation of the recent events in Poland and openly sympathized with the Polish Solidarity movement. A high-ranking party commission was set up to scrutinize the activities of the institute, with the undeclared intention to discredit its staff and oust its director, Nikolai Inozentsev.[10]

Under Brezhnev's authoritarian rule, cultural and academic pluralism remained limited in scope and fell short of real ideological and political pluralism. Nevertheless, the rise of informal interest groups in the post-war USSR was an indication of the important developments in the depths of Soviet society that were beginning to affect and modify its political system. The cultural and scholarly activities of the educated elites were softening the totalitarian monolith gradually, eroding its out-dated ideological and intellectual foundations imperceptibly, sponta-neously, and almost unintentionally. The full effect of these changes would be felt in the Gorbachev period and beyond, when the reformist ideas, aired and developed in the 1960s and 1970s, would spread from the educated society to reach the key decision makers in the government.

Dissidence

Not all members of the Soviet intelligentsia, however, were content to put up with the officially sanctioned limits of cultural and intellectual freedom and keep quiet. In particular, many were deeply concerned that, with the advent of Brezhnev, Krushchev's cultural and ideological "thaw" was substantially curtailed. They feared a return of harsh Stalinist practices, and they had the courage to protest openly against violations of civil liberties. The authorities used a whole arsenal of repressive measures, short of killing dissidents, yet were unable to root out dissidence.

In the 1960s and 1970s dissidents typically expressed their criticisms in letters of protest and appeals to Soviet leaders and law-enforcement agencies. These were typed and copied by their supporters and dissemi-nated among like-minded friends. In the Soviet Union this free under-ground press became known as *samizdat* ("self-publishing"). Through various channels some of this literature filtered through to the West and was published there as *tamizdat* ("over-there publishing").

Two figures in the dissident movement in particular caused constant trouble for the Soviet authorities. One was Alexander Solzhenitsyn (b. 1918), a winner of the Nobel Prize in literature and the author of such novels as *Cancer Ward* and *The First Circle*,[11] widely circulated in *samiz-dat* and *tamizdat*. The other was Andrei Sakharov (1921–89), one of the inventors of the Soviet hydrogen bomb and later a winner of the Nobel Peace Prize. Both rose to personify the Soviet dissident movement.

The writer and the scientist were in opposition to the Soviet regime, but they also disagreed with each other about the path that Russia should follow. Their divergent views bring to mind parallels with the Slavophiles versus westernizers controversy, the intellectual argument that has animated Russian social thought ever since the "great debate" of the 1840s. Solzhenitsyn, with his nationalist views, stood in the succession line to the Slavophiles, whereas Sakharov's ideological preferences were more in tune with the westernizers' liberal orientation. Their ideological differences, however, were of secondary importance. What mattered was their open opposition to the Soviet regime and their determination to free the country from Communist authoritarianism.

Their international reputation to some extent protected them from persecution by the authorities. However, when in 1974 KGB agents discovered a copy of Solzhenitsyn's manuscript *The Gulag Archipelago*, the authorities had had enough. The book, a copy of which had been smuggled to the West and published there, disclosed the chief Soviet secret about the scale, history, and methods of Stalin's terror.[12] Written as a work of political journalism, it was based on interviews with hundreds of victims of Stalinist repressions, as well as the writer's own experience in a labor camp as part of a ten-year sentence as punishment for a critical remark about Stalin made in a letter to a friend. In contrast to Khrushchev's "secret speech," Solzhenitsyn's book was a profound and fundamental condemnation of the entire Soviet system. The writer rejected the notion of Stalinism and treated the events of Stalin's era as part of Lenin's legacy and as a logical development of Bolshevism.

Solzhenitsyn demanded the punishment of individuals still alive who had been accomplices in Stalin's actions, as well as the condemnation of the Communist system that had perpetrated such unspeakable crimes against its own people. Such calls could not be allowed to go unchallenged, and in 1974 Solzhenitsyn was forcibly deported to the West. However, the damage that his book did to the reputation of Soviet socialism was irreparable: with the publication of *The Gulag Archipelago*, nobody in the West could any longer believe in the radiant image of the USSR as the stronghold of progressive humanity and the defender of all the oppressed.

In presenting alternatives to the Soviet regime, Solzhenitsyn did not idealize Western ideological influences that filtered through the "iron curtain." He believed that the West's emphases on democracy and individual freedom were not entirely suited to Russia and advocated instead a benevolent authoritarian regime that would be based on the ideological and spiritual foundation of Russia's traditional Christian values.

In contrast to Solzhenitsyn, with his moderate nationalist views, academician Sakharov personified a westernizing strand within the Soviet dissident movement. This tendency became prominent following the Soviet invasion of Czechoslovakia in 1968 that dashed the hopes of Soviet progressives for the ability of the Soviet system to evolve in the direction of a democratic and humane socialism. The dissident thought now turned to other social systems, in particular, the West.

Sakharov was an outstanding representative of the Soviet scientific community, which in many respects was one of the most influential groups within the post-Stalin society. It comprised scientists who were responsible for making Russia a nuclear power and placed the first man into orbit and who gave Russia its intercontinental ballistic missiles and created the enormous Soviet educational-scientific establishment. Most leading Soviet scientists were also closely linked to their counterparts abroad. They attended international conferences and were familiar with the main currents of Western thought. In his famous essay *Progress, Peaceful Coexistence, and Intellectual Freedom* (1968), Sakharov acknowledged, for instance, that its basic thrust had been inspired by the ideas advanced in the postwar years by "public-spirited and penetrating thinkers—physicists and mathematicians, economists, jurists, public figures, and philosophers," including Einstein, Russell, Bohr, Cassin, and many others.[13]

However, for a westernizer, Sakharov's approach was quite unorthodox. He believed in the "convergence" of socialism and capitalism: eventually the two social systems would come together by retaining the advantages of each and overcoming deficiencies. The West would guarantee wide social provisions, while the socialist system would become thoroughly democratized. The ultimate integration of the Communist and capitalist systems would take the form of "democratic socialism."

Sakharov's "westernism" was evident in his emphasis on emulating the democratic system and technological achievements of the West. In his letters to Soviet leaders reproduced in the underground *samizdat,* Sakharov stressed that the USSR could not develop in economic and technological isolation from the rest of the world and that technological progress was inseparable from the democratization of society. The scientist argued that in the present age no country could resolve its own problems in isolation from global problems and that peace and the prosperity of humankind could only be preserved by the joint efforts of all.

Sakharov's writings contain many of the ideas that would later crystallize into the principles of the "new thinking" of *perestroika.* Striking parallels can be found between the ideas of the Soviet dissident and General Secretary Gorbachev's foreign policy doctrine. As one of the creators of the Soviet hydrogen bomb, Sakharov knew better than others about the threat to the very survival of humankind posed by nuclear weapons. His central idea was that the world could survive only if the United States and the Soviet Union established a cooperative framework, in which they would jointly work at resolving the problems that threatened humankind (Gorbachev would refer to them as "global problems"). According to Sakharov, apart from the universal nuclear war, civilization was imperiled by hunger, overpopulation, and the destruction of the environment:

> In the face of these perils, any action increasing the division of mankind, any preaching of the incompatibility of world ideologies and nations is madness and a crime.[14]

This was, in effect, a plea for the deideologization of international relations that would become the chief principle of foreign policy under Gorbachev.

In his essay *My Country and the World* (1975), Sakharov gave a list of reforms that he felt were necessary "to bring our country out of a constant state of general crisis." Several of the points of his program, such as the calls for *glasnost* (greater openness), economic reform, partial denationalization of all types of economic and social activity, and others, foreshadowed many of the *perestroika* slogans.[15] Indeed, Sakharov's essays constitute a unique body of writings, which contain most of the ideas of the reforms that would later form the basis of *perestroika*. His thoughts on international relations, in particular, reflect almost all the main elements of Gorbachev's new thinking, including the downplaying of ideology and class approach, the inadmissibility of nuclear war, a rejection of the disunity of nations in favor of interdependence and cooperation as the only salvation from the threat of nuclear catastrophe and other global problems, a return to all-human values, and continuous disarmament.

Other important aspects of Sakharov's public activities included his calls for the freedom of emigration and appeals against the use of special psychiatric hospitals by the KGB for the suppression of dissidents. The authorities' patience ran out when Sakharov spoke openly against the Soviet invasion of Afghanistan that began in December 1979. He was stripped of all his state awards and honors without trial and exiled from Moscow to Gorky (now Nizhny Novgorod), a city on the Volga closed to foreign journalists.

Sakharov was to remain outspoken and constant in his views, continuing to warn from exile against Soviet expansionism and the danger of thermonuclear war. It was the Soviet Union that began to change after the election in March 1985 of Gorbachev as general secretary. In

December 1986, Gorbachev personally phoned Sakharov and invited him to return to Moscow.

Observers have often noted how close were some of Gorbachev's utterances to the ideas of the former Soviet dissident. The Soviet leader had, no doubt, read Sakharov's writings and absorbed many of his postulates. Later he came to acknowledge publicly the intellectual ascendancy of dissidents in formulating the guidelines for reform:

> The awareness of the need for changes in society has been growing for a long time and assumed different forms. One of them was a phenomenon, which has received the name of dissident movement. And Andrei Sakharov has been its most outstanding representative. Reading his letters, which have remained unanswered, to the country's former leaders, one can see how very precisely has he defined the causes and effects of our general crisis, how sensible were many of his recommendations.[16]

Thus, *perestroika* marked the ending of the mutual isolation of dissidents, on the one hand, and "within-the-system" reformers, on the other, with the latter being increasingly swayed by the arguments of free-thinking people like Sakharov, who had the courage and moral spirit to stand up for their convictions.

Totalitarianism with Corporatist and Pluralist Subsystems

Contrary to the hopes of Sakharov and other reform-minded intellectuals, both in the USSR and in the West, the Soviet state-socialist system proved incapable of convergence with or evolutionary transformation into a Western-style democracy. Despite a whole number of significant modifications made to the system following Stalin's departure and spanning the period of thirty-odd years until the advent of Gorbachev, the essence of the regime remained practically unchanged. The party-state retained its power monopoly intact and strove to control the entire sociopolitical order; no autonomy unauthorized from above was tolerated. Of the original six characteristics of totalitarianism, only the role of the leader changed, and there was a decline in terror. The ban on independent activity was particularly stringent in the political sphere: all political initiatives from below, even when they seemed to be largely in tune with the party line, were branded "dissidence" and discouraged by various means, from subtle dissuasion to blunt repression.

Any attempts at modernizing the system to make it more flexible and efficient could be sanctioned only from above and were abrogated the moment the regime felt they eroded the totality of party-state control. This was the main reason for the repeated attempts at and failures of the sporadic reforms undertaken under Khrushchev and Brezhnev. On the one hand, Soviet leadership understood that the system was in need of modernization and that the only way to achieve this was to decentralize and infuse it with elements of autonomy and competition. On the other hand, however, all experiments in this direction were quickly abandoned, as even timid steps toward decentralization detracted from the party and state's power monopoly, threatening to undermine the totalitarian foundations.

The fundamental paradox of the Soviet postwar development was that the diversification of economic, social, and political life diluted the classical features of totalitarianism, yet there was no breakthrough into the liberalization of social life or the institutionalization of pluralism.[17] "Pluralism" of interest groups existed only at the level of these groups and did not determine the nature of their relations with the state. The central idea of the pluralist model is not just the existence of plurality of interests, but their independence and the ability to retain their autonomy while interacting with the state. In the Soviet Union interests were completely denied such autonomy.

It is true that pluralism of cultural and academic kinds came to play a significant role in society and in its relations with the state, but it could not modify the system to such an extent that at some point it lost its totalitarian character. Cultural and academic opposition did not pose real danger to the regime, because these groups' primary concern was to gain maximum creative and professional freedom, rather than wield political influence. The authorities tolerated cultural and academic pluralism because it helped to alleviate the corroding demoralization of society. It also provided the leadership with much-needed expert information and advice. As a result, controlled cultural and academic pluralism developed into a significant and influential subsystem within the totalitarian system. All substantial concessions to the intellectuals notwithstanding, real freedom of speech, expression, and research remained an unattainable dream.

Similarly, the corporatist approach that began to form in relations between the state and certain institutional economic interests did not really infringe on the indivisibility of the regime's political power. Soviet state-socialist corporatism did not form a political system or regime of its own, but was also a subsystem within a totalitarian regime.[18] It was set up by the state and functioned under state control. In other words, socialist corporatism represented an interaction not between state and nonstate actors, but almost entirely within state structures themselves ("state-bureaucratic corporatism," as some analysts call it).[19] It gave access to economic decision making to more influential institutional interests, but it also made them answerable to central authorities for the implementation of decisions taken.

Under socialist corporatism conflicts of interests were ironed out and reined in by a single integrating force—the ideological and political decrees of the party. Under Stalin, these decrees were so absolute that the role of interests was almost negligible. Besides, interests simply did not have enough time to form. Stalin's period was the time when the command-administrative system, designed to spearhead the "socialist onslaught," took shape and existed in its "purest" form, almost undiluted by group activity. The development of group interests accelerated significantly only after the dictator's death. Gradually, the command-administrative system was transformed into a more complex setup, in which certain interest groups evolved into "partners" of the party-state. This process was already quite advanced under Khrushchev and strengthened under Brezhnev. During his occupancy the party, state, and economic bureaucracies came into their own: their ever-swelling structures became main repositories of power and privilege. Nevertheless, the role of the central party-state authorities as an integrating and directing force was not abrogated or reduced to that of a mere broker or mediator. The center may have stopped acting like a despot, it no longer suppressed and quashed all interests outright, but, at the same time, it retained its preeminent directing and guiding prerogatives.

The rise of socialist corporatism had certain positive consequences. It led to some relaxation of the regime's extreme rigidity and inflexibility, helping it to respond better to changes in the economy and society. It engaged economic units of lower levels, including enterprises, in the process of accommodation and bargaining, giving rise to a "bureaucratic market" that prepared the soil for the true market, which began to take shape in the *perestroika* and post-*perestroika* period.

Thus, as a result of the postwar evolution of the relations between rising interests and the party-state authorities, the Soviet regime took on a more elaborate configuration. The new setup diluted and modified certain features of Stalin's totalitarianism but did not transform its essence. The most significant change was the evolvement of the corporatist and pluralist elements within the regime. In the post-Stalin Soviet Union corporatism and pluralism were implicitly permitted by the authorities and functioned not as an antithesis to totalitarianism but as its integral parts, or subsystems.

Corporatist and pluralist interaction helped to resolve or alleviate economic and social problems. However, no pluralism was allowed at the level of formulating the regime's political priorities and strategies of sociopolitical development. This was the exclusive preserve and absolute monopoly of the party-administrative apparatus, and here all differences of interests or opinion were reined in and tamed, both institutionally and politically, to serve the regime's objectives.

The development of corporatist and pluralist subsystems under Khrushchev and Brezhnev led to a social modification of totalitarianism, while its political structures remained relatively intact. The dismantling of the totalitarian political system began only in the 1980s as a result of Gorbachev's political reforms. As Soviet totalitarianism crumbled, two deformed siblings rose from its rubble—anarchic pluralism and oligarchic corporatism—both of which bore the distinctive birthmarks of their deceased totalitarian parent. One of the siblings in particular—oligarchic corporatism—appeared to develop into a full-blown system or regime in the early 1990s under President Boris Yeltsin. It remains to be seen whether Russia can evolve in the direction of a more mature pluralism or some form of liberal corporatism.

Part Three

FROM REFORM SOCIALISM TO DEFORMED CAPITALISM

Chapter Fourteen

The Command Economy in Crisis

Internal and External Pressures for Economic Reform

There is no agreement among analysts on when the Soviet economic system showed the first signs of stagnation and decay. Some believe that the origins of its general crisis go as far back as the mid-1950s; others think that it entered the crisis stage in the late 1970s, still others, in the 1980s. One thing is certain: in the final two decades of the Soviet Union's existence, "state socialism" lost its earlier dynamism and vitality and became mired in a drawn-out stagnation. The protracted and creeping nature of the Soviet economic crisis may be explained by the country's huge dimensions: its abundant natural resources could be thrown indefinitely into the furnace of the wasteful command economy to keep it going. Moreover, there were enough resources to enable the state to provide a system of social guarantees, including full employment, housing provision, free health care and education, and old-age pensions. The system of social protection, in combination with police control and ideological indoctrination, helped the regime to forestall for some time any serious outbursts of popular discontent.

However, when the economy showed the first symptoms of decay, the Soviet system began to lose the very rationale it was based on. Economic growth, as the necessary condition for the creation of the material base of the future Communist society, was critical for justifying the system. As long as the economy delivered high growth rates, it commanded loyalty. But the declining economic performance corroded peoples' belief in the ability of the system to create the base for a society of material plenty. The inability to reverse this decline ultimately destroyed the system's legitimacy.

The Stalinist economic policies favored extensive growth, that is, growth by increasing inputs of labor, raw materials, and investment capital into building ever more factories and plants. With a large pool of workers, seemingly endless supplies of oil, gas, coal, and other raw materials, ample land for cultivation, and capital squeezed from the rural sector through collectivization, Soviet planners during the 1930s and 1940s treated inputs as virtually inexhaustible. However, in the late 1950s and 1960s the USSR no longer enjoyed excess labor, land, or capital resources waiting to be exploited. New gains in production had to be achieved through intensive growth, that is, by the more efficient use of existing resources. Economic growth now depended on increases in labor productivity, automation, mechanization, and the application of new technologies.

All this put pressures on Khrushchev's and consecutive Soviet governments to shift away from the Stalinist model of extensive growth. After Stalin's death and until the USSR's collapse the Soviet leadership for over thirty years was engaged in an almost continuous process of reforming the Stalinist system of socialist central planning. The objective of the reform programs of all Soviet leaders from Khrushchev to Gorbachev was to make the economy more efficient and receptive to technological innovation and more responsive to consumer wants, while retaining its socialist character. All the reform programs moved in the direction of administrative decentralization. The reforms made by Khrushchev and Brezhnev came to naught, because they left the essential features of the Stalinist economic system in place. Only under Gorbachev did the reforms make some timid steps toward privatization and marketization of the economy.[1]

By the mid-1980s the internal pressures connected with the domestic economic situation and the limitations of the extensive economic development made the appearance of a bold reformer almost inevitable. Internal problems apart, there were important external factors that compelled the Soviet leadership to embark on a reform course. By the 1980s, as a result of the Soviet Union's dubious efforts to sponsor a "world revolutionary process" in Africa, Asia, and Latin America and the consequent deterioration of the climate of détente, the country had found itself in international isolation. The NATO bloc countries in the West and Japan and China in the East were now united in their hostility to the USSR.

The rise to power of strong-willed and deeply anti-Communist Western leaders, such as Margaret Thatcher in Britain in 1979, Ronald Reagan in the United States in 1981, and Helmut Kohl in West Germany in 1982, only served to amplify tensions in the relations between the USSR and the West. The Western leaders were committed to defeating the Soviet Union both in the economic contest and in the arms race. The military-industrial competition between the USSR and the West intensified at a time when advanced capitalist countries had been able to overcome the economic problems of the 1970s and their economies revived. Under these circumstances, Soviet ideologues found it more and more problematic to prove to their population the virtues and superiority of socialism.

U.S. President Ronald Reagan, in particular, took a strongly anti-Communist stance and even publicly denigrated the USSR, dubbing it "the evil empire." Convinced in the righteousness of his anti-Communist crusade, he inaugurated the largest peacetime military buildup in American history. In 1983 he proposed a program emphasizing the construction of a U.S. strategic defense system in space known as the Strategic Defense Initiative. The SDI, immediately dubbed "Star Wars," was intended to defend the United States from attack from Soviet intercontinental ballistic missiles by intercepting and destroying them in flight. Such an interception would require extremely advanced technological systems, which were yet to be researched and developed. There were serious doubts among Western arms experts about the technical feasibility of constructing a comprehensive defensive system of this kind, and some thought the project was unworkable. Its cost was prohibitive even by the standards of the powerful American economy.

The Soviet leadership, however, appeared to be too unnerved by the news of the American intentions to be able to muster courage and call Reagan's bluff. It was seriously concerned that the national economy might not be able to sustain the new spiral of the arms race and that the West would obtain a technological edge in the military field. The SDI presented a powerful military-technological challenge, posing a real threat to the USSR's superpower status. Whether the danger was real or imagined, the SDI became an important factor that compelled Soviet rulers to contemplate reforms aimed at retaining the country's international standing.

Gorbachev's *Perestroika*

The word *perestroika* is associated with the final stage of Soviet history and with the name of Mikhail Gorbachev (b. 1931). It is applied to the period beginning with his appointment to the post of general secretary in March 1985 and ending with his resignation and the dissolution of the USSR in December 1991. Gorbachev's period in power was marked by complex and conflicting developments in Soviet society. The term *perestroika,* which literally means "restructuring," was itself interpreted in different, sometimes diametrical, ways by various individuals, social groups, and political forces within the Soviet Union. For some, it stood for the dismantling of the Stalinist system and a transition to democracy. Others wanted to limit *perestroika* to replacing some outdated elements of the socialist system, claiming that its foundations were sound. There were also various shades of opinion between these two approaches to what was to be "restructured."

The important thing to note, however, is that, when Gorbachev came to power in 1985, almost all sections of society, all social groups, longed for change. These included certain groups within the party and state bureaucracy that were in favor of moderate reform. They hoped that more dynamic and vigorous actions of the government would rejuvenate the declining economy, reinvigorate the system, and ultimately strengthen their own authority. Gorbachev was sensitive enough to detect these hopes and aspirations, which were already in the air.

Gorbachev's election to the post of general secretary took place at the extraordinary plenum of the Party's Central Committee in March 1985, convened following Chernenko's death. By that time the command system had reached a point at which it was in great need of rejuvenating its geriatric structures. Gorbachev's candidacy was a logical choice in the situation when a younger and reform-minded leader was vitally needed to improve the external image and reanimate the decaying mechanisms of the system. His appointment was received as a natural and necessary step by the Soviet *nomenklatura*.

The change in the country's leadership generated cautious hopes in the Soviet population. The personality and actions of the new general secretary were received with enthusiasm and inspired optimism. Gorbachev's popularity soared rapidly, and his support base quickly became nationwide. His confident manner, unconventional behavior during unscheduled walks about Moscow, even his ability to smile and his sense of humor made him look different from his predecessors and instilled optimism. Gorbachev demonstrated enviable energy both at home and abroad. He conveyed the impression of a modern and dynamic leader, who knew in which direction to lead the country to overcome what he described as a "precrisis situation."

However, with each passing year popular trust in Gorbachev waned and faded. By 1990 Boris Yeltsin (b. 1931) had moved into first place as the most popular politician. A nationwide opinion poll conducted by the All-Union Center for the Study of Public Opinion in February 1991 asked about the qualities that marked Gorbachev as a political leader. The answers revealed that 28 percent of those interviewed thought that

Gorbachev's main characteristic as a political leader was "duplicity and hypocrisy." About 20 percent believed that he had "flexibility and skills of political maneuvering"; a similar number thought that Gorbachev was "weak and indecisive." Eighteen percent believed that the Soviet leader showed "indifference to human suffering," only 7 percent credited Gorbachev with "decisiveness," and just 4 percent thought that he possessed strategic foresight.[2]

Thousands of articles, books, and political portraits have been written about Gorbachev in his own country and abroad. Some were mystified by the seeming unpredictability of his actions. Some said he had a secret plan, which he concealed even from his associates but implemented persistently, often taking by surprise both his friends and his foes. He was extolled by some and vilified by others. In light of *perestroika*'s results, it would perhaps be fair to say that Gorbachev was an innovative leader and a reform-minded politician. However, the scale of his innovations was constrained by the fetters of Soviet ideology.[3] Despite all evidence to the contrary, Gorbachev believed that the core of the system was sound and that Soviet socialism could be reinvigorated. Moreover, he never questioned the viability of the two main pillars of the Soviet economic system: public ownership and planned economy. In his book, *Perestroika: New Thinking for Our Country and the World*, which appeared two years after he took office, Gorbachev continued to swear his allegiance to the socialist ideal:

> Socialism and public ownership, on which it is based, hold out virtually unlimited possibilities for progressive economic processes.[4]

> What is offered to us from the West, from a different economy, is unacceptable to us. We are sure that if we really put into effect the potential of socialism, if we adhere to its basic principles, if we . . . use the benefits of a planned economy, socialism can achieve much more than capitalism.[5]

Gorbachev and his Politburo colleagues were unambiguous about *perestroika*'s objectives. One prominent Politburo member, Yegor Ligachev, for example, saw the essence of *perestroika* in the simple formula "more socialism!" In other words, the reforming leadership believed that socialist foundations were basically sound: the problem was not so much that socialism was flawed, but that its potential was not used to the full.

No wonder that Gorbachev's first moves resembled those of his immediate predecessors—replacing administrative personnel, trying to enforce tighter discipline, inaugurating draconian measures to reduce the consumption of alcoholic beverages, and the like. However, as Gorbachev's perception of the severity of economic problems deepened, his prescriptions for remedies became less traditional. At the Twenty-Seventh Party Congress in February 1986, he declared the need for "radical reform" of the economic mechanism, including a reexamination of the nature of property ownership under socialism. He spoke of the need to make each worker feel like an owner of his or her firm and, contrary to established ideology, suggested an expanded role for producer cooperatives. He called for accelerating the country's development and opening it to the outside world.

Perestroika's Economic Strategies and Their Results

The problem, however, was that most of his reform measures were spontaneous and did not foresee many negative consequences. Several steps, in particular, taken from 1988 on, proved fateful and self-defeating. The first of these was connected with his plan to create financial incentives for enterprises and to encourage them to show more initiative and independence in their economic activity. To this end, the Law on State Enterprises was adopted that came into effect in 1988. The new law's central idea was to allow each state enterprise, no matter how large or small, to dispose of its share of budget allocation independently, without commands and instructions from Moscow. The reformers hoped that if factories were free to administer their own budget and to fix prices for their output, they would have greater incentives to improve their performance and profitability. Moreover, they would be motivated to look actively for their own (and not imposed by Moscow) suppliers and subcontractors, thus setting up effective producer networks within and between regions.

Gorbachev and his economic advisers hoped that the new law would unleash the initiative of enterprise managers and infuse the stagnating socialist economy with elements of competition. However, many company directors were not prepared psychologically to turn into responsible independent managers. Instead of restructuring production and improving quality, they preferred to raise the prices of their products and increase the wages of their work force. Instead of looking for suppliers and partners across the Soviet Union, they turned for help to local party-state administrators. The law increased the dependence of companies on local government, and the supervision of the economy by all-union ministries was seriously undermined. The law dealt a powerful blow to the Communist centralized managerial system before any viable alternative was put in its place.

The next fateful decision concerned the reform of economic management in general. The traditional system established by Stalin had been based on the political supremacy of the Communist Party. Party bodies played a key role in sorting out problems in relations between enterprises. Depending on the scale of a problem, it was resolved by district, city, regional, or republic party committees. If a problem was of an all-union magnitude, it was placed before the party's Central Committee. In short, party structures were the "blood vessels" of the command-bureaucratic system, ensuring its smooth operation.

In the postwar period, as the complexity of the Soviet economy grew, this system became less and less effective. First party secretaries in the regions and even Central Committee officials were often poorly qualified to make important decisions in specialized branches of production. Gorbachev thought that he could make the economy more efficient by curtailing the interference of the party bureaucracy in economic management. He announced that the party's main concern should be ideology and that any intrusion in matters of production should cease.

In addition to undermining the role of the party bodies as economic mediators, Gorbachev sought to liberalize economic management by dismantling all-union ministries, portrayed as "monsters" of the command-bureaucratic economy. Civil servants, working in economic bureaucracies, were disparaged as parasites who produced nothing and yet had the power to determine economic activity across the entire country from a single center. The result of Gorbachev's onslaught on the ministries was a speedy dissolution of less important ministries and drastic job cuts in more important ones. In a year, the staff of central ministries was reduced from 1.7 million to 700,000.[6] This was extolled as a triumph of the reformist leadership over the old command system.

However, the drastic weakening of the central ministries only accelerated the disintegration of interregional ties between enterprises. The substantial reduction of the ministries' functions, as well as the diminished role of the party structures, damaged the "blood vessels" that integrated the economic space of the Soviet Union. Freed from the arbitrary meddling of party officials and the pervasive control of central planners, the Soviet economy, far from being able to revive, began a rapid descent into chaos.

This general chaos and disorganization was precipitated further by the relaxation of fiscal policy under Gorbachev. He put pressure on the

Gosplan to augment significantly industrial investment targets to expand production and accelerate the rate of economic growth. This strategy required substantial budget borrowing, which ran contrary to the instincts of Soviet planners used to fiscal discipline. However, a group of economists close to Gorbachev swayed the argument in favor of borrowing by citing Western examples when budget deficit and inflation were used to stimulate economic growth. Beginning in 1988 the government debt grew and soon spun out of control. The government resorted to printing money and turned to the West for credits. In just two years after 1988, the USSR's foreign debt reached an unprecedented level of $70 billion.[7] However, the reform-minded leadership and pro-Western elements in the Soviet elite saw nothing wrong with foreign loans. Western credits were proof to them of the West's support of *perestroika*, and a factor that bound the Soviet Union and the West in partnership. The experiment with budget borrowing inaugurated spiraling inflation, which proved ruinous for the Soviet economic system.

Finally, the crisis of the Soviet economy was precipitated by the liberalization of foreign trade. The Soviet bloc used to have its own privileged trade zone of countries united in the Council of Mutual Economic Assistance, or Comecon. It was set up in 1949, when the onslaught of the cold war led to the emergence of economic barriers between Eastern Europe and the West. Up to 80 percent of Soviet foreign trade was with the Comecon member states. By the 1970s the socialist countries had established effective economic co-operation, based on their specialization in the production of different types of machinery, equipment, and agricultural produce. In its drive toward greater economic integration, Comecon appeared to be even more successful than the European Economic Community. Starting in 1973 the USSR shielded its Eastern European partners from the shock of the many-fold increase in the price of oil: it supplied it to the Comecon member states at greatly reduced prices. There were few reasons to doubt the beneficial nature of the Comecon cooperation: the Soviet Union provided socialist countries with raw materials well below world prices in return for more technologically sophisticated goods.

With the advent of Gorbachev, when it became clear that the new Soviet government was reluctant to enforce Moscow's political domination over the socialist bloc countries, the internal cohesion of the socialist bloc began to crack. The Comecon member states blamed some of their economic difficulties on the poor quality of products supplied by their neighbors. They believed they could resolve their economic problems by expanding trade with the capitalist West. This, however, was hindered by the lack of hard currency, as transactions within Comecon were conducted in rubles, which could not be used outside the socialist bloc. To put an end to mutual recriminations that soured relations within Comecon, the member states agreed to put trade within Comecon to the test of a convertible currency.

The switch to hard currency was also advocated by some of Gorbachev's advisers. They argued that the Soviet Union would only benefit from selling more oil to capitalist countries at world prices and buying better-quality Western equipment and goods. The Soviet bloc countries would be quickly brought to their senses when they would face the prospect of paying world prices for Soviet oil and would appreciate more the USSR's role of a major donor within Comecon. Persuaded by these arguments, Gorbachev authorized the switch to hard currency accounting within Comecon. The problem, however, was that none of the Comecon countries—from poor Romania to relatively prosperous East Germany, and even to the powerful Soviet Union—had sufficient hard currency reserves.[8] The switch caused the collapse of trade links within the socialist bloc. It deprived the USSR of access to Eastern European markets, compounding its economic self-isolation.

By the early 1990s, as a result of Gorbachev's self-styled economic reforms, the Soviet economy was in worse shape than in 1985. Freed from some of the coercive pressures of the past, the system of central planning eroded without adequate free-market mechanisms to replace it. In an environment of universal shortages and general confusion, state enterprises used their newly found freedom to reduce planned output, to drop low-priced products from production, and to raise prices under the guise of new products. All this added to inflation and exacerbated the perennial shortage of consumer goods. Empty shelves, longer lines, and increased distribution through special channels and on the black market became widespread. Because there was no longer effective control from Moscow at the republic and local levels, rising nationalism, ethnic strife, and regionalism fragmented the economy into dozens of mini-economies. Many republics within the Soviet Union sought independence, others sovereignty, and they all pursued policies of economic self-isolation. Barter was widespread. Goods and food rationing systems had to be set up: Ukraine introduced coupons, and Moscow issued ration cards. By 1990 the Soviet economy had slid into near-paralysis, and this condition foreshadowed the fall from power of the Soviet Communist Party and the breakup of the Soviet Union itself into a group of independent republics in 1991.

Gorbachev's economic strategies were largely to blame for the disappointing record of *perestroika*. His intention was to switch to intensive economic development by adjusting the traditional pillars of the Soviet economic system. After an initial flush of enthusiasm, the task of accelerating economic growth by adjusting the centralized planning system proved to be far more difficult than anticipated. Reform measures were introduced without investigating the roots of Soviet economic difficulties and the reasons why similar reform attempts in the past had failed. Decades of falsified statistics and creative accounting to simulate nonexistent successes had created a situation where even the top Soviet leaders themselves did not have a true picture of the condition of the national economy and the severity of its crisis.

Gorbachev acted out of a firm conviction that the ideological and economic foundations of the Soviet system were fundamentally sound. It would be naive to expect a convinced Communist to advocate liberal economic policies, such as breaking the monopoly of state ownership, withdrawing state subsidies from unprofitable enterprises, allowing genuine market competition, and giving land to peasants in their private ownership. Moreover, radical proposals of this nature would have never received the approval of his Politburo colleagues: a Soviet leader who espoused such views would have been regarded by them as worse than the dissidents and would have risked being locked up in a psychiatric hospital.

Gorbachev's attempt to renovate socialism was limited to tinkering with the old system that only deepened its general crisis. By the end, *perestroika* had reached the stage of a total economic breakdown, with deficits and social upheavals. The goal of creating a socialist regulated market economy, able to satisfy consumers and close the technological gap with the West, was not realized. However, the abysmal economic record of *perestroika* did achieve one thing: it appeared to demonstrate the impossibility of rejuvenating the Soviet model of socialism, pushing it to its final collapse.

Chapter Fifteen

The Collapse of the Political System

"Democratization" and "New Thinking"

By 1987, when his initial efforts to accelerate economic growth had come to nothing, Gorbachev put the blame for the failures of his economic strategy on party officials reluctant to give up the old command-administrative methods. He referred to these conservative elements in the party and economic management collectively as the "braking mechanism" that stalled his plans of "acceleration." He now felt that, without a far-reaching political reform that would sideline or remove these unwilling elements and release the energies of the masses, he would not be able to get ahead with the desired economic restructuring. The emphasis, accordingly, now shifted from economic reform to political democratization, which, together with *glasnost,* became the main catchword and the rallying cry of the second and final stage of Gorbachev's reforms.

Democracy was proclaimed to be the true essence of socialism that was to be reclaimed by transforming the command-bureaucratic system into socialism with a human face, or "democratic socialism." The reforming leadership called for a greater role for workers in the running of enterprises and the greater involvement of the general population in the affairs of state and in the law-making activity. The new reformist strategy implied that a radical economic reform could begin only after society had been reenergized through far-reaching democratization. In practice this meant that the economic restructuring was postponed, surrendering the center stage to the propaganda and promotion of democratic principles.

This shift of emphasis led to a deepening "westernization" of the Soviet reform process, as democratization was impossible without the introduction of certain elements and mechanisms from Western political systems. For some time, however, Gorbachev denied that democratization was aimed at borrowing "bourgeois" values and strove to prove that it was inspired by the ideals of Marx and Lenin. In reality, Gorbachev's "new thinking," as he called it, signified a revision of Marxism-Leninism and an attempt to incorporate certain new principles into Soviet socialist ideology, including civil society, the law-based state, parliamentarism, separation of powers, human rights, and, finally, the market—in other words, all those values that Marx and Lenin regarded as "bourgeois." Gradually, Gorbachev and his supporters began to refer to these principles as "all-human" rather than strictly socialist.

Democratization soon blossomed into the golden age of *glasnost,* leading to the soaring circulation of newspapers and magazines and a general publishing boom. Soviet intellectuals—writers, journalists, economists, historians, and others—were at the forefront of the searching and uncompromising criticism of the "deformations of socialism" in the economy, politics, and culture. For the first time in seven decades they could analyze and criticize openly the defects of command-administrative socialism. Their efforts met Gorbachev's expectations: the intellectual discussion was conducted within a socialist ideological framework, it shamed conservatives resisting the reform of the command system, and it helped to define the principles of an alternative model of "democratic socialism."

However, as the debate participants redoubled their efforts to find an alternative to the command system in Soviet history, probing ever deeper into the origins of Soviet socialism, they uncovered more and more facts, which showed clearly that the brutal suppression of dissidence and democracy was typical not just of the age of Stalin but also of the times of Khrushchev and Brezhnev and even under the "untouchable" Lenin. A pure and unpolluted spring of socialism, which could provide guidance and inspiration for a new generation of reformers, was nowhere to be found in Soviet history. The ever-growing number of intellectuals began to question the very proposition that it was possible to give socialism a human face or that "democratic socialism" could ever be built in the USSR.

Thus, the scathing criticism of the command system, sponsored and encouraged by the reformist Soviet leadership, soon began to break the confines of the *perestroika* ideological framework, leading to outright condemnations of socialism as a whole. The negative view of the potential of socialism to reform itself was instilled even further following the publication of the previously banned works of Russian writers, such as Mikhail Bulgakov, Andrei Platonov, Evgeny Zamiatin, and Alexander Solzhenitsyn.[1] They brought home the message that from the very outset Soviet socialism was harmful and damaging to Russia. Some writers disagreed that there was any difference between Lenin and Stalin, or even between communism and fascism. Their literary works delivered a crushing blow to the ideology of reform socialism and made many people skeptical that democracy under socialism was in principle feasible to achieve.

This growing skepticism notwithstanding, Gorbachev continued to argue that the main reason for the failure of his economic reform was not the Communist system as such but the hard-liners in the political leadership and economic management who should be removed from their positions of influence with the help of political reform, including direct popular elections. This view was translated into the decisions of the Nineteenth Party Conference (end of June–early July 1988), which discussed and adopted concrete measures aimed at democratizing the Soviet political system. The most important of these was the decision to hold multicandidate elections to soviets of all levels at which the voters would for the first time be given the choice of several candidates (previously, each deputy to a soviet was chosen from one candidate). Soviets themselves were to be brought into line with parliamentary conventions, including the transformation of the Supreme Soviet into a proper sitting parliament. The soviets were also to regain their governing functions, which had been previously usurped by the party bodies. The new approach was to be tested during the elections to a USSR Congress of People's Deputies—a superparliament, endowed with the powers to change the constitution—scheduled for the spring of 1989.

The conference decisions had momentous consequences for the Soviet political system and for the fate of the Soviet Union itself. Gorbachev relied on them to remove hard-liners, whose resistance paralyzed his economic modernization. He could never imagine, however, that the population would use the elections not just to vote out retrograde bureaucrats, but also to punish the party apparatus as a whole. The new electoral legislation would set in motion the process of disengaging the state from the party and dismantling the system, under which the party kept state and public organizations under its undivided control.

The Course of Political Reform

In the autumn of 1988 the Soviet political scene entered the stage of dramatic transformation. The formerly united camp of *perestroika* supporters began to split, as groups emerged that demanded more radical and far-reaching reform measures. Nascent radicalism contained two strands, both of which spelled danger for Gorbachev's policies. One strand was represented by national radicalism and was directed by popular fronts set up in most of the Soviet republics. They demanded greater autonomy for their republics and a reform of the Soviet federative structure. The other strand was political and insisted on radicalizing and deepening *perestroika*'s political, economic, and other reform measures. The two strands developed side by side and even overlapped in some of their demands, including the support of private ownership, political pluralism, and a multiparty system, all of which went beyond Gorbachev's original plans of democratization.

In line with the decisions of the Nineteenth Party Conference on the new electoral system, elections were held in March 1989 to the USSR Congress of People's Deputies. The new electoral law was not fully democratic and represented a compromise designed to enable the party to retain its overall influence: two-thirds of deputies were to be elected by direct popular vote, while the remaining one-third was to be elected by public organizations, including the Communist Party. These undemocratic restrictions notwithstanding, for the first time since 1917 the elections were held with genuine competition among candidates. Electoral campaigning roused keen interest among many sectors of the population in the outcome of the elections, resulting in a massive turnout at balloting stations of 90 percent of eligible voters.

The 1989 elections proved to be the first "quiet" popular revolution against the party-state apparatus. They gave a powerful signal about the declining popularity of the regime. Although the Communists gained a parliamentary majority, great damage was done to the party's prestige as many of its high-ranking representatives, the crème de la crème of the Soviet establishment, were rejected at the ballot box. The elections revealed an important pattern: every time the authorities tried to prevent an independent candidate from taking part in the elections, either by means of administrative pressure or by seeking to discredit him, the voters were even more determined to support the "antiestablishment" candidate. In other words, the less popular the candidate's standing with the authorities, the higher his popularity rating with the electorate.

Boris Yeltsin's case was a prime example of this tendency. The party's top hierarchy orchestrated an unprecedented dirty tricks campaign to discredit the former first secretary of the Moscow City Committee, who had been removed from his post in November 1987 for his calls to accelerate reform. However, far from defeating him, the intrigues of the party *nomenklatura* against Yeltsin—which were no doubt approved by Gorbachev personally—actually reinforced his popularity in the

Moscow electoral district, where he was running, bringing him a resounding victory with a record 90 percent of votes and a standing of a popular hero.

The electoral campaigning in the spring of 1989 also gave rise to novel forms of spontaneous collective action and political behavior unthinkable under Gorbachev's predecessors. These included unsanctioned mass rallies, which were a clear indication of the growing radicalization of the popular mood. The rallies featured speakers and protesters whose calls and demands went beyond Gorbachev's controlled liberalization and threatened to destabilize the Soviet regime. For the first time Gorbachev's efforts to elicit popular support for his reform backfired, undermining not just his conservative opponents but also him personally. A threat even more dangerous than mass rallies was the resurgence of the working-class movement. In the summer of 1989 miners' strikes were held. They challenged the very legitimacy of a system established on the claim that it represented the working class. Rapidly, the miners' strikes became overtly political, even revolutionary, demanding an end to the Communist Party's power monopoly.

The USSR Congress of People's Deputies, elected in the spring of 1989, was to play the role of the country's supreme legislative body. This superparliament, comprised of 2,250 deputies, was to be convened twice a year to discuss and settle most important constitutional issues. The Congress in its turn elected out of its deputies a smaller sitting parliament, the Supreme Soviet, which was to carry on the day-to-day legislative work between the sessions of Congress. The sittings of the First Congress, televised across the country, unedited and full of political struggle, were an incredible spectacle for the Soviet people. The entire country stopped working and followed its proceedings on radio and television.

The newly elected parliament also saw the formation for the first time in Soviet history of parliamentary opposition, the Interregional Group of Deputies. It consisted of democratically and liberally inclined intellectuals and politicians, including Boris Yeltsin and Andrei Sakharov. The latter entered parliament as a representative of the USSR Academy of Sciences and quickly emerged as the main ideologist and moral leader of the democratic opposition. His intellectual and political debate with Gorbachev and the Communist majority on the floor of Congress became the main source of political controversy throughout its sittings. It resulted in a dramatic split of the supporters of *perestroika* into moderates led by Gorbachev and radicals united in the Interregional Group of Deputies. From now on Gorbachev ceased to be the single leader of the reform process. He now had to contend with political rivals who offered alternative reform strategies and whose support in society was growing. It is likely that Gorbachev's personal dislike of Yeltsin colored his attitude toward radical democrats as a group.

The schism between Gorbachev and the radicals continued to widen throughout the rest of 1989. The radicals had the support of a number of influential national media outlets and were successful in popularizing their political agenda on national TV. On the whole, their demands remained within the ideological confines of democratic socialism, but the emphasis was now increasingly made on dismantling the authoritarian unitary state. Sakharov, for instance, drafted a new union treaty, which envisaged a loose constitutional structure, uniting the republics more on the principles of a confederation rather than a federation.

By 1990 the radical democrats competed vigorously for power with Gorbachev. In the autumn of 1989 their cause received a powerful impulse from the revolutions that swept across Eastern Europe, leading to the collapse of the Communist regimes there. At the Second Congress of People's Deputies in December 1989 the radicals even made open hints that Gorbachev himself might share the lot of Erich Honecker and Nicolae Ceausescu unless he moved quickly to implement radical reform. With the sudden death of Sakharov at the end of 1989, Yeltsin became the unquestionable leader of the radical opposition.

In March 1990 the body of deputies, gathered for the Third Congress of People's Deputies, elected Gorbachev president of the USSR. Gorbachev garnered less than 60 percent of the deputies' votes. The chief "architect of *perestroika*" did not have the courage to run for the presidency in popular elections. The resultant lack of popular mandate compromised the legitimacy of Gorbachev's new post and was one of the main reasons for his growing political weakness. Nevertheless, the structure of presidential power began to take shape, signaling the curtailment of the domination of the party's central bodies.

Yielding to the demands of the radical democratic opposition, the Congress also changed the wording of the notorious article 6 of the Soviet constitution and removed the definition of the CPSU as "the leading and guiding force of society and a core of the political system." The repeal of the article formally ended the power monopoly of the Communist Party and cleared the way for a multiparty system. The Communist Party would for some time remain the best-organized political force in the land, yet it was now a mere shadow of its former self, and its power and authority were eroded virtually from day to day. The executive and legislative organs of state gradually took over the policy-making and governing functions of the hitherto all-powerful Politburo.

In 1990 the political struggle reached a new high with the elections to the Supreme Soviets of union republics and to local soviets. In the run-up to the local elections, the radical democratic movement in Russia adopted a new political strategy. Russian radicals came to the conclusion that it was futile to wait for the all-union bodies, including the USSR Congress of People's Deputies and the USSR Supreme Soviet, to approve radical reform measures, as the resistance of their conservative memberships was too strong. Russian radicals were now determined to concentrate their efforts on taking power in Russia—the biggest of the republics—by winning the elections to the Congress of People's Deputies of Russia. They would use their electoral victory to proclaim Russia's sovereignty, then proceed to implement reforms, relying on the support of the more democratically inclined population of Russia. To this end, the radicals set up an electoral bloc, "Democratic Russia," the core of which was comprised of members of the Interregional Group of Deputies. The elections in the union republics brought a resounding victory to radicals, of both democratic and nationalist persuasions. In Russia, Yeltsin became head of the Supreme Soviet, while his associates were now heads of the soviets in Russia's two biggest cities, Moscow and Leningrad.

In the summer of 1990 the Supreme Soviet and the government of Russia controlled by Yeltsin's supporters prepared a plan for a radical move toward a free-market economy under the name of the "500 Days Program." It involved the freeing of prices and the private ownership of enterprises, land, services, and so on and had more in common with the "big bang" approach being adopted in Poland than with Gorbachev's intentions of a gradual, step-by-step introduction of a regulated market economy. To the Russian radicals' surprise, Gorbachev agreed to cooperate and submitted the Russian program for the approval of the USSR Supreme Soviet and of the all-union government. The all-union bodies, however, stripped the program of all its radicalism and rewrote it in a form unacceptable to the Russian government.

Yeltsin and his supporters saw the debacle of the "500 Days Program" as a wicked ploy by Gorbachev to derail their reform plans, and they now took the view that any further cooperation with the existing all-union authorities was pointless. They now intensified their struggle for Russia's independence from the union authorities and Gorbachev in order to be able to carry out a radical economic restructuring within Russia separately from the rest of the union. Gorbachev was now left without the support of the leadership of the biggest of the union republics and also without a viable economic policy. Moreover, his wrangling with the radical democrats on the Left did not win him friends on the Right: Gorbachev increasingly came under attack by the conservatives, who now felt that if they applied enough pressure he would always abandon radical reform.[2]

By the early 1990s Gorbachev's political reform had transformed the former party-state monolith into a political arena with many competing actors, including radical democrats, hard-line Communist conservatives, nationalist movements, and even an open anti-Communist opposition. The power of the CPSU was breaking down, no longer able to cement the Soviet political system or hold together the Soviet unitary state. The party's disintegration was both national and ideological. Its national breakup began when its branches in the three Baltic republics of Lithuania, Latvia, and Estonia announced their decision to leave the CPSU and become independent Communist parties. Its ideological division accelerated in 1990 with the appearance of two large groups within its rank-and-file: hard-line Communists and more democratically inclined party members. In his speech at the Twenty-Eighth Party Congress of July 1990, which also turned out to be the CPSU's last congress, Yeltsin, as a representative of the democratic strand, proposed to rename the Communist Party as the Party of Democratic Socialism and to repeal the age-old ban on factions within the party. The conservative majority at the congress, however, rejected his proposals. This prompted Yeltsin to take the floor to declare that he was quitting the party, then to stalk out of the congress hall. His example was followed by a score of prominent pro-democracy Communists, including the heads of the city soviets in Moscow and Leningrad.

Many of the radicals who left the CPSU following its 1990 Congress took openly anti-Communist and antisocialist stands. The result of the inability of the Communist Party's leadership to cast off its outmoded ideology was that rank-and-file members began leaving the party in droves and joining new parties, which were beginning to form and which were soon brought together under the umbrella of the Democratic Russia movement. The majority of the new political parties now advocated capitalist reforms.

This drastic shift of political orientation was a logical outcome of Gorbachev's failure to reform socialism. His continued incantations about the potential of socialism now only irritated in the conditions of widespread shortages of basic goods and food items, including soap, salt, bread, milk, shoes, and cigarettes. More and more people thought that socialism was unreformable and that it was time to emulate the economic and political patterns of the advanced countries of the West.

On 12 June 1991 Yeltsin scored a resounding victory in Russia's first presidential elections. He garnered over 57 percent of the votes, with his four Communist rivals receiving together just over 30 percent. The surge of anti-Communist sentiments was also revealed during the referendum in Leningrad, conducted at the same time as the presidential elections, on the issue of the city's name. The majority of the population no longer desired the city to be named for the founder of the Communist Party and voted in favor of the original name, St. Petersburg.

In July 1991 Yeltsin, now the newly elected president of Russia, decreed that the Communist Party of Russia, the sister party of the CPSU and the largest republican Communist party, must wind down its cells in state organizations and factories. By then the CPSU had already been voted out of government in several of the constituent republics. The Soviet Union had finally reached the point of no return when an unsuccessful coup in August organized by the conservative elements in the Politburo, military, government, and KGB was defeated. That fiasco led to the winding down of the CPSU's central bodies and the complete separation of the state and communism. After the coup of August 1991 and the consequent arrests of the top officials of the all-union state, as well as the ban on the Communist Party in the territory of Russia, the USSR's political system was extinct.

Results of Political Reform

By sponsoring *glasnost* and democratization, the reformist leadership dealt a deathblow to the power monopoly of the Communist Party and thereby destroyed unwittingly its own institutional base. The party sustained a critical loss of authority and faced massive popular hostility, as it was held responsible for all the mistakes and crimes of the Communist period. The flood of publications on the repressions under Stalin and the human rights abuses under Brezhnev caused irreparable damage to the image of socialism, impelling the population to vote against the old corrupt elite. The mass media now portrayed Marxism-Leninism as an ideology that had led the country into a historical dead end. Instead of reinvigorating socialism, democratization eroded the ideological foundations of the Soviet state and delegitimated the party's privileged position as the core of the political system.

The reformist leadership's plan to revitalize the soviets also backfired. The expectation was that popular elections to soviets would provide a new source of legitimacy for the system and that, at the same time, the party would somehow retain its control of the elected governing bodies. These hopes proved unfounded, however, and following the 1990 republican and local elections, real power began to shift from the discredited center to the republics. Moreover, the new-style soviets proved ineffective as governing structures. They were revived under the old Bolshevik slogan of "All power to the Soviets!" designed to make them more independent from the party structures. In practice, this led to the soviets' attempts to grab both legislative and executive powers. The new system failed to act as an effective legislative branch and completely disorganized the executive.

Gorbachev tried to correct the situation and prop up the executive arm by setting up the powerful new office of state president. This, however, made matters worse, as the republics began to replicate the institution of presidency and elect their own presidents. These developments only served to speed up the breakup of the Soviet ruling elite. The climax came on 12 June 1991 with the election of the president of Russia. The Soviet capital of Moscow, which doubled as the capital of the Russian republic, was now the seat of two presidents, Gorbachev and Yeltsin, each vying for political preeminence. Gorbachev was elected to his post by the votes of several hundred deputies of the USSR Supreme Soviet. His challenger had an unshakable legitimacy of the popular mandate conferred on him by the majority of voters in the core republic.

In retrospect, Gorbachev's biggest miscalculation was the decision to allow free elections of republican and local soviets.[3] The 1990 elections took place when the Communist Party and socialism had lost their credibility, when national movements were rising in the constituent republics, and when Eastern European Communist regimes were falling from power. Prior to the local elections, the opposition movements in the republics had relied on the support of the reformist leadership in Moscow in their struggle against local conservatives. However, having defeated the Communists in the local elections, the new republican elites no longer saw the all-union center and Gorbachev as their protectors because they now derived legitimacy from their voting constituencies. Armed with a popular mandate, the victorious opposition changed the emphasis of the political struggle from the "democratic" to the "ethnic" aspect. The goals of national revival and independence, particularly in the Baltic and Transcaucasian republics, came to the fore. As a result, the internal power struggle in the republics gave way to the mounting confrontation between the republics and the Kremlin. The forces that initially had been sponsored and encouraged by the reformist center now turned against it. The newly elected republican parliaments engaged in the "war of laws" against Moscow, insisting on the supremacy of their local laws over those of the Soviet Union. They paralyzed centralist controls even further by declarations of sovereignty and claims of sovereign control over the assets in their territories. The decisive moment came in 1990, when Russia, the biggest of the republics, proclaimed its sovereignty and declared that its laws took precedence over the laws of the USSR. The result of this political reform was the disintegration of the Soviet political and constitutional systems.

Gorbachev's political reform was a belated and inconsistent attempt to save the Soviet system. He sought political reform that would allow authorities to rule, relying on new sources of legitimacy and without constantly threatening their political opponents with repression. This in itself meant a revolution in Soviet politics. It was a desperate and unsuccessful attempt to renovate the facade of the Communist system by preserving many of its fundamental elements. Although it failed to rescue the Communist system from disintegration, it brought about cardinal changes indispensable for further democratization, including the surge of popular participation, the legalization of public and political associations and popular movements, the acknowledgment of the right to strike, the rise of political pluralism, the establishment of regular democratic elections, and the emergence of a multiparty system.

Chapter Sixteen

Unraveling the Unitary State

The Rise of Popular and Nationalist Movements

The public debate of the *glasnost* era created an environment conducive to the reawakening of civil society. A civil society is one in which interest groups can assert themselves and can make the state respect their rights. The introduction of *glasnost* led to the broadening struggle of the independent movement against the administrative system. Civil society soon revealed many aspects and represented many independent groupings and interests, including the nascent entrepreneurial class, freedom of expression, religious freedom, and a multitude of other forces that were suppressed after October 1917. In the more liberal atmosphere of *glasnost* these diverse interests revived, signaling a growing autonomy of society from party-state structures.

What was particularly remarkable about Gorbachev's period and clearly marked a new departure was the toleration of ideological and political activity independent of the authorities. Citizens were allowed to organize into political parties, popular movements, parliamentary oppositions, and so on, and all this was dramatically changing the political landscape. The new forms of civic activity were building links between civil society and the state and acted as primary schools of democracy by training leaders and structuring politics.

Before *perestroika,* dissent had been driven deep underground and had been confined to the activities of small circles of like-minded friends. In the summer of 1986 in cities across the country these groups began to legalize their activities and amalgamate into larger political debate societies. These were set up in major cities, including Moscow, Vilnius, and Riga, and were often called "clubs of public initiatives" or "clubs of socially active citizens." These developments became possible following the authorities' decision to stop arrests on political grounds and to begin the release of political prisoners. Among others, Andrei Sakharov, the dean of the Soviet dissident movement, was allowed by Gorbachev personally to return to Moscow from his internal exile in a closed city on the Volga.

For the first time in decades the Soviet regime tolerated organizations standing outside the party-state structures and engaged in independent political activity. So novel were unsanctioned organizations to the Soviet Union that in the Soviet and foreign press of the *glasnost* era they quickly earned the name of "nonformal" organizations, and their members were referred to as *neformaly* ("nonformals"). The debate clubs aired a variety of political, environmental, and nationalities issues, and their activities were mainly informed by the desire to rally support from below for the reform initiatives of the Soviet leadership. Most of these groups described their ideological leanings as democratic socialism, but some anti-Communist groups also began to take part in political discussions. Most of the leaders and activists of the new political parties that would emerge by 1990 were initiated into politics as *neformaly*.

By the spring of 1988 the membership of all nonformal organizations taken together was no more than several thousand, including several hundred activists. Clearly, in a country the size of the Soviet Union, their collective voice was too weak to alter the existing political system. But their activities had prepared for the rise of mass popular movements that would have enough muscle to bring about fundamental political change.

From 1988 on, mass popular movements began to appear across the country, usually centered in the capital cities of union republics. Typically, they took the form of nationalist movements. The rebirth of a nationalist movement in a given republic was often connected with some concrete grievance or issue. For example, in Armenia and Azerbaijan the explosive issue that prompted national mobilization was the problem of the Nagorno-Karabakh autonomous region. It was predominantly populated by Armenians but had been ceded to Azerbaijan by Stalin. Armenians wanted it back, and they saw *perestroika* as their chance to put right what they believed was a historical wrong. In Moldova nationalist sentiments were roused by the cause of reinstating the Latin alphabet in place of the Cyrillic one. In the Baltic republics nationalist movements mobilized around the struggle to compel the Soviet authorities to admit officially the illegality of the 1939 Molotov-Ribbentrop Pact, which had authorized the Soviet annexation of the three Baltic states.

The result was that nationalist movements emerged in most of the union republics usually under the blanket term "popular fronts." Most of them quickly radicalized their demands, pressing for greater autonomy from the all-union authorities and a reform of the Soviet federation.

The Baltic popular fronts, in particular, were among the better organized and most militant. By the end of 1988 it was clear that they would not be satisfied with greater self-government within the USSR. At their mass rallies and in the media the Baltic popular fronts demanded the setting up of a special commission to investigate the circumstances of the annexation of the Baltic states under the Molotov-Ribbentrop Pact, and they called for the disclosure and publication of the pact's secret protocol. Their ultimate aim was to compel the Soviet authorities to admit that the pact was unlawful and thus give Baltic separatists legal ammunition to demand full secession.

After the Baltic republics, the Transcaucasian region was another major hotbed of nationalist movements. The Armenian popular front fought to bring the Nagorno-Karabakh autonomous region back into the Armenian republic. The Armenian demands led to a sharp deterioration in the relations between Armenia and neighboring Azerbaijan. In Georgia, the popular front led by Zviad Gamsakhurdia engaged in an intense confrontation with the republic's Communist leadership. The tension broke out on 9 April 1989 when the authorities used the army to disperse the mass rally in the center of the republic's capital, Tbilisi. In clashes with soldiers about twenty popular front supporters were killed. The tragic event led to the further nationalist radicalization of the popular front in Georgia.

Popular fronts were an important element of the transition from Communist authoritarianism to a new socioeconomic order. They represented a broad compromise between various sectors of the population united in a bid to change the old system of property and power relations. Such umbrella organizations were typical not only of Gorbachev's Soviet Union but also of Eastern European countries (e.g., Solidarity in Poland and Civic Forum in Czechoslovakia). Popular fronts were called forth when political parties were still too weak to confront the Communist establishment. Only popular movements had the necessary muscle to do this. In the 1990 local elections popular fronts and similar organizations won parliamentary majorities in Latvia, Lithuania, Moldova, Armenia, and Georgia; they entered local parliaments as powerful oppositions in the Ukraine, Azerbaijan, and Belorussia. In the majority of republics the Communist party was rejected, and control over policy was transferred to popular movements and republican leaders.

The 1990 local elections demonstrated how politics could begin to escape the control of the bureaucracy. In August 1991 the central party-state bureaucracy attempted to reassert its political control. The conservatives in the Soviet leadership decided to stage a coup and approached

Gorbachev to lead it. Gorbachev refused and was put under house arrest at his residence in the Crimea. The plotters, who included the Soviet prime minister and the heads of the KGB, Interior Ministry, and Ministry of Defense—eight men in all—formed the State Emergency Committee. On 19 August the plotters took all power in their hands, reintroduced censorship, and banned all newspapers, with the exception of the Communist organs.

The conservative putsch was the final attempt to reinstate centralist controls. Its leaders, however, had underestimated the strength of the new political forces that emerged under *perestroika* and that rallied behind the popularly elected president of Russia, the biggest of the Soviet Union republics. Boris Yeltsin's determination to resist the unlawful coup made him the symbol of popular resistance. The Muscovites built barricades in the center of Moscow, engaging in a tense three-day standoff with troops sent by the coup leaders to suppress resistance. Yeltsin and his supporters unnerved the plotters, transforming the abortive coup into a victorious popular revolution that led to the final collapse of the Soviet Communist Party.

Taking advantage of the ensuing chaos, the republics, one after another, hastened to proclaim their complete sovereignty and secession from the union. On 1 December 1991 a referendum was held in the Ukraine at which the majority of the Ukrainians, the second biggest population after Russians in the Soviet Union, voted in favor of their country's independence. This sealed the fate of the Soviet Union.

On 8 December 1991, at a secret meeting in Belorussia, the leaders of the three Slavic core republics—Russia, Ukraine, and Belorussia—Boris Yeltsin, Leonid Kravchuk, and Stanislav Shushkevich, on their own authority declared the USSR dissolved and announced the formation of the Commonwealth of Independent States (CIS), as a new entity and as a framework for coordinating their economic and strategic relations. On 21 December, at a meeting in the Kazakhstan capital of Alma-Ata, to which Gorbachev was not invited, eight more republics joined the CIS. The Alma-Ata declaration stated: "With the formation of the Commonwealth of Independent States, the Union of Soviet Socialist Republics ceases to exist."

Thus, on the eve of the sixty-ninth anniversary of its creation, the USSR was dissolved peacefully and without bloodshed, simply by the stroke of the pens of eleven leaders of its former constituent republics. Four signatures were missing from the declaration, as the leaders of Georgia and the three Baltic states of Lithuania, Latvia, and Estonia declined to join the Alma-Ata accord. This was not because they were against the dissolution of the USSR, but because they believed that their republics' incorporation into the USSR had been unlawful in the first place and they did not wish to participate in any alliances with the former sister republics (Georgia, however, would join the CIS in 1993). Gorbachev's signature was also absent from the declaration: none of the republican leaders wanted to know his opinion on the fate of the union. The Soviet leader was left without a country to rule and had no choice but to resign, which he did on 25 December 1991.

Key Factors in the USSR's Collapse

The USSR's dramatic and precipitous collapse has given rise to various interpretations, with many of them politically motivated. The politicians who had put their names on the Alma-Ata declaration strove to prove that the Soviet Union was doomed and that the setting up of a loose alliance of independent states to replace it was the only possible way out of a political dead end.[1] Their political opponents attributed the dissolution of the USSR to different reasons, from collusion of the three Slavic leaders, who had signed the fateful agreement of 8 December 1991, to the machinations of "world imperialism." The dramatic upheavals in the period following the disintegration of the USSR have led to a steep rise in the numbers of those who regard the dissolution of the USSR as a tragic mistake or even a crime committed by high-ranking politicians.

It appears that the disintegration of the USSR was caused by a cumulative effect of a number of factors. Surely, the political will and actions of the republican leaders did play a significant role. In particular, the political decision adopted by the Slavic leaders, Yeltsin, Kravchuk, and Shushkevich, in December 1991 made the process of dismemberment of the USSR hard to reverse. Yeltsin's personal dislike of Gorbachev was an important factor, which could have tipped the scales in favor of that decision.[2]

Equally important was the "Gorbachev factor" itself in speeding the USSR towards its inglorious end. His plans and intentions often revealed utopian attempts to combine the incompatible: socialism with capitalism, totalitarianism with democracy.[3] At the start of *perestroika* Gorbachev demonstrated astonishing complacency with regard to the nationalities policy. In 1986 he publicly claimed that the "nationalities question in the USSR had been settled." Any reform program if it was to be successful had to address the federal structure of the Soviet Union first. The failure to realize this was undoubtedly one of the major mistakes of Gorbachev's career as the Soviet leader. His detailed plans for political reform as presented at the Nineteenth Party Conference in 1988 contained little on the question of reforming the federation and showed every sign of intending to retain the basic centralist structures of the Soviet system intact.

The centrifugal tendencies generated by political democratization had caught him by surprise, and he felt hurt by what he saw as the "ingratitude" of the republics. As the nationalist pressures for autonomy increased, Gorbachev was unwilling to make any concessions to separatists. In April 1989 Soviet troops came to the help of the Communist authorities in Georgia to disperse the opposition rally in Tbilisi; in January 1990 they prevented the nationalist forces in Baku from coming to power in Azerbaijan; in January 1991 they seized the state TV station in Vilnius. These military reprisals caused many casualties, and the Vilnius affair was apparently intended as a dress rehearsal for a major crackdown in the Baltic region. The pro-reform forces in Russia and other union republics accused Gorbachev of collusion with antidemocratic forces and of attempting to depose the legitimate popular front governments of the Baltic states.

It took Gorbachev more than five years as the leader of the USSR to realize that, in order to save the union, it was necessary to share power with the republics. Even then he could not make up his mind on the cardinal issue of how much sovereignty should be given to the republics to assuage their appetite for greater autonomy and to preserve the union at the same time. In the spring of 1991 the governments of nine out of the fifteen union republics agreed to take part in talks with Gorbachev on the redistribution of power between the republics and the center (the other six—Lithuania, Latvia, Estonia, Moldova, Azerbaijan, and Georgia—refused to join the negotiations). The negotiations with the leaders of the union republics offered Gorbachev a last chance to reform the country's federal structure and to secure his own position as an influential political player.

The outcome of these protracted and tough negotiations between Gorbachev and the republican leaders was the draft of a new union treaty, which was finally agreed on and made public in June 1991. It envisaged that the country's name, USSR, would have a fundamentally new meaning—Union of Soviet Sovereign (instead of Socialist) Republics—and that the powers of the republics would be substantially augmented. The Soviet Union would be transformed into a genuine federation in which the republics themselves were to decide how much power to delegate to the federal center. The signing of the new treaty, scheduled for 20 August 1991, would have meant the end of the unlimited powers of the center. The conservative August coup was an attempt on the part of the all-union authorities to prevent this and to restore the power of the Kremlin. Following the coup's collapse, the central governing bodies in Moscow were discredited, Gorbachev's authority rapidly diminished, and the republics were reluctant to return to the negotiating table. The coup sealed the fate of the union, putting an end to Gorbachev's efforts to rescue it.

It will always remain a mystery whether the new union treaty would have saved the USSR from disintegration. What is clear, however, is that Gorbachev's authority had considerably eroded even before the fateful August coup because of the permanent failures of his economic reforms. By the end of the 1980s, the Soviet system was facing an economic breakdown more severe and far-reaching than the worst capitalist crisis of the 1930s. Not surprisingly, the unrest aroused ancient nationalist rivalries and ambitions, threatening the dismemberment of the Soviet economic and political empire. Mounting economic problems pushed the republics toward secession, bringing local elites and populations to the conviction that only by freeing themselves from the failed and unreformable socioeconomic system would they be able to find a way out of the Soviet impasse.

The "Gorbachev factor" revealed the basic defect of Soviet authoritarianism: the system's overdependence on the top leader. Gorbachev's enormous powers blocked ways of counteracting his policies, even when these led to the regime's self-destruction.

The USSR's disintegration was further precipitated by the regional fragmentation of the once unitary and strictly hierarchical all-union *nomenklatura* and the consequent weakening of the central party-state authorities. This bifurcation of the *nomenklatura* along ethnic lines accelerated in 1989–90, when the Communist parties of Latvia, Lithuania, and Estonia announced their decision to break away from the Soviet Communist Party. This started a chain reaction of ideological and organizational disintegration of the very foundations of the Soviet political system. Because the CPSU was the backbone of the Soviet political system and the cementing force of the Soviet unitary state, the splits within it could only erode its authority and undermine the unitary USSR. As the old system was crumbling, the party elites in the union republics were able to carve out a considerable degree of bureaucratic autonomy for themselves and to distance themselves from the central authorities.

In addition, new centers of power began to form in the union republics represented by the local parliaments popularly elected in 1990.

In the local legislatures politicians of various political persuasions asserted their local autonomy and often spoke as one in their opposition to the Kremlin. In the spring and summer of 1990 first the Baltic republics and then others, including the biggest of them, Russia, adopted declarations of national sovereignty and thus openly confronted the union state. The "parade of sovereignties" led to a standoff between the federal center and the republics and fueled the "war of laws," as local parliaments strove to reassert supremacy of their local legislation over union laws. The "war of laws" marked the first stage of the constitutional crisis that eventually led to the disintegration of the union.

When in August 1991 Soviet hard-liners attempted to recapture control over the republics, the majority of them either condemned the plotters outright or did not recognize the State Emergency Committee as a legitimate government. Only the central Asian republics and Azerbaijan showed obeisance to the State Emergency Committee, but even they did not recognize it formally. The attempt to restore control over the republics came too late, and in the conditions of August 1991 it could only accelerate the disintegration. Having defeated the plotters and rescued Gorbachev from his house arrest in the Crimea, Russian President Yeltsin compelled Gorbachev to sign a series of decrees, which dissolved the CPSU and the federal cabinet of ministers and made Gorbachev give up his post of CPSU general secretary. The CPSU Central Committee was also forced to dissolve itself. As a result, the Communist regime collapsed like a house of cards, and with it crumbled to dust the party-state structures that had held the USSR together. The August events, which began as a last-ditch attempt to save the Soviet Union, the CPSU, and the power of the old party-state elite, ended as a velvet revolution, destroying the Soviet Union and the CPSU and consolidating the power of the new republican elites.

Chapter Seventeen

Return to a Market Economy

"Shock Therapy" and Its Consequences

The breakup of the Soviet Union will go down in history as a political, social, and economic event, whose dramatic repercussions will be as great as those of the October Revolution of 1917. The scale of the upheaval is revealed in the depth of the economic dislocation, the explosions of interethnic violence escalating into local wars, the pauperization of much of the population, the magnitude of human suffering, and other dramatic developments.

The contemporary Russian state, which emerged after the dissolution of the USSR in December 1991, has no historical precedent. Its borders correspond to no previous historical entity. Of the successor states, only Russia possesses the capacity to become a global power. It comprises 76.2 percent of the entire territory and has half the population of the former USSR, just under 150 million people. The country is richly endowed with natural resources and a skilled work force. Russia has 90 percent of the oil, 80 percent of the natural gas, 70 percent of the gold production, and 62 percent of the electricity output of the former Soviet Union. The great majority of research institutes and educational establishments are also situated here.[1]

All this seemed to give the Russian government many advantages in implementing successful economic reform. The task was nevertheless immense: to dismantle the economic system of state socialism in one of the world's great countries. Russia was great in terms of its territory, population, and sophisticated economic structure. For the second time in a century, Russia was to perform a vast experiment in social engineering, reshaping its state, society, and economy all at once.

International experience suggested two main types of transition from a command-administrative to a market economy: a slow, step-by-step transition and a "shock therapy" or "big bang" approach. The first, gradualist, approach envisaged that the old institutions of the command system would coexist for some time with the new market structures and would gradually be transformed or replaced. The second, radical, solution envisaged a swift introduction of market mechanisms and a determined dismantling of state-administrative structures.

In the autumn of 1991, after the apparent failure of Gorbachev's chaotic reforms, the Russian political establishment favored a radical solution. Even more moderately minded democrats rejected the idea of state regulation of the economy. An absolutely free exchange of goods and services, with economic relations totally freed from state regulation, was seen as a sort of magic wand that would rapidly transform the economy of Russia and propel it to the top of the league of economically advanced countries. President Boris Yeltsin shared these naive expectations. He hoped that a package of administrative decrees would ensure the country's speedy transition to a market economy. This blind belief that a market economy could be introduced with the stroke of a pen and that it would resolve Russia's economic problems as if by magic was not based on any serious analysis of the actual economic, political, and sociocultural circumstances the government had to face in trying to effect such a rapid transformation.

President Yeltsin outlined his proposals for radical economic reforms in October 1991. The chief directions of the government program included (1) economic stabilization based on tight monetary and credit policy, including strengthening of the ruble; (2) price liberalization; (3) privatization and the introduction of a mixed economy, with a growing private sector and accelerated land reform; and (4) reorganization of the financial system, including tight control of budget expenditures, and reform of the tax and banking systems. Yeltsin's program promised quick results in overcoming the crisis and a general improvement in the economy by the autumn of 1992. It was a program of radical changes in both the ownership and the management of the Russian economy, and drew on the prescriptions of the advocates of "shock therapy."

The "shock therapy" reforms were launched in January 1992. They became associated with the young economist Yegor Gaidar (b. 1956), who was appointed by Yeltsin to lead the reformist government. The reforms were to begin with price liberalization: 90 percent of wholesale and retail prices were released from state control overnight. The results were dramatic. Prior to freeing the prices, the government had forecast threefold increase in prices across the board and had planned for increases in wages for budget-sector workers (e.g., civil servants, doctors, teachers, and coal miners), pensioners, and students in accordance with that estimate. However, the moment the prices were freed, they immediately skyrocketed ten- to twelvefold. Overnight Russian citizens found themselves below the poverty line. In addition, their lifelong ruble savings were made worthless by this manifold increase in prices, and the government was unable to recoup their losses. In effect, it was an expropriation comparable in scale to the forced collectivization of agriculture in the 1930s. Its economic consequences were no less devastating, though it was conducted without violence and deportations. Whatever the economic arguments behind "shock therapy" may be, it was inexcusable from a moral perspective. From the very start the reform efforts earned the nickname "robber reforms." The harsh consequences determined the negative attitude of most Russians toward the reforms and made them treat the government's intentions with deep mistrust.

A broad opposition in the Supreme Soviet, a Soviet-style Russian parliament elected in 1990, soon obstructed the implementation of the reforms. It consisted mainly of deputies representing the interests of state enterprises, collective farms, and the military-industrial complex. The liberalization of prices, especially energy prices, and the abolition of government orders and cheap credits made the majority of industrial and agricultural companies unprofitable. Many of them were insolvent and faced the threat of closure. The new economic realities seriously affected the behavior of the Supreme Soviet and led to the spiraling confrontation between the executive branch represented by the president and the reformist government, on the one hand, and the legislature in the form of the Supreme Soviet, on the other.

The Supreme Soviet insisted on financial assistance to industry to avert the economic collapse of entire branches of industry and to prevent mass unemployment, which could lead to a social explosion. The government, on the other hand, saw the way forward in raising the economic efficiency of enterprises by turning them into share-holding companies and insisted that subsidies and cheap credits to unrestructured enterprises would only fuel inflation and give a lifeline to inefficient producers.

This was the essence of the confrontation between the legislative and the executive branches: the Supreme Soviet preferred hyperinflation to the collapse of production, whereas the government sought financial stabilization by any means, even at the cost of the mass closure of industrial enterprises. In their ferocious standoff the government and parliament appealed to two different constituencies: the executive branch sought the support of those sectors of the population that had benefited from the market reforms, and the Supreme Soviet strove to champion the interests of those who stood to lose from the reforms. The conflict between the executive and the legislative branches determined the development of Russian politics in 1992 and 1993 and reached its climax in the bloody clash in October 1993, when Yeltsin ordered the shelling of the parliament building by tanks after the Supreme Soviet had refused to obey his order to dissolve itself.

"Shock therapy" reforms under the leadership of Gaidar lasted for about a year: in December 1992 Yeltsin sacrificed him as a concession to the demands of the Supreme Soviet and replaced him with Victor Chernomyrdin (b. 1938) as head of the government. Chernomyrdin's government admitted that the Russian economy was in shambles and that something needed to be done to stop the sharp decline in industrial production. However, Gaidar's basic monetarist approach, with its emphasis on strengthening the ruble, on financial stabilization, and on the fight against inflation, was retained. Having said that the previous economic policy had been seriously flawed, Chernomyrdin's government was unable to offer an alternative to Gaidar's course and to change the balance of negative and positive effects of the capitalist modernization.

Under Chernomyrdin's government, industrial and agricultural output continued to fall. The lack of investment resulted in a primitivization of industrial production and a return to outdated technologies. The acute underfunding dealt a crushing blow to education, science, culture, health care, and other spheres vital to the functioning of a modern society. The structures of the welfare state created under communism were crumbling. The Russian population was rapidly polarized into the poor and the rich. A sharp deterioration in the standards of living led to a significant decline in the birthrate: for an average family to have a baby became a luxury it could no longer afford.

Millions of workers and intellectuals felt uncertain about their future and feared losing their jobs because of the continuing deindustrialization and sharp contraction of the educational, cultural, and academic establishments. By 1994 the number of fully or partially unemployed exceeded ten million—nearly 14 percent of Russia's entire working population.[2] The mounting socioeconomic problems and the hardships imposed by the reforms were the social cost of the radical transformation. The price for most citizens was exorbitantly high and directly affected the behavior of voters during the 1993, 1995, and 1999 parliamentary elections and the 1996 and 2000 presidential elections.

The results of "shock therapy" were controversial. Gaidar and his circle, the media who supported him and the individuals who benefited from the reforms, appraised them very positively. They pointed out that the release of prices brought the country closer to a balance between supply and demand. Free prices brought most basic goods back on the shelves, putting an end to the omnipresent lines that were a major part of the consumer's life in Soviet Russia. The market mechanism was started. Despite the horrendous rate of inflation, the ruble recovered its function as money, as a means of circulation and payment, that it had nearly lost in the Soviet economy. This helped to restore links between enterprises. Without this, a complete stoppage of production would have been inevitable. The basic institutions of a market economy have appeared with astonishing speed. Until the end of Gorbachev's presidency in 1991, most forms of private business were still illegal. Since then, Russia has seen the rise of a vigorous financial services industry, with hundreds of newly created commercial banks and investment funds. A structural transformation of the economy took place in the early 1990s, with cuts in defense spending. Even as Russia's manufacturing and military industries lay paralyzed, the services sector experienced remarkable growth, rising from one-third of the gross domestic product in 1990 to nearly two-thirds in the late 1990s. For the first time since Stalin's industrialization, the production of services exceeded the production of goods. The reforms gained a self-sustaining character. Powerful interests were now bound up with the continued marketization of the economy.

However, the political opposition and the broad mass of citizens, whose standards of living plummeted, appraised the results of the reform very differently. The "shock therapy" strategy put intolerable strains on the economy and society. It resulted in a rapid impoverishment of the majority of the population. People were subjected to dubious privatization schemes, their lifelong savings made worthless by inflation, and millions suffered from the nonpayment of wages and pensions. The radical monetarist approach advocated by Gaidar failed to achieve its express aim of preventing inflation and showed a complete indifference to the plight of average citizens. Shops almost overnight became stocked with imported goods, which most people were unable to afford. All this abundance only irritated and generated social tensions. Russia's industrial output halved between 1989 and 1994, a sharper contraction than the United States suffered during the Great Depression of the 1930s. A drastic fall in the standard of living for the majority of people was accompanied by the emergence of the super-rich "new Russians," creating an abyss between the very rich and the very poor. The vast majority of the population was impoverished and deprived of a stake in privatized property.

"Shock therapy" was more like a surgical operation on Russia's peculiar economic and social organism. It inflicted great pain but gave little cure. It was a Bolshevik-style attempt to destroy the old economic system to its foundations in the hope that the phoenix of the market would rise from its ashes. This, however, did not happen. The reformist strategy of the government was a utopian attempt to achieve a "great leap" into capitalism. In real life it led to the appearance of such unattractive characteristics of Russian capitalism as the concentration of former state assets in the hands of a small group of financial and industrial magnates and the economy's nontransparent and semicriminalized nature.

"Nomenklatura" Privatization

The task of privatization in Russia surpassed by far the scale of privatization of certain branches of industry undertaken in some Western capitalist countries, such as Britain under Prime Minister Margaret Thatcher. Russia had inherited an economy in which the share of state property was the highest in the world—95.4 percent. Officially, state property in the USSR was described as public property; that is, in theory, all citizens were regarded as equal owners of state assets. In reality, the government and party elite, which actually managed public property, came to regard it as belonging to themselves. They came to see national assets as their *nomenklatura* property. Naturally, they were reluctant to give up power and the assets they controlled, and they had many opportunities to delay and obstruct any real privatization or to conduct it on their terms.

The process of the creeping, unofficial *"nomenklatura* privatization" had started already under Gorbachev. Between 1987 and 1990, when the Soviet system began to disintegrate, the ruling elite was suddenly confronted with the prospect of losing everything it possessed. To prevent this, a series of all-union and then republican laws were enacted that carved up state property and put it under all-union, regional, and municipal control. The new laws divided state assets further by transferring full control over them to different groups of the *nomenklatura,* such as the heads of various economic ministries, company directors, and collective- and state-farm managers. As a result, state assets were "hidden," as it were, from the claims of the rising masses. Instead of one impersonal owner in the form of the state, it acquired numerous "custodians," whom any future potential claimants, wishing to dispute their ownership rights, would have to fight separately.

The essence of what happened is best illustrated by the change in the status of directors of state companies. Formerly, directors were state employees on state salaries, which they could not legally increase by a single ruble. Now they were the de facto owners of their enterprises and had legal rights to dispose of assets and make money any way they wanted. They could now personally set the level of wages paid to workers as well as their own remuneration.

This de facto privatization of assets, which technically were still regarded as public, gave many representatives of the *nomenklatura* unique opportunities and unfair advantages to enrich themselves at the state's expense by exploiting state assets in their control. They were now the new class of the rich, a powerful economic and political elite. All they needed was to legitimate their property ownership in the eyes of the population. The legalization of their propertied status was achieved during the next stage of the ownership transformation, which was officially sponsored by Yeltsin's government.

Russia's official privatization program itself consisted of two stages. The first stage began in late 1991 and was completed by the end of 1994. It was called "people's privatization" or "voucher privatization" and was associated with Anatoly Chubais (b. 1955), the minister in charge of privatization in Gaidar's government. Over three to four years the mass of state-owned enterprises was to be transformed into joint-stock companies, sold to or distributed among the country's citizens. A privatization on such scale and within such time limits was unprecedented in world economic history.

The Russian government strove hard to give the semblance of "people's privatization" to its program. However, it proved to be little more than a simulation of a popular redivision of state assets among the entire population of the Russian Federation. Every single member of Russia's 150 million-strong citizenry, from newborn babies to old-age pensioners, was to be given a privatization voucher, which conferred the right to own shares. The value of the voucher was fixed at the end of 1991, when the government could not foresee the scale of inflation that would be inaugurated by the price liberalization in January 1992. One voucher was worth 10,000 rubles, which at the time was a substantial sum of money, equivalent to approximately half the price of a popular Lada car. The reformers hoped that the voucher's high value would cushion the adverse effects of price liberalization on consumers' savings and thus help to diffuse their resentment. The program envisaged that in 1993 the population would be given the opportunity to either sell their vouchers for cash or use them to buy shares in privatized companies. But price liberalization and the consequent rate of inflation rapidly devalued the voucher. By the end of 1993 it had become worthless: 10,000 rubles could now buy just three or four bottles of vodka.

Chubais's program envisaged several schemes to privatize state assets. The most common scheme was the one whereby the company's management and workers declared it a closed joint-stock company owned 100 percent by themselves. In such companies, shares were not traded. Management exercised de facto control, and in many cases bought back shares issued to workers in exchange for rubles or hard currency. Thus, although a certain amount of the shares of "privatized" enterprises was allocated among numerous small shareholders, the number of real property owners grew insignificantly.

The result of Chubais's voucher privatization was that all Russians for a moment became candidates for property ownership, only to discover the next moment that most of them were effectively excluded from owning a slice of the former state assets. In the chaos of the post-Soviet transition, as traditional public mechanisms of constraint and law enforcement were weakened or dismantled and with few new instruments of public oversight in place, the former *nomenklatura* found itself ideally positioned to reap economic benefits from the deformed market. The transition years became a golden age of opportunity: everything the *nomenklatura* had owned anonymously and illegally was now made fast, not only by the letter of the law but also by the written law of the market: the sacred act of purchase and sale. While the majority of people were locked in the state sector and depended on miserly and irregular wages out of the state budget or employed in enterprises facing bankruptcy, a small group of economic managers and *nomenklatura* capitalists seized the lion's share of state property. Because the type of property ownership forms the foundation of an economic system, the new economic structure, which emerged as a result of government privatization, may be called "*nomenklatura* capitalism."

"Crony Capitalism"

By the mid-1990s Russia formally had a market economy. However, in practice, huge financial resources were still distributed through the state budget. Subsidies and "selective" financial support from the state budget still existed. Railways, massive energy systems, and entire branches of industry were completely or partially state-owned. The state dominated the financial sector. It retained influence in foreign trade, dictating quotas for exported raw materials, granting export licenses, and regulating access to the gas and oil pipe networks. The incomplete nature of Russia's capitalist reforms meant that the state continued to play a major role in running the economy.

Under these conditions, it was extremely important for the business class to establish close relations with state officials at all levels. Russian entrepreneurs realized that, in a country where officials had such extensive powers, it made sense to have good political connections. A handful of the most successful of them thrived on the confluence of power and big business, accumulating enormous political and economic influence and concentrating in their hands control over entire branches of the economy. These magnates soon began to refer to themselves as "oligarchs."

The new oligarchs' rise to prominence began in 1994. By that time a score of leading bankers and entrepreneurs had emerged who had made their fortunes in the period of rampant inflation of 1992–94.[3] The new magnates included Vladimir Gusinsky (the Most group), Alexander Smolensky (the Stolichny bank), Mikhail Khodorkovsky (Menatep-Bank), Vladimir Potanin (ONEXIM-Bank), Boris Berezovsky (the Logovaz group), Mikhail Fridman (Alfa-Bank), and Vladimir Vinogradov (Inkombank).

The next crucial stage in their fabulous enrichment was opened by the second phase of Chubais's privatization, which followed the completion of voucher privatization at the end of 1994. The new phase involved a massive sale of state assets for money rather than vouchers. It opened with "loans for shares" auctions in the autumn of 1995 that did much to discredit even more the market reforms and Chubais as one of its main architects in the eyes of the Russian public. Under the pretext of an urgent need to raise money for the state budget, the last "heirlooms" of the Russian state sector were transferred into the hands of a few well-connected individuals. The scheme was simple: the state transferred into temporary ownership of major commercial banks its controlling interests in attractive companies, such as Norilsk Nickel and major oil companies. In exchange for state shares, the banks were to give loans to the government to finance budgetary expenses. After an agreed period of time, the government had to return the loans to the banks; failing that, the state shares would become the property of the lenders.

To implement this scheme, dubious auctions were set up, at which valuations of state shares were set very low and only the bankers close to the government were allowed to bid. As a result, they gained control over state holdings in lucrative companies. As it turned out, the government had no intention to repay the loans, and the money-spinning enterprises were forfeited to the so-called oligarchs. The "loans for shares" auctions were ostensibly designed to salvage the government's budget, but they turned out to be a ploy that allowed the privatization of lucrative companies in circumvention of the parliament's ban on the sale of state shares in such companies.

The auctions boosted the oligarchs' powerful economic structures, which now included oil companies, mines, and smelters, as well as vast holdings in the banking sector. The new magnates' powerful financial-industrial groups even set up their own private armies with hundreds of security personnel, many of whom were members of Soviet security services in the past, including former high-ranking KGB officers. These formidable security arms were used to shield the groups' economic interests from criminal rackets and to "sort out" defaulters who refused to pay.

Another essential characteristic of the oligarchs was their increasing control of the influential mass media, in particular, TV stations with nationwide coverage (Berezovsky's ORT and Gusinsky's NTV). The ownership of media outlets allowed them to mold public opinion in ways that promoted their interests and to use compromising material to discredit their political and business rivals.

But the crucial defining feature that marked the oligarchs from other successful business leaders was their connections in the Kremlin, especially their personal access to President Yeltsin and members of his family. Only the ability to establish a mutually beneficial alliance with the Kremlin circle elevated a financial tycoon to the sought-after status of "oligarch." The mechanism of the confluence of high officialdom with the oligarchs was simple: the magnates arranged foreign vacations, gave credit cards for the use of government officials or members of their families, and bribed them with gifts of expensive cars, country houses, and even luxurious vacation homes abroad. In return, the oligarchs were able to exercise influence over appointments in the government and state companies, to control key financial decisions, and to use the power of the state to fight competitors and political opponents.

The 1996 presidential elections were the turning point in the transformation of some of Russia's most prominent business leaders into a premier league of oligarchs. On the eve of the elections Boris Berezovsky, Vladimir Gusinsky, and several other top business leaders had agreed to throw their wealth and media resources behind Yeltsin in his uphill battle against a strong Communist challenger, Gennady Zivganov. As a result, their commercial structures became actively involved in financing Yeltsin's presidential campaign to the tune of $300 million.[4] It goes without saying that their investment in promoting the incumbent was recouped manifold through tax concessions and other tokens of government favor. After Yeltsin's reelection, several of the tycoons were rewarded with high government posts (e.g., Vladimir Potanin became vice premier). All of them were handed assets at knock-down prices: for example, Boris Berezovsky was given control over the first public TV station, ORT, and over the country's biggest airline, Aeroflot; and Alexander Smolensky gained control over Agroprombank, which had one of the best local branch networks.

Having assisted Yeltsin's reelection, the oligarchs seriously believed that the state owed them a debt of gratitude, forgetting that a substantial part of their wealth had been gained by plundering state assets in the first place. Because most money-making business was now placed under their control, the oligarchs' financial-industrial empires swelled rapidly, enabling them to enter the ranks of the world's richest individuals, as published in *Forbes* magazine.

As a result of these developments, the "oligarchic vanguard" of Russian business began to define, to a large extent, Russia's foreign and domestic policies. It exerted a powerful influence on the central government's economic strategies, which often neglected national interests for the sake of corporate interests. In an enfeebled state the powerful financial-industrial groups were able to use the resources and capabilities of the state itself to accrue profits. In contrast to countries with developed democratic systems, Russia's small and medium-size businesses were obstructed from playing any significant political role. The lower segments of the business community had no input in decision making at the federal level, and only limited influence at the regional or city level.

The intimate and cozy relationship that developed between big business and officialdom—"crony capitalism," as it is sometimes called—posed a threat not just to the development of free competition but also to Russia's nascent democracy itself. Some of the leading oligarchs claimed that Russia developed not along Western but Asian lines and that it should therefore be run by powerful financial-industrial groups rather than a democratically elected government. Anatoly Chubais quotes Boris Berezovsky as saying that "business should appoint the government."[5] Berezovsky himself boasted on more than one occasion that he was the real "kingmaker" behind the high turnover of prime ministers during Yeltsin's occupancy. Whether his claims were true or not, one thing is certain: the mighty tycoons sought to spread their rights of ownership to the entire country and to elevate themselves above government ministers appointed by the elected president, and above elected officials, such as Duma deputies and local administrators.

With all the internal tensions and rivalry between the oligarchs themselves, they were united as one in their attempts to monopolize all property relations and to close access to other groups and classes of the population to the division or exploitation of privatized spoils. In short, the oligarchs became the enemies of genuine privatization as they strove to ensure that the market and private property should remain under their undivided monopolistic control. Russia's crony capitalism and oligarchic corporatism obstructed the development of a more broadly based private ownership, making a joke of all the talk, so popular in the Russian media, about the desirability of building a "people's capitalism," achieving a wide dispersion of property ownership, expanding the ranks of shareowners, and raising a large middle class.

It remains to be seen whether Russia's current president, Vladimir Putin, who seems determined to break up the exclusive companionship that has been established between big business and corrupt officials, will be able to encourage the emergence of a more civilized form of capitalism.

Chapter Eighteen

Handicaps of Russia's Capitalist Transformation

The Role of National Characteristics

The Russian westernizing government borrowed the ideas for its modernization at a time when Western governments came under the strong influence of the neoliberal ideology. By the 1990s the doctrines of the free market, competition, privatization, and deregulation had captured the commanding heights of world economic thought. As the Iron Curtain was bulldozed, Russia encountered the new liberal orthodoxy at the height of its power and self-confidence. Neoliberalism advocated the complete economic freedom of the individual, the radical denationalization of industry, and the replacement of state enterprises by private companies. If Russian capitalist reforms had begun two or three decades earlier, they probably would have been guided by a markedly different set of principles, such as the emphasis on state regulation and the benefits of state capitalism, which held sway in the West during that earlier period. In any event, the Russian government's abrupt withdrawal from state intervention proved detrimental to the country's economy.[1]

Geographical and Environmental Characteristics

Geographical and environmental factors are of crucial importance for any national economy. With the breakup of the Soviet Union, all of the empire's southern and western republics were lost to Russia. In terms of territory, the country still remains the biggest in the world, but it has now become even more northern. Temperatures of minus forty degrees Fahrenheit unimaginable in major cities of Western Europe and the United States, are quite normal in Ekaterinburg, Tomsk, Irkutsk, and Novosibirsk, and not uncommon in the capital of Moscow. The severity of the Russian climate means that the cost of housing, heating, and lighting is considerably higher than in the West. In addition, the country's vast territory increases transportation costs.

All this means that, even with the most judicious use of energy resources, Russian industrial enterprises will always have bigger outlays than their counterparts in Western Europe, the United States, and Japan. State support of industry, transport, and agriculture was one of the main characteristics of Russia's economic development both during the Soviet era and under the tsars. Western economic models and prescriptions, which envisage sharp contraction of the state's role in these areas, condemn Russian companies to being uncompetitive in world markets.

The notion of capitalism is an abstraction. Many kinds of capitalism coexist in the world: North American, European, Turkish, Japanese, Latin American, and so on. Yegor Gaidar and his team chose to emulate mainly Anglo-Saxon economic patterns, which were not entirely suitable to Russian conditions. The liberal capitalist economy of a country like Britain is a highly complex system, which has evolved over centuries and cannot be transplanted wholesale overnight and set up by "big bang" methods in a culturally distinct environment. Moreover, Russian reformers tended to overlook the obvious fact that the market was by no means the only economic regulator in either Britain or the United States. In the United States, for instance, ever since the Great Depression of 1929–33 the role of the state in controlling the main parameters of the national economy has been far from negligible.

In a sense, the Russian radical reformers strove to surpass even such traditionally "de-etatist" countries as Britain and the United States in cutting back the scope of the central government's control over social, economic, and political processes.[2] In Russia, with its enormous territory, unpredictable agriculture, northern location, and specific economic structure, the regulatory role of the state has always been significant and is likely to remain so. The reforms of the 1990s have clearly demonstrated that a weak state can hardly create conditions for an effective market to emerge.

The Cold War Legacy

For a number of historical, political, and ideological reasons, military production and the needs of the Soviet armed forces were for decades the chief concerns of the national economy. Direct and indirect defense expenditures accounted for no less than 50 percent of the country's budget.[3] Defense ministries oversaw the construction of railways and defense plants, airports, and secret spacecraft launching sites. Dozens of secret closed towns were set up that specialized in designing and producing sophisticated weapons systems. Millions of qualified workers and engineering staff worked in the companies of the military-industrial complex. Most of the think tanks of the USSR Academy of Sciences conducted research for the interests of the defense industry. The standards and quality of production in the Soviet defense industry were comparable to those of the defense sector in the West. The problem, however, was that these high standards were achieved by crippling the civilian branches of the economy and diverting most of the resources into the military field.

Yegor Gaidar's radical reformist approach ignored the huge gap, inherited from the Soviet Union, between the highly advanced space and military systems and the underdeveloped consumer industries and agricultural sector. The end of the cold war presented the reformers with a unique opportunity to implement a large-scale conversion of the defense sector and to transform Russia's military potential into economic might. The implementation of a defense conversion program of such magnitude required a substantial degree of centralized planning, investment, and management. "Shock therapy" methods were hardly compatible with a conversion of this kind. At the same time, the government, starved of cash, made drastic cuts in military procurement. The blow to the defense industry was shattering. As a result, the civilian branches of industry failed to benefit from the resources, the know-how, and the skilled labor force of the converted military-industrial sector. Many enterprises of the light and machine-building industries were unable to modernize production and compete successfully with Western companies.

Lack of Investment Capital

The transition from state socialism to capitalism required enormous financial resources. Gaidar's team hoped that the West, which so enthusiastically hailed the end of communism in Russia and its plan to switch to a market economy, would provide massive financial assistance for Russian reforms. This, however, did not happen on the scale expected by the reformist government. There was no other choice but to drastically cut social expenditures. As a result, the fairly comprehensive system of social protection put in place during the Soviet period was severely crippled. Tight budgetary constraints did not provide adequate social security for the growing army of the unemployed and poor. Chronic underfunding affected such vital areas as national health care, education, and culture, posing a serious threat to the stability of Russian society.

Pinning their hopes on Western aid, Russian reformers lost sight of the brutal fact that global integration and the international division of labor do not cancel competition between countries and economic blocs. The prospect of the emergence of a new powerful rival in the east of Europe and Asia did not necessarily delight Western politicians and business leaders. The Russian government dismantled most of the trade barriers that prevented Western goods from entering the Russian market. As a result, Western companies rapidly established footholds in Russia and in a few years, through their greater efficiency and competitiveness, practically put out of business entire branches of domestic industry, such as the textile industry. Bowed down under the crushing burden of accumulated foreign debt, including the Soviet debt honored by the post-Communist government, Russia found itself in a situation where its very economic independence was at stake. The inability to compete on equal economic terms with the West threatened to relegate the former superpower to the status of a raw materials supplier for Western transnational corporations.

Weakness of the Social Base of Capitalism

In order to be successful, any radical reform must take into account not just the material conditions prevailing in a given country but also the cultural, religious, and psychological makeup of its population. Over centuries Russia has evolved as a Eurasian power with distinctive historical, economic, and political characteristics, and a way of life different from Western norms. Being open to influences from both the East and the West, Russia has always followed its own path. However, the radical westernizers of the early 1990s ignored some of the age-old values and ideals that form the core of the mentality of the Russian people. The attempt to create overnight a bourgeois society of a Western type and establish full-scale capitalist relations in a society that for over seventy years had officially repudiated them was a utopian idea, and doomed to fail. There is little doubt that the social and political system that will ultimately emerge from the post-Communist transition will in many ways be different from Western patterns.

To the average Russian, the idea of social justice has been more important than those of freedom and democracy. The interests of the collective and the state traditionally have taken precedence over those of the individual. The moral code of the Russia Orthodox Church condemns profit hunting and wealth accumulation, preaching instead self-sacrifice for the common good. The Communist doctrine, which replaced Orthodoxy as

Russia's state ideology for much of the twentieth century, equally discouraged capitalist habits of mind. It is clear that Russia needs to find its own model of capitalism with Russian characteristics.

In the late 1980s and early 1990s most Russian people sought improvement in their material and social conditions rather than fight for capitalism. The rank-and-file participants of the democratic movement were inspired by prospects of greater freedom and social justice. The mistake of the Russian government was its failure to engage the citizenry as partners in its modernization attempt. The reformers pushed through radical policies without making a real effort to explain clearly their plans to the people, treating the populace as guinea pigs in a colossal economic experiment. Their biggest mistake, however, was that they did not regard the goal of raising the population's living standards as the main criterion, against which the reforms' success or failure should be judged. By allowing these standards to take a deep dive, they alienated citizens from their capitalist project.

Far from mobilizing the necessary public support for their policies, the reformers' actions threatened to erode the social base of Russia's fledgling democracy itself. Many of the democratically minded people withdrew their support from Yeltsin as early as 1992 when the first devastating effects of "shock therapy" turned the words *democracy* and *market* into terms of abuse. In 1993 President Yeltsin resorted to military force to disband the very parliament that only two years earlier had supported the dissolution of the USSR and vested him with vast powers to implement reform. From 1994 on, the regime's social base of support was restricted to the bureaucracy, which enjoyed unjustified privileges in the climate of corruption, and the big business tycoons. Even the support of the new business community was halfhearted as the government failed to protect entrepreneurs from corrupt officials and criminal rackets. The growth of the middle class, which could have provided a base of stability, was held back by the banking crisis of August 1998, which plunged many of its members into poverty.

The "Survival" Economy

There is no doubt that future generations will be able to arrive at a more balanced evaluation of the cataclysms that rocked Russia at the turn of the twenty-first century. Historical distance will allow future analysts to assess the Yeltsin era more objectively and dispassionately. However, it is clear even now that the price Russian society paid for the post-

Communist modernization and the second transition within one century to a cardinally new system of life was very high. There are examples of reforms in other countries when a cautious and well thought out approach allowed governments to reduce substantially the burdens of radical reforms. In the 1930s, for example, President Franklin D. Roosevelt was successful in bringing about changes that gave the U.S. government a new role in both domestic and foreign policies. To counter the Great Depression, he enlisted the powers of the federal government to promote the economic welfare of the American people. His measures seemed anticapitalist and even "socialist" by American standards. Yet they relatively quickly brought benefits to the middle and lower classes and, far from undermining the capitalist foundations, reinvigorated them. Other examples of relatively painless and swift transitions from totalitarian to liberal-democratic societies include postwar West Germany, Italy, and Japan, as well as Spain of the 1970s.

Somehow Russia has never been able to emulate foreign examples of successful evolutionary transitions. The Russian tradition has never known such precedents. In Russian history transitional periods have invariably been accompanied by the immense suffering of its citizens and have always been very protracted and painful. In this sense, the transitional era opened by Gorbachev's *perestroika* and continued by Yeltsin's liberal reforms conforms fully to the Russian tradition. Neither Gorbachev nor Yeltsin was able to achieve his objectives. The result of both reform efforts was a society in a state of acute economic and political crisis.

However, the Russian tradition has also taught its people how to survive in times of great uncertainty and upheavals. Many Western commentators were puzzled: all formal economic indicators throughout the 1990s clearly showed that the Russian economy was in a deep hole. Plants did not produce output, wages were not paid, the productivity rate fell, and almost all effective institutions of social protection practically collapsed due to underfunding. Yet all these negative processes did not seem to have the impact one would expect on the population's survival. True, the average life expectancy dropped, people's food rations declined, and everyday problems multiplied. But there were no signs of starvation. Life continued as normal, with teachers teaching, doctors treating patients, army officers giving orders, and police officers controlling street traffic. The social and economic survival of its population against all odds appears to be the central paradox of Russia's contemporary history.

The secret of this amazing endurance of Russian society and its considerable stability lies in the high degree of autonomy of everyday economic existence of the majority of the population. Russians have developed the ability to function independently from the actions and decisions of the government. This is reflected in the many jokes they tell about their situation. One of them is about a telephone conversation between Yeltsin and U.S. President Bill Clinton. They are discussing the way their peoples live.

Yeltsin asks:
—Bill, what is your minimal subsistence level?
—$1,000 per month.
—And the average wage?
—$2,000.
—Bill, and what do they do with the rest of the money?
—How do I know?

Clinton asks Yeltsin:
—Boris, and what is your subsistence minimum?
—1,000 rubles.
—And the average wage?
—500 rubles.
—Boris, but where do they get the rest of the money from?
—How do I know?

The authorities themselves seem to recognize the reality of the informal economy, so important for the well-being of the population. It is described with the help of such attributes as "shadow," "underground," "gray," and "black." However, all these terms are inaccurate because they usually imply illegal activity. A "survival"economy helps millions of people to get by without necessarily turning them into criminals and breaking the law.

This phenomenon is difficult to pinpoint as it has been studied very little. But among some of its more basic characteristics are the following: the people's chief preoccupation is survival, not capital accumulation; they are prepared to take any employment, use different methods of earning money, and have several jobs at a time; wage labor is replaced by family labor and by mutual support networks based on close neigh-borly, kinship, and ethnic ties; and money lending is based on kinship and trust rather than formal contractual relations.[4] These features of the informal "survival" economy did not conform to market principles, which the Russian government sought to enforce. On the contrary, they were designed to keep both the state and big business at a safe distance from society to minimize the ruinous effects of their decisions and activities on the mass of Russian families.

Here is an example of a typical self-sufficient family system sustaining three generations of family members. The grandfather and grandmother live in a village. Their children and grandchildren are city dwellers. In summer the grandchildren stay with their grandparents in the village. Their mother and father come down from the city to help their elderly parents during the sowing season, and in the autumn they collect their children along with sacks of potatoes and vegetables to help the family survive over the winter. In return, they supply the elderly couple with goods that are hard to get in the village, such as medicine. As this example demonstrates, the economy of survival is not based on purely economic relations, but is conditioned by noneconomic—personal, family, and social—factors.

Of course, one should not idealize the informal economy. Everyday life in Russia is tough and insecure; the continual struggle for survival generates tensions and vexations. The important thing to note is that this is not a negligible phenomenon or something that has appeared only recently. The Soviet economic system would not have been able to function without the lubricant of the informal economy. Under the Soviet system, excessive centralization, bureaucratic blunders, and difficulties involving distribution and exchange in a climate of universal deficit could only be overcome by an intricate web of personalized relations. The operation of major industrial and agricultural trusts was maintained by a vast network of supply agents, who resolved bottlenecks in the flow of goods with the help of barter and bribes. In agriculture the peasants' small private allotments significantly augmented their meager income, which they earned on collective farms. In towns personal contacts helped overcome perennial shortages of goods and services and generated intricate networks of exchange benefits. People lived in a complex web of connections based on friendship, kinship, or simply good neighborly relations.

Post-Soviet Russia saw a massive expansion of new forms of informal relations caused by the rapid decline of the official economy. Contrary to the expectations of Russian reformers, the state's withdrawal from the economy did not result in a wholesale appearance of capitalist economic forms. When the state socialist economy declined and the capitalist economy failed to replace it, the "survival" economy revived to provide self-protection to the masses.

The "survival" represents one part of the shadow economy, the other being crime syndicates organized along capitalist principles. The two parts can sometimes overlap, but it would be erroneous to equate the two. For the "new Russians," the retreat of the state from its dominant position signified the accumulation of property in their hands by legal or illegal means and rapid self-enrichment. For most Russians, however, it meant falling back on the self-reliant family economy as a vital means of survival.

It was naive, in retrospect, to believe that capitalism in Russia could be built in a decade. The world constructed by the Communist regime was as unique a system as has ever existed. It had its own ideology, institutions, and culture, formed over more than seven decades. In its way it was as internally consistent and highly evolved as its market-based Western counterpart. For those who were adults when Gorbachev's reforms began, an inner core of Soviet habits, beliefs, values, and expectations still remains.

Seen from this broader perspective, the 1990s were only the first chapter of a story that will take at least another generation to finish telling. The Russian economy is still in a no-man's-land, neither socialist nor capitalist. The shoots of the new economic order are deformed and fragile. The transition to a money-based economy and the national market is still only partial, and large parts of the country still stand outside it. Capitalism and the accompanying wealth creation have taken root only in a relatively small part of the country.[5]

The reforms of the 1990s led to the emergence of two Russias. One-tenth of Russians—approximately fifteen million people—inhabit the thriving "Russia Minor" (or what one writer describes as "Russian Luxembourg"[6]). They can afford foreign vacations, credit cards, mobile phones, and imported cars. They do not have to economize on food or their children's education. As a rule, they are young and live in big cities. They work hard, applying their knowledge and skills under the conditions of a capitalist economy, and they have an average individual income of about $750 per month.

However, nine-tenths of the Russian population—the remaining 135 million people—live in "Russia Major," which is a very different country indeed. They need to stock food supplies for winter by cultivating their tiny out-of-town allotments. Their average monthly earnings are about $100. They are often without a permanent job and regular income.[7]

Is there a way to spread the benefits of the new economic system from a few thriving pockets of capitalism to the rest of the country? Can the Russian government find strategies that will allow the expansion of "Russia Minor" into "Russia Major"? The answers to these questions hold the key to Russia's future and to the solution of its economic, social, and political problems.

Chapter Nineteen

The Yeltsin Era

"Democrator"

Following Boris Yeltsin's surprise voluntary resignation on 31 December 1999, just a few hours before the start of the millennium celebrations, analysts were quick to dub the decade of the 1990s in Russia "the Yeltsin era." For better or worse, Boris Yeltsin will go down in history as one of the great figures of the twentieth century. His rule was nothing if not controversial. Like Gorbachev, there were two sides to Yeltsin: the radical reformer condemning the privileges and political corruption of the old *nomenklatura* and the *apparatchik* (i.e., a member of the Communist *apparat*) who was thoroughly imbued with the ethos of the old regime. These two sides were in constant tension. The tug-of-war between the democratic and the authoritarian aspects of his political personality has allowed Russian journalists to describe Yeltsin as a "democrator," a hybrid of *democrat* and *dictator.* This hybrid nature of his charisma and leadership in a distinctive way reflected the ambiguities of the country itself.

In his last televised address to the nation, Yeltsin asked the Russian people for forgiveness. He asked them to forgive him for the failures of his reforms, for his mistakes and illusions. He said he sincerely believed it was possible to overcome quickly the legacy of the totalitarian past and in one great leap to reach a society "with normal civilization." This did not happen, he said.

Indeed, Yeltsin too often turned an eager ear to those who promised him what he wanted to hear. He blindly put his faith in the medicinal effects of "shock therapy" and the magic powers of the market. He believed that it was possible in a few days and with a small military force to establish "constitutional order" in Chechnya (see chapter 20). He believed that Chubais's vouchers would be enough to create overnight effective private ownership. These examples of the economic, political, and military illusions of Yeltsin could be easily multiplied.

Unfortunately, Yeltsin was not unique in his wishful thinking. The last Russian tsar, Nicholas II, dreamed of a small victorious war, but what he got instead was a series of humiliating defeats at the hands of the Japanese and the revolution of 1905. Lenin dreamed of a world socialist revolution, which the Russian proletariat would trigger and which the rest of Europe would support. Even Stalin's "revolution from above," which plunged the country into the worst period of mass terror in its history, was an attempt at one stroke to resolve problems that had remained unsolved for decades. Khrushchev's dream of quickly catching up and overtaking the United States and Gorbachev's ill-conceived campaigns of the *perestroika* period are part of the same tradition. In short, the reform zeal based on false expectations was not unique to Yeltsin. However, he was the only Russian leader in the twentieth century to ask the Russian people for forgiveness.

Yeltsin's original decision to hold a presidential election in 1991 in the Russian Federation, which was then still part of the old Soviet Union, was part of his long-standing rivalry with Mikhail Gorbachev. In the 1991 election, which became the Russian people's first-ever chance to freely elect their leader, Boris Yeltsin was triumphantly elected Russia's first president for a five-year term. At that time, there was no constitution to define his powers, and they literally became his for the taking. As Yeltsin was then seen as the chief guarantor of reform—especially after his firm pro-democracy stance during the failed August 1991 coup—he had a popular mandate to expand his powers in order to implement reforms. However, by the end of 1992, a conflict emerged between Yeltsin and the then Russian parliament, the Supreme Soviet, which had been elected in 1990 before the breakup of the Soviet Union.

In September 1993 Yeltsin dissolved the parliament and began to rule by decree pending a new parliamentary election in December. That led to the first major incident of fighting in the streets of Moscow since 1917, as armed hard-line protesters were besieged in the parliamentary headquarters and later attacked and captured by troops remaining loyal to the president.

The events of October 1993—the first major crisis of Yeltsin's presidency—could be said to have only partly resolved the conflict between Russia's presidency and legislature. The elections of the new parliament, the Federal Assembly, in December of that year failed to produce a reformist majority in the new legislature. Moreover, the majority in the lower chamber of parliament—the Duma—was in the hands of authoritarian parties: Communists, the Agrarian Party, and the woefully misnamed ultranationalist Liberal-Democratic Party headed by right-wing populist Vladimir Zhirinovsky.

DECEMBER 1993 ELECTIONS TO THE DUMA[1]	
Four biggest parties/blocs	*Total seats (%)*
Russia's Choice (a pro-government party led by Yegor Gaidar)	15.6
Liberal-Democratic Party (Vladimir Zhirinovsky)	14.2
Communist Party (Gennady Ziuganov)	10.7
Agrarian Party	7.3

The elections also approved Russia's first non-Soviet constitution. It set clear terms of reference for the branches of power and endowed the president with enormous prerogatives. The Russian president appoints and dismisses the premier and his cabinet ministers and issues decrees and orders that are valid throughout the territory of the Russian Federation. The president orders the elections to the Duma, and he alone can dissolve it. He is also commander in chief of the armed forces. The powers of the new parliament, called the Federal Assembly, are restricted to passing legislation, approving the budget, declaring amnesty, and ratifying international treaties.[2]

The force of Yeltsin's personality and his skill in controlling people shaped the unique character of the Russian presidency. His conflicts with party politicians in parliament and his failure or reluctance to create a party of his own led him increasingly to see the presidency as standing above parties, and almost above politics. His presidency acquired an almost tsarlike quality, which was to have an important impact on the 1996 presidential election. His personal achievement in effecting his astonishing comeback in 1996 should not be underestimated. It will ensure his place in history books as one of the most resilient politicians of the late twentieth century.

However, Yeltsin could hardly be said to have been elected on his record. His early popularity as a spokesman for a new Russia had long been overshadowed by the mistakes he had made, by the widespread disillusionment about the pace and the direction of reform, by the spread of corruption, and, above all, by the countless lives lost in Chechnya. Few people—including those who had benefited from Yeltsin's policies—were truly happy to elect him for a second term. The presidential contest was close: Yeltsin failed to win enough votes in the first round to get elected, but in the second round he managed to beat his Communist rival.

PRESIDENTIAL ELECTION, SECOND ROUND, JULY 1996[3]	
Candidates	*Percentage of votes*
Boris Yeltsin	54.39
Gennady Ziuganov	40.73
Against all candidates	4.88

One of the main reasons for Yeltsin's political longevity was that it was not clear who could replace him. During the *perestroika* period, against the Communist hardliners there had been Gorbachev and the reform Communists; against Gorbachev there had been Yeltsin and the democrats; but against Yeltsin there were various extremist forces that could spell trouble for Russia. In this sense, he became irreplaceable. However flawed Yeltsin might be, the alternatives appeared worse. This was a verdict reiterated by the voters in June–July 1996: "Whatever we say of Yeltsin, even in his condition [having suffered his second heart attack], he is still the only guarantor of democracy and the irreversibility of economic reform." There is no doubt that, for most Russians, he was the only man they could see as their president at the time. Many were against a Communist taking the top job and feared the new uncertainty this could bring to their lives. As a result, Yeltsin's era was prolonged by three and a half years.

To many, Yeltsin's second presidential term, marked by prolonged spells of passivity and ill health on his part, appears to have been in many respects a period of wasted opportunities for Russia. Indeed, for nearly the entire second half of 1996 Yeltsin devoted very little time to performing the duties of office. A heart attack suffered between the first and second rounds of the presidential election in the summer required that he undergo heart bypass surgery, which was performed in November 1996. Preparation for the surgery and recuperation from it, followed by a severe bout of pneumonia, left him unable to make all but the most pressing decisions for well over half a year. He resumed a more normal schedule only in the spring of 1997, but even then Yeltsin was unable to exercise the duties of his office with any consistency or impose a common policy line on the huge presidential administration. The banking crisis of August 1998 and his deteriorating health made him distance himself from control over socioeconomic policies. He concentrated on overseeing the so-called power ministries (such as Defense, Interior, and the Federal Security Service) and on key international policy issues.

A distinctive development of Yeltsin's second term in office was the growing influence of Russia's financial and industrial magnates in Kremlin politics. Beginning in 1996 the so-called oligarchs had actively looked for people in Yeltsin's inner circle who could provide more effective channels for lobbying their interests. They finally found in Tatiana Diachenko, Yeltsin's younger daughter, the key that gave them access to the president. Previously, Diachenko had kept out of politics and the public limelight, but in 1996 she was persuaded to take an official position as the president's image manager. Soon Diachenko became the chief conduit of the oligarchs' influence on Yeltsin. It is doubtful that she possessed the necessary experience or expertise to understand the complex problems facing the nation. It was also rumored that her financial and commercial interests, entangled with those of the oligarchs, could have influenced several important political decisions.

In the final two years of Yeltsin's presidency the effective control over most important decisions and appointments passed into the hands of Yeltsin's inner circle, which the media dubbed the "Family." This preeminent clan was composed of a small circle of Yeltsin's aides and top officials, a few of the oligarchs, and the president's blood relations. The growth of its influence was a direct result of the president's ill health and his inability to fulfill routine presidential duties. Alongside Tatiana Diachenko, the Family was rumored to include Valentin Yumashev, a journalist who had entered Yeltsin's circle in 1990 by helping him to write his first book of memoirs;[4] Alexander Voloshin, an economist who was put in charge of the presidential administration; Roman Abramovich, a talented young businessman and a protégé of Boris Berezovsky; and the ubiquitous Berezovsky himself.

Of all Russia's oligarchs, Berezovsky had the unequaled talent of combining business interests with involvement in big-time politics. Following the 1996 presidential election, he was given the post of executive secretary of the Commonwealth of Independent States. This appointment gave him direct access to the heads of the former Soviet Union republics. His skills in behind-the-scenes intrigues were legendary, leading to the appearance of myths about his omnipotence. Events of any significance, from acts of Chechen terrorists, to scandals in the elections of provincial governors, to Yeltsin's resignation, were directly or indirectly attributed to his unscrupulous and self-serving politicking.

The distinctive political regime that took shape in Russia by the late 1990s can be described as "oligarchic corporatism." Behind its carapace, sections of the state bureaucracy and the governing elite joined the economic groups and "clans" to take advantage of the opportunities generated by the redivision and privatization of the former Soviet state assets. State power was highly fragmented, with the regime mediating between the former Communist officialdom, the old economic monopolies, and the expanding financial-industrial business interests.

It would be naive to ascribe the rise of the powerful corporatist interest groups and their detrimental effect on Russia's domestic development simply to "wickedness" and the unscrupulousness of the oligarchs. Their disproportionate and often insalubrious influence during that period was a direct result of the frailty of Russia's young democracy, with a weak parliament, marginalized trade unions, a financially dependent press, few strong social organizations, and a host of stillborn political parties. All this only served to reinforce the regime's oligarchical tendencies. In particular, the post-Soviet party-parliamentary system proved to be unable to establish a cooperative framework with the government and to provide the necessary support for the executive. In these conditions, the government had to look for an anchor of stability and found it in the corporatist sector. As a result, it grew increasingly dependent on and beholden to influential interest groups, especially the giant industrial-financial conglomerates. The political regime became entwined with powerful economic interests.

Parties and Elections

The limitations of Russia's post-communist democracy were, first of all, conditioned by its failure to evolve a stable and predictable multiparty system. Most parties that emerged after the Soviet collapse were puny movements, focused on single issues, or leader-dominated groups. The formation of political parties with defined constituencies, interests, and programs was slow, and popular organization and participation remained weak. Politics focused on elite struggles of power broking, with economic coalitions contending for access to Yeltsin and the government. This gave rise to strange political formations, such as the Our Home Is Russia movement (NDR in Russian) under the leadership of then Prime Minister Victor Chernomyrdin. It was quickly dubbed the "party of bosses" as it was comprised mainly of members of the state bureaucracy and governing elites. Chernomyrdin's bloc demonstrated the essence of "oligarchic corporatism" at its starkest, combining unashamedly state administration with private capital, and with barely any attempt to couch its appeal in a democratic idiom.

The economic hardships imposed by the 1992 "shock therapy" were also hardly conducive to the entrenching of democratically oriented parties and constituencies. The period between 1993 and 1995 saw what had seemed impossible only a few years before—the reemergence of the Communist Party. In 1993 President Yeltsin lifted the ban, which he had imposed on the party after the failed hard-line coup in August 1991. Renamed the Communist Party of the Russian Federation (CPRF), the party, which by then had lost millions of members, regrouped around a second echelon of functionaries, with a former deputy head of the Central Committee's ideology department, Gennady Ziuganov (b. 1944), emerging as the leader.

Building on a surviving network of activists in the provinces and on a growing nostalgia for the certainties of the Soviet past—especially among the older generation—the Russian Communists quickly restored their grassroot political structures and delivered an impressive victory in the 1995 parliamentary elections. Leaving far behind the hastily constructed pro-government bloc Our Home Is Russia and the 1993 favorite, Vladimir Zhirinovsky, the Communists virtually took control of the lower house, the Duma. The party that formed the core of the pro-reform majority of the old Duma—the liberal Russia's Choice, led by the former acting prime minister Yegor Gaidar—failed even to get the 5 percent of the vote needed to be represented in parliament. That was a clear indication that the 1995 parliamentary elections were a large-scale protest vote against the hardships brought on by the tough program of economic reform.

According to the Duma election rules, contestants vie for all 450 seats in the chamber. Half of them go to the winners in individual constituencies, where candidates are elected on a first-past-the-post system (i.e., on the basis of simple plurality, when the candidate with more votes than any other is elected). The remaining 225 seats go to parties and political blocs (the so-called party-list vote, when the votes are cast for one of the parties listed on the ballot). Parties and blocs must garner more than 5 percent of votes to enter parliament. The Central Election Commission divides the total number of ballots cast for parties and blocs by the number of seats they contest (225). This allows it to establish how many ballots were cast for each seat. Then the number of votes cast for each party is divided by the number of votes for each seat, giving the parties a particular amount of places in the Duma.

Out of the forty-three blocs registered for the 1995 parliamentary election, only four managed to overcome the 5 percent threshold needed to enter parliament. The inability of the overwhelming majority of political parties to gain the required percentage of votes was a clear indication of the fragmentation of the political spectrum. Most parties were still in embryo and were parties in name only. Most of them were

DECEMBER 1995 ELECTIONS TO THE DUMA[5]	
Successful parties/blocs	*Party-list votes (%)*
Communist Party (Gennady Ziuganov)	22.30
Liberal-Democratic Party (Vladimir Zhirinovsky)	11.18
Our Home Is Russia (Victor Chernomyrdin)	10.13
Yabloko (Grigory Yavlinsky)	6.89

centered in the capitals of Moscow and St. Petersburg and had weak regional and national positions. The Communist Party was the only mass party claiming to have the membership of half a million people.

The fact that the Communist opposition represented the biggest political faction in the Second Duma did not affect significantly the main direction of the government's policies, though it helped, to some extent, correct the excesses of Gaidar-style radical liberalism. The biggest blow to economic liberalism was dealt not by the Communist opposition in parliament but by the August 1998 banking crisis. It brought about a steep devaluation of the ruble, a production slump, galloping inflation, and a drop in real incomes. In the immediate aftermath of the financial crash the supporters of liberal reforms seemed completely demoralized and almost obliterated, while their Communist opponents now actively fought to fill government posts with their political allies. The antiliberal forces represented by the Communist, nationalist, and other parties and movements advocating a state-directed economy looked set to expand their electorates on the wave of antireformist sentiments fomented by the crisis.

Even the ruling bureaucracy swung somewhat to the left after the August events and now competed with the Communists in gibes at "bankrupt monetarists." The authority of the president and his administration was badly damaged by the crisis and so, too, was the prestige of the Kremlin-sponsored Our Home Is Russia movement, which had been an instrument in rallying regional elites behind the government. Regional bosses now looked for a new leader capable of consolidating bureaucratic elites, and they found one in Yury Luzhkov, the powerful mayor of Moscow, who had always been a loud critic of Gaidar, Chubais, and the other ideologues of economic liberalism. Governors proceeded to leave Our Home Is Russia and join the new "party of bosses"—the Fatherland (Otechestvo in Russian) movement—that was being set up by Luzhkov. The mayor himself was now seen as one of the favorites to win the next presidential contest, and therefore his claims to leadership in the new party looked legitimate to the Russian bureaucracy. In August 1999 Luzhkov's "Fatherland" joined forces with another "governors' bloc," the All-Russia movement, thus setting up a formidable coalition of regional barons in the run-up to the December 1999 parliamentary elections under the name of Fatherland–All Russia (OVR in Russian). The regional leaders behind the merger—Luzhkov and the president of Tatarstan, Mintimer Shaimiev—invited Evgeny Primakov, the former prime minister and a respected politician, to lead their electoral coalition.

On the liberal side of the political spectrum the effect of the financial crisis was mixed. On the one hand, the crash seemed to strengthen the appeal of Grigory Yavlinsky's Yabloko party (the party's name is an acronym formed from the initial letters of the names of its three founders, including that of Yavlinsky). Ever since 1992, Yavlinsky had consistently criticized the government's reform course, condemning Gaidar's approach as too crude and not suitable to Russia's economic structure. Yavlinsky interpreted the events of August 1998 as a logical result of the implementation of Gaidar's "primitive scheme."[6] In the past, the leaders of Yabloko had always been against blocs with other liberal political groupings. Now they felt that any potential challengers to their domination of the liberal-democratic flank had been terminally undermined. This served to bolster Yabloko's self-confidence and also strengthened its traditional tendency toward self-isolation.

On the other hand, the remaining parties and movements of the liberal and liberal-conservative persuasion felt the need to overcome their disunity and fragmentation. This tendency toward consolidation among liberally and democratically minded Russians was further strengthened following the contract killing of Galina Starovoitova in November 1998. A Duma member and an anticorruption crusader, Starovoitova had been a prominent figure in the democratic movement since Gorbachev's time. Her tragic death galvanized liberal and democratic organizations into action: in December 1998 they set up a single liberal bloc, the Right Cause (Pravoe delo in Russian), that united most of the better-known liberal groupings with the exception of Yabloko. In August 1999 the liberal-conservative coalition regrouped again, forming the election bloc the Union of Right-Wing Forces (SPS in Russian).

By the autumn of 1999 the main contestants in the approaching elections—from Communists to liberals, from local bureaucrats to ultranationalists—were ready to enter the election fray, with the chances of the Communist Party, the Fatherland–All Russia bloc, and Yabloko looking particularly good. It was at this moment, when the process of coalition building across the entire political spectrum seemed to be complete, that the Kremlin suddenly sprang into action and attempted to recapture the initiative in the run-up to the December elections. By that time, the social misery and political gloom of the postcrisis period had largely receded: the economy was picking up, and some social stability had returned. It appeared that the financial crash came with a "silver lining": the ruble devaluation and the collapse in imports from August 1998 created conditions for the revival of domestic production. The presidential administration had little to do with the economic recovery but was quick to take credit for it. It also intended to gamble on the new face in Russian politics—Vladimir Putin (b. 1952)—who had just been appointed prime minister.

In a matter of days the federal administration managed to set up from scratch a new election bloc, the Interregional "Unity" (Edinstvo in Russian) movement. Its core was comprised of local bosses from less economically viable regions, which depended on subsidies from Moscow. These regional administrators had little chance of playing a prominent role in the existing governors' blocs, such as Fatherland and All Russia, led by strong governors from industrialized regions like Moscow and Tatarstan. The new pro-Kremlin bloc was to be led by Sergei Shoigu, the respected emergencies minister. Because of the nature of his job of supervising disaster relief operations during earthquakes, floods, fires, and so on, Shoigu was often in the news and had earned a reputation as an effective and no-nonsense "disaster manager." His election bloc was backed by the new prime minister, Putin, who also showed himself from the start to be a tough administrator, capable of taking responsibility for risky actions, including military operations in Dagestan to repel the incursions of Chechen armed groups and then in Chechnya itself. Thus, the regional bureaucracy, united under the umbrella of the Fatherland–All Russia bloc, suddenly found itself confronted by a powerful regions-based contender, which was competing on the same segment of the electoral field and had the public endorsement of the popular prime minister to boot.

All in all, twenty-six electoral coalitions and blocs took part in the 1999 election campaign. However, only six of them had any real chance of passing the 5 percent hurdle needed to enter the Duma: the Communist Party, Fatherland–All Russia, the Unity bloc, Yabloko, the Union of Right-Wing Forces, and Zhirinovsky's ultranationalists. Out of these leading six, only the Communists seemed to be assured of the stable support of their electorate, which traditionally voted for them out of nostalgia for the times of Brezhnev's "stagnation" and the long-gone certainties of the Soviet era. The rest had to fight for votes in fierce compe-

DECEMBER 1999 ELECTIONS TO THE DUMA[7]	
Successful parties/blocs	*Party-list votes (%)*
CPRF	24.29
Unity	23.32
Fatherland–All Russia	13.33
Union of Right-Wing Forces	8.52
Zhirinovsky bloc	5.98
Yabloko	5.93

tition with other contestants occupying similar ideological and political niches: the Unity bloc pitted against Fatherland–All Russia, the Union of Right-Wing Forces against Yabloko, and Zhirinovsky's "liberal democrats" against a number of smaller ultraradical groupings. The result of this uncompromising struggle, which took the form of a venomous "information war" waged in the national media, saw the "outsiders"— the Unity bloc, the Union of Right-Wing Forces, and the Zhirinovsky bloc—begin to press the favorites—Fatherland–All Russia and Yabloko.

The December 1999 elections significantly changed the balance of political forces in the new Duma in comparison to the previous two, resulting in a more "centrist" parliament. Although the Communists came in first as before, they lost their almost undivided dominance of the lower house. The pro-Kremlin Unity bloc came in a very close second. The steep rise in its popularity ratings cannot be explained only by the support of the military operation against the Chechen separatists or Putin's charisma. The pro-government bloc was able to extract kudos from a general improvement in the economic situation, including growth in production, lower inflation, and the government's efforts to meet wage and pension arrears. The vagueness of its political platform also played a part, as no one knew exactly what the recently appointed prime minister and the movement created almost overnight under his patronage stood for. Yet the voters appeared to be prepared to give Putin a chance and to support the new "party of bosses," as all the old ones had been unable to meet their social expectations. This also explains the modest showing of the Fatherland–All Russia bloc: the coalition of powerful regional bosses, which had predicted a resounding victory only three months before the elections, came in third.

On the liberal flank, Yavlinsky's Yabloko party seemed to have underestimated significant changes in the social base of support of liberal groupings since the 1995 Duma elections. In the mid-1990s the core of its electorate was comprised of somewhat demoralized members of the intelligentsia, disoriented by the loss of the dominant influence they used to enjoy in the *perestroika* era. By 1999, with the rise of the Russian bourgeoisie, the social complexion of people with liberal leanings had changed: "chattering intellectuals" had to make room for the new business elite. In contrast to the Union of Right-Wing Forces, Yabloko was unable to convince Russia's entrepreneurs that it was a constructive party capable of promoting their interests through genuine compromise and cooperation with the government, rather than the party in a perpetual opposition that could only rend the air with empty promises.

The 1999 parliamentary elections revealed significant shifts in Russia's political and ideological landscape over the preceding decade. At the start of the market reforms Russian society had been split into two big camps of Communists and democrats. These ideological labels were imprecise and disguised the conflict between traditionalists (Communists) and reformers (democrats). At that time most of the democrats espoused radical liberal solutions and enjoyed an impressive support of 40 to 45 percent of the socially active population. They proclaimed the supremacy of the "Western" economic and political patterns, denying that the Soviet past could offer any usable elements. The traditionalists, on the other hand, insisted on Russia's "own way" and fought to preserve its identity shaped both by its Soviet and pre-Soviet history.

In the course of the 1990s this ideological polarization was diffused and transformed into a number of ideological-political strands. The most spectacular—threefold—decline was in the ranks of the supporters of radical market reforms, and for obvious reasons. At the start of the reforms of the early 1990s, the democrats had embraced enthusiastically and uncritically a set of attractive but abstract ideas, such as democracy, human rights, and the market economy. By contrast, at the close of the decade the general population had firsthand experience of homegrown liberalism in all its concrete and often unappealing political and economic realities. The disappointment with the liberal prescriptions translated into a general disaffection with the West, blamed for its support of the Russian "shock therapists." As a result, a considerable number of former liberals and "westernizers" went over to the side of the nationalists.

At the end of the decade no single ideology appeared to dominate the minds of Russians. An opinion poll conducted by the Russian Independent Institute of Social and Nationalities Problems (RIISNP),

IDEOLOGICAL PREFERENCES OF VOTERS[8]	
Prepared to support	*Percentage of respondents*
Democrats favoring market reforms	17.2
Russian nationalists in search of the "Russian way"	10.5
Communists, favoring socialism	14.0
Centrists in favor of combining different approaches and avoiding extremes	17.2
Unsure whom to support	41.1

established the following ideological preferences and leanings among the Russian population at the close the twentieth century.

It is significant that the majority of the respondents (41.1 percent) did not align themselves with any of the current ideological-political orientations and that Russian nationalists had the smallest base of support. People's ideological leanings also depended on their social and age group: the majority of the pro-Communist sympathizers came from groups characterized by old age and lower educational levels. Democrats, on the other hand, enjoyed greater support among socially more active sections of the electorate, including city dwellers, younger people, and the intelligentsia.[9]

Despite a general disenchantment with liberalism (or, perhaps, with the idealistic understanding of liberalism, characteristic of the early 1990s), liberal ideology has taken root in Russian society. It is embraced by more dynamic sectors of the electorate; it informs the activity of many key decision makers in the Russian executive branch, including the presidential and governmental structures; it is the dominant ideology of powerful financial-industrial groups; and, most importantly, it has the support of the leading mass media. In addition, the Third Duma, elected in December 1999, had a significant parliamentary faction of "classic" liberals in the shape of the Union of Right-Wing Forces. All this enables the adherents of liberalism to exert considerable influence on the way of thinking of the Russian people.

Yeltsin's Legacy

Ten rulers have stood at the helm of the Russian and Soviet state over the past hundred years. Some of them governed the country for many years, even decades, others stayed in office for a few months. Men as different in their outlook, personality, and political style as Nicholas II, Alexander Kerensky, Vladimir Lenin, Joseph Stalin, Nikita Khrushchev, Leonid Brezhnev, Yuri Andropov, Konstantin Chernenko, Mikhail Gorbachev, and Boris Yeltsin have shaped Russia's destiny. Yeltsin was the only one to be popularly elected. The rest came to power as a result of a revolution, or a coup, or party decisions and conspiracies. All of them occupied office against the will of their predecessor and usually tried to undo his work, promising to lead the Russian people to a new and better order.[10]

The liberal Kerensky, for example, spurned the policies of Nicholas II, whereas the Communist Lenin scrapped all of Kerensky's plans. Stalin extolled Lenin in words while firmly rejecting Lenin's compromise policies of the early 1920s in practice. Khrushchev saw the struggle against Stalin's "personality cult" as one of his main objectives, whereas Brezhnev proclaimed war on Khrushchev's "voluntarism." Andropov did not want Chernenko to succeed him, and Chernenko was against Gorbachev as his heir. Gorbachev made a great effort to overcome the legacy of the "era of stagnation" but soon found himself embroiled in a fierce personal and political rivalry with Yeltsin. The fact that Russia did not have a normal system for the transfer of power was one of the main reasons for its troubles and setbacks. Over the past century five of its ten leaders died in office, three were swept away by revolutions, and one was removed as a result of a conspiracy. Yeltsin was the only one who left the Kremlin voluntarily before the end of his term and handed over power to a successor, Vladimir Putin, who was appointed by him and approved by the parliament precisely as the law required. His departure was a peaceful constitutional procedure and set an important precedent, serving to entrench a system for the democratic transfer of power and thus preserve continuity and stability in politics.

Even more importantly, Yeltsin's period marked a revolution in Russia. An entire order, based on the political, economic, and ideological system of Soviet Marxism-Leninism, was overthrown. The foundations for the command economy and the one-party dictatorship no longer exist. They have been replaced by a new set of economic and political institutions, founded on different constitutional and ideological premises. They are still fragile and uncertain, but they are a world apart from the past.

Despite the many justified criticisms that can be made of Yeltsin's presidency, under him Russia has made enormous strides in the direction of a democratic and market-oriented society. Yeltsin's chief ambition as the leader of the new Russia was to create the conditions under which the revival of totalitarianism would be impossible. The jury is still out, debating the verdict of whether he succeeded in this aim. Yet it is hardly possible to ignore the following positive developments:

A Modern Political and Legal System

Russia now has a modern political system and a constitution that meets international standards and guarantees free elections. It defines the Russian Federation as a democratic, federative, rule-of-law state with a republican form of government. It recognizes ideological and political pluralism, the principle of the separation of powers, and the right of private ownership. It states that "[t]he individual and his rights and freedoms are the supreme value. Recognition, observance and protection of human and civil rights and freedoms are the obligation of the state."[11] The new Criminal Code, conforming to legal standards of civilized countries, and the new Civil Code, enshrining property rights, have also been enacted.

The Spread of Democratic Habits in Russia

Russian democracy is far from perfect, with the parliament in frequent disarray, with an authoritarian style to the presidency, and with corruption scandals succeeding each other in a never-ending stream. But one must not overlook the important process of the steady accustomation with democratic procedures that goes on under the unruly surface. This habit formation affects both the electors and the elected, who get used to certain rules of the game as these rules gain increasing legitimacy.

Contested elections, as one of the vital elements of the democratic process, have become competitive and regular. Between the first contested elections of USSR deputies in 1989 and the presidential election of March 2000, Russian voters went to the polls ten times in nationwide elections:

- 1989, election of USSR deputies

- 1990, election of RSFSR and local deputies

- 1991, March: referenda on preserving union and creating Russian presidency

- 1991, June: election of RSFSR president

- 1993, April: referendum on approval of Yeltsin and government

- 1993, December: election of deputies to new parliament and referendum on draft constitution

- 1995, December: election of deputies to parliament

- 1996, June/July: election of president

- 1999, December: election of deputies to parliament

- 2000, March: election of president

These elections varied in the degree to which they were honest, open, and fair. But the principle of democratic elections as a means of conferring legitimate power on political leaders is now well established, both in political practice and in public opinion.

With all their flaws and deficiencies, the modernized or re-created Russian institutions are nevertheless in continuous function. In the Duma as in other elected bodies, the parliamentarians deliberate, examine laws, formulate proposals, and gradually acquire a deeper understanding of the challenges facing the nation. The mere survival and routine operation of lively parliamentary institutions at different levels contribute to democratic stability and maturity and reinforce the process of sound habit formation among both the rulers and the ruled.

Demographic, Cultural, and Social Forces for Change

Despite the upheavals of the last decade and the widening gap between the haves and the have-nots, Russian society does not appear particularly polarized politically. Surprisingly, Russian sociologists find there has been little change in Russians' basic perceptions and values since the late 1980s. The great changes in society, they say, occurred in the previous two generations, with the move to the cities and the rise of educational levels and standards of living. By the late 1980s a new Russian urban culture had formed, founded on a large professional class, largely free of ideology and potentially supportive of liberal political values.

At the start of the twenty-first century, a new post-Soviet generation is rising to leading positions throughout the country. Many of its members, those in their early thirties today, have lived their entire professional lives in the world of Gorbachev's *perestroika* and the post-Soviet market economy. For this generation, the end of the Soviet era was a liberation they had hoped for. They are familiar with international practices and trends, and they do not hesitate to look to the outside world for models. Increasingly, they are not engineers, but lawyers, accountants, and economists, who understand opportunity and competition and possess the marketing and financial skills needed for business.[12]

At the ballot box, the post-Soviet generation has broadly supported the government's reforms. The problem is that many younger Russians take the changes that have taken place in their lifetimes for granted and often do not care to vote at all. However, if Russia follows the experience of other countries, younger Russians will vote in larger numbers as they grow older and establish families. Meanwhile, at the other end of the age spectrum, the generation of pensioners who are the main constituency of the neo-Communist parties is gradually moving off the stage. In short, demographic change is on the side of the reforms, as it brings forward the generation of people who have never experienced anything else.[13]

Economic Forces for Change

The long-term economic forces for change are even more important. Opportunities for making money by stripping privatized Soviet assets and speculation have already declined, forcing managers to begin looking for efficiency gains instead. After the financial crisis of August 1998, with the devalued ruble staying low, imports have been contained and domestic production has revived. As the economy turns around, it will generate demand for better services in banking, insurance, accounting, legal services, and advertising, causing these sectors, which are the blood vessels of a market economy, to grow and mature.[14]

As the domestic market grows, privatized enterprises will come under increasing competitive pressures to restructure and invest. They are already being forced to think about cutting costs, marketing their products, and developing new ones. There will be growing pressure to extend privatization to areas of the economy where it has been held back until now, especially land ownership and the so-called natural monopolies, such as oil and natural gas extraction and power generation. Many of the key institutions of a market economy now exist. Money has returned to a central role in the economy; the borders are largely open to the flow of people and goods; and hundreds of thousands of new private businesses, both big and small, operate in an environment governed by market forces.

Thus, the reforms seem to have gained a self-sustaining character driven by the new interests created by the vibrant private sector. The wealth of the country has passed largely into private hands. A new class has come to the fore, many members of which, to be sure, are descended from the Soviet administrative class, the *nomenklatura*. But they no longer owe their rank and privileges to the Communist state and the command economy. They are in business for themselves, and their prosperity is now bound up with continued marketization.

Worldwide Political, Intellectual, and Technical Trends

Finally, there is a growing international consensus that democratic procedures, such as free elections and multiparty parliamentarism, are part and parcel of a modern state. The idea of one-party rule is thoroughly discredited and supported by only a handful of nations. Pluralist democracy is no longer seen as a mode of government suitable only for certain wealthy nations, but as one that brings universal benefits.

Moreover, Russia can hardly escape the powerful pressure of such worldwide forces as the revival of liberal economic doctrines in the last generation and the tidal wave of globalization, privatization, and liberalization. Technological change and global competition will continue to act powerfully on Russia, as they have done ever since the time of Peter the Great.

Chapter Twenty

Russia in Search of an Identity

The Commonwealth of Independent States

The Commonwealth of Independent States (CIS) is a free association of sovereign states formed in 1991, comprising Russia and eleven other republics that were formerly part of the Soviet Union. The CIS had its origins on 8 December 1991, when the elected leaders of Russia, Ukraine, and Belarus (Belorussia) signed an agreement forming a new association to replace the crumbling Union of Soviet Socialist Republics. The three Slavic republics were subsequently joined by the central Asian republics of Kazakhstan, Kyrgyzstan, Tajikistan, Turkmenistan, and Uzbekistan, by the Transcaucasian republics of Armenia, Azerbaijan, and Georgia, and by Moldova. (The remaining former Soviet republics of Lithuania, Latvia, and Estonia declined to join the new organization.) The CIS formally came into being on 21 December 1991 and began operations the following month, with the city of Minsk in Belarus designated as its administrative center.

The commonwealth's functions are to coordinate its members' policies regarding their economies, foreign relations, defense, immigration policies, environmental protection, and law enforcement. Its top governmental body is a council composed of the member republics' heads of state (i.e., presidents) and of government (prime ministers), who are assisted by committees of republic cabinet ministers in key areas such as economics and defense.

Russia is the dominant force in the Commonwealth of Independent States. The 1990s were the period when the post-Soviet and postimperial Russian state sought to redefine the boundaries of its national interests. It is hardly surprising that the fate of the twenty-five million Russians in the "near abroad" (meaning the other former republics of the Soviet Union) should be central to the national and state interests of post-Soviet Russia. At the same time, Russian democratic leaders take pains to point out that Russia seeks to construct its relations with the newly independent states of the former union on a basis of equality and mutual respect for sovereignty.

Throughout the 1990s Russia established itself as a peacekeeper and the guardian of CIS borders. The central Asian states, as well as Armenia and Georgia, formally agreed that Russian troops should police their borders jointly with local forces. All states agreed that Russia should send troops to the breakaway Georgian region of Abkhaziya. CIS forces, mainly Russian, remain in Tajikistan. Russia was less successful in getting CIS states to contribute to the costs of the peacekeeping forces.

Over the decade of its existence regular summits have been convened at which the leaders of the CIS member states have sought to overcome numerous disagreements between the former Soviet republics. Presidents and premiers of the CIS member states have signed nearly a thousand agreements and treaties on "deepening the integration." The CIS's main problem, however, is that the adopted decisions are rarely implemented. Less than half of the multilateral agreements have been ratified by all of the member states. Even when the agreements are signed, the states do not always act on jointly adopted decisions. It appears that the difficulties of the post-Communist transition compel most member states to focus their attention on pressing domestic concerns.

After a decade of its existence, the attitude of the leaders of the former Soviet republics to the CIS remains ambivalent. On the one hand, they are aware of the need to settle vital issues of political, economic, and military cooperation. On the other hand, they are reluctant to make serious political commitments to the CIS, regarding them as a diminution of national sovereignty. They are afraid that their CIS obligations may be construed as turning over power to the huge Russian state and thus furthering "Russia's imperial policy." A postimperial syndrome seems to paralyze the CIS collaboration.[1]

This is one of the reasons why over the recent decade the CIS has developed into a multilayered collaborative structure. Bilateral relations and agreements between its member-states appear to be more effective and workable than multilateral treaties. For example, Russia and Belarus have been making steady progress toward reestablishing a close union of the two nations with common citizenship, coordinated security and economic policies, and a single currency. By contrast, multilateral accords, such as the accord between Georgia, Uzbekistan, Azerbaijan, and Moldova (GUAM), appear to be less effective. The CIS member states seem to favor a system whereby the integration of the former Soviet republics can proceed at different speeds. In practice, however, this combination of bilateral and multilateral agreements creates confusion and has not proved successful in harmonizing the interests of the once "brotherly peoples."

Post-Soviet Geopolitics

The extremely complex and diverse geopolitical space of the former USSR can be best analyzed in terms of four main groups of states, singled out in relation to their geographical location, ethnic composition, political leanings, and ideological orientation.[2]

The first group of countries is represented by the Baltic states of Lithuania, Latvia, and Estonia. They are united by their common past, including the experience of independent statehood in the period between the two world wars. Reannexed by the USSR in 1940, they retained their strong pro-Western leanings and, half a century later, seized the opportunity offered by Gorbachev's liberalization and finally broke away from what they regarded as the "imperial center." Having regained their full independence, the three countries declined membership in the CIS. They view as their natural allies the countries of western and northern Europe and therefore strive to join Western political, economic, and military organizations. Their relations with Russia are strained not only because of the security implications of their possible membership in NATO but also because of the substantial ethnic Russian minorities, who found themselves subjected to various discriminatory practices by the governments of the three Baltic states. It is unlikely that in the foreseeable future the Baltic republics will be inclined toward far-reaching economic, political, and cultural reintegration with Russia and other countries of the former Soviet Union.

The countries of the Transcaucasian region represent the second big group of states that have emerged from the ruins of the Communist state. The region includes countries that have gained complete independence, such as Armenia, Georgia, and Azerbaijan, and territories that are part of the Russian Federation but have at present an indeterminate status, like Chechnya. This is the most troublesome region for Russia and a hotbed of political, ethnic, and religious conflicts fraught with unpredictable consequences. The Transcaucasian region is characterized by an extremely diverse ethnic mix of population cemented by the two dominant religions of Christianity and Islam. The Greater Caucasus range that cuts the region from west to east is Russia's natural boundary in the south, serving as a geostrategic barrier that curbs the expansion of pan-Islamism.

Historically, Russia and the Christian peoples of Armenia and Georgia have enjoyed mutually beneficial and friendly relations with one another. Armenia and Georgia's voluntary accession to the tsarist empire preserved their ancient national cultures from forcible assimilation by the Islamic states of Turkey and Persia. In the late 1980s the nationalist movements in Armenia and Georgia actively pushed for secession from the USSR. Following the collapse of the union and in the initial euphoria of their newly found independence, the two republics have distanced themselves from Russia. However, economic, cultural, geostrategic, and religious pressures will almost certainly propel them back into Russia's orbit.

Following the breakup of the Soviet Union, Georgia and Armenia became entangled in bitter political and military confrontations with their Islamic neighbors. Armenia was drawn into an all-out war with neighboring Azerbaijan over the disputed Nagorno-Karabakh enclave. Georgian troops tried unsuccessfully to pacify one of Georgia's constituent parts, the autonomous republic of Abkhaziya, which wants independence from Georgia. The difficulty of the situation for Russia in its efforts to contain or arbitrate these discords is that it cannot be seen as taking sides in the Armenian-Azerbaijani or Georgian-Abkhaziyan conflicts.

Russian peacekeeping actions in the Transcaucasian region are further hampered by a drawn-out conflict in the North Caucasus within its own borders with the Chechen republic, which has unilaterally declared its independence from the Russian Federation. The complexity and intensity of the confrontation with Chechnya casts a dark shadow across the entire Transcaucasian region and beyond. Resolving this conflict is critical for Russia's national interests in the region.

The third group of the former Soviet republics with common geopolitical characteristics is located in central Asia. It includes the four newly independent states of Kyrgyzstan, Turkmenistan, Uzbekistan, and Tajikistan. Their geographical position makes them a buffer zone separating Russia from direct contact with the Islamic countries of Afghanistan, Iran, and Pakistan, and also from India and China. The republics themselves gravitate toward an Islamic orientation. The ethnic, religious, and political makeup of these countries, in particular, of Tajikistan, do not augur well for their long-term stability. The chief cause of the region's volatility is ideological pressures generated by Islamic fundamentalism.

With the breakup of the USSR local Communist elites jettisoned the Communist ideology and managed to preserve their dominant position.

On the whole, they remain friendly and loyal to their big northern neighbor. The four states also retain substantial Russian-speaking populations. The alliance with Russia helps them to keep in check a potentially explosive situation within their own borders. However, the fundamentalist threat has become real following the military successes of the Taliban movement in Afghanistan. Its militant and fanatical followers cause trouble at the borders of Uzbekistan and Tajikistan. Indeed, Tajikistan, which itself has suffered from a violent civil war between Islamic fundamentalists and government forces, has accepted a status akin to that of a protectorate of Russia. It is impossible to predict how long the present pragmatically minded politicians will remain in power in these states. Russia is obviously interested in preserving the buffer of stable central Asian republics as a shield against Islamic fundamentalism. The recent acquisition by India and Pakistan of nuclear weapons has been another dangerous development in the area.

The final group of countries that obtained independence as a result of the breakup of the Soviet Union is of special importance for Russia. It includes Belarus, Ukraine, and Kazakhstan. The former Soviet republic of Moldova can also be considered within this group. The disintegration of the Communist state resulted in a dramatic division of the three East Slavic peoples—Russians, Belorussians, and Ukrainians—which have for centuries lived in one state united by their common ethnic roots, history, culture, and close economic ties. Their similar cultural, historical, and geopolitical characteristics notwithstanding, the members of this group do not have the same political leanings, and their attitude to Russia as the historic heartland of the East Slavic lands is far from uniform.

Belarus has been the first country in the group to overcome its largely artificial separation from Russia and forge a closer alliance with its Slavic sister nation. Under its president, Alexander Lukashenka, Belarus has in fact made union with Russia a principal goal. The two countries are gradually reconstituting a single economic, sociocultural, and military-strategic space. Belarus is the only republic on the western fringes of the former Soviet territories that does not seek NATO membership. A union with Belarus thus improves Russia's geopolitical situation in the west, where it now borders mostly on countries gravitating toward the North Atlantic Alliance.

By contrast, Russia's relations with Ukraine are not as easygoing. The second (after Russia) most powerful former republic of the USSR, both economically and in terms of population, Ukraine experienced a steep decline in living standards after obtaining independence. The main reason for this was the severance of vital ties that used to bind Russia and

Ukraine in a single, unitary economy. Despite the present difficulties in relations between the two countries, prospects for Russian-Ukrainian economic and cultural reintegration remain strong. Economically, Ukraine depends heavily on Russian energy supplies and on the export of its agricultural produce to Russia. Most importantly, blood ties bind the two peoples not just in a metaphoric but also in a direct sense: millions of Russian speakers live in Ukraine, and millions of Ukrainians live in Russia; many thousands of mixed Russian-Ukrainian families have become artificially separated as a result of the breakup of the Soviet Union.

The process of reintegration between Russia and Ukraine, however, is hampered by the legacy of the troubled Soviet past. It includes militant nationalism, rife in Ukraine's western provinces, and the problem of the Crimean peninsula, ceded to Ukraine by Khrushchev on a whim, at a time when the administrative borders between the republics of a unitary empire did not matter. Crimea is vital to Russia as home to its main Black Sea naval base of Sebastopol.

Kazakhstan, which also belongs to this group, is a republic with a vast territory populated by a diverse ethnic mix of Turkic, Mongol, and Slavic populations. Geographically, it occupies a position between Russia and the central Asian republics. Historically, economically, and strategically, Kazakhstan gravitates more toward Russia. These leanings are further reinforced by the fact that ethnic Russians constitute nearly half of its population. Russia's famous Baikonur space-vehicle launching site is also situated in Kazakhstan. The deepening economic, political, cultural, and military integration between Russia and Kazakhstan is vital for the prosperity of both of these states.

Finally, the small republic of Moldova may also be considered as a potential candidate for reintegration with Russia. The majority of its people are ethnic Moldavians, who speak a language that is virtually identical to Romanian. But Moldova is also inhabited by large numbers of Russians, Ukrainians, Gagauz, Romanians, Jews, and others and is often compared to an ethnic powder keg. The process of Moldova's separation from the USSR was agonizing and bloody. Political turmoil was fueled by ethnic tensions between Russians and Ukrainians, on the one hand, and Moldavians, on the other. In 1992 the Russian-speaking populations rebelled against Moldovan authority and formed the breakaway Dniester republic in the so-called Transdniester region. The region is located to the east of the Dniester River and contains large numbers of Russians and Ukrainians. The confrontation escalated into a drawn-out military conflict. Finally, in 1997 the Moldovan authorities and the leadership of the breakaway Dniester region were persuaded to sign a memorandum on normalizing relations. Russia, Ukraine, and the Organization for Security and Cooperation in Europe acted as guarantors of the truce. Since then the tension in the area has been largely contained.

Russian Federalism

The "nationalities question," which had so unsettled the Soviet Union and pushed it to its inglorious end, did not completely go away with the secession of the Soviet republics from Russia. Russia was a federation in its own right, and the reformist government faced the task of restructuring the country's state and political system on genuine federative foundations and establishing a federative structure, which would take into account the country's historical traditions and the realities of modern-day Russia.

Soviet federalism had evolved as a result of two conflicting tendencies: growing national separatism and the Russian tradition of a centralized, unitary state. From the early stages of Russian statehood, the country comprised nationalities and ethnic groups of diverse cultural backgrounds and varying levels of development. In prerevolutionary Russia the unity of the tsarist empire was cemented by the powerful integrating role of the Russian imperial nation and the relatively low level of national development of the mass of the empire's ethnic populations. Even at the start of the twentieth century most of the non-Russian nationalities, which evolved their nationalist movements, did not dream of independent statehood: their most radical demands did not go beyond a desire for cultural autonomy within the Russian empire. Only with the collapse of tsarism and the establishment of the Bolshevik dictatorship did Soviet Russia become a federative state.

Despite being based ostensibly on a national-territorial principle, Soviet federalism was not a result of the integration of national states that had existed before. On the contrary, Soviet republics themselves were typically creations of the federal center. Moreover, the central authorities in Moscow devised a union treaty and set up a federation, which some of these entities joined as union republics, while others remained autonomous territories within union republics. As a result, a complex, multitiered federative structure took shape. Most of the autonomous ethnic-national territories were located within the Russian Soviet Federated Socialist Republic, the Soviet core republic, which itself was an artificial creation similar to other union republics. At the time of the formation of the USSR in 1922, no one could have predicted that the RSFSR's administrative borders would become contours of the new Russia that would emerge at the end of the twentieth century as a result of the Soviet collapse.

Russia's new-style federalism is embodied in the Federative Treaty of 1992 and the constitution of 1993. It is a federalism of a mixed type: the Russian Federation incorporates not only ethnic-national subdivisions, inherited from the Soviet past, but also pure (nonethnic) administrative territorial units, such as regions and even certain cities (Moscow and St. Petersburg). In other words, Russian federalism provides both a framework for managing interethnic relations and a form of the country's territorial organization. As of 2001, Russia comprises eighty-nine constituent territorial units, which in Russian constitutional language are called the "subjects of the federation."

In the years immediately following the Soviet collapse, Russia found it particularly difficult to reestablish the primacy of its own central authority. Conflicts between the regional governments and the Russian federal authorities over the spheres of rights and powers were substantial. They even led some analysts to debate the question of whether Russia itself was in danger of splitting apart. However, the demographic differences between the former USSR and present-day Russia make the prospect of Russia sharing the fate of the USSR unlikely. The Soviet population was more ethnically fragmented than that of the Russian republic. Whereas only half of the Soviet population was ethnically Russian, Russia's population is 81 percent Russian, with ethnic minorities forming a very small proportion of the total. Besides, the national republics of the Soviet Union were all located on the perimeter of the union, and thus bordered other countries. The national territories of Russia are mainly internal to the Russian republic, and thus have less direct interaction with the outside world.

In the past, Russia's internal ethnic-national territories were classified by size and status into autonomous republics, autonomous provinces, and national districts. Today all the autonomous republics are simply termed republics. In many, the indigenous ethnic group comprises a minority of the population. Republics and autonomous districts are units created specifically to give certain political rights to populations living in territories with significant ethnic minorities. Typically, republics enjoy higher constitutional status and are treated as though they had a share of sovereignty. They have the right to adopt their own constitution so long as it does not contradict the federal constitution.

The elevated status of ethnic-national republics is partly the legacy of the early 1990s, when all the republics within the Russian Federation adopted declarations of sovereignty and two of them (Tatarstan and the Chechen republics) made attempts to declare full or partial independence from Russia. In this period, when the new Russian constitutional order was particularly fragile and fears of regional separatism were acute, the central government was compelled to negotiate special arrangements with some of the ethnic-national territories. Moscow signed bilateral treaties with Tatarstan and Bashkortostan under which it conceded special privileges in return for their loyalty. Ethnic-national territories were also able to negotiate special arrangements under which they were exempt from certain taxes, or permitted to retain a higher share of earnings from the exploitation of the region's natural resources.

By contrast, pure administrative subdivisions such as *oblasts* (regions), populated mainly by Russians, have no special constitutional status. Not surprisingly, there is constant rivalry between the *oblasts*, on the one hand, and the republics, on the other. Leaders of *oblasts* complain that republics enjoy special privileges, which enable them to circumvent federal law or receive other benefits in the form of federal subsidies. The tensions between the two kinds of "subjects of the federation" generated by the inequalities in their constitutional status are likely to continue unless the central authorities can find a way of persuading the governments of the republics to relinquish their privileged constitutional status.

Under the Communist regime, federalism in Russia, as in the Soviet Union as a whole, was largely formal. Only in recent years has Russia's constitutional order evolved toward a more meaningful form of federalism, which gives constituent units of the federation a certain degree of autonomy. The bicameral structure of the parliament, introduced by the constitution of 1993, went some way to making federalism real by ensuring that each of the eighty-nine federal subjects had an equal number of representatives in the upper house of parliament, the Council of the Federation. The Council of the Federation was given certain specific rights over matters of direct concern to regions, including the budget and taxation policy. It has strongly defended the prerogatives and interests of the regions, which has helped to mitigate some of the internal problems that fueled regional separatism and to allay nationalist passions that used to drive the movements for separatism in the republics.

The populations of Russia's regions and republics have, by and large, come to recognize that their economies are not likely to benefit from independence. Increasingly, much as in other federal states, the politics of federalism in Russia revolves around a continuous renegotiation of the powers of the center and the constituent members of the federation. The switch from formal to real federalism has enabled the Russian state to preserve itself despite centrifugal pressures from the regions. The sole exception is Chechnya, where the federal government had to resort to force to preserve the unity of the state.

The Chechen Problem

Chechnya is a republic in southwestern Russia, situated on the northern flank of the Greater Caucasus range. It is bordered by Russia proper on the north, the Dagestan republic on the east and southeast, Georgia on the southwest, and the Ingushetia republic on the west. Chechnya's main ethnic group is the Chechen, with minorities of Russians and Ingush. In the mid-1990s its population was about 850,000.[3]

The Chechen and Ingush are both Muslim. Their society is based on clan and tribal relations. Traditionally, the Chechens' chief occupations were farming in the lowlands in the north of the republic and cattle raising in the mountain areas in the south. Oil drilling became increasingly important in Chechnya. It began around the 1890s, when Russia's earlier industrialization drive was successfully launched under the tsarist government. Under the Soviets oil-drilling and refining became the backbone of the Chechen economy. Grozny, the capital of Chechnya, became one of the largest oil-refining centers in Russia. Of even greater economic significance than its industrial capacity is Chechnya's strategic geographical location as a transport junction and transit corridor, which accommodates the railway and highway connecting southern Russia with Baku, the capital of Azerbaijan, and the pipelines supplying oil and natural gas from the Caspian and central Asian regions to Europe.

Chechnya has never known independent statehood, and a Chechen republic has never existed as a state or an administrative unit. In 1922 the Bolsheviks created the Chechen autonomous province within Russia, and in 1934 they merged it with the Ingush autonomous *oblast* to form the Chechen-Ingush autonomous *oblast*. Two years later it was designated a republic. When the Soviet leader Joseph Stalin accused the Chechen and Ingush of collaboration with the Germans during the Second World War, they were deported to exile in central Asia, and the republic of Checheno-Ingushetia was dissolved. The exiles were allowed to return to their homeland, and the republic was reestablished under Nikita Khrushchev in 1957. The hardships of a life in exile had strengthened the habits of mutual support among the Chechens and the tenacity with which they clung to their ethnic traditions. Not all the Chechens, however, chose to return home. A big Chechen diaspora remained scattered across the Soviet Union, and some of its members used their entrepreneurial skills in the shadow economy or joined the criminal underworld as far back as the time of Khrushchev.

Secessionist sentiments emerged in Checheno-Ingushetia in 1991 as the Soviet Union's decline accelerated. A Chechen politician, Dzhokhar Dudayev (1944–96), quickly rose to the position of the chief champion of Chechen independence. He was a former Soviet officer who had risen steadily in the air force to assume command of the strategic air base at Tartu, Estonia, in 1987 with the rank of major general. Dudayev retired from the air force in May 1990 and returned to Grozny to devote himself to local politics. In November 1990 he was elected head of the Executive Committee of the unofficial opposition All-National Congress of the Chechen People, which advocated an enhanced political status for Chechnya as a separate republic within the USSR.

In August 1991, following the collapse of the conspiracy of the Communist hard-liners in Moscow, Dudayev and his supporters carried out a coup against the local Communist government in Checheno-Ingushetia. The union imposed on the Chechen and Ingush by the Soviet authorities was dissolved, and Checheno-Ingushetia was divided into two separate republics: Chechnya and Ingushetia. In October Dudayev was elected Chechen president in the rigged presidential election, in which less than 20 percent of those eligible to vote took part.[4] In November he unilaterally declared Chechnya's independence from the Russian Federation. Russia's supreme legislature of the time—the Congress of People's Deputies—immediately declared the election of the Chechen president illegal and his decrees devoid of legal force.

Although Russia refused to recognize Chechnya's move toward secession, it hesitated to use force against the separatists. In addition, the federal authorities were absorbed by an internal political crisis caused by the fierce confrontation between different branches of power in Moscow in 1992–93. Dudayev exploited the difficult situation in Russia to strengthen his authoritarian regime and to prepare for the time when Russia would be inevitably compelled to turn its attention to the secessionist province. In a short period of time a compact, well-trained, and well-equipped illegal army was built up in Chechnya. Most of its commanding corps was drawn from the former Soviet military, many of whom had had the experience of the Afghan war behind them. Aslan Maskhadov, for instance, the head of staff of Dudayev's armed units, had been a commander of a Soviet artillery regiment during the Afghan campaign. Simultaneously, Dudayev's regime actively recruited mercenaries from the Baltic states, Tajikistan, Azerbaijan, Ukraine, Afghanistan, Turkey, and other countries, selecting, as a rule, fighters with experience in guerrilla and terrorist warfare in mountains and urban areas. Many of the Chechen militants had been tested in armed conflicts in the territory of the former Soviet Union, including Karabakh and Abkhaziya.

Dudayev's regime used psychological and physical terror against the Russian military personnel stationed in the province to provide his army units with modern weapons and military equipment. In 1991–92 Moscow was compelled to withdraw its troops from the province to avoid major bloodshed. However, substantial munitions stores were left behind, including 42 tanks, 270 planes, 139 artillery systems, and loads of other military equipment.[5] All this weaponry was illegally appropriated by Dudayev's clique and distributed to the Chechen armed units. In hindsight, the biggest mistake of the political and military leadership of the Soviet Union and Russia was that it failed to prevent the seizure of huge stocks of modern weapons and military equipment of the Soviet army by Dudayev's detachments. The rebels' military units led by the former commander of a Soviet strategic air force division were equipped on a par with the armed forces of some smaller western European countries.

In 1993–94 the federal government abstained from intervening directly in Chechnya, using instead the tactics of providing military and financial support to armed Chechen opposition groups, which tried repeatedly but unsuccessfully to depose Dudayev by force. Fighting between the Chechen government and the opposition escalated gradually in the autumn of 1994, intensifying sharply at the end of November. On 10 December Yeltsin ordered the borders of Chechnya sealed, and the following day Russian troops entered Chechnya with the intention of disarming the illegal armed detachments of separatists and restoring constitutional order in the province.

Russian troops made slow and very costly progress toward Grozny, the capital, amid a growing chorus of criticism of Russian involvement—in Chechnya itself, among many Russian civilians and politicians, even in the military, and almost universally abroad. Russian troops had not secured Grozny by year's end, as had initially been planned. Augmented Russian forces totaling perhaps 40,000 troops managed to take Grozny in March 1995, but at the cost of heavy civilian casualties. Militarily defeated, the rebels took to the southern hills of

Chechnya and launched daring attacks on the occupying Russian forces. Instead of retaliating with its full military might, the actions of the Russian army remained muddled and inconclusive. With little public support for its mission and without a clear understanding of the war's aims, a demoralized Russian army was bogged down in a humiliating and bitter war for nearly two years.

A rapprochement between the warring sides became possible only after April 1996, when Dzhokhar Dudayev was killed in the fighting. Yeltsin handed responsibility for dealing with the situation in Chechnya to the ambitious retired general Alexander Lebed, who had been appointed secretary of Russia's influential Security Council. He immediately made trips to the breakaway republic to meet with both the Chechen separatists and the Russian military commanders, and by the end of August 1996 he had negotiated a cease-fire that included the agreement to defer a decision on Chechen independence for five years. The cease-fire made it possible for federal troops to withdraw from Chechen territory and for elections to be planned. By the end of the year Russian troops had left the province and Chechnya was, in all but name, an independent state.

In January 1997 former guerrilla leader and Dudayev's head of staff Aslan Maskhadov was elected president of Chechnya. But the territory remained divided among local warlords, and it was questionable how much control Maskhadov exercised outside the capital. Under Maskhadov the breakaway republic continued to assert that it was a sovereign state, but no coherent state structure came into being. The province became split into a maze of small entities, each headed by a warlord. Nearly two-thirds of the republic's population voted with their feet against "independence" forced on them by leaders like Dudayev and Maskhadov.

The chief causes of the war and the reasons that prompted Yeltsin to adopt the military option to resolve the problem of a mutinous territory within Russian borders in December 1994 and again in September 1999 seem to be the following.

"Gangsters' Paradise"

Dudayev's policies were fraught with serious legal, economic, and criminal consequences. They severely undermined or completely destroyed the republic's health care, education, and social security systems. Even before the first, December 1994, invasion, tens of thousands of refugees had fled the province. Dudayev's aggressively nationalistic, anti-Russian policies began to affect not only the Chechen economy, but also Russia as a whole. Russia's economic ties with the newly independent Transcaucasian states of Georgia, Armenia, and Azerbaijan were severely disrupted. Train robberies became common with hundreds of trains and thousands of carriages plundered. Ninety percent of petroleum products produced in Chechnya were sold abroad illegally with the spoils appropriated by the republic's leaders.[6] Chechnya became Russia's main hub of financial fraud, where huge amounts of counterfeit banknotes and fraudulent payment documents were forged causing massive damage to Russia's financial system. From 1991 to 1994 alone, Russia's economic losses caused by the "Chechen factor" amounted to $15 billion.

The removal of all judicial, customs, and tax controls by the Chechen authorities transformed the province into a safe haven for criminals from all over Russia. Each month from 100 to 150 unsanctioned international flights were made from the Grozny airport.[7] Chechnya became a transit base for drugs and weapons smuggling. Some of the Chechen warlords turned drug barons, owning heroine-producing facilities. The illicit drug industry yielded profits comparable to or better than those from oil extraction and refining. Chaos and economic dislocation created ideal conditions for criminal business when the only means of subsistence for many locals became working in hemp and poppy fields or pushing drugs through Chechen criminal networks across Russia, the Transcaucasian region, the Baltic states, and Eastern Europe.

Maskhadov's administration tried to overcome the degradation of Chechen society by attempting to reorient the republic's state and judicial systems toward Islamic tenets and values and even by seeking to institute a code of Islamic laws known as Shariat. The move to Shariat was designed to strengthen the presidential authority by giving it an elevated religious status and to use strict Shariat norms to combat the rising crime rate. However, the introduction of the Shariat code had an opposite effect. Far from propping up Maskhadov's authority, it led to a complete disintegration of the judicial system, as armed groups took the law into their own hands under the banner of enforcing Islamic norms.

The Threat of a Secessionist Chain Reaction

Dudayev's ultimate objective was not just the secession of Chechnya from Russia. He sought to transform the entire North Caucasus into an Islamic republic, in which Chechnya would play a preeminent role. Dudayev's imperial cravings could have resulted in the secession of the entire Russian North Caucasus with a population of some twenty-five million, including Chechnya, Dagestan, Ingushetia, and North Ossetiya. Moreover, the implementation of these messianic ambitions could have led to a major conflagration in the Transcaucasian region as a whole, where Islam is by no means the dominant religion. Yeltsin was swayed by the arguments of his advisers that it was preferable to nip the contagion in the bud in the territory of Chechnya before it spread to the whole of the area. Moreover, Russia's consent to Chechnya's secession could have sparked a separatist chain reaction, threatening to engulf not just North Caucasus, but numerous ethnic territories in other parts of the Russian Federation, including the ethnic-national republics of Tatarstan, Bashkortostan, Kalmykiya, Buryatiya, Tuva, and Yakutiya.

The Oil Factor

From the time of Brezhnev, the Russian economy has come to depend to a considerable extent on the export of oil as one of the main sources of hard currency revenues. Chechnya had substantial oil reserves. Even more importantly, the pipelines were built through its territory to carry oil from the rich fields of Azerbaijan to Russia's seaports. Chechnya provides the gateway to the Caspian and central Asia, which holds a substantial share of world oil and natural gas reserves. The safety of those pipelines could hardly be guaranteed by Dudayev's regime.

Some analysts interpret the events in the region as a global-strategic game played by the major world powers in their struggle for access to natural resources.[8] The competition had begun as far back as the early nineteenth century, when the British began their "Great Game" for the control of the mineral resources of the Caspian region. Their plans, however, were thwarted by the Russian revolution and the creation of the Soviet Union. During the Second World War one of Nazi Germany's key objectives in invading the Soviet Union was to gain control of the Caucasian oil supplies, but their defeat at Stalingrad dashed these intentions. Following the collapse of the Soviet Union, the "Great Game" has revived with new intensity. At present, all major transnational energy companies are involved in the exploration and exploitation of natural resources in the former Soviet republics of the Caspian region.

The independence of Chechnya and its hostility to Russia would automatically exclude or seriously impede Russia's participation in major international projects on transporting the mineral resources of Azerbaijan, Kazakhstan, and Turkmenistan through the Russian North Caucasus into Europe. The turmoil in Chechnya made the old pipeline of Baku–Makhachkala–Grozny–Tikhoretsk–Novorossijsk, which crossed the mutinous territory, unsafe. Russia proposed a new northern route for the pipeline, Baku–Makhachkala–Kizliar–Budyonovsk–Tikhoretsk–Novorossijsk, which would bypass Chechnya. However, some interested countries, including the United States, favored an alternative southern route, which would go through Georgia and Turkey to the Mediterranean, bypassing the Russian territory altogether.

It is possible that secret services of the countries involved manipulated Dudayev's separatists and used Chechen terrorism as a tool in their struggle against the Russian proposal for the oil transportation route. This view of the events in and around Chechnya interprets the two major and high-profile terrorist raids made by the Chechen bandits to Budyonovsk in June 1995 and to Kizliar in January 1996, accompanied by mass hostage taking and the killing of innocent civilians, as attempts to spread the unrest to southern Russia and Dagestan, to prove that Russia was incapable of ensuring the security of the pipeline in its territory and thus frustrate the Russian plan of the northern pipeline bypass.[9] According to this theory, the invasion of Dagestan by the Chechen armed units in August 1999 marked a renewed attempt to destabilize the situation in this part of the Russian Federation, drag Dagestan into an armed conflict, and bury the plan of the northern pipeline bypass for good.

Disaffection with the Results of the "Chechen Revolution"

On 2 August 1999 the Chechen armed detachments invaded Dagestan hoping to destabilize the situation in the neighboring republic by drawing on the support of the large Chechen minority there. Substantial Russian forces were immediately deployed in Dagestan to repel the Chechen armed units. The leaders of Dagestan demanded that Maskhadov dissociate himself from the Chechen warlords who led their units into Dagestan and condemn the invasion. Maskhadov, however, refused to do so. In September the Chechen separatists were blamed for the terrorist acts unheard of in Russian history: four residential blocks were razed to the ground by bomb explosions, one in Dagestan, two in Moscow, and one in southern Russia, causing hundreds of casualties. The Dagestan affair and the horrendous explosions across Russia sealed the fate of Chechen independence. The Russian leadership mounted a large-scale antiterrorist operation involving army units and the police and succeeded in routing organized armed detachments of the separatists.

If in 1995 nearly two-thirds of the Russian population were against the military solution of the Chechen problem, in 1999 an equal share of the population supported the preservation of Russia's territorial integrity by force of arms. The reasons for this turnabout in the popular mood in relation to the Chechnya problem are not hard to figure. Russian society became completely disaffected with the results of the "Chechen revolution," as the so-called fighters for national self-determination revealed their true colors as cutthroats and terrorists, blowing up residential blocks. Tired of economic and political instability and military reverses, Russian society yearned for victory. The news of the military successes of the federal troops in repelling the attacks of Chechen armed bands in Dagestan gave people hope that the Chechen problem could be resolved by military means after all and that the government's strong-armed tactics could work in stabilizing Russia's situation as a whole. These hopes were associated, first of all, with the rising political star of Vladimir Putin, who was appointed prime minister several days after the start of the Chechen invasion of Dagestan.

In addition, NATO's military operation in Kosovo in the spring of 1999 had provided a demonstration to Russian political and military elites of the viability of the military solution. "If the West is allowed to pursue its political objectives by bombing civilian targets in a foreign country, then surely nothing can stop us doing the same in our own country," was the sentiment shared by many among the Russian military.

The cost of the two Chechen campaigns has been very high both for the Chechens and for Russians. Thousands of Russian soldiers and officers have lost their lives, countless innocent civilians have become victims of Chechen terrorism or have been caught up in massive aerial and artillery attacks of the federal troops on rebellious villages and in the capital of Grozny. Nevertheless, the second Chechen war seems to show that the army and Russian society at large now understand more clearly than in 1994–96 what is at stake in this conflict. Separatism may survive in the pacified Chechnya for some time as a political tendency, but it is unlikely to revive as a military-terrorist movement.[10]

Chapter Twenty-One

Prospects for the New Century

Who Is Putin?

When on 9 August 1999 Yeltsin appointed the relatively unknown Vladimir Putin as his fifth prime minister in seventeen months and even designated him as his desired successor, the news was met with disbelief, ridicule, and sarcasm both at home and abroad. Yeltsin's suggestion that Putin was a realistic candidate to succeed him was interpreted as yet another sign of his woeful mental decline. His exuberant description of Putin's qualities and potential as the man best equipped to "renew the great country, Russia, in the twenty-first century" certainly stirred amusement. Most of Moscow's Kremlin watchers warned that, in any case, a seal of approval from such an unpopular president was as good as the kiss of death for Putin's political ambitions. Back then nobody believed it possible that this untested faceless bureaucrat, who never in his life had been elected to any position, could ascend to become head of state within six months, winning the presidential elections in March 2000 with almost 53 percent of the vote.

Putin's rise to power was important beyond the fact that this was Russia's first constitutional presidential succession since the collapse of communism. His accession has brought ideas, approaches to governance, and new faces to the Kremlin that are likely to define the priorities and character of the Russian government for the next decade and even beyond. It has solidified the presence of post-Communist political elites, which support a strong state but not the restoration of the Soviet regime or the undoing of the main accomplishment of the post-Communist era—the division of Soviet state property. The broad support for Putin among Russia's regional bosses, the military, and the business community demonstrates that the post-Soviet elite has found its leader. But so, too, have many ordinary Russians. After the fall of the Soviet regime, Russians were looking for a new identity. They wanted a new face, a young and dynamic leader who would end the chaos but would not reverse the reforms. Putin's first public words and actions made the majority of the Russian people perceive him as their man of the hour.

Putin rose from a relatively obscure position as a Soviet intelligence officer during the cold war. He was born in 1952 to a working-class family in Leningrad (now St. Petersburg). An overachiever, Putin excelled in his studies, particularly German, wrestling, and the humanities. After graduating from the law faculty of Leningrad State University in 1975, he began a fifteen-year career with the KGB's foreign intelligence arm, stationed in Leningrad and East Germany. In the late 1980s, with the Soviet Union facing collapse, Putin retired from the KGB with the rank of colonel and quickly began to build a respectable career in reformist politics.

In the early 1990s, Putin joined St. Petersburg's local government, first as an aide and then as deputy mayor to Anatoly Sobchak, St. Petersburg's first post-Soviet elected mayor. Putin's relationship with Sobchak, an influential leader in the first wave of democratic reformers of the Gorbachev years, was important, allowing him to burrow deeper into the reform movement. An efficient executive, Putin quickly became a key player in the St. Petersburg administration. Sobchak relied heavily on him for day-to-day management of the city's affairs, especially in the area of international investments. Putin was involved in attracting companies such as Coca-Cola and the BNP-Dresdner Bank to St. Petersburg, in setting up the city's first hard currency exchange, and in privatizing state assets, such as hotels. In short, he quickly became the man to see if one wanted to do business in St. Petersburg.

In 1996 Sobchak was voted out of office, and Putin went too, resigning. But his boss's defeat set the stage for Putin's move to Moscow, where he suddenly got onto a remarkably fast career track through the ranks of the Kremlin bureaucracy. First occupying the position of deputy to the powerful Pavel Borodin, the Kremlin's estates manager, he was then named deputy chief of the presidential administration in charge of relations with Russia's diverse regions. This position offered Putin unique influence over regional leaders who were tainted with corruption. In 1998 Putin was promoted to chief of the secret police, the Federal Security Service (better known by its Russian acronym FSB), which was the successor to the KGB's Second Chief Directorate (internal security).

By mid-1999 Putin rose to become one of the most powerful men in the Kremlin—in a quiet, behind-the-scenes way. He performed his tasks, as he had already done in St. Petersburg under Sobchak, as efficiently and discreetly as possible, without a sign of political ambition of his own and in complete loyalty to his superiors. Yeltsin was impressed with

Putin's cold efficiency and entrusted him with the most sensitive missions. In early 1999 he was made secretary of the Security Council, the powerful advisory body that coordinates the activities of Russia's armed forces, security agencies, and police. Putin was instrumental in the firing of Prosecutor General Yury Skuratov, who had authorized the investigations into members of Yeltsin's inner circle for corrupt activities. His extreme loyalty and great energy must have finally convinced Yeltsin that he found in Putin a suitable successor. In early August 1999 Putin was made prime minister and was "officially" named by Yeltsin heir apparent to the presidency.

Determined to boost its protégé's chances, the Kremlin hurled the full weight of government-friendly media behind Putin. A bitter, scandal-mongering campaign was launched against his potential rivals in the presidential race, especially those who were seen as a threat to the Kremlin elite. For example, Evgeny Primakov, a well-respected politician and a former prime minister, was depicted as an old and frail has-been; and Yury Luzhkov, the popular Moscow mayor, was painted as a dishonest crook. But the deployment of the power resources of the "Kremlin Family" to back Putin cannot alone explain the comet-like rise of his popularity ratings. The forty-seven-year-old former KGB officer managed to project an image of a youthful and energetic leader, a man of integrity and quiet dignity capable of putting an end to the drift and chaos of the Yeltsin era.

In almost every respect, he could not be more different from his mentor. Far from charismatic, he rarely smiled and talked with clipped sentences in an immensely popular, no-nonsense style, reinforcing the image of a doer rather than a talker. His most memorable soundbites are coarse, matching his tough image. Pledging to track down Chechen rebels, he promised "to rub them out, even in the toilet." Launching a campaign against corruption, he said officials on the take would be "squashed like rats," Oddly enough, despite having been at the center of Kremlin politics since 1996, he was not regarded as a member of Yeltsin's court cabal and maintained a patina of toughness and incorruptibility associated with his KGB origins. His youthfulness, physical health, and energy were in stark contrast to the aging and ailing Yeltsin. Television images of Putin flying a fighter plane, inspecting a battleship, practicing judo, and skiing down mountain slopes reinforced the message that he was no softy. His youth and vigor quickly endeared him to various sectors of the Russian electorate. Women, in particular, were pleased to see a presidential candidate capable of projecting quite a different image from the traditional Russian stereotype of an unsporty, drinking, and smoking male.

Even more important was the message that his public words and actions conveyed to the people tired of post-Soviet chaos and arbitrary rule. His political thought was made public for the first time at the end of December 1999 in a programmatic article written by staff members of the Center for Strategic Studies, established on his initiative. The article, "Russia at the Turn of the Millennium," was posted on the Internet and was seen by many as his manifesto for the presidency outlining his vision.[1]

Putin's main thesis is that Russia can regain its former status as a "great power" only by combining the principles of a market economy and democracy with Russia's realities. Russia is not yet ready for classical liberalism, and will not soon, if ever, come to resemble the United States or Britain. The experience of the 1990s has shown that mechanical copying of other nations' experience does not guarantee success. Russia needs to find its own model of transformation.

Putin underscores the idea that economic recovery and growth do not result just from economic factors, but are driven even more by fundamental intellectual, ideological, and moral attitudes. He calls for a reform program based on "a new Russian idea," claiming that, by contrast to the Soviet era, this is no uniform, state-imposed ideology, but represents the basic national values that citizens voluntarily support. In effect, this is a call for reforms that take into account the political culture of the overwhelming majority of Russians. This culture is an alloy, which combines "traditional Russian values which have stood the test of the times" with "universal general humanitarian values" that have taken root in Russia as a result of modernization and westernization.

It is those characteristics that Putin singles out as a core of Russian traditional values, which may, perhaps, provide the key to explaining the basic elements of his political views. He puts special emphasis on patriotism, social protection, and a strong state. Putin speaks of positive patriotism, based not on "nationalist conceits and imperial ambitions," but on a "feeling of pride in one's country, its history and accomplishments." It is a patriotism springing from the belief that "Russia was and will remain a great power" as an effect of "the inseparable characteristics of its geopolitical, economic and cultural existence."

Putin also emphasizes Russia's collectivist ethos that has "always prevailed over individualism." Russian collectivism is a form of corporatism, based on paternalistic relations between the state and society. Paternalistic sentiments have struck deep in Russian society: "The majority of Russians are used to connecting improvements in their own condition more with the aid and support of the state and society than with their own efforts, initiative and flair for business. And it will take a long time for this habit to die."

All this has conditioned an exceptionally important role of the state and its structures in the life of the country and its people: "For Russians a strong state is not an anomaly which should be got rid of. Quite the contrary, they see it as a source and guarantor of order and the initiator and main driving force of any change." In Putin's opinion, there is little point speculating whether the Russian tradition of a strong, paternalistic state and collectivist forms of activity is good or bad: "The important thing is that such sentiments exist. What is more, they still prevail. That is why they cannot be ignored."

Some Western commentators have been quick to interpret Putin's emphasis on Russia's established values as the upholding of the decisively anti-Western, antiliberal, and antidemocratic traditions of the tsarist and Soviet history of government and ideas. Putin's message, however, is more complex and stresses the need for a synthesis of traditional national values with what he describes, by drawing on the vocabulary of *perestroika*, as "supra-national universal values." These have entered Russian mentality and political culture in more recent decades and include freedom of expression, freedom to travel abroad, individual property rights, freedom of enterprise, and other fundamental political rights and human liberties. Only on the basis of a fusion of the traditional mores with modernizing influences can Russian society hope to overcome its internal disunity and find a path of development that would be desirable for and attractive to the overwhelming majority of Russians.

It is important to emphasize that Putin's philosophy of a strong state does not hark back to the Soviet era of central planning. He knows that Russia needs a fully functioning, well-regulated, private-sector economy to thrive. At the same time, he has learned the lesson of Gorbachev and Yeltsin's periods, which have vividly shown that Russia needs a strong central government to tackle its problems, from the struggling economy to the unruly regions. Putin sees the state as "an efficient coordinator of the country's economic and social forces that balances out their interests, optimizes the aims and parameters of social development and creates conditions and mechanisms of their attainment." He admits that such a remit exceeds the liberal formula, which limits the state's role in the economy to devising rules of the game and controlling their observance: "With time, we are likely to evolve to this formula. But today's situation necessitates deeper state involvement in the social and economic processes."

Most crucially, Putin's vision draws a decisive line under the recent times of revolutionary upheavals and cataclysms. Putin strongly condemns radicalism of every hue, be it Communist, national-patriotic, or radical-liberal, and vows to offer the nation a "strategy of Russia's revival and prosperity implemented only by evolutionary, gradual and prudent methods." Putin's accent on gradualism emphasizes the need for political stability, social accord, and ensuring decent living standards for Russian citizens.

The image that Putin's article and his subsequent public statements project is that of a rational politician who is both a statist and a liberal conservative. Guided by what he considers to be Russia's national interests, he is a supporter of order and discipline, but one who understands the need for Russia to lure foreign investment and develop market mechanisms. His priorities are a strong Russia, capable of standing up, politically and economically, for itself; a strong state, which has the ability and the will to enforce its authority on the civil society; and a strong center, which keeps the regions under control. His vision of a strong state power does not spell the reversal of the process of political and economic liberalization, but only the removal of the distortions, which had rendered Russia weak.

Putin's vision of a developed, prosperous, and reinvigorated Russia resonates with prevailing attitudes in Russian society. Some compare him to Yuri Andropov and the Chilean general Augusto Pinochet, but his supporters choose instead Charles de Gaulle, the democratically elected patriotic French general with an autocratic style. They say that even in a democratic society a political leader could be strong in enforcing the state authority if his goal is to bring to the people the benefits of the free market without the evils of the corporate jungle and to encourage private firms without letting them dictate to the state. Russia seems to have found in Putin a strong and able statesman who may be able to curb the free-for-all nature of post-communist politics and business practices, and uphold discipline, law, and order.

Recentralizing the State

Putin's ascendancy demonstrated that Moscow was willing to use its massive military might to establish central control and repel any threats to its rule. Even as prime minister, Putin was given far-reaching control over defense, internal affairs, and security. Ostensibly, he received his vast prerogatives to provide effective leadership of the military operation against Chechen-based rebels: in early August 1999 they had invaded next-door Dagestan, a constituent territory of the Russian Federation, trying to declare it an Islamic republic against the will of the Dagestanis. In response to the incursions by Chechen militants, Putin ordered the Russian army to expel them from Dagestan, which they did. Then, in September 1999, blaming the Chechens for a series of terrifying apartment-block bombings in Russian cities, including Moscow, he told the troops to continue into Chechnya, to root out and destroy the rebels. His leadership of the operation was the chief factor in his soaring ratings and allowed Putin to present himself as defender of the fatherland, determined fighter against terrorism, and war leader even before he became president.

Some commentators believe that, by presenting the war in the separatist region as a "counterterrorist operation," Putin cynically used the brutal battle as a platform for his own political ambitions and a military vehicle for electoral victory. Some Russian journalists and politicians even suspect that the authorities might have had a hand in the mysterious apartment-block bombings, which were presented as "terrorist attacks" and used as the war's ostensible justification. There is no hard evidence either way, and Putin calls the very suggestion "immoral." But the media's exaggerated portrayal of the war as righteous self-defense against international Islamic terrorism certainly helped the obscure, newly appointed prime minister to gain rapidly in popularity. In a matter of weeks he won himself such unanimous support on the Chechen issue that any politician who dared to voice doubt about the war risked being branded a traitor.

There is no doubt that the Chechen war played into Putin's hands, transforming him into a national political figure and helping to gain the presidency. Even though the assault on Chechnya was waged brutally, most Russians backed the war for obvious reasons. Chechnya's self-proclaimed independence had turned the rebellious territory into an enclave of lawlessness, hostage taking, and even instances of slavery, and Russia had to address the security challenge that this posed. Indeed, the threat to the integrity of Russia from Chechnya was quite real. As for the military, it embraced the war as a chance to rehabilitate its image following defeats in the Afghanistan war (1979–89) and the first Chechen war (1994–96). The Russian military also saw the war as an opportunity to send a signal to Russia's neighbors, as well as NATO, that Russia would deal with the Islamic rebels in a firm manner without letting itself be ruffled by the criticism of Western governments and human rights organizations. Finally, it was a signal to the Russian Federation's other ethnically based regions that separatism would be crushed with an iron fist. In short, the military success in Chechnya promised big political gains in several directions simultaneously, including reviving territorial unity, boosting national pride, strengthening the military's morale, and upholding Russia's power and international standing.

However, the gains came at a price: thousands of civilians, Russian soldiers, and Chechen fighters have been killed in the war, and an estimated 250,000 people are refugees. Nevertheless, the war remains popular in Russia, and Putin continues to endorse it. By the start of 2001 it looked as if Russian generals had done their part and smashed the rebels' main formations. At the end of January Putin took control of the war away from the Ministry of Defense and gave it to the special services, but he emphasized that Russia's military campaign would continue. Putin's plan appears to be to scale back, eventually, the Russian military presence in the Northern Caucasus republic from the current officially estimated 80,000 troops to a permanent garrison of about 20,000.

Simultaneously, political power is to be gradually delegated to the Kremlin-appointed leaders of Chechnya's administration, while law enforcement will be, little by little, entrusted to armed Chechen police forces. Some see this attempt at "re-Chechenizing" the province (that is to say, putting Chechens back in charge of the civil administration) as an old colonial tactic to try to get local forces to do the fighting for somebody else. Such critics point out that neither "Vietnamization" in the war in Vietnam nor "Afghanization" of the Soviet Union's war in Afghanistan worked properly for either the United States or the former USSR. "Re-Chechenization" could also be part of a propaganda effort designed by the Kremlin to convince Russians and the international community that the war in Chechnya is over and that civil conditions there are normalizing, despite the deadly clashes that are taking place on an almost daily basis.

The reality, however, is that ethnic Chechen administrators who collaborate with the federal authorities become prime assassination targets of the terrorists. Despite the fact that the separatists have been contained militarily, with their organized armed detachments routed or dispersed, hopes of outright victory in the near future remain dim, and landmine and guerrilla warfare is likely to drag on for a long time. Sooner or later, ways need to be found to halt the constant stream of Russian losses and to stem the inexorable erosion of public support for the seemingly endless bloody conflict. It appears that only a political agreement with the Chechens can do this, and Putin may turn out to be the only person in Russia with the credibility to cut a deal with the separatists. There are

signs that the federal authorities are broaching the prospect of negotia-
tion through intermediaries, such as liberals in the Duma.

In his drive to recentralize political authority, Putin's government
sought to deal not simply with Chechnya but with the more general phenomenon of a loosening of control of the center over the periphery.
Under Yeltsin some provincial bigwigs had abused the power, which
they had wrested from Moscow after the collapse of the Soviet Union.
To reestablish a normal state, Putin needed to reverse a decade of fragmentation of Russia's eighty-nine regions and republics and stop the
confederalization of the country, when there were regions, which grew
into independent fiefdoms or even claimed sovereignty.

In his first substantive policy move, Putin acted boldly to rebuild central authority and restructure the federation. He began by decreeing, in
May 2000, a division of Russia into seven federal districts under
Kremlin-appointed governors-general. Their assignment was to establish
"a single legal and economic space in Russia," and the implied brief was
to restrain the power of the regional barons, dismantle regional authoritarian regimes, and bring unruly governors into line by anticorruption
investigations.

In economic terms, many of the regions are minuscule, and there is
little cooperation between them by international standards. It is hardly
surprising that regional bosses have become "oligarchs" on a local scale.
Much of their power stemmed from their control of the local outposts
of federal agencies such as Interior, Procurator's, Federal Security
Service, regional branches of the Central Bank, and tax police. Most of
the local leaders used the regional offices of federal ministries to their
own political and private advantage. Now these agencies were to be
taken out of their hands and put under the control of the president's
plenipotentiaries.

In theory, the new scheme could create a powerful new layer of government, serving as a "buffer" between the president and the regional
leaders and thus diminishing the latter in status and importance. Some
commentators, concerned about the fact that five out of the seven presidential envoys happened to be generals of the security apparatus, interpreted their appointment to supervise the elected governors as an
indication that the president was slowly reverting to the repressive
police-state mentality that ruled the Kremlin in the Soviet Union.
Certainly, the institution of "supergovernors," answerable only to the
president, helps to strengthen the vertical structure, with the Kremlin at
the apex. Whether this will lead to the return of a police state or will
result in more effective government is too early to say. There are encour-

aging signs, however, that the new system does help to curb the arbitrary power of autocratic regional princes in some parts of the country, including the Russian Far East Maritime Province, where Governor Evgeny Nazdratenko's notorious misrule continued unchecked for almost a decade. In February 2001 Nazdratenko was finally "persuaded" by the Kremlin to send in his "voluntary" resignation.

Local governors' autonomy was further significantly cut by the president's regional reform package passed by the Duma in June 2000. The laws stripped the regional governors and the heads of the regional parliaments of their ex officio mandate in the Federation Council and replaced them with regional representatives elected or confirmed by the regional legislatures. As a result, the regional bosses were transformed from serious players on the national political stage to purely local politicians. The loss of direct control over Russia's legislative agenda also meant the loss of bargaining power in negotiations with the different centers of power, especially the federal agencies located in Moscow. What is more, deprived of their seats in the upper house, the governors lost their parliamentary immunity and could now be liable for criminal prosecution. The new laws also gave the president the power to recall regional governors or dissolve regional parliaments that do not observe federal laws.

In the first year of Putin's presidency, his all-out campaign to rebuild the central state has been largely successful and has produced a much more centralized structure, in which once-independent regional governors have been significantly undermined. The new system of vertical power, more tightly controlled by Moscow, is now in force. Legislative changes in the status of governors have led to a clearer delineation of duties between authorities of different levels and curbed the willful and arbitrary rule of certain of the regional bosses. However, given the long and often unsuccessful history of attempts by Moscow to centralize, it is too early to say whether the reform to control the Russian leviathan will work in the long run and will be effective against corrupt governors and in cutting through local vested groups.

"Deprivatizing" the State

During the first year of his presidency, in his efforts to recapture the state Putin pursued a two-pronged strategy, in which the measures to subdue the local princes were combined with an attack on the entrenched interests of semi-criminal financial and industrial magnates, the so-called oligarchs. The oligarchs' unholy alliance with senior members of the

Yeltsin regime had allowed them to fuse power and capital and achieve control over the lion's share of the national economy. Their dominance, especially over banking and the extraction of raw materials for export, had cost the state immense revenues. More importantly, their omnipotence and monopoly played a critical role in preventing the emergence of a working free market and in discouraging foreign investment in Russia. In effect, Putin faced the daunting task of dismantling the system of "robber capitalism," that thrived on Russia's insider privatization, allowing a handful of politically well-connected tycoons to manipulate the post-Soviet sell-off of state assets to their personal advantage.

The dimensions of the challenge that the oligarchs, organized crime, and corruption posed to Putin's leadership can hardly be overestimated. The situation in Russia demanded that Putin be an independent actor, and it was not at all certain whether he would be his own man or a mere puppet of Yeltsin's entourage, beholden to the same oligarchy that captured the Yeltsin regime. In the three months from January to March 2000, while he was acting president, Putin appeared to follow a fine line of honoring his former boss while simultaneously reinforcing his own independence: on the one hand, he signed a decree immunizing Yeltsin from future prosecution on any corruption charges; on the other, Putin fired from the Kremlin staff Tatiana Diachenko, Yeltsin's daughter and a target of corruption allegations. Her dismissal sent a signal that, whatever loyalty he felt, he was now the acting president. Finally, his election as president at the end of March 2000 gave Putin a popular mandate, a political base, and supreme institutional power as Russia's chief executive.

More importantly, in his campaign to take on the tycoons, he could count on the backing of ordinary Russians, fed up with greedy oligarchs, mafia gangs, shady banks that could not be trusted with savings, and other ills of "robber capitalism." His preelection pledge to "eliminate oligarchs as a class" resonated with the prevailing attitudes among the mass of Russian voters, tired of the situation, when crooked businessmen and corrupt politicians were left alone by the police and prosecutors, while a small group of super-rich ran the country. They voted for Putin in the hope that a strong leader would be able to impose law and order and rein in corruption and criminality.

In his first year as president Putin managed to ease the oligarchs' grip by a combination of different methods, including tighter regulation by the state of economic activity; tougher curbs on the power of the monopolies run by the oligarchs; efforts to set up a normal executive branch comprised not of politically ambitious individuals from different financial-industrial groupings and clans, but of technocrats; and, finally, criminal prosecution or the threat of launching criminal investigations to persuade the unwilling tycoons to return part of their ill-gotten assets.

Three cases, in particular, involving some of the more high-profile oligarchs, produced a compelling demonstration effect, enough to cow the rest of the business tycoons into submission. Two of these involve the powerful media barons Boris Berezovsky and Vladimir Gusinsky and the third, Putin's former boss Pavel Borodin. Boris Berezovsky, a friend of Yeltsin's daughter and the mastermind of the Kremlin's election victories since 1996, rewarded for his services with vast holdings in oil, aluminium, and media, became, arguably, one of the biggest casualties of the "antioligarch war." In a 1997 interview Berezovsky boasted that he and six other oligarchs owned economic empires controlling 50 percent of Russia's gross domestic product. He also bragged about his role in persuading ailing former president Boris Yeltsin to resign, and in promoting Putin into office. In the summer of 2000, this previously untouchable insider, who had attained fabulous wealth and influence during the past decade by getting close to the Kremlin, suddenly resigned his parliamentary seat and fled abroad. There is little doubt that he must have acted so promptly out of self-preservation after having got wind of impending charges of embezzlement and money laundering.

Vladimir Gusinsky's media empire was another logical place to start "deoligarchization." Gusinsky's vast media holdings, which included Russia's main independent station, NTV, had been amassed thanks to political connections and, first of all, to the backing his media outlets had provided to Yeltsin in his 1996 reelection campaign. In the run-up to the 1999 parliamentary and 2000 presidential elections the powerful media mogul is rumored to have demanded vast economic and financial concessions from Putin in return for the backing of his media empire. When his demands were met with refusal, Gusinsky's media supported the anti-Putin side in both elections. Following the elections, NTV continued to criticize Putin and his policies, reporting aggressively on the war in Chechnya, official corruption, and the embarrassing scandal surrounding the sinking of the submarine *Kursk* in August 2000.

The clouds over the media tycoon began to gather in the summer of 2000, when Gusinsky was arrested and jailed on charges of financial fraud. After three days, however, he was released, charges against him were dropped, and it looked as if he had agreed to give up his media empire in exchange for immunity from prosecution. Gusinsky then fled abroad, where he resumed the legal battle against NTV's powerful creditor Gazprom, which, goaded on by the Kremlin, strove to declare his business empire bankrupt and take control of the television company. The intense wrangle continued for ten months and involved an extradition battle in Spanish courts. Finally, in April 2001, Gazprom cobbled together a majority of shares in NTV and launched a coup: at an extraordinary meeting in Moscow shareholders unceremoniously fired the board and tossed out the company's general director and Gusinsky's close ally, Evgeny Kiselev. Gusinsky effectively lost control of NTV, but managed to escape criminal prosecution, as Spain refused to hand him over to Russia.

Even more intriguing is the case of Pavel Borodin, the Kremlin's former property manager, who used to control a vast empire of Russian government real estate, cars, and other assets. Under him the presidential property office embodied extravagance, secrecy, and corruption. At a time when Russia was all but bankrupt, Borodin spent hundreds of millions of U.S. dollars on redecorating some historic rooms in the Kremlin. Highly lucrative contracts for Kremlin renovations were awarded to a Swiss construction firm as part of an alleged kickback scheme. But the real source of his considerable behind-the-scenes political influence stemmed from the fact that the presidential property office oversaw the allocation of housing, cars, and other perquisites to members of the federal agencies located in the capital, including the elected Duma deputies and procurator general.

The delicacy of the situation for Putin was that his first Kremlin job, following his move to Moscow from St. Petersburg, was that of a deputy to Borodin. One of Putin's first acts on coming to power was to move Borodin to a different post: the chiefly ceremonial position of state secretary of the Russia-Belarus Union. But Borodin's real troubles began in January 2001, when he was arrested in the United States, under a Swiss arrest warrant for alleged money laundering, on his way to George W. Bush's inaugural celebrations. Borodin was held for three months in the federal detention center in Brooklyn pending a court decision on his extradition to Switzerland. He was finally handed over to the Geneva authorities, which released Borodin on a massive $3 million bail. He returned to Russia with his reputation irrevocably damaged.

It is significant that Putin consistently dodged the matter of defining his stance on the issue of Borodin's predicament at the hands of the American and Swiss law enforcement agencies and was extremely careful in his statements. Some of the explanations in the media of Borodin's arrest put his case in the context of Russia's domestic, rather than foreign, policy. Putin reportedly did not take action against Borodin in Russia to avoid a conflict with Boris Yeltsin's still very influential team, and with the help of Russian secret services "gave up" Borodin to Western justice.

Putin's approach of curbing the oligarchs may seem selective and arbitrary and is open to accusations of using the criminal justice system to cow political opponents and break them to the president's will. Nevertheless, it sent a clear signal that the days of the tycoons, who had been pulling many of the country's political strings, were over: there were now certain restraints on their activities, and they were no longer omnipotent. Putin managed to redefine the alliance with the elites and scale down the oligarchization of power, which had led Boris Yeltsin to a political trap and greatly weakened the federal center. In the first year of his presidency a new system of power was set up that normalized relations between the state and big business.

Putin's "dictatorship of law" may well be necessary to transform Russia from a barter economy run by robber tycoons, corrupt bureaucrats, and crime syndicates to a modern capitalist economy with a transparent civil service and judiciary. His methods of squeezing the oligarchs and frightening the governors cannot always be described as democratic. The problem is that it may well be impossible to create an effective state in Russia by purely democratic methods. As is now recognized even by more conservative free market thinkers, a limited but effective state is absolutely necessary to ensure the conditions for a working free market. Somehow, the power of the oligarchs, corruption, and organized crime have to be curbed, and a measure of discipline and honesty restored to the state service. So when Putin speaks of the need for a stronger state, he is reflecting not just the Russian tradition but also Russian realities.

Instead of unlimited freedom there should be freedom with certain limits, which the governors, oligarchs, and civil servants are obliged to observe. The introduction of rules is a sign not of curtailing liberties but of civilization. It has been noted that "liberal values are threatened just as thoroughly by state incapacity as by despotic power" and that "less state means less freedom."[2] The problem for Putin is whether or not he can rein in corruption without suffocating more acceptable forms of private economic activity. The business community should be able to engage in a dialogue with the state: not in the form of collusion of individual business barons with the authorities, but as a consolidated group able to articulate its common interests. The influential Russian Union of Industrialists and Entrepreneurs, which unites several thousand employers and business leaders, could potentially become a body capable of providing a framework that reconciles the interests of the state and business. The Union cooperates actively with relevant Duma committees and with the government and its ministries. Its members now participate in regular meetings with Putin, ironing out the rules of the relationship between power and business.

The success of Russia's economic reforms depends on Putin's ability to dismantle the system of "robber capitalism," which incubated in the ashes of the Soviet Union, and create the conditions of competition in the market that are equal for all. Russia, he correctly insists, needs a proper legal framework for undertaking the sort of economic reforms that could eventually bring it justice and equity as well as material prosperity. He has sworn to put social concerns at the center of economic policy to provide "more therapy, less shock." He has inducted some genuine reformers into his team. In the first year of his presidency he has made significant moves to reform taxes, to deregulate business, to secure protection for investors' rights, and to reform the land-holding system.

Putin's Russia is considerably more stable than it was during the turbulent end phase of the Yeltsin era. That is largely due to its economic recovery. In 2000 the Russian economy grew at a rate that would have been unimaginable a year before, with the gross domestic product rising 7.5 percent and industrial production, more than 9 percent.[3] Much of this was due to the oil price rise and the collapse in imports from August 1998. But the rapid rise in revenues from exports of oil and gas cannot alone explain the rapidity with which the Russian economy had turned around from its earlier years of shrinkage to an unmistakable tendency to growth. The recovery had deeper economic reasons and meant that Russia was at last beginning to reap some return from the substantial structural reforms it had actually undertaken. The best enterprises in various industries dashed ahead, stimulating significant growth not only in oil and gas extraction but also in industries involved in intermediary goods production and manufacturing, including chemicals, light manufacturing, pulp and paper, and machine building.

All these changes should give greater prominence to a new group of Russian entrepreneurs and small business owners, as well as magnates. They are mainly manufacturers who are interested in production for the market rather than sheer redistribution of the former Soviet state assets. They are getting weary of the leaden bureaucracy, corruption, illegality, and even violence that pervade Russia's business practices, and they rally to Putin's flag of restoring order to the anarchic business sector. They are interested in a transparent legal system and a sound banking system and will demand these reforms as Russia moves to the next stage of growth.

In short, they are Putin's natural allies in his efforts to transform Russia's murky business environment and put the economy on a sustainable growth path.

"Controlled" Democracy

Putin's clampdown on the media moguls, such as Berezovsky and Gusinsky, is part of a more general campaign to change what some analysts describe as a "media-political system," which took shape in the 1990s and which now hinders Putin's pursuit of a strong presidency and an effective state.[4] Under Yeltsin, when state institutions and political structures were enfeebled and unstable, the national TV shaped, to a great extent, the contours of the political system. When the party system was underdeveloped and when only one party—the Communists—could boast mass membership, the main TV stations assumed the functions of political parties. They played out a political show and determined the hierarchy of roles in the political arena. At times of elections, these roles were assigned "brand names" of parties and movements, for which the viewers were enjoined to vote.

In the media-political system the press and television became effective mechanisms of manipulating political power relationships and public opinion, and were used to great effect by the alliance of the media oligarchs and the Kremlin Family to pursue their political and commercial interests. Their concerted efforts brought about a perverted form of democracy—sometimes described as "manipulated democracy"—that dominated Russian politics in the 1990s.[5]

This system was possible as long as the state was prepared to put up with the presence of powerful and even quite independent players in the media-political system. Yeltsin's regime was tolerant toward the media for historical and utilitarian reasons. Following the first wave of privatization, when the mass media had been taken away from the Communists and handed over to the journalists, the media always supported Russia's first president at all key moments when the fate of his regime hung in the balance. With all his faults, Boris Yeltsin remained a guarantor of civil liberties and private ownership for the media community. However, the growing commercialization of the media brought new dangers to its freedom and reputation. Millions of rubles were spent to fan "wars of *kompromat*" and stage character assassinations by publication of compromising material. The oligarchs used their media empires to pursue their political and commercial battles. Through their control of TV and other media, they could create political crises in the country almost at will.

With Putin's appointment as prime minister and the onset of the new war in Chechnya, it became obvious that the media-political system would hardly be able to survive beyond the next parliamentary and presidential elections. The irony of the situation was that Putin owed his own elevation, to a great extent, to the mechanisms of the system. Putin's sudden rise out of nowhere was the work of the Kremlin strategists and their allies in the media, who created his neatly packaged media image, which scored such a success with the voters. Crucial electronic and other media outlets, including Russia's two main television stations, Channel 1 (ORT) and Channel 2 (RTR), controlled either by the government or pro-Putin businessmen, were consistent in promoting both his candidacy and the war in Chechnya. They waged sustained and often vicious attacks against Putin's rivals, the former prime minister Evgeny Primakov and Moscow's mayor Yury Luzhkov.

Having used the instrumentality of "manipulated democracy" to effect his ascent, Putin then proceeded to wrestle the levers of the media-political system from the hands of the media magnates. It is clear that Putin sees the media as a vital tool for shaping public opinion and achieving national accord on major political issues. These include, first and foremost, the war in Chechnya: Putin authorized stronger military controls over the media in the battle zone and appointed a wartime "media tsar," Sergei Yaztrzhembsky, to control the flow of information about the war to the press.

Putin's critics say that the attempts to impose tighter control of the media by the state bode poorly for freedom of speech and the future of the free press in Russia. Some believe that Putin's ultimate goal is not only to harass and intimidate, but also to stop criticism, control competition, and neutralize opposition. As a result of the campaign of taming the oligarchs, the state or its corporate allies now largely control more influential media.

Russian journalists accept that self-censorship is one likely defense strategy to state pressure. They point out that one problem in an underdeveloped civil society is there is no support from society for media freedom. However, most media practitioners think it is unlikely that the genie of media freedom can be put back in the bottle. Russia's major cities have now scores of independent TV stations, which include cable and satellite, providing alternatives or counterweights to the government-controlled TV channels. The news agencies and international broadcasters with their transmissions receivable in Russia also play a role in combating pressures on the media, while international media interests such as the Reuters news agency are now part of the substructure of Russian media and financial sectors. New technologies such as the Internet provide additional sources of information and publication. President Putin himself uses the Internet to publish his articles and speeches and has even announced a nationwide competition for the best design of the presidential Web site after his official site was criticized by one of the participants in Putin's on-line press conference of March 2001 for its boring look.

Putin's efforts to replace "democracy," manipulated by powerful political and economic clans, by a "state-controlled" democracy are seen in his attempts to reshape Russia's party-parliamentary system, as well as the state's relations with the media. The party that borrowed his name in the December 1999 Duma election—the Unity bloc—surprised everybody by almost winning, missing first place, which went to the Communists, by one percentage point. Unity was not a party at all, just a collection of people thrown together and placed on the ballot by the Kremlin spin doctors just a few months before the election. Its electoral success was assured by the support of the government-friendly media, which associated the party with Putin day after day in the news, enabling it to capitalize on Putin's very high public support.

The result of the election was a Duma in which the Kremlin could almost always muster the required number of votes needed to pass important bills by using the mechanism of a shifting coalition, that is, by drawing alternatively on the support of the liberals on the right or the Communists on the left. Virtually all the parties in the Duma, from diehard Communists to economic liberals, sound keen to give him a chance. Putin persuaded the Duma, after years of stalling, to ratify the Start-2 treaty, limiting long-range missiles, and the Comprehensive Test Ban Treaty. The deputies easily approved the 2001 budget with a speed never seen before. Even the seemingly incongruous concoction of state symbols—the classic fifteenth-century double-headed eagle of the Muscovite tsars, the eighteenth-century westernized imperial tricolor (both adopted by Yeltsin by decree), and the Soviet anthem—was overwhelmingly approved by the parliament. In short, the once-combative Duma has been transformed into an obliging mechanism of voting for the president's legislative initiatives.

In just one year of Putin's presidency the political landscape has changed drastically. In the Yeltsin era Yury Luzhkov, the mayor of Moscow, enjoyed unlimited power in the capital and even had presidential ambitions. Now he has thrown in the towel, surrendering completely to Putin's camp, and has even announced the imminent merger of his party Fatherland–All Russia (OVR in Russian) with the president's Unity bloc, his erstwhile archrival. If created, the new parliamentary coalition of Unity and OVR will remove completely any threat of noncompliance in the parliament. Moreover, two smaller factions—Russia's Regions and People's Deputy—hastened to join the two bigger organizers of the merger, also expressing their intention to become part of Putin's voting machine. The coordinating council of the four parliamentary factions will ensure a stable majority to rubber-stamp the Kremlin's legislative initiatives. As the four factions have together over 226 seats, they will be able to garner a simple majority in the 450-seat parliament.

The new coalition leaves out the Communists, who are now accorded the role of the opposition. But Putin has reined them in, and they have remained more or less resigned to his dominance. The liberal faction in the Duma, represented by Grigory Yavlinsky's Yabloko and the Union of Right-Wing Forces, headed by the liberals, such as Boris Nemtsov and Yegor Gaidar, strives to promote itself as a "third force," but has little real influence on the balance of power in the Duma. Moreover, the liberals and the Union of Right-Wing Forces firmly support the president in his initiatives to promote the development of the market economy.

The result of the Kremlin's efforts to reshape Russia's party-parliamentary system is the formation of a powerful center-right coalition designed to dominate the parliament for a long time and to prevent the left-wing forces from stalling reform or coming to power. In one year Putin has achieved support in parliament that Yeltsin could never even dream about. His strong leadership and the backing of the Duma could create a very real opportunity for genuine reform in Russia.

Putin's edifice of "controlled" democracy is now almost complete. Democratic institutions exist and function, but the Kremlin holds them on a tight leash. Opposition in the Duma is demoralized. The upper chamber of parliament—the Federation Council—has been bent to the president's will without putting up any serious resistance. With the governors sent back to mind their provinces and replaced by compliant bureaucrats, the formerly independent assembly of ambitious regional princes has been transformed into just another mechanism of giving approval to presidential initiatives.

It would be misleading, however, to dwell only on the "controlled" aspect of Putin's regime. In contrast to Yeltsin's "manipulated" democracy, which often mocked the very notion of democratic politics, Putin's version of democracy retains significant and real democratic substance. In one year he has been able to expand his political base beyond his initial circle of governors, military generals, and security officials to include the center-right, the nationalists, and some elements of the Communist electorate. He has consistently scored an unbelievable 70 to 75 percent approval rating in public opinion polls. Putin's social base of support is unique and is unlike that of any other leading politician in Russia: his supporters can be found in almost equal numbers in all sociodemographic categories—among men and women, the young and the old, better and less educated, urban dwellers and villagers, and so on. In other words, Putin's electorate is comprised of a remarkably representative cross section of the Russian population.

The secret of Putin's popularity is that for the first time in many decades the authorities have narrowed the gap dividing them from the people and have begun to register and take into account their expectations and problems. Putin is perceived by members of various sectors of the population as "theirs," that is, as someone they can relate to and understand and who knows about their problems and has the resources to address them. All this gives him important advantages if he decides to push through a tough package of major economic reforms.

To a large extent, the president has met the expectations of society to maintain stability and do away with revolutions, cataclysmic changes, personnel purges, and so on. The Russian people, tired of the chaos and injustice of Yeltsin's rule, and the socially dependent sectors of the population in particular (i.e., those groups, such as budget sector workers or pensioners, who rely heavily on the support of the state), have felt improvements in their socioeconomic situation: wages and pensions are regularly indexed to keep up with inflation, and social policies are now given greater priority in line with Russian traditions.

The development of the political system under Putin seems to have revived certain characteristics typical of the traditional Russian state. The prerogatives of the Russian leader—be it Moscow prince, all-Russian tsar, or Soviet general secretary—have traditionally been vast and autocratic and have also been hostile to pluralism. The worship of the leader is also an engrained Russian tradition and a need, which apparently is deeply entrenched in the Russian mentality. Even the suffering inflicted during the years of Stalin's cult has not provided sufficient immunity against a revival of attitudes of adulation and deference toward the supreme leader. Putin and his circle readily draw on these traditions and public attitudes in their efforts to reclaim the state. Analysts comment on the first signs of the leader's cult that became noticeable as the country marked the first anniversary of Putin's inauguration.[6] Books and brochures devoted to the president or describing the childhood years of "little Volodya" (diminutive for Vladimir) have saturated bookstores and newsstands. His portraits are produced in every desired format: one for the desk, another for the wall, and still others for official receptions.

Of course, any direct parallels with the past are superficial or even misleading. Putin rules by modern methods, using democratic processes and institutions. He is strongly against a return to the Soviet system and is committed to economic and judicial reforms. His political style verges on autocratic, but his strong social support among ordinary Russians and his genuine efforts to consolidate society give "Putinism" a democratic face. As a professed "gradualist," Putin realizes that, in light of Russia's historical legacies, it is not to be expected that the necessary institutional framework for good governance can be brought about overnight. Political traditions, customs, and forms of political behavior (e.g., paternalism, collectivism, and patronage networks) will in all probability continue for a long time. Putin understands that attempts to cancel them by decree are doomed to fail.

Finally, today's demand for a strong leader and the current power centralization reflect the weakness and ineffectiveness of the institutions of democracy in Russia. The institutions of a broad civil society—the press, political parties, free associations and others—are not yet well developed. The rule of law has not been well entrenched. In part, these weaknesses are a legacy of the Soviet police state of Putin's early career, when the Communist Party had a monopoly on power. In part, they are a hangover from Yeltsin's years, when the attempts at reformulating the relations between the state and society brought into being civic and media structures, which were taken over by corporatist actors and exploited as instruments of furthering clan and corporatist interests, rather than the public good. In this situation, the state, as it happened on more than one occasion before in Russian history, has to take on social and political functions that in mature democracies are performed by the institutions of civil society. State intervention is capable of solving major political problems and directing vital national efforts, but it can also delay the "coming of age" of public institutions of a fully fledged society.

Putin's ascendancy to power in the Kremlin marks yet another historic transformation in Russia. In a country where the political system has always been dominated by people, rather than laws and institutions, the change in leadership represents a change in direction more so than it would in Western democracies. Like many of Russia's rulers before him, Putin looks set to impose his indelible stamp on the country, and the first year of his presidency has already made his Russia very different from that of the Yeltsin era. His political thought and behavior seem to fit the country's current system, which remains a hybrid of democracy and authoritarianism. What is less known is how well Putin understands that heavy-handed state regulation and pervasive bureaucracy stifle democratic policies and economic freedom. His vision of revitalizing the primacy of the state in Russian lives is designed to overcome the neofeudal fragmentation of state authority inherited from Yeltsin's era, but may come at the expense of human rights, democracy, and media freedom. Does he realize that greater economic liberalism is linked to liberalism of the political kind? Will Putin's state be able to sponsor the development of a nationally conscious community? Can he orchestrate a society-powered remodernization that would be responsive to domestic consumer needs and integrated functionally into the global economy? Does he understand that technological innovation, advanced telecommunications, and venture capital, which are the engines of economic growth in the early twenty-first century, can thrive only in open and free societies? These are the questions, the positive answers to which will ensure Putin's valued place in Russian and world history.

Notes

Introduction

1. See A. K. Sokolov, "Konets sovetskoi istorii" (The end of Soviet history), in *Rossia na rubezhe XXI veka* (Russia on the threshold of the twenty-first century), edited by Yu. A. Poliakov and A. N. Sakharov (Moscow: Nauka, 2000), 238–69; p. 244.

1. "Old Regime" Russia

1. I elaborated on the thesis that the historical development of imperial Russia was predicated on paradoxes in *The Fragile Empire: A History of Imperial Russia* (New York and London: Continuum, 2001), 201–17.
2. See A. N. Sakharov, "Dinastia Romanovykh kak istoricheskii fenomen" (The Romanov dynasty as a historical phenomenon), *Nezavisimaia gazeta* (31 December 1997).
3. S. V. Kuleshov et al., *Nashe Otechestvo* (Our fatherland) (Moscow: TERRA, 1991), 1:202.

2. Political Culture

1. On the concept of Russian patrimonialism, see Richard Pipes, *Russia under the Old Regime* (London: Penguin, 1990).
2. For a detailed study of the effects of the socioeconomic and political changes of the 1990s on the mass consciousness and behavior of Russians, see M. K. Gorshkov, ed., *Rossia na rubezhe vekov* (Russia at the crest of the centuries) (Moscow: RIISNP, 2000).

3. Soviet Ideology

1. See, in particular, Karl Marx and Friedrich Engels, *The Communist Manifesto* (London: Penguin, 1985).
2. Mark 7:14–23, The New Testament (Nashville: The Gideons International).
3. See A. Z. Arabajan, *Notches on Time* (Moscow: Institute of Oriental Studies, 1998), 82.
4. Karl Marx, *Capital,* translated by Ben Fowkes (Harmondsworth: Penguin Books, 1990), 1:229.
5. Cited in ibid., 229–30.
6. Ibid., 254.
7. Ibid., 280.

4. The Soviet Political System

1. Vladimir I. Lenin, "The Proletarian Revolution and the Renegade Kautsky," in *The Lenin Anthology,* edited by Robert C. Tucker (New York: Norton, 1975), 466.
2. Vladimir I. Lenin, "April Theses," cited in Martin McCauley, *Octobrists to Bolsheviks: Imperial Russia, 1905–1917* (London: Arnold, 1984), 105–06.

5. Soviet Nationalities

1. Cited in Martin McCauley, *Octobrists to Bolsheviks: Imperial Russia, 1905–1917* (London: Arnold, 1984), 26.
2. Cited in Vladlen Sirotkin, *Demokratia po-russki* (Democracy Russian-style) (Moscow: MIK, 1999), 385.
3. See Andreas Kappeler, *Rossia—mnogonatsional'naia imperia. Vozniknovenie, istoria, raspad* (Russia as a multinational empire: Origins, history, and disintegration) (Moscow: Progress-Traditsia, 1997), 275.
4. Based on ibid., 292–94.

6. Serfdom—Capitalism—Socialism

1. R. W. Goldsmith, "The Economic Growth of Tsarist Russia," *Economic Development and Cultural Change* 9 (1960–61): 442.
2. Karl Marx, *Capital,* translated by Ben Fowkes (Harmondsworth: Penguin Books, 1990), 1:929.

7. The Beginnings of the Socialist Transformation

1. *History of the Communist Party of the Soviet Union (Bolshevik): Short Course,* authorized by the Central Committee of the CPSU (B.), 1938 (Moscow: Foreign Languages Publishing House, 1951), 343.

8. "Great Leap" to Socialism

1. See Neil Harding, *Leninism* (Basingstoke and London: Macmillan, 1996), 248–50.
2. Based on A. K. Sokolov, *Kurs sovetskoi istorii 1917–1940* (A course in Russian history, 1917–1940) (Moscow: Vysshaia shkola, 1999), 154.
3. A *kulak* household at that time had, on average, 1.7 cows and 1.6 heads of workstock, whereas an average middle peasant household had the same amount of cows and 1.2 heads of workstock. There were bigger differences between these two categories of peasantry in the value of the means of production in their possession. See S. V. Kuleshov et al., *Nashe Otechestvo* (Our fatherland) (Moscow: TERRA, 1991), 2:254.

4. Sokolov, op. cit., 185; V. Khutorskoi, *Istoria Rossii. Sovetskaia epokha (1917–1993)* (A history of Russia: Soviet epoch, 1917–1993) (Moscow: Fazis, 1994), 61.
5. Sokolov, op. cit., 201.
6. Kuleshov et al., *Nashe Otechestvo,* 2:276.

9. Stalinism

1. V. Khutorskoi, *Istoria Rossii. Sovetskaia epokha (1917–1993),* 64.
2. Sokolov, *Kurs sovetskoi istorii 1917–1940,* 256.
3. Cited in Kuleshov et al., *Nashe Otechestvo,* 2:215.
4. S. V. Kuleshov et al., *Politicheskaia istoria: Rossia-SSSR-Rossiiskaia Federatsia* (A political history: Russia–USSR–Russian Federation) (Moscow: TERRA, 1996), 2:383.
5. *Pravda,* 1 February 1935.
6. *History of the Communist Party of the Soviet Union (Bolshevik): Short Course,* authorized by the Central Committee of the CPSU (B.), 1938 (Moscow: Foreign Languages Publishing House, 1951).
7. Sokolov, op. cit., 228.

10. From World War to Cold War

1. Kuleshov et al., *Nashe Otechestvo,* 2:387.
2. Ibid., 2:392.
3. O. A. Rzheshevsky, ed., *Kto byl kto v Velikoi Otechestvennoi voine* (Who was who in the Great Patriotic War) (Moscow: Respublika, 1995), 4.
4. Kuleshov et al., op. cit., 2:402.
5. Rzheshevsky, op. cit., 13.
6. Kuleshov et al., op. cit., 2:415.
7. Ibid.
8. Rzheshevsky, op. cit., 9.
9. G. F. Krivosheev, ed., *Velikaia Otechestvennaia voina. Tsifry i fakty* (The Great Patriotic War: Figures and facts) (Moscow: Prosveshchenie, 1995), 47.
10. V. A. Zolotarev, "Kurskaia bitva: vzgliad cherez polveka" (Half a century after the Battle of Kursk: A reassessment), in *Vtoraia Mirovaia Voina. Aktual'nye problemy* (World War II: Topical issues) (Moscow: Nauka, 1995), 268–69.
11. Krivosheev, op. cit., 105.
12. V. A. Pron'ko, "Tzena pobedy" (The price of victory), in *Vtoraia Mirovaia Voina,* 318.
13. See, for instance, R. C. Tucker, *Stalin in Power: The Revolution from Above, 1928–1941* (New York and London: W.W. Norton, 1990), 225–32.
14. Viktor Suvorov, *Ledokol. Kto nachal vtoruiu mirovuiu voinu?* (Icebreaker: Who started the Second World War?) (Moscow, 1992).
15. *The Speeches of Winston Churchill,* edited by D. Cannadine (London: Penguin Books, 1990), 303.

11. Khrushchev and De-Stalinization

1. N. Khrushchev, *The "Secret" Speech*, introduction by Zhores A. Medvedev and Roy A. Medvedev (Nottingham, England: Spokesman Books, 1976).
2. Ibid., 25–26.
3. Ibid., 58.
4. R. W. Davies, *Soviet Economic Development from Lenin to Khrushchev* (Cambridge: Cambridge University Press, 1998), 70.
5. *XXII s'ezd kommunisticheskoi partii Sovetskogo Soyuza. Stenografi-cheskii otchet* (Twenty-Second Congress of the Communist Party of the Soviet Union. Stenographic minutes) (Moscow, 1962), 3:276.
6. Z. Dolgopolova, ed., *Russia Dies Laughing: Jokes from Soviet Russia* (London: Andre Deutsch, 1982), 11–12.

12. Brezhnev's "Mature" Socialism

1. Kuleshov et al., *Nashe Otechestvo*, 2:490.
2. See, for instance, David Christian, *Imperial and Soviet Russia* (London: Macmillan, 1997), 385; L. Cook, "Brezhnev's 'Social Contract' and Gorbachev's Reforms," *Soviet Studies* vol. 44, no. 1 (1992), 37–56.
3. Dolgopolova, *Russia Dies Laughing*, 20.
4. See Gorshkov, *Rossia na rubezhe vekov*, 238; F. M. Burlatsky, *Russkie gosudari. Epokha reformatsii* (Russian rulers: The reformation era) (Moscow: Shark, 1996), 162.

13. Cracks in the Soviet Monolith

1. C. Friedrich and Z. Brzezinski, *Totalitarian Dictatorship and Autocracy*, revised edition (New York: Praeger, 1966), 22.
2. See *Pluralism in the Soviet Union: Essays in Honour of H. Gordon Skilling*, edited by Susan Gross Solomon (London: Macmillan, 1983).
3. J. Hough and M. Fainsod, *How the Soviet Union Is Governed* (Cambridge, Mass.: Harvard University Press, 1979), 446.
4. J. Hough, "The Brezhnev Era: The Man and the System," *Problems of Communism*, vol. 25, no. 2 (March–April 1976), 14.
5. See Valerie Bunce and John M. Echols, "Soviet Politics in the Brezhnev Era: 'Pluralism' or 'Corporatism'?" in *Soviet Politics in the Brezhnev Era*, edited by Donald R. Kelley (New York: Praeger, 1980), 1–26; Valerie Bunce, "The Political Economy of the Brezhnev Era: The Rise and Fall of Corporatism," *British Journal of Political Science*, 13 (1983), 129–58.
6. V. Konstantinov and V. Naishul', *Tekhnologia planovogo upravlenia* (The technology of central planning) (Moscow, 1986).
7. A. Neshchadin et al., *Lobbizm v Rossii: etapy bol'shogo puti* (Lobbyism in Russia: Stages of development) (Moscow: RSPP, 1995), 13–14.
8. See, for instance, N. N. Inozemtsev, "Problemy sovremennogo mirovogo razvitia" (Issues of contemporary world development), in *XXV*

s'ezd KPSS i razvitie marksistsko-leninskoi teorii (Twenty-Fifth Congress of the CPSU and the development of Marxist-Leninist theory) (Moscow: Politizdat, 1977), 93.

9. S. P. Peregudov et al., *Gruppy interesov i rossiiskoe gosudarstvo* (Interest groups and the Russian state) (Moscow: Editorial URSS, 1999), 58.

10. G. Arbatov, *Zatianuvsheesia vyzdorovlenie, 1953–1985* (Protracted recovery, 1953–1985) (Moscow: Mezhdunarodnye otnoshenia, 1991), 273.

11. Alexander Solzhenitsyn, *Cancer Ward,* translated by Nicholas Bethell and David Burg (London and Toronto: Bodley Head, 1970); *The First Circle,* translated by Michael Guybon (London: Fontana, 1970).

12. A. Solzhenitsyn, *The Gulag Archipelago, 1918–1956: An Experiment in Literary Investigation* (London: Harvill, 1995).

13. Andrei D. Sakharov, *My Country and the World* (London: Collins & Harvill Press, 1975), 4.

14. Andrei D. Sakharov, *Progress, Coexistence, and Intellectual Freedom* (London: Andre Deutsch, 1968), 27.

15. Sakharov, *My Country and the World,* 101–02.

16. Mikhail Gorbachev, *Dekabr'–91. Moia pozitsia* (December 1991: My stance) (Moscow: Novosti, 1992), 189.

17. Richard Sakwa, *Soviet Politics: an Introduction* (London: Routledge, 1989), 197.

18. See Peregudov et al., op. cit., 60–69.

19. Ibid., 66.

14. The Command Economy in Crisis

1. See Gertrude E. Schroeder, "Economic Reform of Socialism," *The Annals of the American Academy,* AAPSS, 507 (January 1990), 35–43.

2. Cited in Kuleshov et al., *Nashe Otechestvo,* 2:567.

3. Ibid., 568.

4. Mikhail Gorbachev, *Perestroika: New Thinking for Our Country and the World* (London: Collins, 1987), 83.

5. Ibid., 86.

6. A. I. Utkin, "Pochemu ischez Sovetskii Soyuz?" (Why did the Soviet Union disappear?), in *Na pereput'e. Novye vekhi* (At the crossroads: New milestones) (Moscow: Logos, 1999), 185–213, p. 207.

7. Ibid., 203.

8. Ibid., 210.

15. The Collapse of the Political System

1. See, for instance, M. A. Bulgakov, *Selected Works* (Oxford: Pergamon, 1972); E. Zamiatin, "We," in *An Anthology of Russian Literature in the Soviet Period from Gorki to Pasternak,* edited by B. G. Guerney (New York: Vintage Books, 1961), 168–353; A. Platonov, "Kotlovan," *Grani* 70 (1969), 3–107; Solzhenitsyn, *The Gulag Archipelago.*

2. In the perverse political spectrum of the *perestroika* period, the Left was the radical democrats whose "democratic socialism" more and more gravitated toward a Western-style neo-liberal outlook, whereas Right was the Communist hard-liners who resisted the reform of the command-bureaucratic system.

3. A. N. Yakovlev et al., *Perestroika: Zamysly i rezul'taty* (Perestroika: Intentions and results) (Rostov: Rostov University Press, 1995), 129.

16. Unraveling the Unitary State

1. See, for instance, Boris Yeltsin, *Zapiski Prezidenta* (President's notes) (Moscow: Ogonek, 1994), 143.

2. Kuleshov et al., *Politicheskaia istoria*, 2:659.

3. See A. Yakovlev, *Predislovie. Obval. Posleslovie* (Foreword. Collapse. Afterword) (Moscow: Novosti, 1992), 169; V. Zamkovoi and M. Il'chikov, *Rossia vchera, segodnia, zavtra!* (Russia yesterday, today, tomorrow!) (Moscow: Griboedov Institute of International Law and Economics, 1998), 51.

17. Return to a Market Economy

1. Richard Sakwa, *Russian Politics and Society,* second edition (London and New York: Routledge, 1996), 30–31.

2. Kuleshov et al., *Politicheskaia istoria*, 2:698.

3. The high inflation rates of 1992–94 were not conducive to industrial investment but benefited bankers speculating in the financial market.

4. Boris Fedorov, *Pytaias' poniat' Rossiu* (Trying to understand Russia) (St. Petersburg: Limbus Press, 2000), 143.

5. A. B. Chubais, ed., *Privatizatsia po-rossiiski* (Privatization Russian-style) (Moscow: Vagrius, 1999), 321.

18. Handicaps of Russia's Capitalist Transformation

1. See Roy Medvedev, *Kapitalizm v Rossii?* (Capitalism in Russia?) (Moscow: Prava cheloveka, 1998), 5–70.

2. Oksana Gaman-Golutvina, "Ot koronatsii k inauguratsii ili ot inauguratsii k koronatsii?" (From coronation to inauguration or from inauguration to coronation?), *Nezavisimaia gazeta* (5 May 2001).

3. Medvedev, op. cit., 21.

4. See Theodore Shanin, "Pochemu do sikh por ne umer russkii narod" (Why haven't the Russian people died yet?), *Ekspert*, no. 1–2 (213) (17 January 2000).

5. A comprehensive account of Russia's capitalist reforms of the 1990s is presented in Thane Gustafson, *Capitalism Russian-Style* (Cambridge: Cambridge University Press, 1999).

6. B. Kagarlitskii, *Restavratsia v Rossii* (Restoration in Russia) (Moscow: Editorial URSS, 2000), 196.

7. See Tatiana Gurova and Valery Fadeev, "Strategia rosta" (Strategy of growth), *Ekspert*, no. 1–2 (213) (17 January 2000).

19. The Yeltsin Era

1. Based on Sakwa, *Russian Politics and Society,* 391.
2. See *Konstitutsia Rossiiskoi Federatsii. Voprosy i otvety* (The Constitution of the Russian Federation: Questions and answers) (Moscow: Iuridicheskaia literatura, 1994).
3. Based on *Maximov's Companion to the 1996 Russian Presidential Elections* (London and Moscow: Maximov Publications, 1996), 254.
4. Boris Yeltsin, *Ispoved' na zadannuiu temu* (Confession on a set topic) (Moscow: Ogonek-Variant, 1990).
5. Based on Sakwa, op. cit., 392.
6. Grigory Yavlinsky, *Krizis v Rossii: konets sistemy? nachalo puti?* (The crisis in Russia: The end of the system? The beginning of a journey?) (Moscow: EPICENTER, 1999), 9–10.
7. Iury Korguniuk, "Izbiratel'naia kampania 1999 g. i perspektivy razvitia rossiiskoi mnogopartiinosti," *Polit.Ru* (17 February 2000).
8. Gorshkov, *Rossia na rubezhe vekov,* 34.
9. Ibid., 35.
10. See Roy Medvedev, "I vse-taki—epokha El'tsina" (It's the Yeltsin era, all the same) *Rossiiskaia gazeta* (6 January 2000).
11. *Konstitutsia Rossiiskoi Federatsii. Voprosy i otvety,* 4.
12. Gustafson, *Capitalism Russian-Style,* 229.
13. Ibid., 229–30.
14. Ibid., 230.

20. Russia in Search of an Identity

1. Mikhail Visens, "SNG na rasput'e: 9 let besplodnogo sushchestvovania" (CIS at the crossroads: Nine years of fruitless existence), *Polit.Ru* (24 January 2000).
2. See Zamkovoi and Il'chikov, *Rossia vchera, segodnia, zavtra!,* 55.
3. *Rossia. Entsiklopedicheskii spravochnik* (Russia: Encyclopedic reference book) (Moscow: Drofa, 1998), 433.
4. Igor' Zadvornov and Alexander Khalmukhamedov, "Posle pobedy" (After the victory) *Nezavisimaia gazeta* (29 February 2000).
5. *Chechenskaia tragedia. Kto vinovat* (The Chechen tragedy: Who is to blame?) (Moscow: RIA Novosti, 1995), 81.
6. Ibid., 32.
7. Ibid., 34.
8. See Wolfgang Gerke, "Chechenskii raund bol'shoi igry Vashingtona" (The Chechen round of Washington's great game), *Nezavisimaia gazeta* (17 February 2000).
9. See A. Kol'ev, *Chechenskii kapkan* (The Chechen trap) (Moscow: Kongress russkikh obshchin, 1997), 32.
10. See Roy Medvedev, "Voina v Chechne i voina na stranitsakh pechati" (War in Chechnya and war in the press), *Rossiiskaia gazeta* (17 February 2000).

21. Prospects for the New Century

1. V. V. Putin, "Rossia na rubezhe tysiacheletii," http://www.government. gov.ru/government/minister/article-vvpl.html (27 December 1999); also available as the English translation "Russia at the Turn of the Millennium."

2. Stephen Holmes, "When Less State Means Less Freedom," *Transitions,* vol.4, no. 4 (1997), 68–75.

3. "Presidentskii god Putina" (Putin's year as president), *Argumenty i fakty* 03 (1056) (17 January 2001).

4. Ivan Zasurskii, "Vy videli, kakie nynche ocheredi v kino?" (Have you seen the lines at the movies lately?), Polit.Ru (11 May 2001).

5. Margareta Mommsen, "The Sphinx in the Kremlin," *Internationale Politik,* 1 (Fall 2000), 21–22.

6. See Klaus-Helge Donath, "Kim II Putin lässt sich feiern" (Kim II Putin condescends to be celebrated), *Tageszeitung* (7 May 2001).

Selected Bibliography of English-Language Sources

Acton, E. *Rethinking the Russian Revolution*. London: Edward Arnold, 1990.
_____. *Russia: The Tsarist and Soviet Legacy*. 2nd ed. London: Longman, 1995.
Adelman, Jonathan A. *Torrents of Spring: Soviet and Post-Soviet Politics*. New York: McGraw-Hill, 1995.
Agursky, Mikhail. *The Third Rome: National Bolshevism in the USSR*. Boulder/London: Westview Press, 1987.
Albats, Yevgenia. *KGB: State Within a State: The Secret Police and Its Hold on Russia's Past, Present and Future*. London: I. B. Tauris, 1995.
Alexeyeva, Ludmilla. *Soviet Dissent: Contemporary Movements for National, Religious and Human Rights*. Middletown, Conn.: Wesleyan University Press, 1987.
Allensworth, Wayne. *The Russian Question: Nationalism, Modernization, and Post-Communist Russia*. Lanham, Md./Oxford: Rowman & Littlefield, 1998.
Amalrik, Andrei. *Will the Soviet Union Survive until 1984?* London: Penguin Books, 1970.
Andrew, C., and O. Gordievsky. *KGB: The Inside Story of Its Foreign Operations from Lenin to Gorbachev*. London: Hodder & Stoughton, 1990.
Andrle, V. *A Social History of Twentieth-Century Russia*. London/New York: Edward Arnold, 1994.
Arendt, Hannah. *The Origins of Totalitarianism*. New York: Harcourt Brace, 1951.
Arnason, Johann P. *The Future That Failed: Origins and Destinies of the Soviet Model*. London: Routledge, 1993.
Ashton, S. R. *The Politics of East-West Relations since 1945*. London: Macmillan, 1989.
Åslund, A. *Gorbachev's Struggle for Economic Reform*, 2nd ed. London: Pinter, 1991.
_____. *How Russia Became a Market Economy*. Washington, D.C.: The Brookings Institute, 1995.
Atkinson, D., and others, eds. *Women in Russia*. Brighton: Harvester Press, 1978.
Ausland, John C. *Kennedy, Khrushchev, and the Berlin-Cuba Crisis 1961–1964*. Oslo: Scandinavian University Press, 1996.
Babkina, M. A., ed. *New Political Parties and Movements in the Soviet Union*. Commack, N.Y.: Nova Science Publishers, 1991.

Bacon, E. *The Gulag at War: Stalin's Forced Labour System in the Light of the Archives*. New York: New York University Press, 1994.

Bahry, Donna. *Outside Moscow: Power, Politics and Budgetary Policy in the Soviet Republics*. New York: Columbia University Press, 1987.

Bailes, K. E. *Science in Russian Culture*. Bloomington: Indiana University Press, 1990.

Balzer, Harley D., ed. *Five Years That Shook the World: Gorbachev's Unfinished Revolution*. Boulder/Oxford: Westview Press, 1991.

Baranovsky, Vladimir. *Russia and Europe: the Emerging Security Agenda*. Oxford: Oxford University Press, 1997.

Barber, J., and M. Harrison. *The Soviet Home Front 1941–1945*. London/New York: Longman, 1991.

Barner-Barry, Carol, and Cynthia Hody. *The Politics of Change: The Transformation of the Former Soviet Union*. London: Macmillan, 1995.

Bialer, S. *Stalin and His Generals*. London: Souvenir, 1970.

————. *Stalin's Successors*. New York: Cambridge University Press, 1980.

————. *The Soviet Paradox: External Expansion, Internal Decline*. New York: Alfred Knopf, 1986.

————, ed. *Politics, Society and Nationality in Gorbachev's Russia*. Boulder, Colo.: Westview Press, 1989.

Billington, James H. *Russia Transformed: Breakthrough to Hope*. New York: Free Press, 1993.

Biryukov, Nikolai, and V.M. Sergeev. *Russia's Road to Democracy: Parliament, Communism and Traditional Culture*. Aldershot: Edward Elgar, 1993.

Blacker, C. D. *Hostage to Revolution: Gorbachev and Soviet Security Policy, 1985–1991*. New York: Council on Foreign Relations, 1993.

Blackwell, W. L., ed. *Russian Economic Development from Peter the Great to Stalin*. New York: Franklin Watts, 1974.

Bloch, Sidney, and Peter Reddaway. *Russia's Political Hospitals: The Abuse of Psychiatry in the Soviet Union*. London: Gollancz, 1977.

Blum, Douglas W. *Russia's Future: Consolidation or Disintegration?* Boulder/Oxford: Westview Press, 1994.

Boettke, Peter J. *Why Perestroika Failed: The Politics and Economics of Socialist Transformation*. London/New York: Routledge, 1993.

Boldin, Valery. *Ten Years That Shook the World: The Gorbachev Era as Witnessed by His Chief of Staff*. Glasgow: HarperCollins, 1994.

Bonnell, Victoria F., and others, eds. *Russia at the Barricades*. Armonk, N.Y.: M. E. Sharpe, 1994.

Bottomore, T., ed. *A Dictionary of Marxist Thought*, 2nd ed. Oxford: Blackwell, 1991.

Bourdeaux, M. *Gorbachev, Glasnost and the Gospel*. London: Hodder & Stoughton, 1990.

Bowker, Mike, and Cameron Ross, eds. *Russia after the Cold War*. Harlow: Longman, 2000.

Bremmer, I., and R. Taras, eds. *Nations and Politics in the Soviet Successor States*. Cambridge: Cambridge University Press, 1993.

_____, eds. *New Nations New Politics*. Cambridge: Cambridge University Press, 1997.

Breslauer, G. W. *Khrushchev and Brezhnev as Leaders*. London: Macmillan, 1982.

Broadman, Harry G., ed. *Russian Enterprise Reform: Policies to Further the Transition*. Washington, D.C.: World Bank, 1999.

Brown, A. *The Gorbachev Factor*. Oxford: Oxford University Press, 1996.

_____, ed. *New Thinking in Soviet Politics*. London: Macmillan, 1992.

_____, ed. *Political Leadership in the Soviet Union*. London: Macmillan, 1989.

_____, and J. Gray, eds. *Political Culture and Political Change in Communist States*. New York: Holmes and Meier, 1977.

_____, and others, eds. *The Cambridge Encyclopedia of Russia and the Former Soviet Union*, 2nd rev. ed. Cambridge/New York: Cambridge University Press, 1994.

Brzezinski, Zbigniew. *The Grand Failure: The Birth and Death of Communism in the Twentieth Century*. New York: Collier Books, 1990.

Buckley, Mary. *Redefining Russian Society and Polity*. Oxford: Westview Press, 1993.

_____, ed. *Perestroika and Soviet Women*. Cambridge: Cambridge University Press, 1992.

Buckley, Richard, ed. *Russia on the Brink: Bandit Capitalism, Social Despair*. Cheltenham: Understanding Global Issues Ltd., 1999.

Bullock, A. *Hitler and Stalin: Parallel Lives*. London: HarperCollins, 1991.

Bunce, Valerie, and John M. Echols, "Soviet Politics in the Brezhnev Era: 'Pluralism' or 'Corporatism'?," in Donald Kelley, ed. *Soviet Politics in the Brezhnev Era*. New York: Praeger, 1980.

Bush, Keith. *From the Command Economy to the Market: A Collection of Interviews*. Aldershot: Dartmouth Publishers, 1991.

Buszynski, Leszek. *Russian Foreign Policy after the Cold War*. Westport, Conn./London: Praeger, 1996.

Butler, William E., ed. *Basic Documents on the Soviet Legal System*, 3rd ed. Dobbs Ferry, N.Y.: Oceana, 1991.

_____, ed. *Basic Legal Documents of the Russian Federation*. Dobbs Ferry, N.Y.: Oceana, 1992.

Buttino, Marco, ed. *In a Collapsing Empire: Underdevelopment, Ethnic Conflicts and Nationalisms in the Soviet Union*. Milan: Feltrinelli, 1993.

Byrnes, R. F., ed. *After Brezhnev: Sources of Soviet Conduct in the 1980s*. London: Pinter, 1983.

Callinicos, Alex. *The Revenge of History: Marxism and the East European Revolutions*. Oxford: Polity Press, 1991.

Carr, E. H. *The Russian Revolution from Lenin to Stalin*. London: Macmillan, 1979.

Carrére d'Encausse, Héléne. *A History of the Soviet Union, 1917–53*, 2 vols. London: Longman, 1981.

_____. *The End of the Soviet Empire: The Triumph of the Nations*. London: Basic Books, 1994.

_____. *The Great Challenge: Nationalities and the Bolshevik State, 1917–1930.* New York: Holmes and Meier, 1992.

Cerf, Christopher, and Marina Albee. *Voices of Glasnost: Letters from the Soviet People to Ogonyok Magazine, 1987–1990.* London: Kyle Cathie, 1990.

Chamberlin, W. H. *The Russian Revolution: 1917–1921,* 2 vols. New York/London: Macmillan, 1935.

Charlton, Michael. *Footsteps from the Finland Station: Five Landmarks in the Collapse of Communism.* St Albans: Claridge Press, 1992.

Chiesa, Giulietto, with Douglas Taylor Northrop. *Transition to Democracy: Political Change in the Soviet Union, 1987–1991.* Hanover: University Press of New England, 1993.

Christian, David. *Imperial and Soviet Russia: Power, Privilege and the Challenge of Modernity.* Basingstoke: Macmillan, 1997.

Chubarov, Alexander. *The Fragile Empire. A History of Imperial Russia.* New York/London: Continuum, 1999.

Clark, Alan. *Barbarossa: The Russian-German Conflict, 1941–1945.* London: Macmillan, 1985.

Cockerham, William C. *Health and Social Change in Russia and Eastern Europe.* New York/ London: Routledge, 1999.

Cohen, Ariel. *Russian Imperialism: Development and Crisis.* Westport, Conn./London: Praeger, 1998.

Cohen, S. *Bukharin and the Bolshevik Revolution.* Oxford University Press, 1980.

Colton, Timothy J. *Transitional Citizens: Voters and What Influences Them in the New Russia.* Cambridge, Mass./London: Harvard University Press, 2000.

_____, and Robert C. Tucker, eds. *Patterns in Post-Soviet Leadership.* Boulder, Colo.: Westview Press, 1995.

_____, and Robert Levgold, eds. *After the Soviet Union: From Empire to Nations.* New York/London: Norton, 1993.

Conquest, R. *Stalin: The Breaker of Nations.* London: Weidenfeld & Nicolson, 1991.

_____. *The Great Terror: A Reassessment.* London: Pimlico Press, 1990.

Cooper, Leo. *Soviet Reforms and Beyond.* London: Macmillan, 1991.

Cox, Terry. *From Perestroika to Privatisation: Property Relations and Social Change in Soviet Society, 1985–1991.* Aldershot: Avebury, 1996.

Crawshaw, Steve. *Goodbye to the USSR: The Collapse of Soviet Power.* London: Bloomsbury, 1992.

Cullen, Robert. *Twilight of Empire: Inside the Crumbling Soviet Bloc.* London: Bodley Head, 1991.

Dallin, Alexander, ed. *Political Parties in Russia.* Berkeley: University of California Press, 1993.

_____, and Gail W. Lapidus, eds. *The Soviet System: From Crisis to Collapse,* rev. ed. Oxford: Westview Press, 1994.

Daniels, R. *Russia's Transformation: Snapshots of a Crumbling System.* Lanham, Md./Oxford: Rowman & Littlefield, 1998.

_____. *The End of the Communist Revolution.* London: Routledge, 1993.

_____. *The Stalin Revolution: Fulfillment or Betrayal of Communism?* 3rd ed. Lexington, Mass.: D. C. Heath & Co., 1990.

Davies, R. W. *Soviet Economic Development from Lenin to Khrushchev.* Cambridge: Cambridge University Press, 1998.

_____, and others, eds. *The Economic Transformation of the Soviet Union, 1913–1945.* Cambridge: Cambridge University Press, 1994.

Dawisha, Adeed, and Karen Dawisha, eds. *The Making of Foreign Policy in Russia and the New States of Eurasia.* Armonk, N.Y./London: M.E. Sharpe, 1995.

Dawisha, Karen, and Bruce Parrott. *Russia and the New States of Eurasia: The Politics of Upheaval.* Cambridge: Cambridge University Press, 1994.

De Nevers, Renee. *Russia's Strategic Renovation: Russian Security Strategies and Foreign Policy in the Post-Imperial Era.* London: Brassey's, 1994.

Deutscher, I. *Stalin,* rev. ed. Harmondsworth: Penguin, 1966.

Devlin, Judith. *The Rise of the Russian Democrats: The Causes and Consequences of the Elite Revolution.* Aldershot: Edward Elgar, 1995.

Dibb, Paul. *The Soviet Union: The Incomplete Superpower,* 2nd ed. London: Macmillan, 1988.

Diuk, Nadia, and Adrian Karatnycky. *The Hidden Nations: The People Challenge the Soviet Union.* New York: William Morrow, 1990.

Djilas, Milovan. *The New Class: An Analysis of the Communist System.* London: Thames & Hudson, 1957.

Dmitrieva, Oskana. *Regional Development: The USSR and After.* London: UCL Press, 1996.

Doder, Dusko, and Louise Branson. *Gorbachev: Heretic in the Kremlin.* London: Viking, 1990.

Donaldson, Robert H., and Joseph L. Nogee. *The Foreign Policy of Russia: Changing Systems, Enduring Interests.* Armonk, N.Y./London: M. E. Sharpe, 1998.

Drobizheva, Leokadia, and others, eds. *Ethnic Conflict in the Post-Soviet World: Case Studies and Analysis.* Armonk, N.Y.: M. E. Sharpe, 1996.

Dukes, Paul. *A History of Russia,* 2nd ed. London: Macmillan, 1990.

Dukes, Paul, *World Order in History: Russia and the West.* London: Routledge, 1996.

Dunlop, John B. *Russia Confronts Chechnya: Roots of a Separatist Conflict.* Cambridge: Cambridge University Press, 1998.

_____. *The Rise of Russia and the Fall of the Soviet Empire.* Princeton, N.J.: Princeton University Press, 1993.

Dyker, D. A. *Restructuring the Soviet Economy.* London and New York: Routledge, 1992.

Eberwein, Wilhelm, and Jochen Tholen. *Market or Mafia: Russian Managers on the Difficult Road towards an Open Society.* Aldershot: Ashgate, 1997.

Eckstein, Harry, and others. *Can Democracy Take Root in Post-Soviet Russia? Explorations in State-Society Relations.* Lanham, Md./Oxford: Rowman & Littlefield, 1998.

Edmonds, Robin. *Soviet Foreign Policy: The Brezhnev Years.* Oxford: Oxford University Press, 1983.

Edmondson, Linda, ed. *Women and Society in Russia and the Soviet Union.* Cambridge: Cambridge University Press, 1992.

Erickson, J. *The Road to Berlin.* London, Weidenfeld & Nicolson, 1983.

————. *The Road to Stalingrad.* London: Weidenfeld & Nicolson, 1975.

Erlich, A. *The Soviet Industrialization Debate 1924–1928.* Cambridge, Mass.: Harvard University Press, 1960.

Eurasia in the 21st Century: The Total Security Environment, vol. 1: *Russia and the West* (Alexei G. Arbatov and others, eds); vol. 2: *Russia, the Caucasus, and Central Asia* (Rajan Menon and others, eds); vol. 3: *Russia and East Asia* (Gilbert Rozman and others, eds). Armonk, N.Y./London: M. E. Sharpe, 1999.

Fainsod, M. *How Russia Is Ruled,* rev. ed. Cambridge, Mass.: Harvard University Press, 1963.

Felshman, Neil. *Gorbachev, Yeltsin and the Last Days of the Soviet Empire.* New York: St. Martin's Press, 1992.

Feofanov, Yuri, and Donald P. Barry. *Politics and Justice in Russia: Major Trials of the Post-Stalin Era.* London: M. E. Sharpe, 1996.

Ferro, Marc. *October 1917: A Social History of the Russian Revolution.* London: Routledge and Kegan Paul, 1980.

Figes, O. *A People's Tragedy: The Russian Revolution 1891–1924.* London: Pimlico, 1996.

————. *Peasant Russia, Civil War: The Volga Countryside in Revolution, 1917–1921.* Oxford: Oxford University Press, 1989.

————, and Boris Kolonitskii. *Interpreting the Russian Revolution: The Language and Symbols of 1917.* New Haven, Conn./London: Yale University Press, 1999.

Filtzer, D. *Soviet Workers and the Collapse of Perestroika.* Cambridge: Cambridge University Press, 1994.

————. *The Khrushchev Era: De-Stalinization and the Limits of Reform in the USSR, 1953–1964.* London: Macmillan, 1993.

Fiorentini, G., and S. Peltzman, eds. *The Economics of Organised Crime.* Cambridge: Cambridge University Press, 1996.

Fish, M. Stephen. *Democracy from Scratch: Opposition and Regime in the New Russian Revolution.* Princeton, N.J.: Princeton University Press, 1995.

Fitzpatrick, S. *Stalin's Peasants: Resistance and Survival in the Russian Village after Collectivization.* New York: Oxford University Press, 1994.

————. *The Russian Revolution: 1917–1932.* Oxford: Oxford University Press, 1982.

————, ed. *Stalinism: New Directions.* London: Routledge, 2000.

Fortescue, G. *The Communist Party and Soviet Science.* London: Macmillan, 1986.

Frankel, E. R., and others, eds. *Revolution in Russia: Reassessments of 1917.* Cambridge: Cambridge University Press, 1992.

Franklin, Bruce, ed. *Essential Stalin: Major Theoretical Writings, 1905–52.* London: Croom Helm, 1973.

Friedrich, Carl, and Zbigniew Brzezinski. *Totalitarian Dictatorship and Autocracy.* New York: Praeger, 1956.

Frydman, Roman, and others, eds. *Corporate Governance in Central Europe and Russia,* vol.1: *Banks, Funds, and Foreign Investors*; vol. 2: *Insiders and the State.* Budapest/London: Central European University Press, 1996.

Gaddis, J. L. *Russia, the Soviet Union and the United States.* 2nd ed. New York: McGraw-Hill, 1990.

———. *The Long Peace: Inquiries into the History of the Cold War.* Oxford: Oxford University Press, 1987.

Gerschenkron, A., "Problems and Patterns of Russian Economic Development," in M. Cherniavsky, ed. *The Structure of Russian History.* New York: Random House, 1970, pp. 282–308.

Getty, J. Arch. *Origins of the Great Purges.* Cambridge: Cambridge University Press, 1985.

———, and R. T. Manning, eds. *Stalinist Terror: New Perspectives.* Cambridge University Press, 1993.

Gill, Graeme. *The Collapse of the Single-Party System: The Disintegration of the Communist Party of the Soviet Union.* Cambridge: Cambridge University Press, 1994.

———, and Roger D. Markwick. *Russia's Stillborn Democracy? From Gorbachev to Yeltsin.* Oxford: Oxford University Press, 2000.

Ginzburg, E. *Into the Whirlwind.* London: Collins, 1967.

Goldman, Marshall I. *What Went Wrong with Perestroika.* New York/London: Norton, 1991.

———. *Lost Opportunity: Why Economic Reforms in Russia Have Not Worked.* London: Norton, 1995.

Gorbachev, Mikhail. *Memoirs.* London: Doubleday, 1996.

———. *Perestroika: New Thinking for Our Country and the World.* London: Collins, 1987.

Grachev, Andrei. *Final Days: The Inside Story of the Collapse of the Soviet Union.* Oxford: Westview Press, 1995.

Graham, Loren R. *Science in Russia and the Soviet Union: A Short History.* Cambridge: Cambridge University Press, 1993.

Granville, Brigitte, and Peter Oppenheimer. *The Russian Economy in the 1990s.* Oxford: Clarendon, 2000.

Green, Barbara B. *The Dynamics of Russian Politics: A Short History.* Westport, Conn./London: Praeger, 1994.

Gregory, Paul. *Restructuring the Soviet Economic Bureaucracy.* Cambridge: Cambridge University Press, 1990.

Gustafson, Thane. *Capitalism Russian-Style.* Cambridge: Cambridge University Press, 1999.

Hahn, Jeffrey W., ed. *Democratization in Russia: The Development of Legislative Institutions.* Armonk, N.Y.: M. E. Sharpe, 1995.

Hajda, Lubomyr and Mark Beissingen, eds. *The Nationalities Factor in Soviet Politics and Society.* Boulder, Colo.: Westview Press, 1990.

Handelman, Stephen. *Comrade Criminal: The Theft of the Second Russian Revolution.* London: Michael Joseph, 1994.

Harding, N. *Leninism.* London: Macmillan, 1996.

Hart, Gary. *The Second Russian Revolution.* London: Hodder & Stoughton, 1991.

Hasegawa T. *The February Revolution: Petrograd 1917.* Seattle: University of Washington Press, 1981.

_____, and Alex Pravda, eds. *Perestroika: Soviet Domestic and Foreign Policies.* London: Sage, 1990.

Heller, M., and A. Nekrich. *Utopia in Power: A History of the USSR from 1917 to the Present.* London: Hutchinson, 1986.

Hewett, Ed A., and Victor H. Winston, eds. *Milestones in Glasnost and Perestroika: Politics and People.* Washington, D.C.: The Brookings Institution, 1991.

_____, eds. *Milestones in Glasnost and Perestroika: The Economy.* Washington, D.C.: The Brookings Institution, 1991.

Hoffman, D. L. *Peasant Metropolis: Social Identities in Moscow, 1929–1941.* Ithaca/London: Cornell University Press, 1994.

Holloway, David, and Norman Nalmark, eds. *Re-examining the Soviet Experience: Essays in Honor of Alexander Dallin.* Boulder, Colo.: Westview, 1996.

Holmes, Leslie. *The End of Communist Power: Anti-Corruption Campaigns and Legitimation Crisis.* Oxford: Polity Press, 1993.

Hopf, Ted, ed. *Understandings of Russian Foreign Policy.* University Park: Pennsylvania State University Press, 1999.

Hosking, Geoffrey. *A History of the Soviet Union,* rev. ed. London: Fontana, 1990.

_____. *Russia: People and Empire, 1552–1917.* London: Fontana, 1998.

_____. *The Awakening of the Soviet Union,* rev. ed. London: Mandarin, 1991.

_____, and others, eds. *The Road to Post-Communism: Independent Political Movements in the Soviet Union 1985–1991.* London: Pinter, 1992.

_____, and Robert Service, eds. *Reinterpreting Russia.* London: Arnold, 1999.

Hough, J., and others. *The 1996 Russian Presidential Election.* Washington, D.C.: Brookings Institution Press, 1996.

Hough, J., and M. Fainsod. *How the Soviet Union Is Governed.* Cambridge, Mass.: Harvard University Press, 1979.

Huber, Robert T., ed. *Perestroika-Era Politics: The New Soviet Legislature and Gorbachev's Political Reforms.* Armonk, N.Y.: M. E. Sharpe, 1992.

Hudelson, Richard H. *The Rise and Fall of Communism.* Boulder, Colo.: Westview Press, 1993.

Hughes, J. *Stalin, Siberia and the Crisis of the New Economic Policy.* Cambridge: Cambridge University Press, 1991.

Jowitt, Ken. *New World Disorder: The Leninist Extinction.* Berkeley: University of California Press, 1992.

Kagarlitsky, Boris. *Farewell Perestroika: A Soviet Chronicle.* London: Verso, 1990.

_____. *The Disintegration of the Monolith.* London, Verso, 1992.

_____. *The Thinking Reed: Intellectuals and the Soviet State from 1917 to the Present.* London: Verso, 1988.

Kaiser, Robert G. *Why Gorbachev Happened: His Triumphs and His Failure.* New York/London: Simon and Schuster, 1992.

Kaminski, Bartlomiej. *Economic Transition in Russia and the New States of Eurasia.* Armonk, N.Y.: M. E. Sharpe, 1996.

Kampfner, John. *Inside Yeltsin's Russia*. London: Cassell, 1994.

Karklins, Rasma. *Ethnic Relations in the USSR: The Perspective from Below.* London: Allen and Unwin, 1986.

Katkov, George, and others, eds. *Russia Enters the Twentieth Century, 1894–1917*. London: Temple Smith Ltd., 1971.

Keeble, Curtis Sir. *Britain, the Soviet Union and Russia*, new ed. Basingstoke: Macmillan, 2000.

Keep, John L. H. *Last of the Empires: A History of the Soviet Union, 1945–1991*. Oxford: Oxford University Press, 1996.

Kenez, Peter. *The Birth of the Propaganda State: Soviet Methods of Mass Mobilization, 1917–1929*. Cambridge: Cambridge University Press, 1985.

Kerblay, B. *Modern Soviet Society*. London: Methuen, 1983.

Khrushchev Remembers: The Last Testament, trans. S. Talbott. London: Deutsch, 1974.

Khrushchev, Sergei. *Khrushchev on Khrushchev: An Inside Account of the Man and His Era, by His Son*. Boston: Little Brown, 1992.

Knight, A. W. *The KGB*. Boston, Unwin Hyman, 1988.

Kochan, I, and R. Abrahams. *The Making of Modern Russia*, 2nd ed. London: Penguin Books, 1990.

Kort, Michael. *The Soviet Colossus: History and Aftermath*, 4th ed. Armonk, N.Y./London: M. E. Sharpe, 1996.

Kozlov, Victor. *The Peoples of the Soviet Union*. London: Hutchinson, 1988.

Kryukov, Valery, and Arild Moe. *The New Russian Corporation? A Case Study of Gazprom*. London: Royal Institute of International Affairs, 1996.

Kubalkova, V., and A. A. Cruickshank. *Marxism-Leninism and the Theory of International Relations*. London: Routledge and Kegan Paul, 1980.

Kux, Stephan. *Soviet Federalism: A Comparative Perspective*. New York: Westview Press, 1991.

LaFeber, Walter. *America, Russia, and the Cold War, 1945–1996*, 8th ed. New York/London: McGraw-Hill, 1997.

Laird, Robbin, and Erik P. Hoffmann, eds. *Contemporary Issues in Soviet Foreign Policy*. New York: Aldine, 1991.

Lampert, N. *Stalinism: Its Nature and Aftermath*. London: Macmillan, 1991.

_____. *The Technical Intelligentsia and the Soviet State*. London: Macmillan, 1979.

Lane, David. *Soviet Society under Perestroika*. London: Routledge, 1992.

_____, ed. *Russia in Flux: The Political and Social Consequences of Reform*. Aldershot: Edward Elgar, 1992.

_____, ed. *Russia in Transition: Politics, Privatisation and Inequality*. Harlow: Longman, 1995.

Lapidus, G. W., ed. *The New Russia: Troubled Transformation*. Boulder, Colo.: Westview Press, 1994.

_____, and V. Zaslavsky, eds. *From Union to Commonwealth: Nationalism and Separatism in the Soviet Republics*. Cambridge: Cambridge University Press, 1992.

Laqueur, Walter. *The Dream That Failed*. Oxford: Oxford University Press, 1994.

_____. *The Long Road to Freedom: Russia and Glasnost.* London: Unwin Hyman, 1989.

Lavigne, Marie. *The Economics of Transition: From Socialist Economy to Market Economy,* 2nd ed. Basingstoke: Macmillan, 1999.

Ledeneva, Alena V. *Russia's Economy of Favours: Blat, Networking and Informal Exchange.* Cambridge: Cambridge University Press, 1998.

Lewin, M. *Lenin's Last Struggle.* London: Pluto Press, 1975.

_____. *The Gorbachev Phenomenon.* Berkeley: University of California Press, 1989.

Lieberman, Sanford R., and others, eds. *The Soviet Empire Reconsidered: Essays in Honor of Adam B. Ulam.* Boulder, Colo.: Westview Press, 1994.

Lieven, Anatol. *Chechnya: Tombstone of Russian Power.* New Haven, Conn./London: Yale University Press, 1999.

Likhachev, Dmitry S. *Reflections on the Russian Soul: A Memoir.* Budapest: Central European University Press, 2000.

Lincoln, W. B. *Red Victory. A History of the Russian Civil War.* London: Sphere Books, 1991.

Linden, Carl. *Khrushchev and the Soviet Leadership.* Baltimore: Johns Hopkins University Press, 1990.

Little, Richard D. *Governing the Soviet Union.* New York: Longman, 1989.

Lockwood, David. *The Destruction of the Soviet Union: A Study in Globalization.* Basingstoke: Macmillan, 2000.

Longley, David. *The Longman Companion to Imperial Russia, 1689–1917.* Harlow: Longman, 2000.

Lowenhardt, John. *The Reincarnation of Russia: Struggling with the Legacy of Communism, 1990–94.* Harlow: Longman, 1995.

Lynch, Allen. *The Cold War Is Over—Again.* Boulder, Colo.: Westview Press, 1992.

Lynch, Michael. *Reaction and Revolutions: Russia 1881–1924.* London: Hodder & Stoughton, 1992.

Malcolm, N., and others. *Internal Factors in Russian Foreign Policy.* Oxford: Oxford University Press, 1997.

Male, Donald J. *Russian Peasant Organisation before Collectivisation: A Study of Commune and Gathering 1925–1930.* Cambridge: Cambridge University Press, 1971.

Malia, Martin. *Russia under Western Eyes: From the Bronze Horseman to the Lenin Mausoleum.* Cambridge, Mass./London: Belknap, 2000.

_____. *The Soviet Tragedy: A History of Socialism in Russia.* New York: The Free Press, 1994.

Mandelshtam, N. *Hope Against Hope: A Memoir.* London: Collins and Harvill, 1971.

Marx, Karl, and Friedrich Engels. *The Communist Manifesto.* London: Penguin, 1985.

Mastyugina, Tatiana, and Lev Perepelkin. *An Ethnic History of Russia: Pre-Revolutionary Times to the Present.* Westport, Conn./London: Greenwood Press, 1996.

Matlock, Jack F., Jr. *Autopsy on an Empire.* New York: Random House, 1995.

Matthews, M. *Privilege in the Soviet Union: A Study of Elite Life-Styles under Communism*. London: Allen & Unwin, 1978.

Mawdsley, F. *The Russian Civil War*. Boston and London: Allen & Unwin, 1987.

McAuley, Alistair, ed. *Soviet Federalism: Nationalism and Economic Decentralisation*. Leicester/ London: Leicester University Press, 1991.

McAuley, Mary. *Russia's Politics of Uncertainty*. Cambridge: Cambridge University Press, 1997.

————. *Soviet Politics, 1917–1991*. Oxford: Oxford University Press, 1992.

McCauley, M. *Gorbachev*. London: Longman, 1998.

————. *Stalin and Stalinism*, 2nd ed. London: Longman, 1995.

————. *The Khrushchev Era 1953–1964*. London: Longman, 1995.

————. *The Origins of the Cold War 1941–1949*, 2nd ed. London: Longman, 1995.

————. *The Longman Companion to Russia since 1914*. London: Longman, 1998.

————, ed. *The Russian Revolution and the Soviet State 1917–1921: Documents*, rev. ed. London: Macmillan, 1995.

McGwire, Michael. *Perestroika and Soviet National Security*. Washington D.C.: Brookings Institution Press, 1991.

McNeal, R. *Stalin: Man and Ruler*. London: Macmillan, 1988.

Medvedev, R. *Khrushchev*. Oxford: Blackwell, 1984.

————. *Let History Judge*, rev. ed. Oxford: Oxford University Press, 1989.

Merridale, Catherine, and Chris Ward, eds. *Perestroika: The Historical Perspective*. London: Edward Arnold, 1991.

Mickiewicz, Ellen. *Changing Channels: Television and the Struggle for Power in Russia*. New York/Oxford: Oxford University Press, 1997.

Millar, James R., ed. *Cracks in the Monolith: Party Power in the Brezhnev Era*. London: M. E. Sharpe, 1992.

Miller, John. *Mikhail Gorbachev and the End of Soviet Power*. Basingstoke: Macmillan, 1993.

Milner-Gulland, Robin. *The Russians*. Oxford: Blackwell, 1999.

Moon, David. *The Russian Peasantry, 1600–1930: The World the Peasants Made*. London: Longman, 1999.

Morrison, John. *Boris Yeltsin: From Bolshevik to Democrat*. London: Penguin Books, 1991.

Motyl, A. J. *Sovietology, Rationality, Nationality: Coming to Grips with Nationalism in the USSR*. New York: Columbia University Press, 1990.

————. *The Post-Soviet Nations: Perspectives on the Demise of the USSR*. New York: Columbia University Press, 1995.

————, ed. *Thinking Theoretically about Soviet Nationalities*. Oxford: Oxford University Press, 1992.

Moynahan, Brian. *The Russian Century: A History of the Last Hundred Years*. London: Pimlico, 1994.

Murray, Donald. *A Democracy of Despots*. Boulder, Colo.: Westview Press, 1996.

Nagy, Piroska. *The Meltdown of the Russian State: The Deformation and Collapse of the State in Russia*. Cheltenham: Edward Elgar, 2000.

Nahaylo, Bohdan, and Victor Swoboda. *Soviet Disunion: A History of the Nationalities Problem in the USSR.* London: Hamish Hamilton, 1990.

Nelson, Lynn D., and Irma Kuzes. *Radical Reform in Yeltsin's Russia.* Armonk, N.Y.: M. E. Sharpe, 1995.

Neumann, Iver B. *Russia and the Idea of Europe: A Study in Identity and International Relations.* London: Routledge, 1996.

Nichols, Thomas M. *The Russian Presidency: Society and Politics in the Second Russian Republic.* Basingstoke: Macmillan, 1999.

Nicholson, Martin. *Towards a Russia of the Regions.* Oxford: Oxford University Press for the International Institute for Strategic Studies, 1999.

Nogee, J. L., and R. H. Donaldson. *Soviet Foreign Policy since World War II,* 4th ed. New York: Pergamon, 1992.

Nove, A. *An Economic History of the USSR,* 3rd ed. Harmondsworth: Penguin, 1992.

———. *Stalinism and After: The Road to Gorbachev,* 3rd ed. Boston: Unwin Hyman, 1989.

Owen, T. C. *Russian Corporate Capitalism from Peter the Great to Perestroika.* Oxford University Press, 1996.

Pankin, Boris. *The Last Hundred Days of the Soviet Union.* London: I. B. Tauris, 1995.

Pavkovic, A., and others, eds. *Nationalism and Post-Communism: A Collection of Essays.* Aldershot: Dartmouth, 1995.

Petro, Nicolai N. *The Rebirth of Russian Democracy: An Interpretation of Political Culture.* Cambridge, Mass.: Harvard University Press, 1995.

Pilkington, Hilary, ed. *Gender, Generation and Identity in Contemporary Russia.* London: Routledge, 1996.

Pipes, Richard. *Russia under the Old Regime.* London: Penguin, 1990.

Posadskaya, Anastasiya. *Women in Russia.* Oxford: Blackwell, 1994.

Pravda, Alex. *Russian Foreign Policy in the Making.* London: Pinter, 1995.

Puffer, Sheila M., and others. *The Russian Capitalist Experiment: From State-Owned Organizations to Entrepreneurships.* Cheltenham: Edward Elgar, 2000.

Rabinowitch, Alexander. *The Bolsheviks Come to Power.* London: NLB, 1979.

Radzinsky, E. *Stalin.* London: Hodder & Stoughton, 1996.

Ragsdale, Hugh. *The Russian Tragedy: The Burden of History.* Armonk, N.Y./London: M. E. Sharpe, 1996.

Reddaway Peter, ed. *Uncensored Russia: The Human Rights Movement in the Soviet Union.* London: Cape, 1972.

Reed, J. *Ten Days That Shook the World.* Harmondsworth: Penguin, 1966.

Reiman, M. *The Birth of Stalinism.* Bloomington, Ind.: Indiana University Press, 1987.

Remington, Thomas F. *Politics in Russia.* New York/Harlow: Longman, 1999.

———, ed. *Parliaments in Transition: The New Legislative Politics in the Former USSR and Eastern Europe.* Boulder, Colo.: Westview Press, 1994.

Remnick, David. *Lenin's Tomb: The Last Days of the Soviet Empire.* New York: Random House, 1993.

Riasanovsky, Nicholas V. *A History of Russia,* 5th ed. Oxford: Oxford University Press, 1993.

Richter, J. G. *Khrushchev's Double Bind.* Baltimore, Md.: Johns Hopkins University Press, 1994.

Rigby, T. H. *The Changing Soviet System: Mono-Organisational Socialism from Its Origins to Gorbachev's Restructuring.* Aldershot: Edward Elgar, 1990.

Riordan, James, ed. *Soviet Youth Culture.* London: Macmillan, 1989.

Robinson, Neil. *Ideology and the Collapse of the Soviet System: A Critical History of Soviet Ideological Discourse.* Aldershot: Edward Elgar, 1995.

_____. ed. *Institutions and Political Change in Russia.* Basingstoke: Macmillan, 2000.

Rogger, H. *Russia in the Age of Modernisation and Revolution, 1881–1917.* London: Longman, 1983.

Roxburgh, Angus. *The Second Russian Revolution: The Struggle for Power in the Kremlin.* London: BBC Books, 1991.

Ruge, G. *Gorbachev: A Biography.* London: Chatto and Windus, 1991.

Russian Federation, 1999–2000. Paris: O.E.C.D., 2000.

Rywkin, Michael. *Moscow's Lost Empire.* Armonk, N.Y.: M. E. Sharpe, 1994.

Rzhevsky, Nicholas, ed. *The Cambridge Companion to Modern Russian Culture.* Cambridge: Cambridge University Press, 1998.

Saikal, A., and W. Maley, eds. *Russia in Search of Its Future.* Cambridge: Cambridge University Press, 1995.

Saivetz, Carol R., and Anthony Jones, eds. *In Search of Pluralism: Soviet and Post-Soviet Politics.* Boulder, Colo.: Westview Press, 1994.

Sakharov, A. D. *Sakharov Speaks.* New York: Knopf, 1974.

Sakwa, Richard. *Gorbachev and His Reforms, 1985–90.* Hemel Hempstead: Philip Allan, 1990.

_____. *Russian Politics and Society,* 2nd ed. London: Routledge, 1996.

_____. *Soviet Politics: An Introduction.* London/New York: Routledge, 1989.

Sandle, Mark. *A Short History of Soviet Socialism.* London: UCL Press, 1999.

Schapiro, L. *The Communist Party of the Soviet Union,* 2nd ed. London: Methuen, 1970.

_____. *Totalitarianism.* London: Pall Mall, 1972.

Schwartz, Donald, ed. *Resolutions and Decisions of the Communist Party of the Soviet Union,* vol. 5: *The Brezhnev Years.* Toronto: University of Toronto Press, 1982.

Sedaitis, Judith, and Jim Butterfield, eds. *Perestroika from Below: Social Movements in the Soviet Union.* Boulder, Colo.: Westview Press, 1991.

Sergeyev, Victor, and Nikolai Biryukov. *Russia's Road to Democracy: Parliament, Communism and Traditional Culture.* Aldershot: Edward Elgar, 1993.

Service, R. *Lenin: A Political Life,* 3 vols. London: Macmillan 1991–95.

_____. *The Bolshevik Party in Revolution: A Study in Organizational Change, 1917–1923.* London: Macmillan, 1979.

_____. *The Russian Revolution 1900–1927,* 2nd ed. Macmillan, 1991.

Seton-Watson, H. *The Russian Empire: 1801–1917.* Oxford University Press, 1967.

Shanin, T. *The Awkward Class: Political Sociology of Peasantry in a Developing Society: Russia, 1910–1925.* Oxford: Clarendon Press, 1972.

Sharlet, Robert. *Soviet Constitutional Crisis: From De-Stalinisation to Disintegration.* Armonk, N.Y.: M. E. Sharpe, 1992.

Shatz, M. S. *Soviet Dissent in Historical Perspective.* Cambridge: Cambridge University Press, 1980.

Shaw, D. J. B. *Russia in the Modern World: A New Geography.* Oxford: Blackwell, 1999.

_____. *The Post-Soviet Republics: A Systematic Geography.* London: Longman, 1995.

Shlapentokh, V. *Public and Private Lives of the Soviet People: Changing Values in Post-Stalin Russia.* New York: Oxford University Press, 1989.

Shleifer, Andrei, and Daniel Treisman. *The Economics and Politics of Transition to an Open Market Economy: Russia.* Paris: OECD, 1998.

Shukman, H., ed. *The Blackwell Encyclopedia of the Russian Revolution,* rev. ed. Oxford: Blackwell, 1994.

Simon, Gerhard. *Nationalism and Policy Toward the Nationalities in the Soviet Union: From Totalitarian Dictatorship to Post-Stalinist Society.* Boulder, Colo.: Westview Press, 1991.

Skilling, H.G., and Franklyn Griffiths, eds. *Interest Groups in Soviet Politics.* Princeton, N.J.: Princeton University Press, 1971.

Smith, Alan. *Russia and the World Economy: Problems of Integration.* London: Routledge, 1993.

Smith, Gordon B. *Reforming the Russian Legal System.* Cambridge: Cambridge University Press, 1996.

_____. *Soviet Politics: Struggling with Change,* 2nd ed. London: Macmillan, 1991.

_____, ed. *State-Building in Russia: The Yeltsin Legacy and the Challenge of the Future.* Armonk, N.Y./London: M. E. Sharpe, 1999.

Smith, Graham, ed. *The Nationalities Question in the Post-Soviet States,* 2nd ed. Harlow: Longman, 1995.

_____, ed. *The Nationalities Question in the Soviet Union.* London: Longman, 1990.

Smith, H. *The New Russians.* New York: Random House, 1990.

_____. *The Russians.* London: Sphere Books, 1983.

Solzhenitsyn. Alexander. *Rebuilding Russia: Reflections and Tentative Proposals.* London: Harvill Press, 1991.

_____. *The Russian Question at the End of the Twentieth Century.* London: Harvill Press, 1995.

Sperling, Valerie. *Organizing Women in Contemporary Russia: Engendering Transition.* Cambridge: Cambridge University Press, 1999.

Stalin, Joseph. *Works.* Moscow: Foreign Languages Publishing House, 1955.

Starr, S. Frederick, ed. *The Legacy of History in Russia and the New States of Eurasia.* Armonk, N.Y.: M. E. Sharpe, 1994.

Steele, Jonathan. *Eternal Russia: Yeltsin, Gorbachev and the Mirage of Democracy.* London: Faber & Faber, 1994.

_____, and Eric Abraham. *Andropov in Power.* New York: Doubleday, 1984.

Strayer, Robert W. *Why Did the Soviet Union Collapse? Understanding Historical Change.* Armonk, N.Y./London: M. E. Sharpe, 1998.

Suny, G. *The Revenge of the Past: Nationalism, Revolution and the Collapse of the Soviet Union.* Stanford, Calif.: Stanford University Press, 1993.

Sutela, Pekka. *Economic Thought and Economic Reform in the Soviet Union.* Cambridge: Cambridge University Press, 1991.

Szajkowski, B., ed. *Political Parties in Eastern Europe, Russia and the Successor States.* London: Longman, 1994.

Szporluk, Roman, ed. *National Identity and Ethnicity in Russia and the New States of Eurasia.* Armonk, N.Y.: M. E. Sharpe, 1994.

Talbott, S. *At the Highest Levels: The Inside Story of the End of the Cold War.* London: Little Brown, 1993.

Taranovski, Theodore. *Reform in Modern Russian History: Progress or Cycle?* Cambridge: Cambridge University Press, 1995.

The Territories of the Russian Federation. London: Europa, 1999.

Thompson, John M. *Russia and the Soviet Union: An Historical Introduction from the Kievan State to the Present,* 3rd ed. Oxford: Westview Press, 1994.

Ticktin, Hillel. *Origins of the Crisis in the USSR: Essays on the Political Economy of a Disintegrating System.* Armonk, N.Y.: M. E. Sharpe, 1992.

Tismaneanu, Vladimir, ed. *Political Culture in Russia and the New States of Eurasia.* Armonk, N.Y.: M. E. Sharpe, 1995.

Tokes, Rudolf L., ed. *Dissent in the USSR: Politics, Ideology and People.* Baltimore/London: Johns Hopkins University Press, 1976.

Tolz, Vera. *Russia.* London: Arnold, 2001.

_____. *The USSR's Emerging Multiparty System.* New York: Praeger, 1991.

Tompson, W. J. *Khrushchev: A Political Life.* London: Macmillan, 1995.

Treadgold, Donald W. *Twentieth Century Russia,* 9th ed. Boulder, Colo./Oxford: Westview Press, 2000.

Trotsky, L. *The History of the Russian Revolution.* London: Pluto Press, 1977.

_____. *The Revolution Betrayed.* New York: Pathfinder, 1977.

Tucker, Robert C. *Political Culture and Leadership in Soviet Russia.* Brighton: Wheatsheaf, 1987.

_____. *Stalin as Revolutionary, 1879–1929.* Chatto & Windus, 1974.

_____, ed. *The Lenin Anthology.* New York: Norton, 1975.

Ulam, A. *Expansion and Coexistence: Soviet Foreign Policy, 1917–73.* New York: Praeger, 1974.

_____. *The Communists: The Story of Power and Lost Illusions, 1948–1991.* New York: Macmillan, 1993.

Urban, Joan Barth and Valerii D. Solovei. *Hammer, Book and Sickle: Communism in Post-Soviet Russia.* Boulder, Colo.: Westview Press, 1996.

Urban, Michael, ed. *Ideology and System Change in the USSR and Eastern Europe.* London: Macmillan, 1992.

_____, and others. *The Rebirth of Politics in Russia.* Cambridge: Cambridge University Press, 1997.

Vaksberg, Arkady. *The Soviet Mafia.* London: Weidenfeld & Nicolson, 1991.

Valenta, J. *Soviet Intervention in Czechoslovakia, 1968: Anatomy of a Decision.* Baltimore/London: Johns Hopkins University Press, 1979.

Volkogonov, D. *Lenin: Life and Legacy.* London: HarperCollins, 1994.

_____. *Stalin: Triumph and Tragedy.* London: Weidenfeld & Nicolson, 1991.

Von Laue, Theodore H. *Why Lenin? Why Stalin? Why Gorbachev? The Rise and Fall of the Soviet System,* 3rd ed. New York: HarperCollins, 1993.

Voslensky, Michael. *Nomenklatura: The Soviet Ruling Class.* Garden City, N.Y.: Doubleday, 1984.

Wade, Rex A. *The Russian Revolution, 1917.* Cambridge: Cambridge University Press, 2000.

Wailer, J. Michael. *Secret Empire: The KGB in Russia Today.* Oxford: Westview, 1994.

Walicki, A. *A History of Russian Thought from the Enlightenment to Marxism.* Stanford, Calif.: Stanford University Press, 1979.

_____. *The Slavophile Controversy.* Oxford: Oxford University Press, 1975.

Walker, Rachel, *Six Years That Shook the World: Perestroika—The Impossible Project.* Manchester: Manchester University Press, 1993.

Ward, C. *Stalin's Russia.* London: Edward Arnold, 1993.

Webber, Mark. *The International Politics of Russia and the Successor States.* Manchester: Manchester University Press, 1996.

Westwood, John. *Endurance and Endeavour. Russian History 1812–1992,* 4th ed. Oxford: Oxford University Press, 1993.

White, James D. *The Russian Revolution 1917–1921: A Short History.* London: Edward Arnold, 1994.

White, S. *Gorbachev and After,* 3rd ed. Cambridge, Cambridge University Press, 1992.

_____. *Russia Goes Dry: Alcohol, State and Society.* Cambridge: Cambridge University Press, 1996.

_____. *Russia's New Politics: The Management of a Postcommunist Society.* Cambridge: Cambridge University Press, 2000.

_____, and others, eds. *Developments in Soviet and Post-Soviet Politics.* London: Macmillan, 1992.

_____, and others, eds. *Developments in Russian Politics 4.* Basingstoke: Macmillan, 1997.

_____, and others. *The Politics of Transition: Shaping a Post-Soviet Future.* Cambridge: Cambridge University Press, 1993.

Williams, Beryl. *Lenin.* Harlow: Longman, 2000.

Wood, Alan. *The Origins of the Russian Revolution, 1861–1917,* 2nd ed. London: Routledge, 1993.

Woodby, Sylvia, and Alfred B. Evans Jr., eds. *Restructuring Soviet Ideology: Gorbachev's New Thinking.* Boulder, Colo.: Westview Press, 1990.

Wyman, Matthew. *Public Opinion in Postcommunist Russia.* London: Macmillan, 1996.

Yeltsin, Boris. *Against the Grain: An Autobiography.* London: Jonathan Cape, 1990.

_____. *View from the Kremlin.* London: HarperCollins, 1994.

Young, J. W. *The Longman Companion to Cold War and Détente.* London: Longman, 1993.

Zaslavskaya, T. *The Second Socialist Revolution: An Alternative Strategy.* London: I. B. Tauris, 1990.

Zaslavsky, Victor. *The Neo-Stalinist State: Class, Ethnicity, and Consensus in Soviet Society.* Armonk, N.Y.: M. E. Sharpe, 1982.

Zubkova, Elena. *Russia after the War: Hopes, Illusions, and Disappointments, 1945–1957.* Armonk, N.Y/London: M. E. Sharpe, 1998.

Selected Bibliography of Russian-Language Sources

Агафонов В. и Рокитянский В. *Россия в поисках будущего*. М.: Прогресс-Культура, 1993.

Александров-Агентов А. М. *От Коллонтай до Горбачева*. М.: Международные отношения, 1994.

Алексеев С. В. и др. *Идеологические ориентиры России (Основы новой общероссийской национальной идеологии)*. Т. 1-2. М.: Книга и бизнес, 1998.

Алексеева Л. *История инакомыслия в СССР*. Вильнюс/Москва: Весть, 1992.

Андреев С. *Один год из жизни страны. Результаты и перспективы*. М.: Прогресс, 1990.

Антонов-Овсеенко А. *Портрет тирана*. М.: Грэгори Пэйдж, 1994.

Арабаджян А. З. *Зарубки на времени (вместо воспоминаний)*. М.: ИВ РАН, 1998.

_____. *Истоки духовности. Религия и атеизм*. М.: Наука, 1993.

Арин О. *Россия в стратегическом капкане*. М.: Флинта, 1997.

_____. *Россия на обочине мира*. М.: Линор, 1999.

Архив русской революции. Изданный Г. В. Гессеном. Т. 1-12. Репринтное изд. М.: ТЕРРА, Политиздат, 1991.

Архипова Т. Г. и др. *История России. Новейшее время 1945-1999*. М.: Олимп, Астрель, 1999.

Бажанов Борис. *Воспоминания бывшего секретаря Сталина*. СПб.: Всемирное слово, 1992.

Байбаков Н. К. *От Сталина до Ельцина*. М.: ГазОил пресс, 1998.

Бакатин Вадим. *Избавление от КГБ*. М.: Новости, 1992.

Баранец Виктор. *Ельцин и его генералы. Записки полковника генштаба*. М.: Совершенно секретно, 1998.

Барсенков А. С. и др. *Русский вопрос в национальной политике. XX век*. М.: Моск. Рабочий, 1993.

Безбородов А. Б. и др. *Материалы по истории диссидентского и правозащитного движения в СССР 50-х - 80-х годов*. М.: РГГУ, 1994.

Бердяев Н. А. *Истоки и смысл русского коммунизма*. М.: Наука, 1990.

Бережков Валентин. *Как я стал переводчиком Сталина*. М.: ДЭМ, 1993.

Березовская Л. В. и Ковалев А. М. *Россия на пороге XXI века: философско-социологическое исследование.* М.: МГУ, 1998.

Березовский Е. В. *Политическая элита российского общества на рубеже веков. Часть I (1991-1996): историко-социологическое исследование.* М.: МГУ, 1999.

Бернштейн Эдуард. *Возможен ли научный социализм? "Ответ Г. Плеханова".* Сост. М. В. Конкин и Л. Б. Шульц. М.: Философское общество СССР, 1991.

Богомолов О. Т. *Моя летопись переходного времени.* М.: Экономика, 2000.

Борев Юрий. *Краткий курс истории XX века в анекдотах, частушках, байках, мемуарах по чужим воспоминаниям, легендах, преданиях и т. д.* М.: Звонница - МГ, 1995.

Бурлацкий Федор. *Вожди и советники: О Хрущеве, Андропове и не только о них...* М.: Политиздат, 1990.

_____. *Русские государи. Эпоха реформации.* М.: Шарк, 1996.

Бушин В. *Честь и бесчестие нации.* М.: Республика, 1999.

В поисках своего пути: Россия между Европой и Азией. Хрестоматия по истории российской общественной мысли XIX и XX веков. Сост. Н. Г. Федоровский. 2-е изд. М.: Логос, 1997.

Валентинов Н. *Малознакомый Ленин.* М.: На боевом посту, 1992.

Вдовин А. И. и др. *Русский народ в национальной политике. XX век.* М.: Русский мир, 1998.

Верт Н. *История советского государства. 1900-1991.* М.: Прогресс-Академия, 1994.

Вехи: Сборник статей о русской интеллигенции Н. А. Бердяева и др. Репринтное изд. 1909 г. М.: Новости, 1990.

Вишневский А. *Серп и рубль. Консервативная модернизация в СССР.* М.: ОГИ, 1998.

Военная реформа: Оценка угроз национальной безопасности России. Под ред. Г. А. Зюганова. М.: РАУ-Университет, 1997.

Вождь: Ленин, которого мы не знали. Сост. Г. П. Сидоровнин. Саратов: Приволж. кн. изд-во, 1991.

Волков О. И. *Континент Россия. XX век: Иллюзии, политика, аферы.* М.: Русское слово, 1998.

Волкогонов Д. А. *Семь вождей.* Кн. 1-2. М.: Изд-во АСТ, Новости, 1999.

Волобуев О. и Кулешов С. *Очищение: история и перестройка. Публицистические заметки.* М.: АПН, 1989.

Вторая мировая война. Актуальные проблемы. Отв. ред. О. А. Ржешевский. М.: Наука, 1995.

Гайдар Егор. *Государство и эволюция.* М.: Евразия, 1995.

_____. *Дни поражений и побед.* М.: Вагриус, 1997.

Геворкян Н. и др. *От первого лица. Разговоры с Владимиром Путиным.* М.: Вагриус, 2000.

Глазьев Сергей. *Геноцид. Россия и новый мировой порядок. Стратегия экономического роста на пороге XXI века.* М.: Астра семь, 1997.

Головатенко А. *История России: спорные проблемы.* М.: Школа-Пресс, 1994.

Голос народа. Письма и отклики рядовых советских граждан о событиях 1918-1932 гг. Отв. ред. А. К. Соколов. М.: РОССПЭН, 1998.

Горбачев М. С. *Декабрь - 91. Моя позиция.* М.: Новости, 1992.

_____. *Размышления о прошлом и будущем.* М.: ТЕРРА, 1998.

Городецкий Габриэль. *Миф "Ледокола." Накануне войны.* М.: Прогресс-Академия, 1995.

Горшков. М. К. *Российское общество в условиях трансформации (социологический анализ).* М.: РОССПЭН, 2000.

Гранкин И. В. *Парламент России.* М.: Консалтбанкир, 1999.

Грачев А. *Дальше без меня... Уход Президента.* М.: Прогресс – Культура, 1994.

Громов Б. В. *Ограниченный контингент.* М.: Прогресс – Культура, 1994.

Громов. Е. С. *Сталин: власть и искусство.* М.: Республика, 1998.

Джилас Милован. *Лицо тоталитаризма.* М.: Новости, 1992.

Дьяков Ю. Л. и Бушуева Т. С. *Фашистский меч ковался в СССР: Красная Армия и рейхсвер. Тайное сотрудничество. 1922-1933. Неизвестные документы.* М.: Сов. Россия, 1992.

Ельцин Борис. *Записки президента.* М.: Огонек, 1994.

_____. *Исповедь на заданную тему.* М.: Огонек, 1990.

_____. *Президентский марафон.* М.: Изд-во АСТ, 2000.

Жириновский Владимир. *Последний удар по России.* 2-е изд. М.: ЛДПР, 1998.

Замковой В. и Ильчиков М. *Россия вчера, сегодня, завтра!* М.: ИМПЭ, 1998.

Замятин Л. М. *Горби и Мэги. Записки посла о двух известных политиках - Михаиле Горбачеве и Маргарет Тетчер.* Люберцы: ВИНИТИ, 1995.

Здравомыслов А. Г. *Межнациональные конфликты в постсоветском пространстве.* М.: Аспект Пресс, 1997.

Зевелев А. и Павлов Ю. *Созидатель или разрушитель? Б. Н. Ельцин: факты и размышления.* М.: Новая игрушечка, 1998.

Из глубины: Сборник статей о русской революции С. А. Аскольдова и др. М: МГУ, 1990.

Ильин В. В. и Ахиезер А. С. *Российская государственность: истоки, традиции, перспективы.* М.: МГУ, 1997.

Ингерфлом К. С. *Несостоявшийся гражданин. Русские корни ленинизма.* М.: Ипол, 1993.

Иного не дано. Перестройка: гласность, демократия, социализм. Под ред. Ю. Н. Афанасьева. М.: Прогресс, 1988.

Исаев И. А. и Золотухина Н. М. *История политических и правовых учений России XI-XX вв.* М.: Юристъ, 1995.

Исторические исследования в России. Тенденции последних лет. Под ред. Г. А. Бордюгова. М.: АИРО-XX, 1996.

История и сталинизм. Сост. А. Н. Мерцалов. М.: Политиздат, 1991.

История Отечества в документах, 1917-1993 гг. Сост. А. Г. Колосков и др. Ч. 1-4. М.: ИЛБИ, 1994-95.

История политических и правовых учений. XX в. М.: Наука, 1995.

История политических партий России. Под ред. А. И. Зевелева. М.: Высшая школа, 1994.

История России (IX-XX вв.). Отв. ред. Я. А. Перехов. М.: Гардарики, 1999.

История России, 1917-1940. Хрестоматия. Под ред. М. Е. Главацкого. Екатеринбург: Уральский лицей, 1993.

Кагарлицкий Борис. *Реставрация в России.* М.: Эдиториал УРСС, 2000.

Каппелер Андреас. *Россия – многонациональная империя.* М.: Прогресс-Традиция, 1997.

Капустин Б. Г. *Идеология и политика в посткоммунистической России.* М.: Эдиториал УРСС, 2000.

Кара-Мурза А. А. и Поляков Л. В. *Русские о большевизме. Опыт аналитической антологии.* СПб.: РХГИ, 1999.

Караулов Андрей. *Вокруг Кремля.* Т. 1-2. М.: Слово, 1993.

Качановский Ю. В. *Куда идет Россия?* М.: Информпечать, 1999.

Киселев В. Н. и др. *Полвека назад: Победа.* М.: Просвещение, 1995.

Кожинов В. *"Черносотенцы" и Революция (загадочные страницы истории).* 2-е изд. М.: Прима В, 1998.

_____. *Судьба России: вчера, сегодня, завтра.* М.: Воениздат, 1997.

_____. *Победы и беды России. Русская культура как порождение истории.* М.: Алгоритм, 2000.

Козлов В. А. *Массовые беспорядки в СССР при Хрущеве и Брежневе (1953 – начало 1980-х гг.).* Новосибирск: Сибирский хронограф, 1999.

Кольев А. *Чеченский капкан.* М.: Конгресс русских общин, 1997.

Конституция Российской Федерации. Вопросы и ответы. М.: Юрид. Лит., 1994.

Коржаков Александр. *Борис Ельцин: От рассвета до заката.* М.: Интербук, 1997.

Костиков Вячеслав. *Роман с президентом. Записки пресс-секретаря.* М.: Вагриус, 1997.

Котеленец Е. А. *В. И. Ленин как предмет исторического исследования. Новейшая историография.* М.: РУДН, 1999.

Кочетков А. П. *Россия на пороге XXI века.* М.: Христианское изд-во, 1998.

Красильщиков В. А. *Вдогонку за прошедшим веком. Развитие России в XX веке с точки зрения мировых модернизаций.* М.: РОССПЭН, 1998.

Кривошеев Г. Ф. и др. *Полвека назад: Великая Отечественная война: Цифры и факты.* М.: Просвещение, 1995.

Кругов Михаил. *Тайны военной реформы. Заметки менеджера.* М.: ДеКА, 1998.

Кто был кто в Великой Отечественной войне 1941-1945: Краткий справочник. Под ред. О. А. Ржешевского. М.: Республика, 1995.

Кулешов С. В. и др. *Наше Отечество. Опыт политической истории.* Т 1-2. М.: Терра, 1991.

Лебедь Александр. *За державу обидно...* М.: Московская правда, 1995.

Лебина Н. Б. *Повседневная жизнь советского города: Нормы и аномалии. 1920-1930 годы.* СПб.: Нева – Летний Сад, 1999.

М. А. Гареев и др. *Полвека назад: лидеры войны.* М.: Просвещение, 1995.

Медведев В. Т. *Человек за спиной.* М.: РУССЛИТ, 1994.

Медведев Р. А. *Капитализм в России?* М.: Права человека, 1998.

_____. *Загадка Путина.* М.: Права человека, 2000.

_____. *Личность и эпоха. Политический портрет Л. И. Брежнева.* М.: Новости, 1991.

_____. *О Сталине и сталинизме.* М.: Прогресс, 1990.

Медведев. В. А. *Распад. Как он назревал в "мировой системе социализма".* М.: Международные отношения, 1994.

Мунчаев Ш. М. и Устинов В. М. *Политическая история России. От становления самодержавия до падения Советской власти.* М. : НОРМА - ИНФРА-М, 1999.

На перепутье (Новые вехи): Сборник статей. М.: Логос, 1999.

Неизвестная Россия. XX век. Главн. ред. В. А. Козлов. Т. 1-3. М.: Историческое наследие, 1992-93.

Некрасов В. Ф. *Тринадцать "железных" наркомов.* М.: Версты, 1995.

Несокрушимая и легедарная: В огне политических баталий (1985-1993 гг). Под ред. М. К. Горшкова и В. В. Журавлева. М.: ТЕРРА, 1994.

Николаевский Б. И. *Тайные страницы истории.* М.: Изд-во гуманит. лит-ры, 1995.

Новый "Октябрь" в оценке историков. М.: Институт российской истории РАН, 1993.

Оболонский А. *На государевой службе: бюрократия в старой и новой России.* М.: Институт государства и права РАН, 1997.

Октябрь 1917: величайшее событие века или социальная катастрофа? Под ред. П. В. Волобуева. М.: Политиздат, 1991.

Октябрьская революция: Мемуары (Революция и гражданская война в описаниях белогвардейцев). Сост. С. А. Алексеев. М.: Орбита, 1991.

Оников Леон. *КПСС: анатомия распада. Взгляд изнутри аппарата ЦК.* М.: Республика, 1996.

Орлов А. С. и др. *История России с древнейших времен до наших дней.* М.: Проспект, 1999.

Отечественная история. XX век. Под ред. А. В. Ушакова. М.: Агар, Рандеву-АМ, 1999.

Павлюченков С. А. *Военный коммунизм в России: власть и массы.* М.: РКТ-История, 1997.

Пантин И. К. *Россия и мир: историческое самоузнавание.* М.: Эдиториал УРСС, 2000.

Парламентаризм и многопартийность в современной России. К десятилетию двух исторических дат. Под ред. В. Н. Лысенко. М.: ИСП, 2000.

Пашенцев Е. Н. *Оппозиционные партии и движения современной России.* М.: Информпечать, 1998.

Певзнер Я. А. *Вторая жизнь.* М.: Марьина роща, 1995.

————. *Крах коммунизма и современные общественные отношения.* М.: Наука, 1999.

————. *Экономическое учение Карла Маркса перед судом двадцатого столетия.* М.: ИМЭМО, 1996.

Первая мировая война: дискуссионные проблемы истории. Под ред. Ю. А. Писарева и др. М.: Наука, 1994.

Перегудов С. П. и др. *Группы интересов и российское государство.* М.: Эдиториал УРСС, 1999.

Политическая история России в партиях и лицах. Сост. В. В. Шелохаев и др. М.: ТЕРРА, 1994.

Политическая история России: Россия - СССР - Российская Федерация. Коллект. авт. под рук. С. В. Кулешова и др. Т. 1-2. М.: ТЕРРА, 1996.

Политические партии России в контексте ее истории. Коллект. авт. Ростов- на-Дону: Феникс, 1998.

Политология на российском фоне. Коллект. авт. под рук. В. В. Рябова. М.: Луч, 1993.

Попов Г. Х. *Будет ли у России второе тысячелетие.* М.: Экономика, 1998.

Попцов Олег. *Хроника времен "царя Бориса".* М.: Совершенно секретно, Берлин: Edition Q, 1996.

————.*Тревожные сны царской свиты.* М.: Совершенно секретно, 2000.

Поспеловский Дмитрий. *Православная Церковь в истории Руси, России и СССР.* М.: Библейско-Богословский Институт св. Апостола Андрея, 1995.

Поцелуев В. А. *История России XX столетия.* М.: ВЛАДОС, 1997.

Рапопорт В. Н. и Геллер Ю. А. *Измена родине*. М.: РИК "Стрелец", 1995.

Ратьковский И. С. и Ходяков М. В. *История Советской России*. М.: СПб.: Изд-во Лань, 1999.

Роговин В. *Была ли альтернатива?: "Троцкизм": Взгляд через годы*. М.: ТЕРРА, 1992.

Российская историческая политология. Курс лекций. Отв. ред. С. А. Кислицын. Ростов-на-Дону: Феникс, 1998.

Российская история. Под ред. Г. Б. Поляка. М.: Культура и спорт, ЮНИТИ, 1997.

Российская элита. Психологические портреты. М.: Ладомир, 2000.

Россия в XX веке. Проблемы национальных отношений. Под ред. А. Н. Сахарова и В. А. Михайлова. М.: Наука, 1999.

Россия на рубеже XXI века. Оглядываясь на век минувший. Отв. ред. Ю. А. Поляков и А. Н. Сахаров. М.: Наука, 2000.

Россия на рубеже веков. Отв. ред. М. К. Горшков. М.: РНИСиНП, РОССПЭН, 2000.

Россия регионов: Трансформация политических режимов. Под ред. В. Гельмана и др. М.: Весь мир, 2000.

Россия у критической черты: возрождение или катастрофа. Социально-политическая ситуация в России в 1996 году. Под ред. Г. В. Осипова и др. М.: Республика, 1997.

Россия, которую мы не знали, 1939-1993. Хрестоматия. Под ред. М. Е. Главацкого. Челябинск: Южно-Уральское книжное изд-во, 1995.

Россия-2000. Современная политическая история (1985-1999 годы). Т. 1: Хроника и аналитика. 3-е изд. Под ред. А. И. Подберезкина. М.: Духовное наследие, РАУ-Корпорация, 2000.

Рудинский Ф. М. *"Дело КПСС" в Конституционном Суде*. М.: Былина, 1999.

Русская идея. В кругу писателей и мыслителей русского зарубежья. Т. 1-2. М.: Искусство, 1994.

Русская интеллигенция. История и судьба. Сост. Т. Б. Князевская. М.: Наука, 1999.

Русский узел евразийства. Восток в русской мысли. Сборник трудов евразийцев. М.: Беловодье, 1997.

Руцкой А. В. *Аграрная реформа в России*. М.: РАУ-Корпорация, 1993.

Сахаров А. Д. *Тревога и надежда*. 2-е изд. М.: Интер-Версо, 1991.

Семенникова Л. И. *Россия в мировом сообществе цивилизаций*. 2-е изд. Брянск: Курсив, 1996.

Сироткин Владлен. *Демократия по-русски*. М.: МИК, 1999.

Скрытая правда войны: 1941 год. Неизвестные документы. Сост. П. Н. Кнышевский и др. М.: Русская книга, 1992.

Собчак А. А. *Хождение во власть. Рассказ о рождении парламента.* М.: Новости, 1991.

Советская историография. Под ред. Ю. Н. Афанасьева. М.: Российск. гос. гуманит. ун-т, 1996.

Советское общество: возникновение, развитие, исторический финал. Под ред. Ю. Н. Афанасьева. Т. 1-2. М.: Российск. гос. гуманит. ун-т, 1997.

Согрин В. *Политическая история современной России. 1985-1994: От Горбачева до Ельцина.* М. : Прогресс-Академия, 1994.

Соколов А. К. *Курс советской истории. 1917-1940.* М.: Высш. шк., 1999.

_____ и Тяжельникова В. С. *Курс советской истории. 1941-1991.* М.: Высш. шк., 1999.

Солженицын А. *Россия в обвале.* М.: Русский путь, 1998.

Союзники в войне. 1941-1945. Под ред. А. О. Чубарьяна и др. М.: Наука, 1995.

Средний класс в современном российском обществе. Под ред. М. К. Горшкова и др. М.: РНИСиНП, РОССПЭН, 1999.

Степанков В. Г. и Лисов Е. К. *Кремлевский заговор.* М.: Огонек, 1992.

Стреляный Анатолий. *Сходит затмение.* М.: Новости, 1991.

Судоплатов Павел. *Разведка и Кремль. Записки нежелательного свидетеля.* М.: ТОО "Гея", 1997.

Судьбы российского крестьянства. Под ред. Ю. Н. Афанасьева. М.: Российск. гос. гуманит. ун-т, 1996.

Сульянов А. *Арестовать в Кремле. О жизни и смерти маршала Берия.* Минск: Славяне, 1991.

Суханов Лев. *Три года с Ельциным. Записки первого помощника.* Рига: Вага, 1992.

Таланов Виктор. *Психологический портрет Владимира Путина.* СПб.: Б&К., 2000.

Тарасов А. Н. и др. *Левые в России: от умеренных до экстремистов.* М.: Институт экспериментальной социологии, 1997.

Трансформация цивилизационно-культурного пространства бывшего СССР (тенденции, прогнозы). Отв. ред. В. А. Корецкий. М.: Фонд Форос, 1994.

Третьяков Виталий. *Горбачев. Лигачев. Ельцин. Политические портреты на фоне перестройки.* М.: Корона-принт, 1990.

Троцкий Л. *Сталинская школа фальсификаций.* М.: Наука, 1990.

Трудные вопросы истории: Поиски. Размышления. Новый взгляд на события и факты. Под ред. В. В. Журавлева. М.: Политиздат, 1991.

Трукан Г. А. *Путь к тоталитаризму: 1917-1929 гг.* М.: Наука, 1994.

Угол зрения. Отечественные востоковеды о своей стране. Сборник статей. М.: Наука, 1992.

Федоров Борис. *Пытаясь понять Россию*. СПб: Лимбус Пресс, 2000.

Фроянов И. Я. *Октябрь семнадцатого: Глядя из настоящего*. СПб.: Изд. С.-Петербургского ун-та, 1997.

Хрущев С. Н. *Рождение сверхдержавы: Книга об отце*. М.: Время, 2000.

Хуторской В. Я. *История России. Советская эпоха (1917-1993)*. М.: ФАЗИС, 1994.

Чеченская трагедия. Кто виноват. М.: РИА "Новости", 1995.

Чубайс Анатолий, ред. *Приватизация по-российски*. М.: Вагриус, 1999.

Чубайс И. Б. *Россия в поисках себя. Как мы преодолеем идейный кризис*. М.: Изд-во НОК "Музей бумаги", 1998.

Шаталин С. С. и др. *Рыночная экономика: выбор пути*. М.: Профиздат, 1991.

Шафаревич И. Р. *Русский народ на переломе тысячелетий. Бег наперегонки со смертью*. 2-е изд. М.: Русская идея, 2000.

Шишкин В. А. *Россия в годы "великого перелома."* СПб: Дмитрий Буланин, 1999.

Шмелев Г. И. *Аграрная политика и аграрные отношения в России в XX веке*. М.: Наука, 2000.

Шоль Е. И. *Прослойка, или истоки революций и перестроек*. М.: МАИ, 1996.

Шрейдер Михаил. *НКВД изнутри. Записки чекиста*. М.: Возвращение, 1995.

Штурман Д. *О вождях российского коммунизма*. Кн. 1-2. Париж: YMCA-PRESS, М.: Русский путь, 1993.

Шульгин. *"Что НАМ в НИХ не нравится..." Об антисемитизме в России*. СПб.: Хорс, 1992.

Шульман Сол. *Власть и судьба... Личные судьбы правителей Кремля от его основания до наших дней*. М.: Остожье, 1998.

Явлинский Григорий. *Кризис в России: конец системы? начало пути?* М.: ЭПИцентр, 1999.

Яковлев А. Н. *Предисловие. Обвал. Послесловие*. М.: Новости, 1992.

————— и др. *Перестройка: замыслы и результаты*. Ростов-на-Дону.: Изд. Рост. Ун-та, 1995.

Яковлев Н. Н. *Полвека назад: Судьба полководца: Жуков, Макартур, Роммель*. М.: Просвещение, 1995.

Index